S0-FJM-286

Youth Group Management: A Multi-Functional Approach

By
Bernard Lesser

a TECHNOMIC® publication
TECHNOMIC Publishing Co., Inc.

Youth Group Management: A Multi-Functional Approach

By
Bernard Lesser

a TECHNOMIC® publication

265 Post Road West, PO Box 913
Westport, CT 06881

Printed in USA
LCC - 82-051065
ISBN 87762-315-5

Preface

Being intimately involved in youth work as a group worker, advisor, supervisor, planner, and trainer for one-third of a century, the author has found a paucity of appropriate training material available for the neophyte group worker (that is, material that lends itself specifically and unilaterally as a singular, albeit multifunctional, training resource). This deficiency impacts directly on the development, or lack thereof, of volunteers and quasi-profesionals (part timers), many of whom are expert in other disciplines.

Although adolescents of any generation have much in common with their counterparts of other times and places, there is much that is characteristic of each generation in and of itself. One generation of youth is replaced by another about every two-to-three years. Therefore, those working with young people should be adjusting and refining techniques and procedures in order to stay as current with the present constituency as possible.

The youth group workers are pivotal figures. It is their responsibility to set the scene and provide the matrix within which the youths themselves plan, execute, and evaluate their programs (whether in a school, community, or religious environment). The youth worker is a catalytic agent helping foster emotional growth and maturity amongst those with whom he works.

In addition to writing an updated text, I will attempt to integrate principles of management with those from the fields of psychology and social work. In so doing, I hope to make available a more complete training reference for group workers. It is also my intent to make the latter feel more comfortable with a multifunctional application in dealing with various groups and their constituents on a day-to-day approach.

The author relies on available literature, which is plentiful, on a discipline-by-discipline basis. However, this project was prompted by that the fact that there is limited resource material available that combines the various specialty areas into a singular manual for training group workers.

In moving toward the aforementioned direction, I also relied on my own experiences, as articulated in my prior writings, along with my more recent experiential findings. This information has been allied with some of the current expositions on the sociological and psychological impact of society on groups.

In the ensuing pages of this book, I will also attempt to integrate some of the lessons and techniques of organizational management with the other disciplines needed for the successful guidance of youth groups, regardless of setting, sponsor, or affiliation.

Much of a group worker's job cannot be taught by others, let along through the written word. As in many other instances, in the human relations field, a successful group worker's qualities are intuitive, pragmatic, and highly elusive to articulate. The worker needs to bring to the job sensitivity, generosity, optimism, and a love for young people. Yet there remain certain techniques, warnings of pitfalls, simple short cuts, and other helpful hints that a text like this can reasonably and objectively spell out for the group worker.

Bibliographical references and other suggested readings are placed, in alphabetical order, after each chapter. In each instance, the references relate to the subject matter contained in that chapter.

The Author

ACKNOWLEDGMENTS

I am most grateful to colleagues, who have helped me with this undertaking, by making suggestions and providing encouragement. My thanks, especially, to Dr. Sam Rowe, currently of the University of Southern California, for his candor, insight and time, both here in the United States and in England, which permitted me to pursue this project with confidence. To him and the thousands of youth and students, who were my pride and joy as well as my teachers and inspiration, I am greatly indebted.

I mention my understanding and loving family—my wife Dorothy, the children—Sharon, Bill, Gerri, Kenneth and Neal and the grandchildren—Jordana, Jarah, Dale, Joshua and Brian.

B.L.

Dedicated to:

The memory of my loving wife, Dorothy

About the Author

Dr. "Bernie" Lesser, a top-level government manager is currently serving as the Internal Revenue Service's Examination Division Chief in the state of New Jersey.

An Air Force veteran of World War II, Dr. Lesser graduated with a B.S. degree in Business Administration from Rutgers University. He also holds an M.A. degree from Central Michigan University with a specialty in public administration and a doctorate in education with a specialty in counseling from Pacific States University. Among the many management development training programs completed by Dr. Lesser were those conducted by the Rutgers University Institute of Management and Labor Relations, the Civil Service Executive Seminar Center at the University of California as well as other programs sponsored by various government and professional groups at places such as Lehigh and Seton Hall Universities.

Professional background and experience include a stint as a public accountant, ten years as an Internal Revenue Agent and over twenty-six years as a mid and top-level manager in the I.R.S. Dr. Lesser also serves as an adjunct faculty member at Fairleigh Dickinson University's College of Business Administration. He has been a teacher of religion, youth advisor/counselor and youth program director in the state of New Jersey for over thirty-five years.

Dr. Lesser has authored three books on youth group management, has served as the Dean of a Youth Advisors Training Institute, on the Board of Directors of a Youth Academy and on a multitude of youth advisory groups. He headed up a pre-college teacher training program in South Orange, N.J., and has seen service on two special municipal commissions combating drug-abuse problems.

Bernie Lesser has lectured extensively to academia and professional groups on tax administration, political science, management and youth counseling. In addition he has chaired numerous tax seminars. He also has served as an advisor to the Federal Bar Association, consultant to the New Jersey Civil Service Commission and as Chairman, New Jersey Council (UAHC) Youth Activities Committee.

In addition, Dr. Lesser has made many appearances on television and radio relative to tax administration, has been involved as a chief negotiator in management-labor negotiations and held an appointment on the Government-wide Security Hearing Board roster.

He has received twenty-one major awards and numerous other commendations for significant contributions to the efficiency of the Treasury Department.

Included therein were received four special awards with national and/or regional implications to wit:

- Citation from the president of the United States in 1973 for youth work, particularly in the area of drug abuse.
- Special award from the Secretary of the Department of the Treasury in 1969 for fostering mutual understanding and exchange of information among various religious and ethnic groups. Also, for organizing and directing tutorial programs for disadvantaged youth.
- The Regional Commmissioner's Award (I.R.S.) for development of an outstanding integrity program – 1980.
- One of the most recent awards, for which Dr. Lesser is selected, is the Treasury Department's E.E.O. (Equal Employment Opportunity) award of the year. This was presented to Dr. Lesser in 1981 for outstanding contributions to the E.E.O. program in the I.R.S. through persistent and successful counseling of current and potential minority and female employees, as well as pursuing programs involving the hiring of disabled employees and part-time working mothers, all of which made a difference in changing the composition of the workforce. (Dr. Lesser received a similar award in 1982 conferred by the local E.E.O. Committee.)

Dr. Lesser has been admitted to the following national honor societies:

- SIGMA IOTA EPSILON, national honor society in management, conferred at Central Michigan University (1979).
- CHI GAMMA IOTA, national veterans honor society, conferred at Central Michigan University (1978).
- DELTA MU DELTA, national honor society in Business Administration. Honorary membership conferred on Dr. Lesser as a person with exceptional business ability and a record of significant community and university involvement and accomplishment. Bestowed by Fairleigh Dickinson University in 1981.

Dr. Lesser was also the recipient of many awards and commendations, throughout the years, for his accomplishments and efforts in the areas of religious education and youth group direction.

Bernie Lesser has been married to the former Dorothy Tevelow for thirty-seven years. He has three children: Sharon Moesch, Gerri Olin and Neal Lesser. Grandchildren include: Jordana, Jarah and Joshua Moesch; and Dale and Brian Olin.

Contents

Chapter 1

Introduction

In dealing with teenagers, the group worker, by being an adroit listener, can from time to time recognize anxieties and other problems troubling the youngsters. However, the worker must be cautioned not to assume the role of analyst and/or therapist. He must convey his observations to the appropriate sponsoring officials and/or parents for their consideration, evaluation, and action. It would be counter-productive and sometimes downright dangerous for an unschooled worker to experiment or dabble in even the most basic forms of therapy.

In a similar vein, the same cautions apply to workers confronting "drug" problems. The likelihood of any drug leading to abuse varies chiefly with the user's personality and motivation. With every mood-changing drug known to man, there is probably some proportion of people who can use it without apparent side effects or without developing a habit, and those who cannot.

Note the drinkers of alcohol who remain social tipplers all their lives while others become alcoholics. Still, no drug is totally without danger. Therefore, it is strongly suggested that the group worker pass a problem of this type along to an expert in the field.

In the rapidly moving and changing organizational world, with its increasingly complex workings and problems, managing and relating to personnel and the application of the techniques attendant thereto are a must for the sophisticated, updated group worker, who must deal with equally sophisticated teenagers and action-oriented youth groups.

Some of the data utilized in this text were gathered via nondirective interviews of group supervisors. C. R. Rodgers describes such interviews as an attempt to develop a very permissive atmosphere in which the respondents feel perfectly free to express their feelings without fear of disapproval (this, as opposed to channeling the interview in certain directions).

The author raises many questions in terms of techniques and philosophies. He expresses his views in relation to such questions with an eye toward todays teenage mores and thinking. He also uses the check-sheet approach so that the youth worker can engage in a series of self-evaluative exercises to determine the need for additional skills and/or training. Some of the questions addressed follow (the answers are interspersed through the text in the appropriately related chapters):

Chapter 1

A. Basic Qualifications of a Youth Group Worker

- Who should be a youth group worker?
  What duties are involved?
- What characteristics, attributes, and competencies should we seek of such workers?
- How essential is a "job description" for the group worker?
  What are the components of such a "job description?"
- Is it a good idea to use volunteers and geographically mobile workers of the part-time professional persuasion in a teenage group setting?
  What are the pros and cons?
- To what extent should the group workers train themselves to identify "drug" problems?

B. Group Interaction

- Who is the teenager?
  Why do they join groups?
- Why form a youth group in the first place?
- Is it possible to use basic principles of management in guiding a youth group?
- What role should the group worker play in the identification and referral of the emotionally troubled teenager?
- In what way should he/she attempt counseling?
- How does the group worker communicate with teenagers?
- How does the group worker relate to the parent organization (church, school, community, center, etc.) officials and authority figures?
- What does the youth group worker look for in groups? (Participation? Influence? Informal leadership? Unmotivated members? Norms? Attitudes? Feelings? etc.)
- Is it a good idea to use student (high school or college) volunteers?
- Is it possible to develop an action guide to motivating teenagers in a group setting?

C. Organizational Management

- How can PBO (Planning by Objectives) and attendant evaluations and measuring be utilized in a youth group setting?
- Comprehensive listening–what does it mean? When and how can it be applied in a youth group setting?
  Is there an art or technique in listening?
- In what ways does Abraham Maslow's "hierarchy of needs," leading to self-actualization, also apply to teenagers?

- Is group worker involvement helpful at all times?
  When should the worker pull back?
- What is the distinction between a natural and a designated leader?
  What is the role of the informal leader in a group setting?

D. Counseling

- Can we find a place for Transactional Analysis in improving communication and attitudes at the teenage group level?
- Is there a place for vocational guidance in a typical group setting?
- What are the teenage sexual mores of the day?
- Should venereal disease information be included in the group worker's training?
- How much background information must the group worker assimilate about teenage alcoholism?
- To what degree should the group worker be versed in typical teenage health problems, such as skin care and teeth care?
- In what way can a limited use of catharsis play a role in the counseling of group members?

David Marsland[1], who teaches and does research work in the Department of Sociology, Brunel University, Uxbridge, England, makes certain assumptions that stipulate most aptly the general social position and political situation of young people today.

In brief, these assumptions are as follows:

- Despite obvious diversity among young people (for example, in terms of sex, class and education), there is also a substantial and important commonality in the situation of all young people.
- The concept of youth is an analytical category designed to refer to all that is common to all young people and all that is shared by them. It is an indispensable and useful concept referring to real and important phenomena.
- Youth is part of the age system of society and only makes sense when it is construed as such. The age system as a whole, whose main components are childhood, youth, adulthood, and old age, is itself merely one part—but an important part—of the sytem of society in its totality. Because of this, the age system is continually and unavoidably affected by all the other important social and cultural forces that constitute society. In turn, these forces are all affected by the age system.
- If we are to understand the situation of young people adequately, it is not enough to focus on the way that young people themselves see it from the

[1]Reprinted with permission of National Youth Bureau, Leicester, England.

inside and the meaning that youth takes on for them. This is necessary, but an adequate account has to go beyond this to explore the fundamental characteristic of youth, which is a transition between childhood and adulthood, a path on the way between two more stable situations in the process of life as a whole.

- Adequate analysis of youth absolutely requires that we take account equally and alike of biological, psychological, and sociological forces and facts. Anything short of this is bound to be one-sided and misleading.
- Relationships between young people and adults are, in the nature of the species, always difficult and problematical to a degree. In some situations, the order of difficulty unavoidably escalates, and conflict between age groups/generations becomes a serious social problem. Such a situation exists today.
- The contemporary youth problem is not trivial, and it cannot be dismissed as merely an example of a perennial and cyclical phenomenon. The situation of youth presents a real and serious challenge.
- In the light of the preceding assumptions, and taking into account the meaning of service and professionalism as they have developed vis-a-vis other areas of need, the problem of youth requres the attention of a specialist professional youth service. This has to be more than a mere "fire-brigade" service dealing with the particular problems that particular categories of young people may have or may present. An adequate analysis of the general contemporary situation of young people points unambigously to the requirement of a service capable of attending to the generic needs of all young people as they develop in a context that is problematical for them across the board of their living as a whole.

This text was developed, not to test a specific hypothesis, but to provide a multi-functional training medium for group workers, be they teachers, clergy, students, social-workers, or parents, whether volunteers or part-time quasi-professionals. Group activity pretty much falls into the sphere of social science. It has been postulated by some that social science suffers from a well-known and serious difficulty, to wit: It is usually impossible (for practical and moral reasons) to test social laws by controlled experiments. Corroboratory significance of social experience in relation to social laws is often quite doubtful. It is to be repeated, then, that no hypothesis will be proved, nor social experiment attempted, in this material. The sole objective is to enhance the knowledge and skills of those who work with youth in a group setting.

Much of what is articulated in this text is directed to the volunteer—those with no or limited experience. We are advised by the federal government's National Student Volunteer Program (ACTION) that thousands of college and graduate students search for ways to be of service to the communities surrounding their campuses. We are further advised that educational institutions themselves have begun to recognize that work in the community could benefit the student's overall education and could help make the institution more responsive and relevant to student needs. The result has been:

- increased school support for student volunteers,
- the establishment of comprehensive, school-based student volunteer programs,
- and, in some cases, the granting of academic credit to students for volunteer work done in the community.

Identification of resource organizations and material available from such organizations, for the benefit of the group worker and/or the group members, is given special attention by the author.

Motivation and Related Leadership Skills

One of the basic problems in any environment is how to motivate people to work. George Strauss and Leonard R. Sayles pointed out that in a modern society this is not an easy task, since many people derive only slight personal satisfaction from their jobs and enjoy little sense of accomplishment or creativity. In large organizations, people must work together, follow orders that they may neither understand nor approve, and obey instructions from superiors whom they had no part in selecting and may rarely see. The group worker must assiduously labor to prevent the youth group from becoming a model prototype or junior edition of these larger organizations. How can our group worker motivate teenagers who are bored? How can they create a situation in which the young people can satisfy their personal needs while contributing to the goals of the group? There are a number of alternative methods available for motivating people. An interesting approach to this problem will be offered in this text, wherein an "Action Guide to Motivating People" available to the business world has been converted and adapted by the author for use in a youth group setting and will serve as a motivational and/or influence self-check list for the group worker. The chapter on motivation will help answer the questions posed above.

The 1972 *Annual Handbook for Group Facilitators* supports the contention that in all human interactions there are two major ingredients—content and process. The first, content, deals with the subject matter or task upon which the group is working. The second ingredient, process, is concerned with what is happening between and to group members while the group is operating. In most interactions, the focus of all concerned is on content, whereas little attention is directed toward process, even when it is a major cause of ineffective group action. The author feels that group process (or dynamics) is the key to successful group operations. Therefore, much space will be devoted to this key activity throughout the text.

Part of the text will deal with findings developed by the U.S. Civil Service Commission about groups and leadership in general. We will want to find a common denominator in terms of what characteristics are common to all groups. Leadership theory and research will be discussed in order to determine the practical relationship between the concepts of leadership and supervision.

Some space will be devoted to acquaint the group worker with the concept of Planning by Objectives (PBO). The Federal Government's ACTION adherents maintain that it can be utilized by almost any group worker, in that "PBO will help you figure out where you're going and point out the road most likely to get you there." PBO is a system for stating what the group worker plans to accomplish with the group and then planning the means to achieve these goals. The author feels strongly that the PBO concept can and should be adapted, with transitory ease, to group work.

Knowledge of the mechanics and intricacies of Interpersonal Relations is a must for those individuals who work with and guide groups of teenagers. An exposition of "The Johari Window" (a graphic model of awareness in interpersonal relations, developed by Joseph Luft and Harry Ingham) will tend to direct the neophyte group worker to examine his/her own behavior in relation to others. Luft feels that many people get along fine working with others without thinking about which foot to put forward. But when there are difficulties, when the usual methods do not work, when we want to learn more—there is no alternative but to examine our own behavior in relation to others. However, it is difficult to find ways of thinking about such matters, particularly for people who have no extensive backgrounds in the social sciences. The "Johari Window" illustrates relationships in terms of awareness and seems to lend itself well as a device for speculating about human relations.

The basic elements of psychodrama and sociodrama will be touched upon, primarily because the author feels that these techniques of therapy are misunderstood by many group workers and conceivably are being inadvertently misused in the group setting in the guise of unrelated role-playing. Adam Blatner, a psychiatrist and advocate of psychodrama, describes the latter as a method by which a person can be helped to explore the psychological dimensions of his problems through the enactment of his conflict situations, rather than by talking about them. Sociodrama is a form of psychodrama enactment that aims at clarifying group themes rather than focusing on the individual's problems. Dr. Blatner cautions, and the author reiterates, that psychodramatic (as well as sociodramatic) techniques can be very powerful, and it behooves practitioners to develop their skills with humility and commitment. The therapist or group leader must build a wide spectrum of skills and a depth of ability to apply them, for mere technique is not enough. An experienced or incompenent group worker can do much more harm than good by experimentation in this sphere.

Without attempting to moralize, it is important to recognize that the so-called sexual revolution and the change in community mores relative to sexual contacts among young people have not bypassed the teenager. Some training and knowledge in the area of venereal disease is therefore incumbent for those working with youth. The American Council for Healthful Living, a nationally recognized leader in the development and implementation of V.D. education for health educators and others, cites nine common sexually transmitted diseases: Gonorrhea, Syphilis, Herpes Simplex II, Non-Specific Urethritis, Trichomonas Vaginalis, Monilial Vaginitis, Venereal Warts, Pediculosis Pubis, and Scabies. It is important for all concerned, particularly the worker, to get to know more about V.D. and other health problems of the teenager (i.e., alcoholism, drug abuse, skin care, teeth care, teenage pregnancies, and the like). These will be covered in the text.

The group worker is often called upon to write recommendations for young people in the latter's quest for jobs or college admission. It behooves the group worker to acquire some basic knowledge of resource materials and persons available in the community to aid in college placement and the securing of jobs. Various guides to college selection and to financing a college education are available in most community libraries and bookstores (note the various guides put out by Barrows). A summary of scholarships, fellowships, grants, loans, jobs, and other aids can be easily obtained from publications such as Fine and Eisenberg's *How to Get Money for College*.

Those youngsters who bypass college and want to enter into the job market need special counseling on how to deport themselves at employment interviews. The importance of such personal characteristics as "oral expression" and "poise" at interview sessions will be covered in the chapter on Vocational Guidance.

Although direct contact with teenagers having emotional problems leading to alcoholism, suicide, and the runaway syndrome is foreign to many group workers, the ability to recognize such problem situations is incumbent upon such workers. The amount and extent of intervention possible in these situations will be explored in separate chapters.

How to get off dead-center at youth group functions—ice-breakers and the like—are made the subject of special attention in the text.

Community project lists and citizen-directed group activities are also discussed at some length.

Therapies, including some rather unusual approaches, are covered for the edification and education of group workers who may find themselves in the position of making suggestions to group members with problems.

Chapter 1

REFERENCES

American Council for Healthful Living (formerly Venereal Disease Service Organization) Orange, N.J. "Nine Commonly Sexually Transmitted Diseases," 1979.

Annual Handbook for Group Facilitators - 1972. "What to Look for in Groups."

Blatner, Howard A. *Acting-in-Practical Applications of Psychodramatic Methods*. Springer Publishing Co. Inc., 1973.

Bureau of Business Practice, Waterford, Conn. *Action Guide to Motivating People,* 1973.

Eskow, Seymour. *Barron's Guide to the Two Year Colleges*. Barron's Educational Series, 1960.

Federal Bureau of Labor Statistics. *Occupational Outlook Quarterly.*

Fine, Benjamin and Eisenberg, Sidney A. *How to Get Money for College*. Doubleday and Co., 1964.

Lesser, Bernard. *The Youth Advisors Handbook*. Nealco Publishing Co., 1970.

Luft, Joseph. *Human Relations Training News,* 1961.

Luft, Joseph. *Of Human Interaction,* National Press Books, 1969.

Mali, Paul. *Managing by Objectives*. John Wiley and Sons, 1972.

Marsland, David. *Sociological Explorations in the Service of Youth. National Youth Bureau, Leicester, England, 1978.*

National Student Volunteer Program (ACTION). Planning by Objectives.

Rodgers, C. R. "The Nondirective Method as a Technique for Social Research." *American Journal of Sociology,* 1945.

Strauss, George and Sales, Leonard R. *Personnel – The Human Problems of Management*. Prentice Hall Publishing Co., 1972.

Student Volunteers. "It's Your Move – Working With Student Volunteers." *A Manual for Community Organizations.*

U.S. Civil Service Comission. "Leadership and Supervision." *A Survey of Research Findings,* 1955.

Weisner, Paul. Director, V.D. Division, Federal Center for Disease Control, Atlanta, Ga. Pictoral story. "In His Own Words," *People Magazine,* 10/1/79.

Chapter 2

Who Should Be A Youth Worker?

Long before a program is established, the success or failure of a youth group is all but assured by a decision made, not by the youth, but (and rightfully so) by the clergyman, youth board or committee, or school principal. I speak of the choice of the group worker. An ill-equipped worker with inappropriate background, motivation, and skills can quickly destroy a well-functioning youth group and often do harm to its individual members, who look to him/her as a model. We must then first appraise the persons who assume this mantle, be they professionals or lay workers, salaried or volunteer. What type of people shall we seek to fill this role? What are their philosophies? Their experience and training? Their personal qualities and attributes? All too often we designate an untrained (not always necessarily fatal) and/or unmotivated person to act in this capacity. As often as not, there is little rapport or identification with the youth group, and certainly only limited guidance and direction emanating from such a person, well-intentioned as he or she may be. The ensuing discourse will deal with the requisite qualities necessary for the youth group worker, the person who is basically responsible for the successful operation of the youth group. This will permit the incumbent as well as the aspiring worker an opportunity for self evaluation.

Generally speaking, the worker should have the tireless energy of a bill collector; the curiosity of a cat; the tenacity of a bulldog; the assurance of a college boy; the determination of a taxi driver; the patience of a self-sacrificing wife; the enthusiasm of a rock n' roll fan; the good humor of a court jester; and the diplomacy of a wayward husband. The author personally would seek as many as possible of the following attributes (although, with full candor, he recognizes that we must usually settle for less. Nevertheless, the more of these attributes that we seek and can find in one person, the finer youth program that we shall ultimately have and the more skills the worker will acquire.) Use the following interrogatory for self-assessment purposes and identification of areas that need improvement.

I. Characteristics of the Worker — Self Evaluation:

A. Interrelationship Factors — Do I have?	Yes	No
• Integrity, sincerity, a sense of fair play, equity, and impartiality.	☐	☐
• A warm and positive feeling about being a group worker.	☐	☐
• As much knowledge as possible about the lay or religious group with whom I am working.	☐	☐
• A firm belief in the value and goals of the aforementioned group.	☐	☐
• A deep sense of responsibility and loyalty to my employers and to the youngsters of the youth group.	☐	☐
• Faith and confidence in the ultimate value of the group members' and my own endeavors, individually and collectively.	☐	☐
• The capacity to like and empathize with people, respect their attributes,worth, and dignity, and to be tolerant of their faults; ability to translate my warmth into purposeful and meaningful relationships.	☐	☐
• At least a rudimentary understanding of the basic skills of human relations, group dynamics, and administration.	☐	☐
B. Personality Factors — Do I have?		
• A sense of humor and an even temper.	☐	☐
• The ability to be friendly, gracious, and cordial.	☐	☐
• A high level of maturity, emotional stability, self-awareness, and insight, allowing me to be attuned to the group and its needs.	☐	☐
• Humility, recognizing my own limitations.	☐	☐
• The ability to inspire.	☐	☐
• Imagination and perspective.	☐	☐
• The trait of decisiveness wherein I do not delay in making decisions but take the initiative with courage and confidence.	☐	☐
• Energy and persistence born of faith and optimism.	☐	☐
• Thoroughness, paying attention to details and not relying on chance.	☐	☐
• Open-mindedness and receptivity to new ideas.	☐	☐

II. Job Description Elements — Check List:

As contained in the job description of a youth worker, I must:

A. Contacts with the Youth

- Become an authority on youth. Through reading books and articles, watching TV specials, etc., I should always be *au courant* as possible with the nature, problems, and concerns of youth. ☐
- Acquire as much knowledge as possible of the structure of the youth group, the personality traits and habits of the officers, key members, and as many of the general membership as possible. ☐
- Counsel and advise youth group members so that they actively participate in youth group functions and develop their own activities. ☐
- Guide individual members involved in special "growth" endeavors, such as participating in the year-round Community Betterment programs. Occasionally, do personal counseling. ☐
- If asked, prepare college recommendations for high school seniors. ☐
- Be alert to identify and report apparent emotional or other problems to parents or program director. This can be a very sensitive area, and great caution and discretion must be exercised. ☐
- Contact those members who are habitually absent to make sure that it is not the fault of the group, that it has failed to sufficiently utilize the talents of the youth or slighted him/her in some way. In such instances, I should take corrective action. ☐
- Maintain sustained liaison with group officers and committee chairmen, attend executive meetings, and be available for consultation in the planning of youth meetings. ☐
- Follow-up with officers and members entrusted with responsibilities to assure that assignments are clear and that the individuals involved or the group as a whole are not harmed by failure to procrastination in following through on specific tasks. ☐
- Attend all general meetings, aiding the youth group members to make decisions democratically (without getting embroiled in "over-parliamentarianism"), with due consideration for the intersts of every member of the group and the sponsoring organization (Sisterhood, the Church, recreation department, etc.). The worker is the final arbiter on health, welfare, safety, and reputation of the organization. ☐
- Be dynamic as a catalyst, helping youth to analyze their activities and to establish their goals and the means toward attaining them, bringing new knowledge, attitudes, and ideas to the group. ☐
- Be a resource person with knowledge and ideas for effective programming. He/she should develop contacts within the community and establish contacts with outside organizations and service bodies that can supply speakers, films, panels, etc., to fit the needs of the group. ☐

B. Contacts with Officials and Others

- Maintain continuous liaison with the program director so that there is congruence of understanding as to the nature and goals of the youth group. ☐
- If a religious group, maintain contain liaison with the congregation's religious school principal or director of education so that activities and schedules can be coordinated. ☐
- If a religious group, maintain continuous liaison with key congregational leaders and staff members, coordinating activites, making the youth group as functional as possible as a member of the religious family, and keeping the parent organization aware of youth group activities and needs. ☐
- Maintain continuous liaison with and attend meetings of the appropriate sponsoring youth committee or commission so as to project new programs, review past and present programs, analyze problem areas, seek logistic support, and clarify policy matters. ☐
- Become acquainted with as many parents as possible; they can become a source of help for chaperones, home hospitality, chauffeuring, cooking and, often, substantive help advising specific committees, helping to get speakers, etc., etc. ☐
- Become acquainted with the home communities and schools of the youth group members. School schedules should be consulted before scheduling youth activities. ☐
- Make initial contacts with youth leaders, workers, and representatives of other groups in the community. ☐

C. Specific Task Requirements

- If working with a religious group, ascertain (through contact with appropriate congregational figures) where and how the group can best serve the congregation in needed activities and services (nothing can contribute more to the deterioration of interest in and concern for a program than the manufacturing and engineering of unneeded and artificial "keep busy" activity). ☐
- Guide and monitor the various youth group projects dealing with service to the community, ascertaining if the recipients of such services are *bona fide* organizations actually in need of the services to be provided. ☐
- Oversee youth group finances. I should participate in the planning of the youth group's segment of the parent body's budget and should endeavor to stay within the approved budget allocation for youth activites. As far as the group's own funds are concerned, I must oversee the books and the budgets. ☐
- Oversee internal and external communications and publications. I

should satisfy myself that all text is appropriate and in good taste. ☐

- Work toward building up interest among pre-teenagers and other potential members, meeting (when feasible) with teachers and parents of potential members. ☐
- Be responsible for all premises used by the group, ensuring that they are left ssecure, clean, and in good condition. I must report any damage or loss of equipment to the appropriate authorities. ☐
- Be the first to arrive and the last to leave any group function. ☐
- Be sure that the sponsoring organization has adequate insurance and bonding for all events on or away from the premises. ☐
- In case of accident, attend the injured person and immediately advise the appropriate authorities. ☐
- Be intimately involved in any disciplinary aciton meted out to those who violate local or regional codes of conduct. ☐
- When invited, participate as a lecturer or panelist on any local or regional programs where I feel I have the competence to do so. ☐
- Accompany the group on out-of-town trips and attend some portion of all camp weekends, conclaves, leadership institutes, etc. ☐
- Attend professional leadership courses and classes and, where they are established, participate in professional betterment courses leading to certification, where available. ☐

This list certainly seems to be overpowering for a part-time job. However, many of these items happen simultaneously, and one often fulfills several in a single given situation. Also, much of this activity may, as we shall see, be delegated to parents, assistants, and even youth.

The behavioral sciences encouraged the sophisticated use of the concept of group dynamics, with its focus on the group members rather than solely on the group worker. The importance of youth group member involvement and participation in decision making is today one of the accepted precepts in group dynamics. The methodology of highly directive leadership has been relegated to the ash heap in favor of motivational approaches and concern with human relations. Today's group worker must understand this concept in order to be effective.

The group worker must be flexible in approach and must exert a pattern of involvement that would best benefit the particular group with which he/she is working.The spectrum of the worker's behavior extends from an almost autocratic approach to complete permissiveness. The ideal today falls somewhere in between. Let us look at the various images of the group worker that today represent our prototypes: Which category do you, as a group worker, fall into?

- The autocratic worker who makes decisions without consultation and blandly announces them at meetings; ☐
- the worker who in essence makes his/her own decisions and who tries to "sell" them to the group; ☐
- the worker who makes tentative decisions, but is willing to discuss them with the group and might possibly alter them subjet to the group's will; ☐
- the worker who presents ideas and invites discussion and questions and then unilaterally makes his/her own decisions; ☐
- the reactive worker who does not participate in initial deliberations, but who lashes into the youngsters, singularly or collectively, privately or publicly, whenever they make errors of commission or omission; ☐
- the worker who presents ideas, defines limits and asks the group to make decisions; ☐
- the worker who disassociates entirely from the decision making, and pursues a passive role, being available for comment only if called on for that purpose. ☐

The autocratic worker generates resentment, whereas the completely permissive worker might well be the cause for indecision and apathy within the group. As indicated before, the course of action to be followed by the worker today should all somewhere between, without him/her abdicating responsibility for disseminating ideas and giving guidance.

The author has known group workers with extensive education, experiential background and infinite skill who almost destroyed normal, functioning groups by an authoritarian demeanor and by publicly criticizing youngsters for errors of omission and commission. The situations were such that the criticism was generally valid. However, the younsters who were made the subject of constant public excoriation built up such a defensive posture that the existing learning process terminated completely, as did the rapport and warm relationship with the group worker involved. As a result, subconsciously (and often overtly), the members create general hostile attitudes that are ultimately expressed in rejection of the worker's ideas, talents, and wealth of information. Obviously, this adverse climate, unknowingly initiated by the worker but perpetuated with great relish by the teenagers, destroys almost every vestige of group *esprit de corps.*

One can envision that, on occasion, a group might band together in such an adverse environment and antithetically develop an *esprit de corps* and series of interrelations that were lacking theretofore. At first blush, this seems to reflect accomplishment of a primary group goal, albeit motivated by retaliatory concerns. However, the foundations built in this manner not only lack perpetuity, but presage limited continuity. A group built primarily on such tenuous, devisive, and shallow precepts must ultimately erode.

It is evident that the group workers described above had little empathy with the youth with whom they were working. They evidently could not identify with or respond to the emotional needs of the young people, and, as a result, broke down what should have been a genuinely warm relationship.

The youngsters, particularly if left to their own devices, will surely come up with their fair share of errors, foolish acts, and excesses. An able worker, unlike those described above, will accept this and spare the youngsters humiliation, for all life is trial and error. The purpose of discipline, *per se,* at all levels of our society is to prevent the repetition of indiscretions and offenses. Therefore, criticism in the youth group environment should be constructive. Wanton pulling apart or tearing down will bring about a distaste for the original rule, project, etc., to say nothing of the persons doing the criticizing.

Inasmuch as we have taken the time to earmark criticism as a privotal point in the group worker's professional life, it might be well to examine some of the mechanics and guideposts involved.

Criticism must always begin with praise and candid appreciation for the positive things that the youngster, or group, have accomplished. This, then, is followed by commentary on how the "good job" might have been done "even better" or differently. An earnest desire by the worker to be helpful in this way creates an empathetic image and generally appeals to the youngster.

Mistakes made by the youngsters must be accepted as evolutionary steps in the process of learning and growing up. They will not attain perfection, and any group that reflects perfection in most aspects of activity is either putting on a well-coached performance for visiting firemen or is engaged in a superficially structured program, without the necessary depth that engenders "trial and error" – the incubator of learning and accomplishment. The worker must always keep in mind the old cliche that nobody ever learns except by making mistakes. It is, for instance, almost axiomatic in the world of business management that the better a man is the more mistakes he will make, because of the many new ideas that he will invoke and experiment with in order to produce a higher quality and quantity of work.

Potential group workers, and incumbents as well, can review the seven basic types of workers outlined in this chapter and decide which grouping they fall into. Is the approach that is used good for both you and the youth group? Or is it time for a personal reassessment?

In assaying his own lifetime experiences with youth, the author would tend to identify four major bodies of knowledge or groupings of skills that would be of utmost vlaue to the group worker or club advisor, to wit:

- Organizational management and development
- Counseling (limited)
- Training
- Recognition and handling of stress and stress situations.

It would be patently unfair and unsopisticated to expect our volunteers or part-time quasi-professionals to be expert in all or any of the above groupings. However, the more information that the group worker can assimilate about these subjects, the more effective he/she can become in group process.

Organizational Management

Hackman and Suttle, in a 1977 work, emphasized the equitable enforcement of rules in reference to supervisors' relationship to workers. An analogy can be drawn in terms of the group worker's relationships with group members.

- Disciplinary action should be invoked only for violations of known and accepted rules, and the degree of such action should not exceed expections.
- First-time violations, unless serious, should receive only a warning.
- An appeals apparatus should be provided.
- No discipline is to be applied arbitrarily or inconsistently.

Personnel texts stress that considerate supervisors (in our case, group workers) avoid nagging or repeated criticism for trivial inadequacies; that they wait to hear the group member's side of the story before imposing discipline. Learning theory is in agreement with these points, in that it suggests that praise is a more effective motivator than punishment. Very often, peer discipline (or pressure) is more effective than supervisory discipline—something a group worker must take into consideration on a case-by-case basis.

What are some of the characteristics of a skilled manager (group worker)? One of the chief functions of a manager (group worker) in our parlance, according to Nathaniel Cantor, is the responsibility to help the growth of the people that they manage. Effective help is based upon knowledge of what occurs between people working together and upon an understanding of how to make use of that knowledge in a multidimensional context.

The outstanding qualities of a skilled group worker are as follows (How many of these do you, the worker, have?):

- Refrains from making narrow moral judgments about associates or group members. ☐
- Keeps personal needs under control. ☐
- Recognizes the importance of group member's and/or learner's feelings. ☐
- Starts where the learner is. ☐
- Accepts differences (permissive atmosphere). ☐
- Recreates himself. ☐
- Encourages group members to develop through his/her help. ☐

Counseling Skills

We expect our group workers to have at least a modicum of counseling skills or to at least recognize situations that call for a minor degree of counseling. Leona Tyler tells us that counseling is an intensely personal sort of activity. The results of research studies comparing methods, techniques, or theories run up against the fact that differences between counselors are greater than any of these systematic differences in procedure. However, successful results seem to depend as much upon what a counselor is as on what he or she says or does. Effective counselors have come from a variety of professions and business situations—therefore, it is most difficult to identify the type or the desired background of a person who would be adept at counseling.

The most authoritative guidelines found in the policy statement prepared by the Professional Preparation and Standards Committee of the American Personnel and Guidance Association for the practicing counselor (i.e., Master's Degree based on two years of graduate work) are generally beyond the reach of the volunteer group worker. Yet counseling is a key aspect of youth group work. We must therefore distinguish between the limited everyday routine type of counseling that the group worker should and can be doing and the deep-seated problem type of counseling that is beyond his or her range of skills. As mentioned many times in various contexts in this work, the truly professional type of counseling should be left to those who can best handle it.

If one subscribes to the view that the most significant element that the counselor brings to the relationship, despite the limitations of a group worker, is oneself, then the way that group worker-counselors see themselves and their roles is paramount in this personal process. Johnson and Vertermark comment that, with the counselor who sees his/her responsibilities in a restricted light, such as extending to educational and vocational matters only, there can be no personal-social counseling. This is self-evident in that the counselor who cuts off personal matters (such that the group worker would encounter in normal group intervention] limits any possible effectiveness in helping the group members in educational and vocational decision making, the very areas in which the counselor,in this case, sees the greatest potential for contribution to the group. The group worker becomes less effective in areas of his/her own expertise (if they have any) by dancing around group members' day-to-day personal problems. The latter may have to be resolved before both counselor and teenager can resolve the former.

Conversely, some group worker-counselors view themselves as being highly competent in counseling individuals with primarily personal problems. They do not think that they are really counseling unless they can uncover a "good problem." The danger here is all too obvious. A later chapter will center on counseling to a greater degree.

Training Skills

Matthew B. Miles identifies the trainer (worker) as a person with special responsibility for helping individual and group members learn from their experiences. The trainer's role is to facilitate learning about better group behavior, basically a teacher, they usually deal more in the analysis of here and now behavior than do most teachers. In essence, the trainer-group worker facilitates learning. When the youth group gets bogged down, becomes apathetic, or is involved in internal strife, the trainer-group worker's job is not necessarily to help the group "get out of the mess," but to help them learn from the mess. In brief, the trainer must act as a planner prior to a training activity, as a guide during the operation of the activity, and as an evaluator during the planning of new activities.

Stress Conditions

The description of organizational stressors is by no means exhaustive, and it should be noted that these forces interact with others that are present in the life of a group worker. Jere E. Yates[2] of Pepperdine University wrote in the September 1979 issue of *Management* magazine that a major source of stress in organizational life is role conflict, such as conflict between one's personal values and what the work role calls for. If group workers' abilities are not utilized by the organization, they are unchallenged and often feel that their education was wasted, this causes stress. Job insecurity also causes stress, as does uncertainty about one's profesional status. Insufficient authority for the responsibility that the group worker has creates stress. So do exhorbitant work demands.

Conflict can occur between the group worker's role as a family member and his/her work role, for instance, frequent travel and unusual hours may prevent one from spending time with one's children. Role ambiguity, the uncertainty of what one's job is or what needs to be done in order to be effective, can lead to stress.

The other major kinds of stressors are personal ones. These are more a product of the group worker's own internal conflicts and perceptions than of pressures stemming from the outside. Yates cites a series of individual stressors that are representative of the many pressures that we (and this would apply to the group worker as well) face today:

- A feeling that the job lacks relevance.
- Frustrated ambitions.

---

[2]Reprinted with permission of Jere E. Yates, Chairperson, Business Administration, Pepperdine University, Malibu, California.

- Belief that younger people moving into the organization are better educated and better prepared and, as such, pose a threat to one's position. (Ironically, although this is often untrue, it may become a self-fulfilling prophecy if stress is permitted to interfere with job performance.)

Excessive, prolonged stress could possibly lead to physical or emotional disorders. The important thing is to head off trouble by noticing early warning signs of stress before the group worker winds up with a full bundle of serious woes. Yates lists the following symptoms as possible warning signs of excessive stress.

- Insomnia
- General irritability
- Anxiety and depression
- Fatigue
- Loss of appetite or excesssive appetite
- Increased smoking
- Impulsive behavior
- Speech changes
- Nervous laughter
- Nervous ticks
- Pounding heart
- Dry mouth
- Alcohol and drug dependence
- Decline in the quality or quantity of work produced
- Pain in the neck or lower back
- Headaches
- Upset stomach
- Inability to concentrate
- Nightmares
- Accident prone
- Neurotic behavior.

One or more of these symptoms, particularly if they persist, may well be strong indicators of stress-induced problems caused by heavy stress loads (before reaching finite conclusions, a consultation with a physician is in order to rule out other causal possibilities).

Stressful situations will not generally disappear on their own. The alternatives left to the group worker are to decrease the amount of stress or learn to live with it and manage it. Being able and willing to take things in stride is a great personal characteristic. The group worker has some power at his/her disposal in determing whether normal stressors become distressful, for one's individual and controlled response to a stressor is by far the greatest factor in how stressful a particular event will become for that person. One person may look upon a particular event as a time of excitement, stimulation, and new opportunities; the second person may experience the same event as distress—a time of fear, anxiety, uncertainty, and upheaval. What makes their responses so different is their differing perceptions, which are often based upon their own abilities and levels of self-confidence. If group workers can change their perceptions of the cause and effect of potentially stressful situations, they will be well on the way toward managing stress.

Relaxation is the physiological antithesis of stress. Relaxation techniques of various kinds appear to be useful for stress reduction, to wit:

- Exercise is a way of using stress to defeat the ravages of distress because it not only builds cardio-vascular fitness (when properly done), but it forces the body to relax afterwards (caution: an exercise program should not be begun or resumed without a physician's clearance).
- It will be most helpful to the group worker if he/she thoroughly enjoys the job. The more one enjoys t work, the better the chance of the stressors producing positive reactions.
- We must tenaciously hold on to some stability in life. The more change there is, the more stress. One must think twice before giving up the stability that one gets from friends, job, family, or religion.
- Values must be periodically clarified and one's life must be matched with such values to ensure harmony. A life that goes against the grain of its value is likely to suffer stressful wear and tear.
- Options must be kept open by keeping oneself as professionally up-to-date as possible. Knowing that one has options is a great asset in dealing with stress.
- Good nutrition is to be practiced. A healthy, well-nourished, and well-exercised body can take more stress than a weak, poorly nourished one.

Group workers, in order to manage stress, must initially identify the sources of their distress and seek to eliminate them or at least blunt their force. Identification of the problems can, as in many other disciplines, go a long way toward solving them.

Yates concludes that stress is not to be avoided; it is to be managed. A certain amount of it is needed to keep people alert and alive. By trial and error, we can learn how much can be tolerated before backing off. As each group worker begins to recognize his or her own unique danger signs of not coping well, he/she will be in a position to take constructive action to manage stress rather than becoming its victim.

REFERENCES

Cantor, N. *The Learning Process for Managers.* Harper and Row, 1958.

Hackman, J. R. and Suttle, J. L. Improving Life at Work – Behavioral Science Approaches to Organizational Change. Goodyear Publishing Company, 1977.

Johnson, D. E. and Vestermark, M. J. *Barriers and Hazards in Counseling.* Houghton Mifflin Co., 1970.

Miles, M. B. *Learning to Work in Groups.* Teachers College Press, Columbia University, 1967.

Tyler, L. E. *The Work of the Counselor.* Meredith Corp., 1969.

Yates, J. E. "Managing Stress." *Management* (a magazine for government managers), September 1979.

Chapter 3

Who Is The Teenager?

Obviously, no text such as this dares to ignore the composition of the product that we are dealing with – today's tenager. many modern-day essayists, journalists, and poets have "waxed eloquent" on the subject "what is a teenager?" But a glib description, however beautifully articulated, cannot really do justice for our needs any more than one could adequately characterize a child, an adult, or a golden-ager in a paragraph or two.

There are basic processes – physical and mental – that the teenager shares in common with all human beings; there are other traits, emphases, and mannerisms that are more characteristic of the adolescent than of people in other stages of their development.

First of all, a teenager is a person. "Teenager" refers to a stage in development, not a separate and different basic character type. Eacch of us adults was once a teenager; we have not altered our basic personality or changed our identity from those days. There is the ever-present danger of considering teenagers as a specific, separate, unique class of individuals, different in kind from all other people. This can produce difficulties, particularly for the worker, since one cannot empathize with something totally different from oneself. There is also the problem of categorizing people and then "pidgeonholing" or filing them away. While some generalizations will prove helpful, it would be most unfortunate if we generalized to the point where we lost sight of the fact that each member of our youth group is a unique individual. He/she is not a member of a faceless class or a roaming band of strange creatures in jeans with trendy styles and incomprehensible dialects committing anti-social actions. They, like all other people, have their own ambitions, hopes and dreams, disappointments, frustrations and confusions, inspirations and joys, and anxieties and fears.

Physically, the teenager of fourteen to eighteen may still be growing. While some of our youth group members have already attained their full growth and physical development, others will still experience spurts of growth, change of voice, development of secondary sex characteristics, etc., which may cause some self-consciousness or even emotional stress. Most youth are energetic, requiring a good deal of sleep and food. Teenagers drink tremendous amounts of milk; they eat more than adults. Thus, teenagers who eat voraciously are not necessarily "piggish" or "orally fixated" but, rather, are fueling a perpetual-motion machine. It is also for this reason that we must be on the lookout for compulsive dieters, particularly amongst the girls – growing people need adequate food.

Today's youth live in a world where technological, economic, and social change are not evolutionary but border on the revolutionary. Changes are being wrought so quickly that the teenage generation not only differentiates theirs from previous generations, but also at times from slightly older contemporaries.

At home, the teenagers with whom we deal most likely have their own record players and perhaps their own TV sets. Those old enough to drive probably have either the use of a family car from time to time or even a car exclusively for their own use. Most do not work but have a weekly allowance. A significant percentage have their own charge accounts and credit cards. Thus, unlike their grandparents who, when children, worked to bring in family income, our typical youth of today, by and large, are consumers causing an economic drain on the family coffers. For example, college may cost from $5,000 to $8,000 per year. This sense of not being needed and not being a partner in the maintenance of the family can, according to many psychologists, cause a sense of insecurity and guilt that can be projected as resentment and hostility toward the parents.

The chances are that the youth of today are members of families that do not spend as much time together as did families in former times. This is due to the realities of suburban and exurban living, with long and wearisome commutation incumbent upon the breadwinner, emancipation of the housewife, and the high degree of community organization. Television and cablevision further cut down conversation within the household. Thus, many relationships that would formerly have existed within the home are now established with the peer group or with adults outside the home.

In school, youth work harder and more hours than did their parents. The explosion in the publishing field and the new methods in education serve to put additional pressure on the student, which may or may not be commensurate with the quality of education or its relevance to teenagers' life problems and needs as they see them. There seems to be coincidentally, more cheating in school (with, probably, less concomitant guilt attached to it). Schools are being transformed more and more into knowledge factories, and the depersonalization of the student becomes increasingly demoralizing. Interested adults with necessary skills, time, and desire to spend time with youth are rarer and rarer commodities.

Youth are more cosmopolitan. A greater number of young peole have the opportunity for travel and other exciting and broadening vacation and summer educational experiences.

Youth are, at least superficially, more sophisticated. With the automobile providing mobility and an always available back seat, sexual experiences seem to be more frequent and intense with this generation.

Socially conscious and concerned youth are feeling more and more that they have new power in this country, and many are attempting to exercise this power. Some of this is promoted and encouraged by the mass media, some by Madison Avenue.

Youth, undergoing the transition from the world of childhood to the world of adulthood, participate in aspects of both; as a result, they are mercurial, often unpredictable, intense, energetic, impatient, idealistic, optimistic, simplistic, engrossed with self, and volatile. They often feel alienated from the adult world and ill at ease in the presence of the older generation; thus, they flock to their peers and conform to the fads of their own subculture.

David Marsland[3], in his study of the habits of young people in England, makes certain observations that seem to fit foursquare with a profile of American teenagers, to wit:

- The earning power of young people has never been anywhere near so high as it is today.
- The spending power of youth is immense, to the extent of dominating and shaping some markets.
- Young people are spared involvement in the rigors and discipline of work which, until very recently, even children had to bear. The continuing growth of education absorbs a larger and larger proportion of young peole up to and beyond the age of eighteen.
- Changes in acceptable styles of authority, and of social relationships generally, relieve contemporary youth of the harshness of earlier forms of supervision, punishment, etc., which were used routinely on young people with even less compunction than on children.
- Hours of work, whether in school, college, or place of employment, are trivial by comparison even with as little as two decades ago. Free time is available in plenty.
- Contemporary youth are the first heirs to wholesale mass-production's effects on supply and on prices. Even in the midst of inflation, luxury goods are easily and cheaply available.
- Above all, youth is free. The established bases for control of their behavior in religion; in widely shared, morally restrictivist values; and in the community context of living have, to all intents and purposes, evaporated. Without "preachers," "moralizers," and "snoopers," young peole can do as they wish, untrammelled.
- Youth has been recognized as a special category in its own right, with the

[3]Reprinted with permission of National Youth Bureau, Leicester, England.

consequence that all sorts of special public and private provision is made for their needs. Claims made by them and on their behalf are increasingly acknowledged as reflecting their rights. At most formal and official levels, special legislative arrangements attend to the needs and rights of young people.

- One effect of the extension of education through schooling (but also, and perhaps more powerfully, through the media) is to equip young people with a level of knowledge that defuses adult myths and cripples the power of customary controls. In regard to religion, politics, sex, work, and all the other fundamentals, young people are "in the know" and out of reach at least of simple trickery, which has worked in the past.
- The geographical and social world is opened up to young people in a way and to a degree that has never been remotely possible in the past. Through the media, through transportation on the local scene, and through tourism, access to new worlds has been vastly increased.

In looking at a broad picture of the impact of youth on society, it would seem that youth is disproportionately represented in the unemployment rolls as well as in the crime statistics. Also included in the negative statistics, as represented by youth, we find inordinate numbers of young people involved with drug and alcohol abuse, V.D., and illegitimacy. There is some degree of homelessness affecting the young. In some quarters, young people are permitted to leave home and move about in pursuit of learning, work, or somewhere meaningful to belong.

One of our weekly news magazines, *Newsweek* (September 17, 1979), focused on the TV industry's preoccupation with the likes and dislikes of young people by pointing out, in an article titled "The Year of the Teen," that twelve of the twenty-one new series arriving that week were targeted at a state of mind bordered by the sixth and twelfth grades.

Herman Peters points out that adolescents, paradoxically, rebel against dependency on and conformity to parental systems, only to substitute a fierce conformity and deep involvement in peer relationships. Teenagers yearn to make real choices in what, to them, appears to be a closed system of behavior. They are becoming aware of the possibility of openness in human relations and of a continuing dialogue with others. To neglect guidance of teenagers in this area of living at this time of their lives is to render sterile other types of guidance in the educational and vocational spheres.

Peters further states that adolescence is the emergence of the spirit of the sense of the self as a distinct, singularly unique being. Adolescence is the process of turning from the security afforded by the outer world to that of being with and relating to others, and of learning to regard these relations as supportive and supplementary, rather than basic and complementary.

Authentic selfhood is emerging in adolescence, even though it is not visibly evident. Their recognition of being startles them into doubting the reliability of people and things that they depended on in childhood for security. They are hampered by awkwardness in relating, as well as functioning physically. They begin to doubt adults, and often they hear them but do not listen. They go through a stage of disillusionment in regard to people and things that they once thought to be firm and fixed.

Youth and early adulthood, according to Peters, involve the integration of being and existing with others. Young persons need opportunities to examine their newly manifested selfhood. They engage in an inner dialogue with themselves. They also yearn for dialogue with others, including various counselors in school and outside the school. The positive outcome of this process of integrating and finding oneself is a part of the continuing creation of a responsible adult. The group worker, therefore, plays a key role in this maturation process and as a developer of human resources.

REFERENCES

Marsland, D. *Sociological Explorations in the Service for Youth.* National Youth Bureau, England, 1978.

"New Fall T.V. Review," *Newsweek Magazine,* (9/17/79).

Peters, H. J. a paper entitled "The Counselor as a Developer in Counseling and Guidance in the Twentieth Century."

Chapter 4

Why a Youth Group?

Throughout history, people banded together in groups for all manner of reasons, from social interaction to survival. Social scientists, however, do not agree among themselves about the definition of a group—notwithstanding the fact that their professional efforts are directed toward analysis of group behavior.

J. R. Hackman and J. LLoyd Suttle of Yale University have proposed a definition of a "group" that the author has found most interesting.

"A human group is a collection of individuals

- who have significantly interdependent relations with each other,
- who perceive themselves as a group by reliably distinguishing members from nonmembers,
- whose group identity is recognized by nonmembers,
- who have differentiated roles in the group as a function of expectations from themselves, other group members, and nongroup members, and
- who, as group members acting alone or in concert, have significantly interdependent relations with other groups."

A. Historical and Philosophical Implications

Hackman and Suttle feel that the idea of significantly interdependent relations among members does not imply that all members must have face-to-face interaction with each other. It does mean that members share common concerns. Further, a collection of individuals known only to each other is not a group. For a group to exist, some nonmembers must know that there is a group in which they are not members. This knowledge is necessary for the group as a whole to relate to its external environment.

The survivial and vitality of a group depends on the evolution of roles to manage the internal and external problems of group life. If the internal concerns of group members are not satisfied, members will drop out, and eventually the group will cease to exist.

Anthony T. Palisi[4] of Seton Hall University proposes that an adaptation of

[4]Reprinted with permission of Heldred Publications, Washington, D.C.

Cattell's (1948) definition of a group can provide a frame of reference for the group worker to organize his/her perceptions *of process*. Cattell held that three aspects must be taken into account in defining a group:

- Syntality traits.
- Characteristics of internal structure.
- Population traits.

Syntality refers to the group acting as a group. It is behavior or inferences drawn from behavior from which the group is perceived as acting as a totality upon its own environment or, conceivably, on the environment of other groups. Casual commentary about a group's "activeness" or "aggressiveness" relates to group syntality (the group acting as an entity). Syntality may be compared with the Gestalt principle that the whole is greater than the sum of its parts. Syntality, "group personality," is more than a summation of the behaviors of individual members.

The idea that a group acts as a unit is reflected in the work of group theorists; Bion described group culture, Bennis and Shepard advanced a theory of group development, and Schutz saw a parallel between individual and group development.

Cattell's second aspect, characteristics of internal structure, refers to the formal and informal networks that affect relationships among members. Forming committees to mobilize and channel individual energy for the attainment of a group objective is an example of a formal group structure. Crystallized and widely accepted norms, such as shared expectations for behavior, is an example of an informal structure. Informal structures are not only valid, but often the key to a successful group. Therefore, it is not surprising that group theorists have paid so much attention to informal structures along with the formal. Jackson, in 1960, offered a schema that conceptualizes group norms. In that same year, Gibb did a study on the behavior of individuals as it related to group climate, and Moreno, back in 1934, devised sociometry as a means to identify those social realities within the group that affect relationships among members.

Finally, Cattell used the panel population traits to define the average or model member of the group. For Cattell, population traits were averaged individual characteristics. However, other group theorists, perhaps not so measurement-oriented as Cattell, addressed themselves to population traits from directions other than the arithmetical means.

Palisi continues with a reference to Redl's explanation, wherein some theorists have speculated that members' common response to one central person is a sufficient condition for group syntality. For example, political action groups have been known to form with the only bond uniting members being their shared feelings toward a particular candidate. Remove the candidate, the central person, and the group disintegrates.

Bion explained population traits in terms of valency, which he defined as member readiness to participate in a particular group culture. In the Bionic tradition, population trait refers to a common need, not typically in conscious awareness, which influences group syntality in a particular moment of group history.

Another group of theorists, as represented by Benne and Sheats, have concentrated on members behavior, organizing these into roles designed to facilitate –

- task achievement
- group history
- personal service

If members' behaviors were typically viewed as fostering any one of the above, an outsider could well determine the nature of group syntality, i.e., hostility, friendliness, satisfying needs of the individual.

Population traits have been accounted for from four standpoints –

1) The arithmetic mean of members' characteristics.
2) The members' shared feelings about a central person.
3) The members' predominating feelings at a given moment in history.
4) The goal directness of role behavior.

The youth group worker can use the adaptation of Cattell's three aspects in two ways –

1) To organize in a consistent way his/her own perceptions of group process.
2) To evaluate the completeness of theories attempting to explain group process.

Essentially, you, the youth group worker, using Cattell's aspects, should ask several questions. How would I describe this group acting as a group? What networks and what population traits tend to support the group in this syntality?

You may evaluate the completeness of other theories by examining them in the light of the three aspects. You will probably discover that many of these theories seem to describe syntality but tend to omit details with regard to either characteristics of internal structure or population traits.

Much of the above tends to articulate concepts for the needs of groups in a broad sense. The youth group worker might tend to look for specific particularization as it applies to their collection of teenagers. What are the syntality traits, internal structure characteristics and population traits of their group?

B. Practical Implications

If one were to take a poll as to why there is need for a youth group, I expect that the nature and type of replies would be almost as varied as the number of ballots sent out. The clergyman looks for, among other things an identification and relationship with the religious and cultural life of the church or synagogue, the parent is interested in his child establishing and continuing day to day contacts with youngsters of his own religious or social background, particularly when it comes to establishing meaningful relationships with youngsters of the opposite sex; the youth worker sees it as an experiment in social interaction, group dynamics and community activity.

To state it rather succinctly, the author feels that we have youth groups because through fostering informal education, these ethical, experiential and sometimes religious workshops in community interaction enable the individual members to grow up with values. Youth groups supply the matrix, the environment and the tools for the maturation process to take place—but a maturation with and through existing community mores and standards.

Let us be even more specific. We must have youth groups to enable their members to:

- develop a sense of self-respect and pride.

One cannot respect someone who does not respect himself. A sense of confidence, worth and mission is vital for every young person. He would want to feel, as Whitney Griswold put it,"that knowing the good, he has done it; knowing the beautiful, he has served it; knowing the truth, he has spoken it." Hopefully, through the youth group he would be motivated toward further development of self-control, scrupulous integrity and a heightened sense of responsibility. Through available, competent, interested adults they could receive counseling and personal help ... either directly or through referral.

- develop sensitivity and respect for others.

Through conducting a model community at youth group and at camp individual members learn through precept and example to treat their fellows as ends and not as means. The youth develop empathy and compassion for others as well as respect for the rights of their neighbors. "Thou shall love thy neighbor for he is as thyself." One learns social skills, meets peers from the other side of town and from the other side of the world with varying outlooks, problems and philosophies, who nevertheless share much in common with him. One also develops his ability to relate constructively with youngsters of the opposite sex.

- develop new organizational and leadership skills.

One learns to show initiative, follow others, take on and fulfill responsibilities, organize, use various office equipment, handle finances sensibly, organize logistics, plan programs, work with publicity and public relations, prepare and conduct meetings and to lead from a vantage of being an authority, instead of being in authority.

- discover and develop various abilities and aptitudes in music, art, literature, dance, dramatics, photography, crafts, public speaking, athletics, etc.
- learn through formal and informal education, discussions, programs, conferences and travel about their own heritage, its beliefs, literature, people, institutions, history, culture and ceremonies.

- develop a commitment to one's own religion (if a religious group) and to its observances through action, experimentation and project activities. Youth often develop dispositions for prayer, worship services, study, philanthropic and service activities, singing, dancing, etc.
- learn of their mission as human beings and of the many unfinished tasks and unfulfilled needs in the world.

Youth of religious groups study social problems and try to understand what their religion has to say relevant to the myriads of issues from abortion to zoning. Wherever possible and feasible, they take action against the evils of society. Commitment brings action and action leads to deeper commitment.

Certainly the time is a time of crisis for both the world and the community and just as certainly the time of youth is the fruitful time educationally and also from the point of a real-politik to learn to experiment and to act intelligently and with purpose.

One sees that the Youth Group environment provides the opportunity for unusual learning experiences that should dramatically broaden the horizons of the individuals in the group. However, let us not fall prey to naivete by recognizing that, despite the loftiness of aims and fullness of program, we are not going to accomplish all of the above for every child in any one year or in four years for that matter.

Learning has been defined as a change in behavior resulting from practice. Conditioning has been described as the simplest form of learning. The conditioning of youth group members to broaden all of the horizons cited above is virtually impossible, keeping in mind the limited number of hours available and the part-time nature of the worker's job. The worker must first analyze the general quality and background of the youngsters, his own education and experiences and the resources of the community. After evaluating these factors, he must make a decision as to which areas he wants to emphasize, keeping in mind the general good of the group rather than specific individuals. The emphasis could and should change from year to year and possibly every few months. The approach in a small school or community with a limited number of youth group members would differ markedly from the methodology used with a big city, large membership, type of group.

C. Other Objectives

In addition to the parochial and other objectives cited in this Chapter, the well rounded youth group has still other concerns in relation to its members such as:

- To develop and nurture wholesome attitudes and ideals dealing with life in general. This is an impressive sounding objective, but what does it mean? What is an acceptable attitude or approach in one society may not be so in another.

The worker may on occasion be required to walk a tightrope in encouraging youngsters to concern themselves with such things as social action and community improvement, then in turn discourage the support of various and sundry misdirected causes introduced by members. The group and the people representing the group, are not autonomous. They are usually an arm of a much larger parent body. The worker must, first of all, acquaint himself with the philosophies, including political if any, of the sponsoring organization and secondly, ensure that the youth group does not cause embarrassment or bring discredit to the parent body, by espousing a cause antithetical to the latter's beliefs. Sometimes this is difficult as it may raise the spectre of censorship and limitation of free speech and action.

- To help develop emotionally stable personalities and to aid the youngsters in achieving personal enjoyment through the various programs provided.

The latter aim is self-explanatory. The former, dealing with the development of stable personalities, requires a great deal of thought. Howard H. Kendler, in his Basic Psychology, states that the test of a theory of personality lies in its ability to predict the behavior of an individual in real life situations. This portends a degree of behavioral consistency when thinking in terms of stability. Consistent behavior is the rule rather than the exception.The worker, in working with the youngsters over an extended period of time, undoubtedly exerts some degree of influence on such youngsters which in turn represents a contribution to their behavior patterns. The youth worker in most instances is not a psychologist, so here again he must tread with caution and not overstep his bounds. He can best serve this cause by alertly recognizing those situations where the behavior pattern is erratic or inconsistent. Very often the reason for it may be fairly obvious. Other times it is not. He must use good judgment when relaying his observations to the parents or program director.

- To help the youngsters in learning to live in a group and to function democratically in relation to other people through group activities which give individual members the experience of planning together with others for the benefit of the entire group.

This is perhaps the key function of the youth group because without first establishing the above relationships, the remainder of the aims and objectives may fall by the wayside. Here, we seek to develop leadership ability as well as intelligent followership. Interaction within the environment of the group gives meaning and very often direction to the lives of many teenagers. Personal adjustment by a teenager made for the benefit of the group is a very valuable learning experience.

There seemed for a time to be a growing tendency among our college youth, and spilling over to the high schooler, antithetical to formally structured youth groups. This, no doubt, had evolved from the preoccupation of some of our young people with "doing their own things." The effect of this philosophy on our structured youth groups is still difficult to evaluate, although it is evident that some impact had been made, witness the increasing demise of or lack of interest in many secular, school and religious youth groups for a time.

The worker should, as a result, consider the possibilty of subjugating the central theme approach (such as monthly or weekly programs) involving the entire youth group to a multidirectional program fragmented into smaller special interest units.The latter could be geared only towards those youngsters in the group especially intersted in or oriented toward that particular mini-activity such as arts and crafts, drama, athletics, charity and community work, teacher aid, etc.

REFERENCES

Benne, K. D. and Sheats, P. "Functional Roles of Group Members." *Journal of Social Issues,* 1948.

Bennis, W. G. and Shepard, H. "A Theory of Group Development." *Human Relations,* 1956.

Bion, W. R. *Experiences in Groups.* Basic Books, 1959.

Cattell, R. B. "Concepts and Methods in the Measurement of Group Syntality." *Psychological Review,* 1948.

Gibb, J. R. "Sociopsychological Processes of Group Instruction." The Dynamics of Instructional Groups – *NSSE Yearbook,* 1960.

Jackson, J. M. "Structural Characteristics of Norms." The Dynamics of Instructional Groups – *NSSE Yearbook,* 1960.

Kendler, H. H. *Basic Psychology.* Appleton-Century-Crofts (Educational Division – Meredith Corp.).

Lesser, B. *Youth Advisor's Handbook.* Nealco Publishing Co., 1970.

Moreno, J. L.*Who Shall Survive?* Beacon House, 1934.

Palisi, A. T. *Structuring Perceptions of Group Process* Psychotherapy and Psychodrama. Beacon House, 1972.

Redl, F. "Group Emotion and Leadership." *Psychiatry,* 1942.

Schutz, W. C. FIRO: *A Three-Dimensional Theory of Interpersonal Behavior.* Holt, Rinehart and Winston, 1960.

Suttle, J. L. and Hackman, J. R. *Improving Life at Work.* Behavioral Science Approaches to Organizational Change. Goodyear Publishing Co., 1977.

Chapter 5

Interaction Between Group Worker and Group Members

The youth worker attends and chairs such an array of meetings where he takes on conference leadership duties, that the author feels compelled to touch on some of the techniques of leading conferences and meetings. This feeling is bolstered by the knowledge that the youth group and committee meetings are also run by similar rules, which makes it incumbent upon the worker to impart these self-same techniques to his young officers and committee chairmen. The following then applies to both the youth group worker as well as key youth group personnel.

The chairman directs the meeting using a non-authoritarian approach, one that does not dominate the meeting, but places responsibility for coming up with solutions on the participants without abdicating his initial coordinating function. Adults and teenagers are alike in that they like to talk things over with their neighbors and friends. This is a treasured constitutional right (free expression) and traditionally we have learned to respect the views of others, albeit different from our own. When people gather in organized discussion they generally get results. The keyword herein is "organized" for productive group discussion just does not "happen" by itself. It involves careful planning and skillful guidance. The chairman, adult or youth, must make the meeting as effective an instrument as possible for solving problems, making plans and arriving at joint decisions.

Duties of the Chairman

- **Open the meeting.** State the purpose of the meeting and introduce the subject matter to be discussed. Motivate the participants' thinking about the subject matter and attempt to arouse a desire in each to make a contribution toward solution of the problem or the formulation of a plan.
- **Define and clarify problem or plan.** Identify obstacles confronting them and the objective to be reached. Cite facts and conditions which will affect the solution of the problem or formulation of a plan.
- **Keep meeting going.** As soon as the problem or objective is stated and agreed upon, ask a question which will get discussion started. Ask for opinions and don't offer your own. The conference leader's job is primarily to draw infor-

mation and opinions from the group—to aid participants in coming to an agreement on a course of action. If discussion drifts away from the subject, the chairman brings it back as smoothly as possible.

- **Include many participants.** In any group will be found those who dominate the discusion and those who are less verbal. The chairman's prime concern herein is to draw out the quiet ones so that the group can benefit from the ideas of all.
- **Clarifying.** The chairman must continually repeat the contribution made by the individual participants so that it is constantly kept before all members for evaluation and analysis. They must see to it that all facts are brought out and-must aid the members in organizing the contributions according to their relation to the topic under discussion. The chairman encourages the group to investigate all possible solutions and select the most desirable one. This means thinking out the problem.
- **Summarizing.** When the group has resolved its problem and arrived at specific conclusions, all members of the group must know what these conclusions are and just what they have accomplished. The chairman summarizes the conclusions in a series of brief statements. If the meeting is one of a series on the same subject, the chairman reflects the relationship between it and past meetings.

This summing up should not be limited to the closing segment of the meeting. Frequent summations throughout aid the members in organizing their thinking and helps the leader keep the discourse on subject.

- **Arbitrating.** This is perhaps the most difficult of all techniques used. Very often the group will propose several good ideas, and each faction will stress its own. It is the duty of the chairman to glean the best portions of each of the ideas and after everything is talked out, to suggest a compromise without detracting from the effectiveness of the ultimate solution.

There is a school of thought among behaviorists that the committee or organization size has some effect on the human relations interplay of the group. The feeling is that the larger the group, the higher the general index of member dissatisfaction, and the lower the morale. The larger a functional or working group or committee is, the less opportunity for significant involvement of all participants. This breeds reduced morale on the part of and ultimately evolves into a pattern of increased absenteeism. Please keep in mind that this is merely a tendency which in itself does not presage automatic absenteeism. However, the worker would do well to ensure that the size of the committees and other subunits in the youth group are so structured as to encourage meaningful and productive interaction among their members. Keep in focus the incontrovertible fact of life, that efficiency of the unit will be impaired almost in direct proportion to the time consumed in added internal coordination and its attendant problems.

The Informal Organization

The worker will soon learn of a phenomenon called the "informal organization" which can be turned into a positive adjunct to effect a smooth-running group. Beneath the mantle of close formal relationships, there often exists a system of informal relations among the members. This informal organization generally evolves from spontaneous interaction of the youth apart from the formal organization. Informal authority attaches to the teenager, where upon the formal authority vests with the office or position held by the elected or appointed member. The informal leader may be the group's most personable member, the star athlete, the best dancer, the "brain," etc., etc. Although one holds no formal position in the group, they do exert an influence on the others. An observant worker will soon be able to identify such a person(s). Inasmuch as leadership and the formal structure did not create this being, it would be fruitless, and essentially unwise, to contain them. In lieu of attempting to destroy this member's role in the group, it would be exceedingly more beneficial to work with the informal leader to assure that their leadership is furthering the group's objectives.

Although we recognize the informal group's existence and tend to convert it for the benefit of the formal organization, we must also be cognizant of the negative role it plays in developing cliques and being an active conduit for the rumor mill. The worker by building up the status of and role of the formal organization can often stem the undesirable manifestations of the informal organization. Of particular concern would be the loss of substantial members who oppose or were not taken into the informal clique. In order to retain such members, they must be given important functions, stimulating a sense of purpose, in the formal organization.

Confidence in the Worker

The author, over the years, has encountered many foundering youth groups, which initially had all the earmarks of healthy, forward-moving entities. However, an undercurrent of discontent was soon noted, which could be directly traced to an unhappy marriage of worker and group. There generally had developed a signal lack of respect or confidence in the worker on the part of the teenagers.

The rapport between worker and group, often taken for granted, must be predicated on a basic respect, not necessarily affection, for the worker. The latter inspires this in many ways; however, a good starting point is with the new youth group enrollee. The worker sees to it that the new member is put at ease. The new enrollee initially should be questioned as to what he knows about the group. Preconceived misconceptions can at this point be altered, but more important, it gives the worker and officers a base from which to describe the functions, philosophy and aims of the group. The new recruit's interest should be ascertained early in the game and he should be given an opportunity to develop such interest. Group programs and activities must be framed out for him, one step at a time, with emphasis placed on key areas. As time goes on, assignments are directed to him commensurate with his interest and skills. The worker follows up with the new member as well as with officers of the group to ensure that the neophyte's early enthusiasm does not go for naught. During the early weeks the new member may not feel comfortable in his new environment. The worker, at frequent intervals, can help him make the necessary adjustment during this transitory period.

The nature of the role played by the worker at meetings often is cause for a ruptured and/or inhibited relationship with group members. It is often difficult for the worker to play the subdued role required. The tendency, at times, is to be somewhat vocal and, yes, overbearing, in trying to keep the teenagers from going overboard on some of their ideas. The worker, however, must contain and envision himself as a ship's rudder, gently keeping the group on course.

The worker must follow certain principles of personal deportment. Cheefulness is contagious. Pains, worries and disappointments must be camouflaged. As worn as the approach has become, it is important that the worker thinks and reacts in a positive posture. A disappointing turn-out at a program can be awfully disheartening to teenagers and may well presage a dampening of spirit. The worker, while working with the members in critiquing how and where things "went wrong" must nonetheless attempt to keep the failure in proper perspective and avoid being hypercritical of the group itself. There is a tendency on the part of the teenagers to deride and lose confidence in their own group, during less happy ventures, and when things are at a low ebb. The worker needs consummate skill and patience, at this juncture, to keep morale up. An unsuccessful program or project should be followed, if scheduling permits, by a sure-fire hit program. Although the activity calendar is usually considered and prepared far in advance, it should contain suficient flexibility, to take care of changes and/or substitutions brought on by emergency or opportunistic conditions. The latter cannot always be pulled out of the hat. However, every community has status individuals (psychiatrists, vocalists, disk jockeys, jazz combos, etc.) who would help draw a crowd if featured at a meeting. As indicated in a prior chapter, the worker takes an inventory of available community resources, skills, talents, etc. It might be wise to identify at least one such resource, early in the year and use that person or group in case of special need such as that indicated. They should be used, calendar permitting, at the event following the failure, so as to help revive the spirits of the group.

Workers Characteristics in Relation to Group Functioning

The worker must preserve an open mind on all debatable questions. He/she should discuss matters but not argue with the youngsters. The workers virtues should speak for themselves, and they must make it a point to refuse to talk of others' vices. Gossip should be discouraged. The worker can show the way in this area by steadfastly refusing to engage in this type of talk. One must be careful of others' feelings, particularly the sensitive individuals in the group. Wit and humor at the other fellow's expense are rarely worth the effort, and may have a lasting, albeit unnoticed, effect on those involved.

This entire books appears to be filled with do's and don'ts, and the author will succumb again by reducing the aforementioned principles to seven easy to follow axioms affecting the worker's relationship with the group.

- He is an advisor: never a driver.
- He is forceful when necessary but not arrogant.
- He is helpful without being patronizing.
- He is friendly without being familiar.
- He is considerate without being unduly easy-going.
- He is sympathetic without being sentimental.
- He is confident without being dogmatic.

The author does not wish to convey the idea that the worker at all times remains entirely passive and never exerts authoritarian pressures, for this would be contrary to nature and the human equation. However, authoritarian methods should always be extremely limited to those situations where a lesson can be learned. The worker establishes and defines his directive limits in advance. They certainly should exercise authoritative demeanor in such matters affecting health, welfare, safety and reputation of the organization. However, the youngsters will understand and accept the workers methods under such conditions and will not question his motives. Other than for the reasons cited above, the worker should generally attempt to steer away from highly directive techniques.

It should be reiterated that those in positions of advising youth never do too much listening. However, it is not enough to listen and observe: one must examine and appraise. By looking at the ideas and suggestions from the teenage viewpoint, the worker can perceive the objections to their proposals, if indeed there are any, and can logically articulate the pitfalls so as to be acceptable to the youth. At the outset the worker must be prepared to meet resistance, when throwing cold water on a "hot" idea conceived by the members. In rebuttal they must offer something more concrete than generalities, otherwise one will find that the proponents will champion their cause in a series of off-premises coteries and a festering problem may have been incubated. The worker's rebuttal can be presented so as to obviate the undisciplined suggestions offered by the youngsters, but the rejection must be presented in terms of the teenagers interests, giving the latter the opportunity to evaluate the problem and turn it down in their own manner. To illustrate, we will quote from Lord Macaulay, "It is not by his own taste, but by the taste of the fish, that the angler is determined in the choice of bait.

At the risk of being uncommonly redundant, it is well to reemphasize that to enjoy good human relations, the worker must recognize the craving of young people, in fact of all humanity, for personal recognition and prestige. By giving them a sense of importance we elicit their interest and concern for group activities and make them eager to help bring the goals of the group to fruition.

Chapter 6

Group "Process" at Work

"Process," in a group setting, concerns itself with what is happening between and to group members, while the group is functioning.

Ken Heap of the Diakonhjemmets School of Social Work, Oslo, points out that interaction has been defined as "the mutual influence of persons who are in contact and communication with each other." With this in mind, consideration is given during group composition to such factors as group size, commonality of needs, aims of membership, and available time, among others.

The 1972 Annual Handbook for Group Facilitators[5,6] contains some excellent observation guidelines to help a group worker process analyze group behavior, which in turn will point out some of the organizational needs and areas ripe for remedial action. Such guidelines include:

Participation

One indication of involvement is verbal participation. Look for differences in the amount of participation among members.

- Who are the high participators?
- Who are the low participators?
- Do you see any shift in participation, e.g., highs become quiet; lows suddenly become talkative. Do you see any possible reason for this in the group's interaction?
- How are the silent people treated? How is their silence interpreted? Consent? Disagreement? Disinterest? Fear? Etc.
- Who talks to whom? Do you see any reason for this in the group's interactions?
- Who keeps the ball rolling? Why? Do you see any reason for this in the group's interactions?

---

[5]Reprinted from: J. W. Pfeifer and J. E. Jones (Eds.) *The 1972 Annual Handbook for Group Facilitators,* San Diego, California: University Associates, 1972. Used with permission.

[6]This structured experience and the accompanying observation guide were contributed by Philip G. Hanson, V.A. Hospital, Houston, Texas.

Influence

Influence and participation are not the same. Some people may speak very little, yet they capture the attention of the whole group. Others may talk alot but are generally not listened to by other members.

- Which members are high in influence? That is, when they talk others seem to listen.
- Which members are low in influence? Others do not listen to or follow them. Is there any shifting in influence? Who shifts?
- Do you see any rivalry in the group? Is there a struggle for leadership? What effect does it have on other group members?

Styles of Influence

Influence can take many forms. It can be positive or negative; it can enlist support or cooperation of others or alienate them. How a person attempts to influence another may be the critical factor in determining how open or closed the other will be toward being influenced. The following items are suggestive of four styles that frequently emerge in groups.

- **Autocratic:** Does anyone attempt to impose his will or values on other group members or try to push them to support his decisions? Who evaluates or passes judgment on other group members? Do any members block action when it is not moving in the direction they desire? Who pushes to "get the group organized?"
- **Peacemaker:** Who eagerly supports other group members' decisions? Does anyone consistently try to avoid conflict or unpleasant feelings from being expressed by pouring oil on the troubled waters? Is any member typically deferential toward other group members—gives them power? Do any members appear to avoid giving negative feedback, i.e., who will level only when they have positive feedback to give?
- **Laissez faire:** Are any group members getting attention by their apparent lack of involvement in the group? Does any group member go along with group decisions without seeming to commit himself one way or the other? Who seems to be withdrawn and uninvolved; who does not initiate activity, participates mechanically and only in response to another member's question?
- **Democratic:** Does anyone try to include everyone in a group decision or discussion? Who expresses his feelings and opinions openly and directly without evaluating or judging others? Who appears to be open to feedback any criticisms from others? When feelings run high and tension mounts, which members attempt to deal with the conflict in a problem-solving way?

Decision-Making Procedures

Many kinds of decisions are made in groups without considering the effects of these decisions on other members. Some people try to impose their own decisions on the group, while others want all members to participate or share in the decisions that are made.

- Does anyone make a decision and carry it out without checking with other group members? (Self-authorized) For example, he decides on the topic to be discussed and immediately begins to talk about it. What effect does this have on other group members?
- Does the group drift from topic to topic? Who topic-jumps? Do you see any reason for this in the group's interactions?
- Who suports other members' suggestions or decisions? Does this support result in the two members deciding the topic or activity for the group (handclasp)? How does this effect other group members?
- Is there any evidence of a majority pushing a decision through over other members objections? Do they call for a vote (majority support)?
- Is there any attempt to get all members participating in a decision (concensus)? What effect does this seem to have on the group?
- Does anyone make any contributions which do not receive any kind of response or recognition (plop)? What effect does this have on the member?

Task Functions

These functions illustrate behaviors that are concerned with getting the job done, or accomplishing the task that the group has before them.

- Does anyone ask for or make suggestions as to the best way to proceed or to tackle a problem?
- Does anyone attempt to summarize what has been covered or what has been going on in the group?
- Is there any giving or asking for facts, ideas, opinions, feelings, feedback, or searching for alternatives?
- Who keeps the group on target? Who prevents topic-jumping or going off on tangents?

Maintenance Functions

These functions are important to the morale of the group. They maintain good and harmonious working relationships among the members and create a group atmosphere which enables each member to contribute maximally. They insure smooth and effective teamwork within the group.

- Who helps others get into the discussion (gate openers)?
- Who cuts off others or interrupts them (gate closers)?
- How well are members getting their ideas across? Are some members preoccupied and not listening? Are there any attempts by group members to help others clarify their ideas?
- How are ideas rejected? How do members react when their ideas are not accepted? Do members attempt to support others when they reject their ideas?

Group Atmosphere

Something about the way a group works creates an atmosphere which in turn is revealed in a general impression. In addition, people may differ in the kind of atmosphere they like in a group. Insight can be gained into the atmosphere characteristic of a group by finding words which describe the general impressions held by group members.

- Who seems to prefer a friendly congenial atmosphere? Is there any attempt to suppress conflict or unpleasant feelings?
- Who seems to prefer an atmosphere of conflict and disagreement? Do any members provoke or annoy others?
- Do people seem involved and interested? Is the atmosphere one of work, play, satisfaction, taking flight, sluggishness, etc.?

Membership

A major concern for group members is the degree of acceptance or inclusion in the group. Different patterns of interaction may develop in the group which give clues to the degree and kind of membership.

- Is there any sub-grouping? Sometimes two or three members may consistently disagree and oppose one another.
- Do some people seem to be "outside" the group? Do some members seem to be "in"? How are those "outside" treated?
- Do some members move in and out of the group, e.g., lean forward or backward in their chairs or move their chairs in and out? Under what conditions do they come in or move out?

Feelings

During any group discussion, feelings are frequently generated by the interactions between members. These feelings, however, are seldom talked about. Observers may have to make guesses based on tone of voice, facial expressions, gestures, and many other forms of nonverbal cues.

- What signs of feelings do you observe in group members: anger, irritation, frustration, warmth, affection, excitement, boredom, defensiveness, competitiveness, etc.?
- Do you see any attempts by group members to block the expression of feelings, particularly negative feelings? How is this done? Does anyone do this consistently?

Norms

Standards or ground rules may develop in a group that control the behavior of its members. Norms usually express the beliefs or desires of the majority of the group members as to what behaviors should or should not take place in the group. These norms may be clear to all members (explicit), known or sensed by only a few (implicit), or operating completely below the level of awareness of any group member. Some norms facilitate group progress and some hinder it.

- Are certain areas avoided in the group (e.g., sex, religion, talk about present feelings in group, discussing the leader's behavior, etc.)? Who seems to reinforce this avoidance? How do they do it?
- Are group members overly nice or polite to each other? Are only positive feelings expressed? Do members agree with each other too readily? What happens when members disagree?
- Do you see norms operating about participation or the kinds of questions that are allowed (e.g., "If I talk, you must talk"; "If I tell my problems you have to tell your problems")? Do members feel free to probe each other about their feelings? Do questions tend to be restricted to intellectual topics or events outside of the group?

Edgar H. Schein makes some further commentary as to what to look for in a group that is valuable to the neophyte worker to wit:

Communication

One of the easiest aspects of group process to observe is the pattern of communication:

- Who talks? For how long? How often? Whom do people look at when they talk? Others who may support them? The group as a whole? The trainer? No one? Who talks after whom? Who interrupts whom? What style of communication is used—assertions, questions, tone of voice, gestures, support or negation?

The kinds of observations we make give us clues to other important things which may be going on in the group, such as who leads whom or who influences whom.

Decision-Making Procedures

Whether we are aware of it or not, groups are making decisions all the time, some of them consciously and in reference to the major tasks at hand, some of them without much awareness and in reference to group procedures or standards of operation. It is important to observe how decisions are made in a group in order to assess the appropriateness of the method to the matter being decided on, and in order to assess whether the consequences of given methods are really what the group members bargained for.

Group decisions are notoriously hard to undo. When someone says, "Well, we decided to do it, didn't we?" any budding opposition is quickly immobilized. Often we can undo the decision only if we reconstruct it and understand how we made it and test whether this method was appropriate or not.

Some methods by which groups made decisions follow:

The Plop: "I think we should introduce ourselves" ... silence. (Group decision by omission.)

The Self-Authorized Agenda: "I think we should introduce ourselves, my name is Joe Smith..." (Decision by one.)

The Handclasp: "I wonder if it would be helpful if we introduce ourselves?" "I think it would, my name is Pete Jones..." (Decision by two.)

"Does Anyone Object?" or "We All Agree." (Decision by a minority–one or more.)

Majority-Minority Voting: (Decision by majority.)

Polling: "Let's see where everyone stands; what do you think?"

Consensus Testing: Exploration to test for opposition and to determine whether opposition feels strongly enough to be unwilling to implement decision, not necessarily unanimity but essential agreement by all.

The procedure can be tricky. For example, it sometimes happens that a decision to poll–which looks very democratic, because polling is considered democratic–can be made by self-authorization or by handclasp. At such a point, the alert group member will realize what is going on and insist that the group be clear on its decision-making style. Actually, the decision a group makes about how it will make decisions can be the most important single element with respect to how it works as a group.

Task or Maintenance Behavior Vs. Self-Oriented Behavior

Behavior in the group can be viewed from the point of view of what its purpose or function seems to be. When a member says something, is he primarily trying to get the group task accomplished (task), to improve or patch up some relationships among members (maintenance), or to meet some personal need or goal without regard to the group's problems (self-oriented)?

The theoretical types of behavior relevant to the group's fulfillment of its task, and which follow, can be most helpful to the group worker.

Initiating: Proposing tasks or goals; defining a group problem; suggesting a procedure or ideas for solving a problem;

Seeking information or opinions: Requesting facts; seeking relevant information about group concern; requesting a statement or estimate; soliciting expressions of value; seeking suggestions and ideas;

Giving information or opinion: Offering facts; providing relevant information about group concern; stating a belief about a matter before the group; giving suggestions and ideas;

Clarifying and elaborating: Interpreting ideas or suggestions; clearing up of confusions; defining terms; indicating alternatives and issues before the group;

Summarizing: Pulling together related ideas; restating suggestions after the group has discussed them; offering a decision or conclusion for the group to accept or reject;

Consensus testing: Asking to see whether group is nearing a decision; sending up trial balloon to test a possible conclusion.

Types of behavior relevant to the group's remaining in good working order, having a good climate for task work, and good relationships which permit maximum use of member resources, i.e., group maintenance, are as follows:

Harmonizing: Attempting to reconcile disagreements; reducing tension; getting people to explore differences;

Gate keeping: Helping to keep communication channels open; facilitating the participation of others; suggesting procedures that permit sharing remarks;

Encouraging: Being friendly, warm, and responsive to others; indicating by facial expression or remark the acceptance of others' contributions;

Compromising: When own idea or status is involved in a conflict, offering a compromise which yields status; admitting error; modifying in interest of group cohesion or growth.

Standard setting and testing: Testing whether group is satisfied with its procedures or suggesting procedures; pointing out explicit or implicit norms which have been set to make them available for testing.

Every group needs both kinds of behavior and needs to work out an adequate balance of task and maintenance activities.

Emotional Issues: Causes of Self-Oriented, Emotional Behavior

The processes described so far deal with the group's attempts to work, to solve problems of task and maintenance; but there are many forces active in groups which disturb work, which represent a kind of emotional underworld or undercurrent in the stream of group life. These underlying emotional issues produce a variety of behaviors which interfere with or are destructive of effective group functioning. Groups often ignore such an issue or wish it away, which can be detrimental to their task-accomplishment as well as to the growth of the individual(s) whose behavior is based on self-oriented needs. The effective group will recognize what is going on, try to identify the issue, and then work with it in ways which permit these same emotional energies to be channeled in the direction of the group's effort.

What are these emotional issues or basic problems?

Identify: Who am I in this group? Where do I fit in? What kind of behavior is acceptable here?

Goals and needs: What do I want from the group? Can the group goals be made consistent with my goals? What have I to offer to the group?

Power, control, and influence: Who will control what we do? How much power and influece do I have?

Intimacy: How close will we get to each other? How personal? How much can we trust each other? Can we achieve a greater level of trust?

What kinds of behaviors are produced in response to these problems?

Dependence-counterdependency: Opposing or resisting anyone in the group who represents authority.

Fighting and controlling: Asserting personal dominance, attempting to get own way regardless of others.

Withdrawing: Trying to remove the sources of uncomfortable feelings by psychologically leaving the group.

Pairing up: Seeking out one or two supporters and forming a kind of emotional subgroup in which the members protect and support one another.

These are not the only phenomena which can be observed in a group. What is important to observe will vary with what the group is doing, the needs and purposes of the observer, and many other factors. The main point, however, is that improving our skills in observing what is going on in the group will provide us with the important data for understanding groups and increasing our effectiveness within them. Often, the most effective and useful group member will be the one who can function as "participant/observer," contributing to the group's task accomplishment, yet still able to use a "Third eye" to observe how the group is working–information which he shares with the group at appropriate times in an effort to help it deal with maintenance issues and blockages arising out of self-orientated needs.

Every group worker will soon become exposed to individuals in groups, who for many reasons are uncooperative or show little in the way of growth or maturity. Most of the individual resistances that are manifest in the situations described above impact negatively on group process. A listing of the individual resistances the worker may encounter follows:

- **Intellectualization:** thinking about, not acting on, feelings and wishes, hyperabstract, circumstantiality (variations).

- **Rationalization:** avoidance of "unworthy" motives, by giving other reasons.
- **Isolation of affect:** splitting off (and repression) of emotional components from an idea; little awareness of feelings.
- **Magical thinking:** focusing on an internal system of logic, in which one or several elements are unrelated to reality—assumptions or data.
- **Undoing:** an attempt to nullify an act (even a fantasized one).
- **Obsession:** avoiding conflict (and expression thereof) by focusing attention on irrelevant detail or an inanimate object. (Uses displacement, undoing, etc.
- **Repression:** a basic process; the unconscious and involuntary exclusion from awareness of painful or conflictual thoughts, impulses or memories.
- **Displacement:** redirecting feelings toward a more acceptable, less threatening object, e.g., phobias, prejudice, caricature, etc.
- **Reaction Formation:** transforming a feeling/impulse into its opposite. A kind of overcompensation for unacceptable impulses, e.g., excessively prudish, prurient, deferential: cruelly treating husband's friend to whom she's attracted.
- **Counter-phobic:** excessively or precipitously engaging in a feared activity, to master and alleviate anxiety: "I'm not scared of...," taking foolish "dares," "Let's get it over with..."
- **Compensation:** trying to make up for an imagined or real deficiency (physical, psychological, or both). Can be healthy if consciously chosen.
- **Dissociation:** "splitting off" of parts of self, sometimes large groups of independently functioning processes; compartmentalization. Can cause fugues, period of time with amnesia; multiple personalites: Jekyll-Hyde, 3 faces of Eve, Sybil...
- **Conversion reactions:** symbolic expression of conflict in body functions: Paralysis, numbness, blindness, pain reactions, twitches, tics, etc. ("original" neurotic paradigm: becoming unusual in psychologically-minded areas).
- **Regression:** under stress or frustration, returning to a protected/familiar/satisfying activity; e.g., illness (a demanding dependent state), sleepiness, overeating, neurasthenia (tiredness), drug abuse or intoxication, infantile behavior, etc.
- **Projection:** attributing one's unacknowledged feelings to others. Very basic phenomenon: can be erotic love, dependency, paranoia, etc.
- **Schizoid Fantasy:** withdrawal into one's private world ("autistic"), to avoid conflict or gratify unmet needs for personal relationships.
- **Hypochonriasis:** emotional conflict, experienced as something wrong in the body; focus on transient sensations (not fixed, as in conversion reactions).
- **Passive-aggressive:** frustrated autonomy expressed through indirect chan-

nels: procrastination, self-sabotage, passivity, masochistic (victim/martyr) behavior.

- **Acting out:** expression of a major behavior that clouds the issue (often a direct expression of an unconscious impulse), in order to avoid becoming aware of related, more painful, emotions, e.g., losing temper, delinquency, drug use, perversion, promiscuity, denial of vulnerability, confusion.
- **Denial (very pervasive):** failure to recognize obvioius consequences of thought, action, or situation. May relate to a particular idea, or denial of an entire experience (or its memory); may replace it with another fantasy, e.g., hypermanic, "pollyanna," hysterical character, etc.
- **Projective identification:** inducing another person to express or become a disavowed aspect of the self (requires a "willing other," usually in a continuing relationship, e.g., marriage, mother-child, etc.). Associated with the idea of *superego lacunae,* "holes in the conscience," e.g., driving a daughter into promiscuity by excessive accusations, goading another on indirectly, etc.
- **Withdrawal/avoidance/ego construction:** Very common, avoiding the situation instead of having to expend energy in dealing with it. Includes changing the subject, diversion, etc.
- **Introjection:** assimilation of other's qualities or attitudes into one's own self and conscious (reduces any feeling of separateness); often the earliest-practiced mechanism.
- **Identification:** unconscious modeling of one's own behavior, body image, attitudes and values on those of another (also reduces separateness); "I am like," but not "I am;" identifying with the qualities of an "injured" to reduce guilt, with an "aggressor" to avoid vulnerability, etc.
- **Aim inhibition:** to accept a modified fulfillment ("all I want is companionship"); a variant: substitution: replace an unacceptable wish with a more acceptable.
- **Idealization:** unconscious overestimating the attributes or aspects of another.
- **Symbolization:** substituting one idea; image formation.
- **Altruism:** vicarious constructive and gratifying service to others.
- **Humor** (requires a bit of observing ego): expression of feelings without hurting others.
- **Suppression:** a **conscious decision** to postpone **conscious** impulses or conflicts; e.g., decision to be optimistic, brave in the face of fear, avoid an issue.
- **Sublimation:** expression of feelings and impulses without loss of pleasure, through alternative channels/diverse interests: art, sports, etc.; creative elaboration: use of symbols, dreams, fantasies, myths, et al., to work out new relationships, i.e., play.

Specific guidance in how to deal with the problem group member will be found in the chapter on motivation.

The changing teenager, as refreshing and stimulating as he is, requires perhaps more guidance and direction than ever before. Than changing mores of his community, the increasing complexities of the world around him and the pressures of his peer groups put him in a posture of constant decision-making and selection of alternatives to both prime and peripheral considerations.

The unfortunate aspect of this concern is that ready-made guidance is not always available when most needed. A poorly trained or insensitive worker sometimes is worse than no worker at all. The economic factors that force the better workers into a state of continued transience impede the all-important continuity necessary to maintain a year-in, year-out balanced youth program. Do we therefore settle for a program infused with half-hearted, phlegmatic mediocrity and idle gestures, or do we move into an improvisational but cogent and well-informed guidance role? Obviously, the latter must prevail. The evolutionary sequence of this conclusion will take us directly to the layman. The community-minded parent or congregational worker, whatever the motivation, will, as time goes on, assume more responsibility in youth work. We dare not look at these people as unpaid fill-ins or stop-gap substitutes until a particular situation, financial or otherwise, rights itself. No, these people, properly trained, will ultimately give us the continuity and the degree of purpose we are seeking. Regardless of the skills the worker brings to the group, if he cannot properly relate to the group there will be difficulties. One of the first training chores for a worker, volunteer or professional, is to absorb some of the basic principles of managing so that, at the proper time, conversion to practical application merely becomes a question of adjustment to the youth group situation.

Management proclivity and adeptness is not a new panacea. Industry, government and our schools have long adhered to its principles. Both our undergraduate and graduate schools equate the teaching of management with that of the other professions. Thus, what will be recited herein is not new in concept, but merely new in its adaptation to part-time youth work.

Functions of Management

What is management? It is a process of accomplishing desired results or objectives through human effort and available resources.

The working functions of management in our context are:

- Establishing the objectives of the youth group.
- Planning the overall program and other work to be done, including, determination of source of funds and facilities.
- Organizing to put the plans into operation including the placing of responsibility with the human resources, followed by the assembly of all resources.

- Motivating the youngsters to execute the plan by inspiring and guiding them.
- Directing the operation and performance of the work to be done.
- Controlling the activities in accordance with the plan and appraising and measuring of the results.

Objectives

In setting, or in helping to set the objectives of a youth group, the policy makers must at the outset pre-determine the posture of the group relative to the areas to be emphasized and their relationship to the whole. Whether the group be primarily religiously, socially, service, social action or academically oriented, it is of utmost importance that this be stipulated in the beginning so that the worker can help establish an overall youth group philosophy and direction. The objective may often be influenced by the policy and the framework of the parent or sponsoring group, (men's club, School Board, etc.) therefore, it is most important to ascertain this before embarking on the development of objectives for the first time.

The important message to be gleaned from this, is that our youth groups dare not operate in a vacuum to the extent that direction and purpose become post facto manifestations to be decided only after a series of disoriented meetings and morale destroying program failures. We must be sure that we know where we are going at the outset, albeit the vehicles for getting there may be as diverse as creative thinking permits them to be.

Planning

The planning function is the basis for all intelligent action. We must consider and establish related facts and assumptions in advance in order to achieve the desired results. The group worker has the overriding responsibility for the efficient operation of his group. Once the objective has been crystallized, the planning function takes over for the purpose of blueprinting the varied programs and activities to promote such objective. In order to effect the aforementioned programs and activities, the worker has at his/her disposal manpower, (the teenagers), a fair quantity of materials, some equipment, limited time and usually adequate space. In order to ensure that these resources are used to their greatest advantage with minimal waste, it will require planning.

It is most desirable that the youngsters be encouraged and trained to plan their own individual events, however, the worker must be alert to extend his/her guidance and superimpose their knowledge when it becomes evident that one of the aforementioned resource items is about to be substantially abused or mishandled. The unbound enthusiasm of our youngsters sometimes overshadows the available resources to accomplish the projected activity. The workers must keep in mind that notwithstanding delegative prerogatives, the overall functional responsibility for group action vests with them alone. As highly pernicious as this may sound to the unitiated, it is a decided must. Any divestiture of exclusive authority or the proclamation of divided or diluted responsibilty will tend to weaken the image of the worker and may well be obstructive in the execution of the plan.

Most teenagers, of their own initiative, will not tend to conserve materials to the utmost or put their time to the most productive use. They must be shown how. Whereas a certain amount of uninhibited thinking or "brain-storming" is most desirable for problem solving, we must be cognizant at all times of the time limitations placed upon us.

If the worker or youth group officers are run ragged trying to get their work done, poor planning must be suspected as the cause. Overextension of activities and an unusual plethora of programs might be examples of poor or incorrect planning as would be a paucity of these elements.

Some Other Evidences of Poor Planning

- Target dates not met; follow-up actions not taken.
- Some of the teenagers are involved in many activities, whereas others are involved in hardly any at all.
- Youth group members with specialized skills in art, music, writing, etc., not being utilized at all or being utilized only on routine work.
- Quarreling, bickering, buck-passing, and confusion.
- Youngsters fumbling on jobs – possibly indicative of poor briefing or lack of guidance.

Evidences of Good Planning

When there is good planning, everything flows with a minimum of consternation. The members are busy but not rushed. There is concern for good housekeeping and cooperation among the various committees. There is generally a healthy respect for youth group officers, the worker and the sponsoring institution.

The difference between good planning and poor plannig is the difference between order and confusion, between things being done on time and not being done on time, between cooperation and conflict and between pleasant working relationships and a series of conflicts.

In order to achieve the desired results the planner or planning group must first ascertain the following (visualization and imagination required):

- What action is necessary to achieve desired results?

- Why is the action necessary?
- Who will be responsible for the action?
- Where will the action take place?
- When will the action take place?
- How will the action take place?

Planning requires knowledge, foresight, judgment and experience.

The youth group workers must have foresight in that they must know how to anticipate difficulties and thus avoid them. They must know how to break down a big program into smaller cohesive operations. One must know the length of time the preparatory aspects of each program and/or activity take and must allow a margin of safety in order to meet target dates.

All planners must have judgment. They must weigh various factors and make decisions. They must be able to balance the short and long range benefits, and-must have a good sense of priorities, putting first things first.

Other Planning Principles

The author would like to cite several other principles which are most useful in planning.

- Principles of opportunity cost. This measures the cost of taking any one course of action by that which was given up to make that course possible. In essence, was it worthwhile?
- Principle of alternative planning. When faced with alternative courses of action, the planner must take that course which yields the greatest net gain to the entire youth group. It might be wise to utilize the alternatives in the preparation of emergency "standby" plans should some unforeseen factor prevent execution of the primary plan.

There is a conceptual tool of planning which the worker should have at least a passing accquaintance with – that is – decision making. This is an integral part of a systematic approach to problem solving.

Whenever a problem is manifest, small or large, it will, at its inception, impede the youth group's progress toward reaching its objective. The worker and/or the youngsters themselves should consider the following decision-making approach for overcoming or negating the problem in a group setting.

- State problem clearly – define its ramifications.
- Identify the various alternatives to be taken.
- Encourage unrestricted thinking or brainstorming.
- Gather all the facts of all the alternatives. Analyze them, synthesize them and permit time for thought.
- Consider the consequences of the solutions considered.
- Evaluate consequences of each action against a standard – time, manpower cost, materials, quality of activity or program, impact on congregation or community, etc.

- Be prepared to arrive at intelligent compromise.
- Decision for action.

Problem Solving

The worker will, at the outset, discuss the technique of problem-solving with the committee chairman or president, and will give him the necessary guidance and together chart the course of action to be taken at the problem solving session. The worker must guard against the tendency to "take over" the meeting, if and when the youthful committee head wanders from the format and begins to lose the benefit and effectiveness of the method. At this junction it is best that the worker maneuver a "break" or short recess so that they can review, with the chairman, where and how the digression took place and how to bring the discussion and approach back in line. When the above occurs, sagacity on the part of the worker becomes paramount.

A negative fault-finding demeanor is a poor substitute for the judgment and proper guidance at a time when the inexperienced and young committee chairman is foundering. Good taste tempered by the amenities of a cultivated and understanding being must be maintained.

The worker during these problem-solving sessions, must convey the impression that he is dealing with the committee in a supportive role; perhaps helping to clarify the problem, but dependent upon the effectively functioning committee to arrive at a reasonable and intelligent solution.

The problems faced by a youth group can be major or minor, long-range or immediate, functional or philosophical, single program or annual activity. In other words the youth group will face the typical problems besetting any formally structured group in our society. For instance, the problem may well center on the type of program the group will sponsor at the very next meeting, or it may well concern itself with the posture, philosophy and direction of the youth group for the entire year. Does the youth group take in non-affiliated members? What should be the ratio between social, educational, religious, and service-type programming? How does the group raise funds to maintain high quality activity? How does the group combat loss of membership? How can it enhance rapport and relations with other youth groups in the community? How can they spur increased parental interest? These are only a few of the types of problems concerning many youth groups for which solutions must be found via the above techniques.

In summing up the advantages of the planning function, we keep in mind that it:

- Provides purposeful action toward achieving the objectives.
- It enables the youth group to avoid mistakes and errors that a hit or miss approach would surely generate.

- It husbands and keeps under control the various cost factors involved in the running of a youth group.

A more detailed exposition of problem solving will be found in the chapter on "Participation."

Organization

Organization is the next function in terms of the sequential managerial process. Organizing is the youth group worker's responsibility for establishing the proper relationships between the various activities and programs, among the youth who are going to do the work and the physical plant involved. In essence this means guiding into operation the plans formulated for accomplishing the objectives.

There are a number of important definitions of "organization" that management experts, teachers and writers have distinguished. The author, however, will touch on only two, the traditional view and the behavioral view, which as stated later, can be used in complementary vien, by astute workers, in their application to youth group structuring.

Traditional View

According to the traditional view of organization, the function of organizing includes the establishment of relationships among the work, the teenagers and the work place, as previously cited. The organization structure, according to this view, is composed of such elements as authority to carry out the plan, responsibility for so doing, accountabilty, hierarchy, chain of command and span of control. The ways of dividing work at each level of organization involve a series of alternative combinations of decisions on the basis of:

1. The activity or program to be performed.
2. The processes involved. Can the youngsters carry it off themselves? How much adult help is needed? Example: Do we need charter transportation facilities or car pools?
3. The number and type of youth to be served.

Authority is the power to act officially. Responsibility carries with it the obligation to perform successfully and accountability is the obligation of reporting to higher authority successes, failures and rates of progress.

The organization process, traditionally speaking, as applied to youth groups would tend to encourage the division of the group into as many units or committees as possible, steer the best talent into the chairmanships, and develop a system of coordination so that each unit can strengthen and support the other.

Behavioral View

The latter leads us into the behavioral view which places the stress on establishing a system of cooperative relationships. This includes concern and attention to individual and group feelings, sentiments, interactions and perceptions. We must then keep in mind that paramount in the organization element is the mandate to satisfy human and personal needs and wants while en route to the accomplishment of the objectives.

In order to effect a successful youth group, the worker can often interchange the traditional and behavioral views in an attempt to increase unit or committee cohesiveness. This can be accomplished by:

1. Increasing members' status within the committee.
2. Increase of pleasant interaction among committee members.
3. The existence of cooperative activities (as opposed to increase of competition among committee members).

Meshing The Views

For instance, youth group member Carl volunteered to serve on a tutorial committee charged with the responsibility of soliciting members interested in tutoring and making contacts with the leaders of the community to be served.As time went on Carl's interest in the program became limited to the actual tutoring activity itself. His attendance at committee meetings was sporadic and his attendance at youth group meetings dwindled to rare occasions. Worker discussions with this young man indicated that he was a bright and conscientious individual who was fully active in school and other neighborhood programs. It was also apparent that in time he would become inactive as far as the youth group was concerned because he felt he wasn't really needed.

In this particular case the committee chairman analyzed and solved the problem himself, not too unusual a feat for today's teenager. Carl was given the responsibility for contacting and meeting with the community leaders interested in the tutorial program. He worked out the details with them, arranged the scheduling, solved transportation problems and made assignment of youth group personnel to the various aspects of the program. Carl, with his talents being properly utilized, became an avid and dedicated youth group member. His pride in the group, and vice-versa, became such that he eagerly volunteered, as an extra hand, in many other areas of youth group activity, whenever extra help was needed. Personal security and self-realization were the key factors in his development.

Eddie came to youth group meetings because his parents pressured him to do so. He often left early and generally was critical, albeit quietly, of the youth group and what it stood for. On several occassions Eddie demonstrated an interest in the operation of a movie projector and other visual-aid equipment. Further probing by the worker drew from Eddie the fact that he was a "bug" on all things electronic. A subsequent discussion between the worker, and the youth group president resulted in Eddie being appointed to head a special fund raising committee which used electronic equipment as their stock in trade. The prime source of income earned by this committee was from the taping of weddings and other events. Eddie assumed responsibility for writing to and personally soliciting the taping jobs from the parents in the community. He took great pride in presenting to the youth group treasurer the checks respresenting the fruit of his labors. Eddie had further trained the individuals on his committee, all who were non-participating members, in the use of the equipment. All committee members worked as a well-drilled team on every job and were constantly thinking of and developing new ideas, wherein their particular skills were put to use for the benefit of the youth group. Eddie and the members of his committee in turn won the respect, and to some degree the adulation, of the youth group for the quasi-professional results they had achieved. The committee members, all who made a valid contribution in their own right, with an element of pride, readily identified themselves with this project. Eddie had learned to delegate a number of duties to his committee members, thus enhancing their personal development and training, while increasing their status in the eyes of the youth group.

It is fairly obvious that Eddie had become a valuable youth group member because of a new sense of fulfillment, recognition by the youth group members and possibly the filling of a psychological need. The individuals on his committee who, as indicated, were non-participating (as opposed to inactive) members, were also able to attain new status within the committee and in the youth group in general.

Knowingly or unwittingly, the worker in the above case-studies meshed elements of both the traditional and behavioral approaches, benefitting the youngsters involved and the youth group in general.

If all of the committees and special interest units of a youth group can be made to function in the above manner, while retaining an identity with the group proper, the worker will be well on the way toward a fairly successful overall program.

Negative Interaction

Thinking along antithetical lines, there are also factors to be guarded against which tend to decrease the unit or committee cohesiveness; such factors include:

- Uncontained and unrestrained member disagreement that take on personal manifestations and evolve into continued unpleasant interaction among committee members.
- Low prestige of the committee resulting in a low degree of outside competition for membership on the committee.
- Lack of sufficient reason for existence. No challenging goal or contribution to be made.

Motivation

Motivation is a term which has taken on an aura of sophistication in today's business and education circles. If we can find the key to this lock, it is generally assumed that the worker will become more productive, the student will achieve better grades, etc., etc. This is fine if we can develop the magic formula. The author has often wondered as to the degree a worker motivates his youth group members vis-a-vis the degree of self-motivation on their part.

Drives and motives are biological and social. Some psychologists tell us that the social motives, of which the desire for social approval is the most important, are built upon physiological drives present at birth. Failure at a task may be due to lack of ability or to lack of motivation. Success, on the other hand, requires a high degree of motivation coupled with a very liberal sprinkling of ability. So it would seem that best performance requires a high degree of motivation plus above average ability.

Social motives include desires for accomplishment for approval, for recognition and status, for community service, etc., all conditions which will react to external stimuli. To what extent can the worker supply such stimuli, which in turn will generate activity on the part of the youngsters? They certainly should be able to make a valuable contribution. The purpose of them motivating is to create and sustain the desire of all youth group members to achieve the prestated objectives in accordance with the formulated plans. What are some of the benefits from proper motivation?

Motivational Benefits

- More effective and expeditious completion of the assigned tasks, programs and other activities.
- Greater sense and feeling of accomplishment by all concerned.
- Better cooperation.
- Economy in utilization of time and all resources.
- Development of personal abilities.

The worker's job is enhanced if he/she has some knowledge as to what the youngster's basic and secondary needs are in order to take the first step in motiving them. A needs hierarchy has been established by A. H. Maslow. These needs are:

- Basic physiological needs (physical)
- Safety from external danger (security)
- Love, affection, and social activity (social)
- Esteem and self-respect (egotistic)
- Self-realization and accomplishment (self-actualizaton)

These need levels are not interchangeable, the premise being that they are sequential in that the needs further down the ladder do not dominate until the initial needs above have been reasonably achieved.

The fifth basic need, self-realization and accomplishment, being able to achieve and accomplish, is often the motivational drive of our youth group members and one which the youth group can help satisfy. The teenagers will couple this need with projects that need doing – social action, community and church service, etc., in order to establish an interest factor. Here, the worker by encouragement and counseling can steer the members into a purposeful, meaningful and satisfying endeavor.

Perhaps the most important concept we can draw from management experts and psychologists is that the workers' concern for motivating cannot be relaxed. Since the teenager's needs and wants change with the growth factor and time, motivational approaches must also be altered to meet the changing sociological and environmental conditions.

Operating Principles

As one can readily deduce, human relations is a pivotal area allied to the motivational process. Some operating principles for the worker in this area include:

- Respect for the individual, whether he be a member of the youth group or connected with the policy-making group.
- Encourage the desire to excel for the benefit of the group.
- Recognize a job well done.
- Ensure fair play in every respect.

Human relations problems are certain to arise. Internal squabbles among the youngsters, youth committee members, etc., will in varying degrees be ever-present. We are dealing with the human element and the reactions to specific situations will evoke typically human responses. The worker then should equip himself with a guide to handling human relations problems. Some of the mechanics of such a guide follow.

Guide to Human Relations Problems

- Obtain all the facts possible, making use of available records and applicable institutional policy.

- Fill in these facts gathering the opinions and feelings of the individuals concerned and all parties related to the condition.
- Fit the facts and opinions together.
- Decide what action is possible and all of the alternatives. Consider the affect of such actions on the individuals involved, the youth group in general and the institution.
- Take action or decide who is to take action. Select the proper time and place. Explain to the persons affected, why such action was taken.
- Follow through. Watch for changes in attitudes and relationships among the youngsters or others. Be prepared to adjust or modify such action, if the welfare of the entire group is affected.

Directing

The fifth management function, directing is in essence interrelated with every other concept and function. It so happens that directing is the classical, most easily distinguishable manifestation of the various leadership qualities.

The youth worker often is aided by a staff of volunteers, drawn from the ranks of the community. This is most desirable and in many cases integrally related to the successful operation of the group. Delegation of tasks to such people becomes essential for accomplishment of the group objectives.

To the non-management oriented worker, the delegation process can very well be misunderstood and singularly abused. Delegation is not complete abdication of either authority or responsibility. It merely permits the worker to extend his influence beyond the limits of his own personal time and energies. The person accepting the delegated tasks becomes the worker's representative in helping to implement a specific sphere of the youth program. Often the inability to delegate may very well impede a worker's progress. Some workers feel that delegation means giving something up, which in turn may detract from their position or image. On the other hand, we have the worker who is such a perfectionist that they trust no one else to carry out the mechanics of even the simplest tasks. Neither reaction is desirable in a dynamic, forward-looking organization. A program that depends solely on the availability of one person tends to sputter, whereas if the tasks were decentralized the group would function more like a well-oiled machine. Notwithstanding the above, indiscriminate delegation without a basis for such delegation borders on irresponsibility. Before delegation is effected the worker must assure that the chosen person:

- Understands the policies of the sponsor and the objectives of the youth group.
- Understands fully his own specific role and tasks to be accomplished and how they relate to the whole.

- That an effective avenue of communication be established, up and down, between the worker and the delegatee.
- That a system for feedback and effective control of action be agreed upon by both parties.

Control

The sixth and final management function, control, is a system of checks and balances ensuring proper follow-up action to assure that actual performance is consonant with planned performance. The worker, as indicated before sets up a procedure calling for periodic feedback and reports, both formal and informal, at meetings and via telephone, involving all adult aides, youth group officers, and committee chairmen.

The key activity herein is recipt of "information." This permits one to adjust their activity to a predetermined plan, should this become necessary and corrective action indicated. Though objectives, plans, programs and special skills are indispensable to the efficient management of the group, they are for naught if a system of checks is not formulated to observe if suitable progress is being made and if the necessary steps are taken to correct any deviations.

The control function is of particular importance to the group worker where there has been extensive delegation to adult helpers, and obviously where the youth have rightly assumed their fair share of execution responsibility. The worker's accountability to the parent organization is not negated nor diminished by virtue of such delegation. This means a constant checking of progress and results.

Another aspect of the control function concerns itself with t financial structure and budgetary considerations of the group. The execution of plans and programs are closely allied to the availability of funds, from whatever source to carry them out. The worker, ascertains the sources and amounts of the funds to be made available (from the parent organization's treasury, fund raising projects, from the youth group's dues structure, etc.). He then projects the expenditure of the funds in relation to the planned programs of the youth group. The control function comes to bear in the monitoring of the expenditures of funds, assuring that there is a relationship between the expended funds and the projections for such expenditures.

As can be seen, control is bound up with the planning function. In comparing execution with the plan, to identify deviations, we are actually measuring and evaluating progress and results. This is essential before corrective action is effected. Periodic evaluation and critiques are part and parcel of control and should include all interested parties, including volunteer aides and the teenagers themselves. Honest evaluation, bringing out both the positive and negative aspects of the condition being studied, creates, in most instances, a healthy climate and work situation.

The feed-back to the worker rarely takes the posture of a related, coherent and understandable whole. This is understandable in that the information does not emanate from one exclusive source. The worker does not have the wherewithal to install an integrated, choesive and logical reporting system, such as some of our wide-spread and progressive corporate giants use to effect internal control. Therefore, the worker must acquire an added sense, which comes with experience, to weed out non-pertinent or exaggerated data. He must keep in mind that in dealing with youngsters and parents, there are many occasions when the feedback information is tainted by personal or emotional considerations. Evaluations of progress must see that such factors are taken into consideration and given proper weight.

Group Workers and Time Management

Effective group workers, that is, those who get the right things done, have learned to manage their time. How well a worker does it depends upon their own goals, personaltiy, self-image, background, and experience. Time is not something that one can turn on and off like a light bulb. It is going on all the time at much greater cost than a light bulb, and one is doing something with it all the time.

To help readers appreciate the value of time, Peter Drucker describes the characteristics of time. It is unique in that everyone has the same amount, 24 hours a day, 168 hours a week, and so on. It is not elastic, it cannot be stretched or stored; when lost, it cannot be regained. It is irreplaceable; you cannot substitute another resource for it. It is the only universal condition; everything happens in time.

Group workers who use time to best advantage have learned to take the steps that Alan Lakein recommended in a 1973 work.[7]

Concentrate on their vital few decisions. A small percentage of causes bring the most results, in 80/20 proportion, that is 80 percent of value comes from 20 percent of items. For example, 80 percent of file usage is in 20 percent of the files. The moral is to concentrate on high-value items and not get bogged down on low-value activities.

Do first things first. Plan. Write a DO list of priorities. Do the most important one first, and do one thing at a time. Alan Lakein proposed the ABC method of coding priorities, A for high value, B for medium, and C for low.

Analyze what one did with time. Workers should keep a record of how they spend their time, as it happens, and then analyze it. If you know the problem is constant interruptions, another method is to keep a log of the interruptions. They will probably fall into 80/20 proportions.

---

[7]Reprinted with permission of David McKay Co., Inc. from the book *How To Get Control of Your Time and Your Life,* by Alan Lakein, copyright 1973.

Treat time like money. Verify Cost/Benefits. Distinguish between High-Opportunity Cost Time and Low-Opportunity Cost Time and relate to values. Determine the cost of an hour, 15 minutes, 5 minutes, and how much of the workers time was invested in the last report.

Slough off the past. In reviewing a program, group workers should ask, "If we were not already doing this, would we start it now?" They drop programs that are no longer productive, including yesterday's successes, to make way for productive new ones.

Set mini, midi, maxi goals. Plan a schedule for getting parts of a job done by certain dates and thereby insuring that it will be finished on time. Build in these checkpoints that provide opportunities for good feelings of accomplishment.

Conquer procrastination. Poke holes in it by Lakein's "Swiss Cheese" method. If you cannot get started on a big A-1 priority, make yourself do something related to it even if you have only ten minutes. Pick instant tasks that you can do to make so many holes, the job will seem less difficult than you thought, so you can get going on it.

The foregoing steps in managing time are not theories expounded by a few experts. They are practical actions that managers take every day to accomplish results and meet the goals of their organizations. These steps work.

If a group worker has not used them, a good way to start and keep on the beam is to ask and go on asking:

"What is the best use of my time right now?"

REFERENCES

Drucker, P. *The Effective Executive.* Harper and Row, 1967.

Lakein, A. *How to Get Control of Your Time and Your Life.* McKay, 1973.

Lesser, B. *The Youth Advisors Handbook.* Nealco Publishing Co., 1970.

Maslow, A. H. *Motivation and Personality.* Harper, 1954.

Schein, E. H. *What to Observe in a Group.*

Strauss, G. and L. R. Sayles. *Personnel: The Human Problems of Management.* Prentice-Hall, 1972.

Taylor, D. W. and P. Berry and C. H. Block. "Group Participation, Brain Storming and Creative Thinking." *Administrative Science Quarterly,* Vol. 3, No. 1, 1958.

The Annual Handbook for Group Facilitators. *What to Look for in Groups.* 1972.

Chapter 7

Communicating With Teenagers

To deal with teenagers requires, as with all people, the ability to communicate thoughts and ideas. This is a two-way phenomenon in that the youth worker cannot possibly put across his philosophies, ideas, etc., if any are already in the minds of the youngsters. The latter must understand what the worker is trying to do before they can be counted upon for a modicum of, if not always enthusiastic, support. This means that both the policy-makers and the worker must have exceedingly clear in their own minds what they are trying to convey, or else they will be the authors of confusion, frustration and in some instances, contempt.

The next step is to convey the message to the members in such a manner as to blunt any dictatorial implications. The teenagers, as indicated before in this book, do not generally take to the idea that they are being ordered to do something. They would prefer to think that they are executing their own ideas. The adroit worker will infuse his own message into the mainstream of the youngsters' discussions and deliberations so as to make it seem that his idea is but one of many that have evolved from the give and take of the discussion.

The author feels that close to 75% of the workers job is in the communication area, primarily, both talking and listening. The experts tell us that up to 50% loss of meaning takes effect after the message goes through several channels (Remember the game called "Telephone."). This then becomes a very important consideration for those people, such as youth workers, whose very existence is dependent upon communication. If the above premise has any validity, it means that certain intermediary steps are incumbent upon the worker so that the message is properly carried to those teenagers who ultimately do the work. A certain amount of test-checking and even a greater amount of follow-through must be instituted by the worker with officers, committee heads, sub-committee heads and helpers to be sure that the original message was comprehended and that it is being executed according to plan.

Much of the above checking and follow-up action is conducted by telephone. Since face-to-face contact is more conducive to better communication, the telephone becomes a subsidiary, albeit essential, method of conveyance. Because of the lack of face-to-face contact, while using the phone, such telltale indicators of miscomprehension as facial expression and attitude are lost.

Speech-rate, tone and modulation of voice and telephone courtesy become all-important in the accurate transmission of the message. Both syntax, the arrangement of sentences and words, and semantics, the choice of words, must be considered. When using the phone, simplification in both syntax and semantics is essential. Reduce the message to its simplest form to avoid lack of comprehension.

The worker had best remember that meanings are found in people not in words themselves. A word or series of words often take on a new meaning by virtue of an inflection given to a particular word or a pause inculcated at a propitious moment. Therefore it is important that the worker listen to what people, particuarly the young people, are meaning, rather than what they are saying. Feedback and testing are also important in this concept; for what becomes meaning to one doesn't necessarily hold the same meaning for another. In addition, we must keep in mind that not all people comprehend a message immediately. Some people often haven't had sufficient time to analyze the meaning or even be aware that they are unsure of the message. It follows, then, that on certain occasions we must give people time to think and find out whether or not they understand the essence of the message.

The worker, in order to effect the best communicative posture with his youth group, must permit the members to know him and how he acts. He should generally always be frank so that the youngsters can reasonably predict his actions. Communications often take place without a word being spoken. The author feels that this is conceivably the best kind, but can take place only when the worker and the youngsters get to know and appreciate each other and are attuned to each other philosophically.

Communications requires a chain of interdependence in order to be effective – the following links in the chain were once cited by a mid-Western professor, whom the author met in a training situation:

- Physical – we need each other to listen, lest we wind up talking to ourselves.
- Thermostat – conveying of ideas through talk – to be turned off and on in an orderly manner.
- Empathy – almost predicting what a person will do before he does it – this comes from development of the close relationship mentioned above.
- Interaction – this is reciprocal empathy and is what the social workers used to call "process" – people working together.

This chain of interdependence has pertinence and applicability for the worker-youth group relationship in that the stock in trade for both is communication of thoughts and ideas and the resulting responses; working together for a common goal and the mutual understanding that evolves from the 'give and take' attendant thereto; and interpretive exercise evolving from anticipatory reaction brought about by a communion of purpose. In effect we are speaking of the team approach, wherein the worker and youth group members understand their own and each other's roles and how they relate and depend on each other.

Strauss and Sayles[8] exposition on "communication," in their book on the human problems of management, is most adaptive to a group worker's concerns and way of life. The following concepts have been converted and applied to the group worker's role in his relationship with teenagers.

Technical Applications of Communication

Almost everything a group worker does involves communications, and yet it is only too easy for them to assume this involves no problems. After all, they have been communicating all their life; ever since they learned as an infant that to get something or to make his feelings known they had only to speak up. We all have the power of speech: to communicate.

On the surface, face-to-face communications would seem to be simple. Have you ever listened to two old friends talking together? Rarely do they use complete sentences; often a single word, a grunt or a groan, or a raised eyebrow communicates as much meaning as lengthy speeches would convey between casual acquaintances. A few syllables go a long way.

The basic problem in communications is that the meaning which is actually received by one person may not be what the other intended to send. The speaker and the listener in a group are two separate individuals often living in different worlds; any number of things can happen to distort the messages that must pass through these stages:

SPEAKER		LISTENER	
Intent	Expression	Impression	Interpretation
(Motive)	(What is said)	(What is heard)	(Meaning assigned)

The human sensory apparatus does not transmit an exact duplicate of reality from the outside world into the mind of the observer. Our needs and experiences tend to color what we see and hear. Messages we don't want to accept are repressed. Others are magnified, created out of thin air or distorted from their original reality.

What are the causes of breakdowns in communications in group activity? What can be done to overcome them? We shall consider each of these questions in turn.

Why Communications Break Down

- **Hearing what we expect to hear.**

[8]Strauss/Sayles, Personnel: The Human Problems of Management, ©1972, pp. 205-215. Reprinted by permission of Prentice-Hall, Englewood Cliffs, N.J.

What a worker hears or understands when someone speaks to them is largely shaped by their own experience and background. Instead of hearing what people tell them, they hear what their minds tell them they have said. These may be the same things or very different. We all tend to have preconceived ideas of what people mean; when we hear something new we tend to identify it with something similar that we have experienced in the past.

An extreme form of letting expectations determine communication content is stereotyping. For example, we may expect athletically inclined, big-muscled people to be rather dull, and when they say something we say to ourselves, "Well there is another typical remark made by someone who is all brawn and no brain." We grow up believing that minorities (or some other group) are shiftless and lazy. Bill Jones is a minority. When Jones comes up with an intelligent short cut on his job which took a great deal of time and energy to develop, we take it as proof that "he's always looking for a chance to loaf, just like al the rest of them." Though ridiculous, such stereotypes are subbornly preserved even in the face of conflicting evidence.

- **Ignoring information that conflicts with what we already "know."**

Some group workers like the rest of us resist change. They tend to reject new ideas, particularly if the ideas conflict with what they already believe. In some ways our communications receiving apparatus (sense organs and brain) works like an efficient filter. When we read a newspaper or listen to a political speech, we tend to note only those things that confirm our present beliefs. On the other hand, we tend to ignore everything that conflicts with our beliefs; sometimes our filters work so efficiently we don't hear new information at all. And even when we do hear it, we either reject it as a fallacious notion or find some way of twisting and shaping its meaning to fit our preconceptions. Because we hear and see what we expect to hear and see, we are rarely disappointed.

Not only does the receiver evaluate what he hears in terms of his own background and experience, but he also takes the sender into account. How reliable is he as a source of information? Does he have an axe to grind?

- **Halo effect – its negative aspects.**

One aspect of stereotyping and evaluating the source is the tendency to ignore the "greys" and to react in "black and white" terms. Thus, when someone is speaking who has gained our trust or who begins a speech by saying something with which we agree, we will hear nearly everything he says as good and correct. On the other hand, someone we distrust will be ignored or heard to say nothing worth attending to. The failure to make appropriate discriminations between the "good" and "bad" that may be intermixed both within a single person and his comments is often called the "halo effect."

- **Words mean different things to different people.**

This is the so-called "semantic" problem. Essentially language is a method of using symbols to represent facts and feelings. Strictly speaking we can't convey meaning; all we can do is convey words. And yet the same words may suggest quite different meanings for different people. The meanings are in the people, not in words.

● **Nonverbal communication – unintentional messages.**

In trying to understand what another person is trying to say to us (and thus to predict their future behavior) we use many cues beside language – what has come to be called "body language." Looking at the eyes, the shape of the mouth, the muscles of the face even bodily posture may tell us more about what the other person really thinks than the words he uses. The reverse is that we ourselves often communicate things unintentionally. Arriving at the group meeting angry because of a traffic jam, a disgruntled group worker may be "telling" the members by his general appearance that he is dissatisfied with their progress, although that was never intended.

● **Emotional context – insecurities.**

When we are insecure, worried or fearful, what we hear and see seems more threatening than when we are secure and at peace with the world. Rumors of all sorts spring up when the worker makes a change of any kind without adequate explanation, even a change as simple as moving furniture around the room. This is particularly true during periods of strife and tension. Then statements and actions that under less trying circumstances would have passed unnoticed become grounds for fear.

By the same token, when we are angry or depressed, we tend to reject out of hand what might otherwise seem like reasonable requests or good ideas. Our gloom and despair color everything we do and see. And while we are engaged in arguments, many things said are not understood or are badly distorted. Similarly, when elated, we may not "hear" problems or criticisms.

● **Noise – inability to tune out.**

Living in a world of words and being deluged by sounds all the time, individuals learn to "tune out" many things.

There are many types of "noise" interfering with accurate reception. In addition to the noise with which we're all familiar – that is, irrelevant, distracting sounds that make hearing difficult – there are also other types of noises covering up or muffling the receiver's words.

Thus when the noise level is high, the listener simply hears unmeaningful sound that contributes no new information.

Among other things, good communications requires solving simultaneously two quite different problems. The group worker must learn to improve his transmission; what words, ideas and feelings he actually sends to the members. At the same time he must cope with his own reception; what he perceives the members' reactions and statements to be.

● **Adjusting to the world of the receiver – contraditions.**

In communicating, the temptation is to adjust to yourself. You have the need to say something and to say it in a particular way. In fact, often you communicate when your emotional needs to speak are strongest and the odds of being understood the lowest.

It is extremely difficult to get through to a listener when what you are trying to communicate contradicts his expectations and predictions.

In short, you must be sensitive to the private world of the member (receiver); the worker should try to predict the impact of what one says and does on the members' feelings and attitudes, and tailor their messages to fit the receiver's vocabulary, interests, and values. Workers who advise a variety of groups in an organization must learn techniques of simultaneous translation to avoid misunderstandings. The greater the gap between their background and experience and that of the receiver, the greater the effort they must make to find some common grounds of understanding.

- **Critical timing – too early or too late.**

Messages can come too early or too late; theoretically there is an ideal time when the odds are greater that the message will get through.

Communications are too early when they presume to deal with problems or subjects which the listener hasn't experienced: "I didn't understand a word you were saying about human relations problems because I had never worked and certainly had never been a group worker." On the other hand, when a group member has a problem which frustrates him he may be highly receptive to new ideas.

Communications come too late when opinions have already hardened or the subject has become a battleground between groups or individuals. One way of limiting the amount of noise or distortion is to communicate your message before those other beliefs or attitudes come into play. Then the communication will meet less resistance and your chances of getting it accepted will be greatly increased.

It is a waste of time to try to communicate during an argument or bitter debate, when the person has to define his preconceptions. During such acrimonious discussion, to concede (or even to "hear" accurately) would mean admitting that you are less worthy than the other person.

The group worker must take the initiative in encouraging the teenager to come to them with their problems. They must convey to them, early on, that they will receive a receptive ear. If the initial interview is a pleasant experience for the youngster, he will tend to become more candid and trusting in terms of future relationships. The group worker must understand that some of the teenagers who seek him out will be more communicative than will be others. They must then go out and make contact with those in the group that are more timid and are reluctant to come to them.

The Art of Listening

The author, over the years, has noted a series of communicative pitfalls and barriers that afflicts many youth groups. It is apparent that the group worker, in many of these situations, is deficient in the art of listening. A great deal of time spent by the group worker is taken up by listening. But do they listen comprehensively to what others say?

The Royal Bank of Canada in its January 1979 Monthly Letter points out, very aptly, that we confuse hearing with listening, believing that, because hearing is a natural function, then listening must be effortless. American speech communications expert, Dr. Harrel T. Allen is quoted to prove that the opposite obtains to wit: "Listening is hard work and requires increased energy—your heart speeds up, your blood circulates faster, your temperature goes up." Listening then is a kind of activity that requires effort and concentration. Those who aspire to be good listeners must turn it from an unconscious activity to a conscious one. We often listen to other people through a thick screen of physical and psychological distractions which can only be penetrated by deliberately applying the power of the mind.

Physical distractions are often easily enough dealt with, although few people bother to do so—shutting a door or window, moving out of hearing range of other people, cutting off telephone calls. The distractions generated within one's own head are far more difficult to manage. For the act of listening has a built-in dilemma, which is that the speaker cannot keep pace with the workings of the listener's mind.

The average rate of speech is about 125 words a minute; the average person thinks at a rate nearly four times faster. With all that slack time at their disposal, people on the listening side of a discussion are likely to be carried away by their own thoughts.

It is said that "the mind wanders" while one person hears another talk; actually it darts ahead and off the track like a runaway race horse. This helps to explain why people jump to conclusions. They anticipate what is going to be said instead of following what is being said in the present. In this regard we might do well to remember the admonishment of a rough-and-ready tycoon as he started a meeting: "Now listen slow."

It takes a concerted effort of will to deal with some of the other impediments to listening that clog the mind, the more so since they spring from perfectly normal human feelings. For example, everyone's range of interest has its limits, so we all have a tendency to resist ideas that are of no personal interest to us. It is natural to conclude that complex thoughts outside of our own field of experience are beyond our comprehension, so we make no effort to digest them. And no one is immune to boredom; the first couple of sentences uttered by a dull speaker are enough to make us want to "tune out" all the rest that he says.

Dr. Ralph G. Nichols[9] of the University of Minnesota brought a different dimension to the subject in his article "Listening is a 10 Part Skill" in the July 1957 issue of *Nation's Business.* In this article Dr. Nichols in essence established a "10 commandments," for effective and meaningful listening. These 10 guides may well be adopted by the group worker as an aid to help them in the day to day communication process by controlling their mind and keep it from wandering–

- Find an Area of Interest – (What's being said that the listener can make use of)
- Judge Content – Not Delivery
- Hold Your Fire (Do not get overexcited or overstimulated)
- Listen for Ideas (Focus on central ideas)
- Be Flexible
- Work at Listening
- Resist Distractions
- Exercise Your Mind (Develop an appetite for hearing a variety of presentations difficult enough to challenge your mental capacities)
- Keep Your Mind Open
- Capitalize on Thought Speed. Note: Use your spare thinking time to advantage–
    a) Try to anticipate what a person is going to talk about.
    b) Mentally summarize what the person has been saying.
    c) Weigh the speaker's evidence by mentally questioning it.
    d) Listen between the lines for unspoken messages (watch body movement, facial expressions, tone and volume of voice).

In bringing this chapter to a close, the group worker must be reminded of the relationship between communication, attitudes and perception within the youth group. This relationship is reciprocal and interlocking. Perceptions of what is being communicated is influenced by attitudes. Communication may help to clarify perception and may bring about changes in attitude. Communication of attitudes frequently colors or prevents the communication of oral or written information. Communication, in a practical sense, must be understood to include what the group worker or group member says, does and feels.

There are professional "Effective Listening" courses and programs available to the youth group worker and others. Xerox Learning Systems,[10] for one, has a training program for the public titled "Strategies for Effective Listening" that is pointed toward–

- Strategies to help ensure that one retains key points of a speaker's message while he/she is listening.

---

[9]Permission granted to reprint "Listening Is A 10 Part Skill" by the Chamber of Commerce of the U.S. taken from Nations Business Issue of July 1957, Ralph G. Nichols, author.

[10]Reprinted with permission from Xerox Learning Systems, One Pickwick Plaza, Greenwich, CT 06830. Copyright©1977 Xerox Corporation, All Rights Reserved.

- Strategies to help identify and retain the critical content of spoken messages.
- Strategies to help ensure that the message one receives is clear and complete before one acts on it.

The Xerox company program on listening outlines the following strategies for effective listening which, when joined with other recommendations in this chapter, should give the group worker a plethora of guidelines in striving for improvement in this key area on communications.

The aforementioned strategies are broken down to specific skills for both active and interactive listening which are learned and practiced through both oral and written messages.

Again drawing from the Xerox company program there follows a summation of the many factors that may influence one's listening ability.

Listening Environment

- Acoustics –
  Barriers – Background noise, interruptions, poor amplification.
  Aids – quiet, away from traffic flow, speaker heard anywhere.
- Physical –
  Barriers – Too hot or cold, poor ventilation, inadequate or uncomfortable seating.
  Aids – Comfortable temperature, good ventilation, adequate and comfortable seating.

Barriers to effective listening are many in number. The aforementioned Xerox Strategies For Effective Listening course has many tips and techniques to help both speakers and listeners overcome other barriers.

REFERENCES

Lesser, B. *The Youth Advisors Handbook.* Nealco Publishing Co., 1970.

Nichols, R. G. "Listening is a 10 Part Skill." *Nations Business,* The Chamber of Commerce of the United States, July 1957.

Strauss, G. and L. R. Sayles. *Personnel – The Human Problems of Management.* Prentice Hall Inc., 1972.

The Royal Bank of Canada Monthly Letter. "The Art of Listening." Vol. 60, No. 1, January 1979.

U.S. Civil Service Commission. *Leadership and Supervision: a survey of research findings. 1955.*

Xerox Learning Systems. Strategies for Listening. Program Book, 1977.

Chapter 8

The Strategy of Planning by Objectives

One of the greatest challenges facing a group worker is to reconcile and integrate human effort, resources, and facilities toward achieving common goals while avoiding mismanagement, discord and disaster. Many approaches to solving this problem have been tried to wit:

- The "hunch and seat-of-the-pants" approach.
- Emulation of practices of predecessors.
- Employment of fads.
- Use of traditional process of management.
- Use of planning and managing by objectives.

The author is of the opinion that the last approach is finding more and more acceptance in recent years and is worthy of extensive consideration by the group worker—that is use of planning and managing by objectives.

Definition

Paul Mali defines managing by objectives (M.B.O.) as a strategy of planning and getting results in the direction that management wishes and needs to take while meeting the goals and satisfaction of its participants.

Planning by objectives (P.B.O.) which is closely allied to M.B.O. is a system for stating what the program is to accomplish and planning means to achieve these goals (per ACTION'S National Student Volunteer Programs).

Setting the Objectives

Edward C. Schleh warns that a common error in approaching objectives is to define activity instead of results. To be sound, objectives should be as specific as possible in amounts, time, percentage, quality, etc. Stating objectives in such terms as "complete a project as scheduled," "carry out plan," is often not really setting objectives at all. It merely points up a general area of activity for the individual. A person may then engage in a tremendous amount of activity and feel he is doing the job, when they really added little of value to forward the objectives of the group. In fact, his activity may have actually retarded other worthwhile achievements. Let's examine how a group worker would implement P.B.O. and some of the impeding considerations.

Problems of Management

One reason group workers often define activity instead of objectives is that they find it difficult to set up precise measurements. In practice, however, extreme accuracy is not critical. Estimates are satisfactory; broad measurements will work. These measurements can become more and more perfect as you learn to work with them, but in the meantime they are still effective as objectives.

Another common error is to make a catalog list of all the things you wish to have achieved by each person. This is done in the mistaken belief that every little accomplishment to be made by a person must be covered by specific objectives or the program will fail. The fact is, however, that too many objectives can take most of the steam out of an objective program.

As a working rule, no job or project should have more than two to five objectives. If there are more, they should be combined in some way so that they can be stated more simply. A program with too many objectives tends to highlight the minor ones to the detriment of the major ones. There is also a tendency for people to pass up the more important (and usually more difficult) objectives, secure in the feeling that they are completing so many minor ones. Ordinarily, any objective that is less than 10 or 15 percent of the job should be combined with another one.

Planning by objectives as indicated above, is a system for stating what you wish your program to accomplish and planning means to achieve those goals. This systems contains four elements, all interrelated, according to a manual put out by ACTION – (which the author thinks is an exceedingly fine product and which is the base of much of what is contained in this chapter).

- Purpose
- Long-term Objectives
- Short-term Objectives
- Planning

P.B.O. Element I – Purpose:

Every organization has a purpose, a reason for being. The people in the organization may be unaware of the purpose or unclear about it. They may have different opinions of what the purpose is. But its there—regardless of its obscurity or the form in which it is stated.

The first task in using P.B.O. is to articulate that purpose in the form of a concise purpose statement. The purpose statement is the broadest possible statement of why the group is in business. It reflects the organization's desire to fill a need of something that is missing. It implies that without the organization there would be an unsolved problem or an unmet need.

If a group worker is starting a program or project from scratch, he/she can arrive at a statement of purpose by making a needs assessment to determine exactly what is missing. Then they can write a purpose statement reflecting a desire to provide that which is missing. So the first step is to determine what the group members need and what the community needs.

What do you do about an existing program? Many who work with groups are thrust into leadership roles in established organizations and asked to give that organization direction focus. They are handed an organization for which they have responsibility, and must work toward the definition of its purpose without the hard data that a needs assessment would provide. Even so, the process must begin by defining the purpose of the organization, using whatever data and good sense is available.

The Value of a Purpose Statement

Preparation of a purpose statement is not simply an intellectual exercise. It has real value even apart from a Planning by Objectives system. For example:

One may be surprised to find that your leadership have divergent ideas as to why your organization exists. These philosophical differences have resutled in conflicting efforts. By agreeing on a purpose statement, the organization ferrets out all the hidden agendas and begins to focus on its activities. The result is less confusion and a greater sense of accomplishment.

A statement of purpose can serve as an introduction to others and can be used in publications describing the group's work. It tells more about the organization than a list of all activities and services because it tells why the group exists, and why it does what it does. Since it is timeless, its inclusion in printed materials does not date them.

A statement of purpose is useful in seeking funds. Potential contributors can see at a glance whether the group's purpose is consistent with theirs.

If the worker can state their organization's reason for being, they improve their ability to recruit volunteers. People are usually attracted to groups whose members and leaders know why they are working together.

As others understand the group's purpose, the number of requests for inappropriate help will diminish. If people understand that the group is a short-term manpower service, they won't bother to call the organization for tutors or soccer coaches.

Understanding the group's purpose enables the members to develop criteria for choosing among the various projects they are asked to undertake, and they will be able to explain clearly and objectively the reasons for reaching a certain decision.

Understanding the group's purpose increases the prospects of doing a few jobs well rather than many jobs poorly.

The development of a purpose statement and a clear understanding of the purposes of other organizations can help the members avoid the unnecessary confusion and conflict issuing from alliances with people or groups whose purposes are in conflict with theirs.

A purpose statement *does* the following things:

- It tells whom the group serves—who the clients are.
- It tells, in general terms, what is done for them.
- It provides broad boundaries that indicate what the group logically would do and would not do.
- It tells why the group is in business.

A purpose statement *does not:*

- List specific activities – Like tutoring, counseling, painting houses.
- Mention time or set deadlines.
- Tell how much will be done.
- Serve as a goal or objective. It is something the group heads toward but can never fully achieve.

A purpose statement is a general, timeless statement that provides the organization with an on-going sense of direction. Conceivably, a statement of purpose could last the organization forever.

Here is an example of a well-written purpose statement:

"The fix-it-up-clean-it-up project provides free manpower services to low-income individuals and families in the greater metropolitan area so that they can maintain their homes."

It indicates who the clients are (low-income individuals and families in the greater metropolitan area) and indicates the *general* nature of the service (providing free manpower). It does not mention time. It does not tell what exact means are used in providing free manpower; it does not say specifically that the group paints houses and rakes yards. It does tell *why* the project exists.

P.B.O. Element II – Long Term Objectives:

The second element of Planning by Objectives is setting long-term objectives (LTO's). LTO's are statements of targets the group seeks to hit, accomplishments to be achieved at some time in the future. LTO's group out of the purpose statement. They are concrete statements of what the group wishes to accomplish in the realization of that purpose.

There are two basic types of objectives: client-centered objectives and organization-centered objectives.

Client-centered objectives are statements of what is going to be accomplished in serving the clients. Organization-centered objectives are statements of what kinds of organization building and resource gathering are necessary to provide those services to the clients.

Both kinds of objetives (client-centered and organizational-centered) must meet certain criteria. Objectives must be:

- Feasible – Objectives must be feasible, possible, and reasonable. The worker's experience or the advice of others must suggest that they can be accomplished.
- Dated – The objective must be set within a time frame that indicates an end date by which time something is to be accomplished.
- Measurable – The group and the worker must be able to tell whether or not they have hit the target. Usually the objective itself suggests the specific means of measurement.
- Indicative of an Acceptable Level of Achievement – They tell exactly how much of the desired result must be achieved to consider the effort successful (Three out of four; 85 percent.).

Foggy Targets

Sometimes a program has unstated or unwritten long-term objectives. Its objectives are vague, poorly defined, foggy. Here are some examples:

to have varied projects;
to have committed volunteers;
to provide a real service to the community.

One of the most difficult tasks that may face someone working with volunteer programs is translating those hazy, unwritten wishes into well-defined long-term objectives and thereby increasing the likelihood that the organization will achieve its objectives. What do you do with such foggy targets: The key is to ask questions – the right ones.

P.B.O. Element III – Short-Term Objectives

Short-term objectives have all the characteristics of long-term objectives, except that they are in a shorter time frame. They contribute directly to long-term objectives.

Short-term objectives:

- directly contribute to the long-term objectives and are feasible.
- are dated (and is a less-distant date than the LTO).
- are measurable – you can tell when they are done.
- set a level of acceptable achievement.

Practical Avantages

Short-term objectives have several very handy uses:

- They break large targets up into less overwhelming smaller targets. They create possibilities out of seeming impossibilities.
- They help the worker see what needs to be done in the near future, in order to accomplish something at a later date. They let the worker know how the group is progressing toward long-term objectives. If the short-term objectives are well thought out, and if they are met on schedule, the group will probably accomplish their long-term objectives.
- They present negotiable small packages; when somebody walks into the worker's office, wanting to help, he can say, "Sure you can help. What I need most is a tutoring recruitment poster with a male tutor on it. Can you design it for me?" And before you know it, he has what he needs. And he has it because he has a clear idea of what he needs, why he needs it, and when he needs it.
- They help set and explain priorities. Suppose somebody wants to put out a newsletter, but it is not part of any of the group's short-term objectives, nor does it look like it would contribute to any of the long-term objectives. The worker can say, "we realy don't need a newsletter as badly as we need a campaign to recruit male tutors. How about helping us on that?"

Traps, Pitfalls and Misuses

Nothing's perfect, and people can get tangled up in using short-term objectives. Here are some examples:

- Sometimes people over-define a level of acceptable achievement. The worker should require detail only as needed.
- Sometimes people choose short-term objectives without being sure that they will contribute to the long-term objectives. If training a volunteer doesn't increase his chances of staying with the project, its foolish to set up training as a short-term objective to contribute to retention. The worker must ensure their assumptions about impacts are correct.
- Sometimes people meet the letter rather than the spirit of the short-term objective. For example, if the short-term objective of the tutoring project is for every male tutor to recruit a friend, the fellow who drags a pal to the orientation promising, "You don't have to do anything, just show up this once and you'll get me off the hook," is only meeting the letter of the objective. Nothing is really being accomplished.
- Sometimes people fail to complete their short-term objectives, so they give up on the long-term objectives and junk the whole thing. If the group fails to achieve a short-term objective, the worker must not give up. Ask why things are not moving faster. Adjust deadlines as necessary.

P.B.O. Element IV – Planning Details:

We have moved through the first three levels of a Planning by Objectives system; purpose, long-term objectives, and short-term objectives. We are now at the final and most immediate stage–planning details. We've been breaking the work of the organization into smaller and smaller packages. Planning details are the smallest package. They must be met in order to accomplish a short-term objective, which contributes to a long-term objective, which, in turn, enables your organization to realize its purpose.

Planning details may be described as tasks that must be completed in the near future in order to achieve a short-term objective. Planning details have the following characteristics:

- They contribute directly to a short-term objective.
- They are feasible.
- They are dated, indicating a completion date that is more immediate than that of the short-term objective to which they contribute.
- They are measurable–you can tell when they are done.
- They indicate details of a project, major details, like completing a mailing, or taking bids on a bus–but no miniscule details.

Planning details could be called by a lot of other names such as:

–immediate objectives;

–tasks;

–activities.

Whatever one calls them, they are the more detailed, more immediate, smaller element of the Planning by Objectives system.

These planning details are the actions that common sense and experience indicate are necessary to the completion of a short-term objective.

If planning details are so logical, so simple, so easy to write, why write them down at all? Here are some reasons:

If planning details are written down, the worker will be less likely to forget what they are and when they need to be done. Things won't sneak up or get away from them.

If planning details are written down, one can see when they have too many activities and details bunched together, and they can arrange these activities or tasks and deadlines to make better use of slack time, so one ends up with a less cyclical organization, a calmer, more organized program or project.

Writing down planning details enables one to check those details more closely and make sure they fulfill all the criteria.

Written planning details enables one to divide up a short-term objecive among other staff (volunteer or paid) and still have accountability.

Some planning details do double-duty. They contribute to two short-term objectives at once. For example, if one person is working on a mailing that must go out by January 1 (and it contributes to one short-term objective) and you have another mailing to go to the same group a few days later (which contributes to another short-term objective) you can combine the two mailings and save time, money, and energy. If, however, your planning details are not written down or recorded somewhere, the person who is responsible for one mailing may not realize that there is another mailing planned for the same group. Then you have duplication of effort and wasted resources.

Objectives Must Be Attainable

The author feels compelled to cite one last caution if the group worker is to be successful utilizing the Planning and Management by Objectives approach—a reminder that the objectives must be attainable.

Mali states that the formal statement of the objective must be subjected to a validation procedure. This procedure determines the confidence one (in this case the worker and the group members) has that the objective can be reached in the stated time. Risks, assumptions, and changing requirements are checked and analyzed to determine if any faults or failures can occur during implementation. The validation procedure simulates in a "dry run" effects of errors or great difficulties that may emerge. It permits the establishment of alternatives within the objective in order to cover contingencies.

The validation procedure assures that resources, facilities, materials, methods, people and the group worker are ready and willing (as well as committed) to reach a desired goal.

REFERENCES

ACTION, National Student Volunteer Program. "Planning by Objectives." A manual for people who work with student volunteer programs.

Mali, P. *Managing by Objectives*. John Wiley and Sons, Inc., 1972.

Schleh, E. C. "Management by Objective." *Management Review,* Nov. 1959.

Chapter 9

Participation

Responsible participation is an oft-cited but underworked activity for those involved in youth work.

Keith Davis, defined participation as "mental and emotional involvement of a person in a group situation which encourages him to contribute to group goals and share responsibility in them."

Group participation in this context relates to an involvement of mind and emotion rather than muscular or task participating activity. The latter situation often creates an involvement wherein the teen-agers go through the motions of participation only. This type of activity is called "busy work" and is not true participation. The teenagers must project their own ideas in planning sessions, seek to implement them, make their own mistakes and be permitted to evaluate their own program to be true participants!

It is most important that youngsters be permitted to contribute to a given situation. Participation motivates such contribution and acts as a release valve in terms of their own creativeness and initiative channeled toward the group's long-range goals and immediate objectives. It is evident then that participation is more than a vehicle seeking the assent of the youngsters for something that has already been decided. It is a multi-directional, social and psychological relationship among the youth and the group worker, rather than an avenue for the imposition of ideas emanating from the worker.

As the youngsters begin to accept responsibility for group activities, they become more receptive to the team approach. This idea of manifesting the teamwork concept is the key in the development of a well integrated, albeit not entirely homogeneous, youth group. Participation engenders responsibility and a feeling of common concern and active endeavor for the benefit of the whole group. The group must be primed to work actively with the worker, instead of reactively against him.

It is relatively simple for non-initiated persons to grab at this concept as the panacea for all of the deficiencies evident in their youth groups. However, certain prerequisites must be present for participation, in the sense that we have described, to be truly effective. The conditions are:

- There should be ample time to participate before the action phase takes place. Participation doesn't lend itself to unplanned emergency situations, i.e. plan ahead.

- Communication is a key factor. There must be mutual understanding of participants' language and ideas.
- The subject of the participation must be relevant to the youth group's activities and the participants' personal interests, lest it be interpreted as "busy work."
- The participants should be in the position of confidently engaging in this activity without fear of recrimination or loss of status vis-a-vis the worker or the officials of the parent organization.
- The participants must be made cognizant of and understand the restrictions on their recommendations. The group cannot make decisions which violate policy, community legal requirements, health, safety and welfare rules.

Advantages of Participation

What are the principal advantages or benefits that evolve from participation? A few such benefits accruing to the youth group are:

- Encouragement of better decisions.
- Improvement of morale.
- Encouragement to accept responsibility.
- Utilization of creativity of participants.
- Engendering human relations fundamentals of dignity, motivation, and mutual interest.
- Encouragement of acceptance of change and deviation.
- Encouragement of better attendance at meetings.
- Discouragement of negative attitudes, conflicts and grievances.

The benefits of participation cited above have direct application to the youth group itself and its subsidiary committees. Like many aspects of the advisory function, it becomes incumbent upon the worker to learn the principles involved so that he can guide the youngsters toward their acceptability and implementation in the youth group setting.

Malcolm and Hulda Knowles speak of a "Participation Pattern." At any given moment every group has a particular participation pattern, which may be one-way (leader talking to the members); two-way (leader talking and members responding) or it may be multi-directional (with all members speaking to one another and the group as a whole). Many studies show that on the whole, the broader participation among members of the group the deeper the interest and involvement will be.

Hackman and Suttle maintain that participation results in the development of better and easier ways of doing group tasks, so that a given degree of effort will result in higher performance. This may occur because the participative atmosphere permits group members to suggest and implement valuable new ideas that will make the organization more efficient. The participative atmosphere may also permit group members to question the group workers' ideas or provide them and group officers with additional information that can be used in making decisions. Practice in participation may lead group members to develop valuable new skills.

In a prior chapter we discussed the various images portrayed by the prototype group worker. Characteristics such as autocratic or permissive were ascribed to the general behavior tendencies of the worker. The author at this time would like to point out to the neophyte group worker, that at the outset the choice is his in terms of the participation quotient of the group. This is done by the types of management decision styles one utilizes, notwithstanding their own ingrained personality traits. One has a choice every time a decision has to be made, and the worker can draw from the following alternatives depending on the attending circumstances.

Autocratic Approach:

The worker solves the problem or makes the decision him/herself, using information available at the time.

The worker obtains the necessary information from the group members, then decides on the solution to the problem. The worker may not tell the members what the problem is. The role played by the group members in making the decision is clearly one of providing the necessary information to the worker, rather than in generating or evaluating alternative solutions.

Consultive Approach:

The worker shares the problem with relevant group members individually, getting their ideas and suggestions without bringing them together as a group. Then the worker makes the decision which may or may not reflect the members' influence.

The worker shares the problem with the members as a group, collectively obtaining their ideas and suggestions. Then, the worker makes the decision which may or may not reflect the members influence.

Group Participative Approach:

The worker shares a problem with the members as a group. Together they generate and evaluate alternatives and attempt to reach agreement (concensus) on a solution. The role of the worker is much like the chairman. He/she should not try to influence the group to adopt their solution and must be ready to accept and implement any solution which has the support of the entire group.

Delegative Approach:

Group members are completely free to make a decision on their own without or with little guidance from the worker.

Whereas, the author tends to shy away from the (autocratic) approaches, he recognizes that on occasion the group worker will be forced to invoke an autocratic decision, i.e. where time is a key factor and where the health, safety or well-being of group members are at stake.

It is quite obvious that the more times the group participative and delegative approaches are used the greater the ultimate acceptance of the decisions will be reflected by group members.

In as much as the group participation technique is the approach most desirable among the decision-making approaches, a check-list type of guide is provided for group workers to aid them in the use and evaluation of the process. This is an adoption from "Outline of the Democratic Technique" found in the *Principles of Human Relations* by Norman R.F. Maier.

Outline of the Group Participation Approach

Study the Problem:

Check your responsibility.

- Consider each problem that arises to see how it involves your responsibility and authority.
  a) Is it a problem to be dealt with directly? Is it in your own area of freedom?
  b) Should it be discussed first with your own supervisor?
- Problems that you would have a right to handle autocratically should be given consideration for democratic handling. This may also give a clue on area of freedom.
- Check your responsibility towards units at the same level as yours.

Analyze the situation.

- How to do the job—not whether it shall be done—may apply to a great many activiites. (So often we assume that the job is specified from above. Note that the how extends the area of freedom. Many jobs are specified as must but there is generally leeway on how to do them.)
- Problems must concern the group.
  a) Reactions to situations or anticipated reactions may make problems important to the group (planning, assignments, schedules, etc.).
  b) Some problems may not apear to concern the group, and yet we later find strong attitudes about them.
  c) If the group is indifferent to a problem or its solution it is not a matter for the group participation technique.

- Attempts to solve some problems may reveal the presence of others. This is why free discussion is desirable.

Check your attitude.

- Are you willing to encourage the group to solve the problem? You do this when you ask for help on a problem: "You are close to the project" or "I'd like to the benefit of your experience."
- Will you have them consider long-range results as well as immediate results and have them look at the problem from various angles?
- Will you deal on a man-to-man basis, respecting the views of everyone and avoiding paternalism?
- Can you give a "yes" to these questions?
  a) Do you believe the group is capable of solving the problem?
  b) Will you be willing to accept their solution even though it differs from one you might have in mind?

Plan your presentation.

- Finding a good way to present the problem will require study and preparation.
- It is essential to have the problem clearly in focus—know why it is a problem.

Sharing the Problem:

State the question.

- Present it in positive terms rather than in terms of objecting to something.
- State the problem in such a manner that there is mutual interest.
- Make the statement so that it stimulates interest in solving the problem rather than giving rise to defense reactions.
- It may be possible to present the problem in a two-column approach, using the easel or blackboard.
  a) Develop with the group a number of the advantages of the situation under discussion. List these in one column on the easel.
  b) Then develop a list of disadvantages.
  c) Now our problem is how to reduce the disadvantages without losing too many advantages.
- The problem may be presented in terms of fairness.

Furnish essential information.

- Present facts. If opinions are important to an understanding of the situation state them but label them as opinions.
- Look on information as ground rules for the game of problem solving.
  a) Ground rules should not be used to eliminate free expression.
  b) Basic information should be supplied at the outset and should not be used to discredit suggestions.
  c) If a suggested solution is contradictory to some fact that you forgot to include in presenting the problem, list it as a possible solution and have

the group search for other possibilities, or state frankly that you forgot to mention certain facts which the suggested solution does not recognize.
d) A worker does not lose face if he has to get certain facts from higher management during the meeting.
e) Exercise care that "your" ground rules do not stem from a preconceived solution you have in mind.

- Share with the group the fact that you are trying to increse their participation in solving problems that concern them.

Discussing the Problem:

Encourage free discussion.

- Establish an atmosphere of permissiveness (interest in having everyone have his say without criticism).
- A permissive atmosphere exists when the individual feels free to say whatever is on his mind.
- Pay special attention to the feeling part of any statement and respect this feeling.
- An informal, relaxed spirit about the meeting will encourage free discussion.
- Remember that the position a worker holds gives him prestige regardless of his personality.
- Raising of eyebrows, a shrewd glance, and other expressions of blame or doubt can destroy the atmosphere of permissiveness.
- Permissiveness does not mean a laissez-faire situation, in which the group is turned loose without a leader.
- Let members of the group do most of the talking and answering of each other.
- The worker can sense those who want to talk.
- Cross flow is a good indication of a permissive atmosphere.
- It may be hard to get discussion at first. The group may regard the worker with an attitude of suspicion: "What does he want us to say?"
- Members should be encouraged to assume a feeling of responsibility for the success of the solution.
- The worker should avoid stepping into the discussion and ruling out some idea that looks impossible to him. If there are flaws in the ideas let the group rule them out.
- The worker can get weak ideas eliminated by asking such questions as, "How would that be done?", "How would that work out?", "Let us analyze that from various angles."
- Write the various suggestions on the board. This gives a person recognition and permits the discussion to continue: "Now are there some other possibilities?"

Get everyone to participate.

- Participation means more than just getting a word of approval from every person. Encourage them to enter the discussion in an active way—to think and speak with the group.
- Ask quiet people for their views: "The group is interested in your views, Joe." But do not press for expression, particularly at first. It is best if group members ask a quiet person for his views.
- If some reticent member says he "doesn't care," be sure to give him a chance to voice interest later.
- Exert influence by getting everyone in the discussion, but avoid calling on them in consecutive order. Avoid putting anyone on the spot. Remember that he may have private reasons for not wanting to talk.
- The member who says he "won't" talk may say so because he feels he does not belong to the group. As more meetings are held he will be helped to feel that he does belong.
- Try to develop an attitude in the group that each person has the responsibility for giving his views. Let the group discuss this phase of a member's responsibility.
- Getting everyone to participate is a way of preventing certain individuals from dominating the discussion.

Keep discussion on the point.

- This is the spot where the worker exerts control. A group of individuals if left entirely "on their own" will tend toward confusion rather than democratic operation. In such situations a member of the group may actually function as a leader to get the discusion back to the point.
- Individuals need to feel free to talk about many things, and this should be permitted within certain limits. This does not imply wide digression from the topic at hand. Remember that other members in the group will want to stay on the subject.
- The group should experience progress; wide digressions prevent this.
- Distinguish between this type of control and dominance. A dominating worker would rule out solutions that did not fit his preconceived notions by limiting discussions under the pretext of "keeping on the beam." This is an easy rut to get into.
- If the group appears to be digressing discussion should still be allowed to go far enough to be sure it is not pertinent to the main topic.
- If you feel that a contribution is unrelated to the problem ask the person if his idea relates to the problem. If he feels it does he is not off the subject. If he feels it is not related ask his permission to take up his problem on a later occasion.
- If group members feel "responsible" they will tend to keep a discussion "on the beam." As participation increases, this feeling of responsibilty

grows. Thus discussions improve with experience. Both the leader and the group learn.

Respect minority opinions.

- Failure to respect minority opinions may cause individual members to feel they "don't belong." Respect for minority opinions can pull back into the group those who feel they do not belong: "Your idea gives us a new slant on things, Sam" or "Let's get your idea down and see how it works in with the others."
- If a group worker aligns himself with the majority they may feel that they have his consent to rule out the minority.
- Sometimes a minority opinion wins out. If the group has a chance to hear what the minority has to say it may be sympathetic and decide in that direction. Good ideas are frequently minority ideas.
- Respecting a minority idea permits a person to stop defending it.
- Minority opinions often are hostile. Expressing hostility gives relief. Treat such an expression objectively: "That's what we're here for, to get all our ideas and feelings on this question" or "That's Ed's view on the problem, and if we have different slants that is all to the good. We are here to iron our differences.

Solving the Problem:

The solution is a meeting of the minds.

- It contains some of each person's thinking. The solution thus grows out of the group. Some solutions, however, are compromises.
- This differs from a voting process, where a majority rules. In that situation, ideas are not developed.
- The democratic solution results from the interplay of forces in group (social pressures) which produce a meeting of the minds. The solution may be one that no individual held at the outset.
- A solution derived in this way involves the best interests of the group rather than the interest of any one individual.

The group worker should summarize and check for group agreement.

- As suggestions come out and are discussed by the group, the worker can sense when a conclusion has been reached.
- Summarizing the points that have been made gives the group an experience of progress and clarifies the issues.
- In checking for group agreement the worker permits individual attitudes to be expressed: "Is this what you all understand is the feeling of the group?" or "Am I interpreting this right?"
- As points are summarized the group feels they have arrived at a basis for exploring the problem further.
- Summarizing allows social pressure to act, since the group has a chance to learn who is for and who is against the suggestion. This points up the differences that remain as problems.

- In summarizing, such remarks may be used as: "We have had such and such a suggestion. How do you feel about it?" or "We have had some discussion on this suggestion. Do you feel it is the answer to our problem?"

The solution should specify action.

- The group may agree that something definite should be done, but the time for initiating the action should also be included.
- If solution involves members taking turns the pattern of rotation should be specified.
- Some discussion may be concerned with what should be done, but unless the how is included misunderstandings may occur.

The group should feel free to request a reopening of the subject.

- The group may have set goals at the wrong level (too high or too low) or may not have fully considered the long-range results of its decisions. This may not be apparent until the solution is tried out.
- An attitude of permissiveness allows for the fact that the group may not have hit on the ideal goal at their first try.
- A democratic group worker will understand that decisions are not made for all time. He will appreciate the need to rediscuss the problem if the group so desires.
- The group should be told that the door is open to reconsider the problem if any member should feel it necessary.
- The best solution is tailor-made to fit the group and the circumstances existing at the time.

In the climate of open and democratic participation is the area of receiving and giving feedback by the group worker. Dr. George F. J. Lehner of the University of California has developed a series of aids for giving and receiving feedback which the author has applied to the group worker.

Some of the most important data the workers can receive from others (or give to others) consists of feedback related to behavior. Such feedback can provide learning opportunities for each worker if they can use the reactions of others as a mirror for observing the consequences of behavior. Such personal data feedback helps to make all of us more aware of what we do and how we do it, thus increasing our ability to modify and change our behavior and to become more effective in our interactions with others.

Feedback Factors

To help the group worker develop and use the techniques of feedback for personal growth it is necessary to understand certain characteristics of the process. The following is a brief outline of some factors which may assist the worker in making better use of feedback, both as the giver and the receiver.

● Focus feedback on behavior rather than the person. It is important that we refer to what a person does rather than comment on what we imagine he is. This focus on behavior further implies that we use adverbs (which relate to actions) rather than adjectives (which relate to qualities) when referring to a person. Thus we might say a person "talked considerably in this meeting," rather than this person is a loudmouth." When we talk in terms of "personality traits" it implies inherited constant qualities difficult, if not impossible, to change. Focusing on behavior implies that it is something related to a specific situation that might be changed. It is less threatening to a person to hear comments about his behavior than his "traits."

● Focus feedback on observations rather than inferences. Observations refer to what we can see or hear in the behavior of another person, while inferences refer to interpretations and conclusions which we make from what we can see or hear. In a sense, inferences or conclusions about a person contaminate our observations, thus clouding the feedback for another person. When inferences or conclusions are shared, and it may be valuable to have this data, it is important that they be so identified.

● Focus feedback on description rather than judgment. The effort to describe represents a process for reporting what occurred, while judgment refers to an evaluation in terms of good or bad, right or wrong, nice or not nice. The judgments arise out of a personal frame of reference or values, whereas description represents neutral (as far as possible) reporting.

● Focus feedback on descriptions of behavior which are in terms of "more or less" rather than in terms of "either-or." The "more or less" terminology implies a continuum on which any behavior may fall, stressing quantity, which is objective and measurable, rather than quality, which is subjective and judgmental. Thus, participation of a person may fall on a continuum from low participation to high participation, rather than "good" or "bad" participation. Not to think in terms of "more or less" and the use of continua is to trap ourselves into thinking in categories, which may represent serious distortions of reality.

● Focus feedback on behavior related to a specific situation, preferably to the "here and now," rather than to behavior in the abstract, placing it in the "there and then." What you and I do is always tied in some way to time and place, and we increase our understanding of behavior by keeping it tied to time and place. Feedback is generally more meaningful if given as soon as appropriate after the observation or reactions occur, thus keeping it concrete and relatively free of distortions that come with the lapse of time.

● Focus feeback on the sharing of ideas and information rather than on giving advice. By sharing ideas and information we leave the person free to decide for himself, in the light of his own goals in a particular situation at a particular time, how to use the ideas and the information. When we give advice we tell him what to do with the information, and in that sense we take away his freedom to determine for himself what is for him the most appropriate course of action.

● Focus feedback on exploration of alternatives rather than answers or solutions. The more we can focus on a variety of procedures and means for the attainment of a particular goal, the less likely we are to accept prematurely a particular answer or solution—which may or may not fit our particular problem. Many of us go around with a collation of answers and solutions for which there are no problems.

● Focus feedback on the value it may have to the recipient not on the value or "release" that it provides the person giving the feedback. The feedback provided should serve the needs of the recipient rather than the needs of the giver. Help and feedback need to be given and heard as an offer, not an imposition.

● Focus feedback on the amount of information that the person receiving it can use, rather than on the amount that you have which you might like to give. To overload a person with feedback is to reduce the possibility that he may use what he receives effectively. When we give more than can be used we may be satisfying some need for ourselves rather than helping the other person.

● Focus feedback on time and place so that personal data can be shared at appropriate times. Because the reception and use of personal feedback involves many possible emotional reactions, it is important to be sensitive to when it is appropriate to provide feedback. Excellent feedback presented at an inappropriate time may do more harm than good.

● Focus feedback on what is said rather than why it is said. The aspects of feedback which relate to the what, how, when, where of what is said are observable characteristics. The why of what is said takes us from the observable to the inferred, and brings up questions of "motive" or "intent."

It is maybe helpful to think of "why in terms of a specificable goal or goals—which can then be considered in terms of time, place, procedures, probabilities of attainment, etc. To make assumptions about the motives of the person giving feedback may prevent us from hearing or cause us to distort what is said. In short, if I question "why" a person gives me feedback I may not hear what he says.

In short, the giving (and receiving) of feedback requires courage, skill, understanding, and respect for self and others.

Capacity to Interrelate

Group participation often is directly related to the capacity of group members (and sometimes the group worker) to interrelate with each other. When there are problems in the sphere of interpersonal relations of any kind, it might be well for the worker to explore the Johari Window: A graphic model of awareness in Interpersonal Relations developed by Ingham and Luft.[11]

---

[11]Permission to reprint granted by Mayfield Publishing Co., Palo Alto, California.

Many people get along fine working with others, without thinking about which foot to put forward. But when there are difficulties, when the usual methods do not work, when they want to learn more—there is no alternative but to examine their own behavior in relation to others. The trouble is that, among other things, it is so hard to find ways of thinking about such matters, particularly for people who have no extensive backgrounds in the social sciences.

The Johari Window

	KNOWN TO SELF		NOT KNOWN TO SELF	
KNOWN TO	Area of Free Activity	I	Blind Area	II
NOT KNOWN	Avoided or Hidden area	III	Area of Unknown Activity	IV

When Harry Ingham and Joseph Luft first presented The Johari Window to illustrate relationships in terms of awareness, they were surprised to find so many people, academicians and nonprofessionals alike, using and tinkering with the model. It seemed to lend itself as a hueristic device to speculate about human relations. It is simple to visualize the four quadrants which represent The Johari Window.

Quadrant I, the area of free activity, refers to behavior and motivation known to self and known to others.

Quadrant II, the blind area, where others can see things in ourselves of which we are unaware.

Quadrant III, the avoided or hidden area, represents things we know but do not reveal to others (e.g., a hidden agenda or matters about which we have sensitive feelings).

Quadrant IV, the area of unknown activity. Neither the individual nor others are aware of certain behaviors or motives. Yet we can assume their existence because eventually some of these things become known, and it is then realized that these unknown behaviors and motives were influencing relationships all along.

The Quadrants and Changing Group Interaction

In a new group, Quadrant I is very small; there is not much free and spontaneous interaction. As the group grows and matures, Quadrant I expands in size and this usually means we are freer to be more like ourselves and to perceive others as they really are. Quadrant III shrinks in area as Quadrant I grows larger. We find it less necessary to hide or deny things we know or feel. In an atmosphere of growing mutual trust there is less need for hiding pertinent thoughts or feelings. It takes longer for Quadrant II to reduce in size, because usually there are "good" reasons of a psychological nature to blind ourselves to the things we feel or do. Quadrant IV perhaps changes somewhat during a learning laboratory, but we can assume that such changes occur even more slowly than do shifts in Quadrant II. At any rate, Quadrant IV is undoubtedly far larger and more influential in an individual's relationships than the hypothetical sketch illustrates.

The Johari Window may be applied to intergroup relations. Quadrant I means behavior and motivation known to the group and also known to other groups. Quadrant II signifies an area of behavior to which a group is blind; but other groups are aware of this behavior, e.g., cultism or prejudice. Quadrant III, the hidden area, refers to things a group knows about itself but which are kept from other groups. Quadrant IV, the unknown area, means a group is unaware of some aspect of its own behavior, and other groups are also unaware of this behavior. Later, as the group learns new things about itself, there is a shift from Quadrant IV to one of the other quadrants.

Principles of Change

- A change in any one quadrant will affect all other quadrants.
- It takes energy to hide, deny, or be blind to behavior which is involved in interaction.
- Threat tends to decrease awareness; mutual trust tends to increase awareness.
- Forced awareness (exposure) is undesirable and usually ineffective.
- Interpersonal learning means a change has taken place so that Quadrant I is larger and one or more of the other quadrants has grown smaller.
- Working with others is facilitated by a large enough area of free activity. It means more of the resources and skills in the membership can be applied to the task at hand.
- The smaller the first quadrant, the poorer the communication.
- There is universal curiosity about unknown areas, but this is held in check by custom, social training, and by diverse fears.
- Sensitivity means appreciating the covert aspects of behavior in Quadrants II, III, and IV and respecting the desire of others to keep them so.
- Learning about group processes as they are being experienced helps to increase awareness (larger Quadrant I) for the group as a whle, as well as for individual members.
- The value system of a group and its membership may be noted in the way unknowns in the life of the group are confronted.

Chapter 9

REFERENCES

Davis, K. *Human Relations at Work.*

Hackman, J. R. and J. L. Suttle. *Improving Life at Work.* Goodyear Publishing Co., Inc., 1977.

Knowles, M. and H. Knowles. *Introduction to Group Dynamics.*

Lesser, B. *Youth Advisors Handbook.* Nealco Publishing Co., 1970.

Luft, J. *Of Human Interaction.* National Press Books, 1969.

Maier, N. R. F. *Principles of Human Relations.* John Wiley and Sons, Inc., 1952.

Chapter 10

Motivation — A Theoretical View

Motivation, by which the needs of a person (group member) give rise to behavior, is one of the most important concepts in the management of the group as a whole. How teenagers perform as members of a group and how they relate to each other depends on their motivation.

Motives are active, driving needs. Some needs are *primary* in that they are part of our basic physiological makeup. However the *socially acquired* needs are those to which we must pay attention. Ignorance of individual group members needs and inability to enlist member support for organizational needs have caused many problems for youth group workers.

Intensity or strength of need in different group members is often difficult to measure. Needs vary with different social and educational groupings. Many differences in need are also due to variations in values and familly background. Needs also change within a group member, as he grows intellectually, emotionally and sometimes occupationally.

The term "motivation" is often used as a synonym for unusual productivity or energetic behavior. As we shall see, this represents a most simplistic assessment and the group worker should be wise to guard against this view.

Selected Behavioral Science Theories[12]

Behavioral science is the systematic study of human behavior which seeks to predict how most people are likely to behave under a given set of conditions. It is this predictive ability that has led many group workers to turn to behavioral science for help in solving recurrent personnel and organizational problems. Frequently, this attention has focused on the area of motivation, with the dual intent of achieving greater organizational effectiveness and satisfaction through the optimal use of group resources.

Motivation-Maintenance Theory

Developed by Frederick Herzberg, the theory postulates two sets of factors

---

[12]Adapted from Gellerman, Saul W., MOTIVATION AND PRODUCTIVITY (New York: American Management Association, Inc., 1963) pp. 48-142.

that operate simultaneously and independently. One set, the maintenance factors (sometimes called hygiene factors or dissatisfiers), cannot cause job satisfaction or motivation, per se. They only have the potential to negatively affect performance, that is, to create dissatisfaction if they are not dealt with. These factors all pertain to job context rather than to the nature of the work performed. The other set of factors, the motivators or satisfiers, cannot cause dissatisfaction, per se, if they are not present at work, but employees lack motivation. The motivators all pertain to job content, the work itself.

Satisfiers	**Dissatisfiers**
Achievement	Company policy and administration
Recognition for	Supervision achievement
Work itself	Working conditions
Responsibility	Interpersonal relations
Advancement	Salary
Growth	Status
	Job security

Attention to either set of factors can result in increased performance and productivity; but, in the case of the maintenance factors, the increase will be due to improvement of the work environment, making it easier to do the job. Because the improvement rests on a hygiene factor, a need that does not stay met, performance may not stay improved unless further improvement on hygiene is made (what have you done for me lately). In the case of the motivators (satisfiers), the increase will be due to providing more satisfaction of the individual's internally generated needs through the work itself. When performance improves because motivators or satisfiers increase, the improvement is likely to be more permanent because it is due to the work itself rather than an external factor.

At the heart of the theory, then, is the concept that the factors which cause employee *dissatisfaction* are different from the factors which cause employee *satisfaction* and that management (or group worker) must work on both sets of factors, not only to avoid discontent, but also to provide the conditions for continued employee (or group member) motivation.

Job Enrichment

Job enrichment is based on the Motivation-Maintenance Theory developed by Frederick Herzberg. It is the process of restructuring jobs by building in higher-order responsibilities and authority and more challenging content. This is done so that an individual has the opportunities for achievement, recognition, and growth that make a job a satisfying, meaningful experience which the employee (or group member) is motivated to perform well. The whole approach is based on the assumption that group members will respond positively to challenging, responsible work.

Needs Hierarchy

The late Abraham Maslow described people as a goal-seeking or need-fulfilling beings. Lowest level goals or needs emphasize preserving the body—physiological needs; highest level goals emphasize realizing potential—self-actualization mentioned in prior chapters. Maslow divided these goals or needs into a Hierarchy of Needs. From lowest to highest this hierarchy is:

- Physiological—food, water, air, sex, rest, etc.
- Safety and Security—actual physical safety and feeling safe from injury, both physical and emotional.
- Belongingness and Love—need to feel part of a group or to belong to and with someone. Implies the need to give and receive love.
- Esteem (self and from others)—need for self-respect, a feeling of personal worth and the need for respect and status in the eyes of others.
- Self-Actualization—the recognition of one's real or true self and the process of working toward the expression of that self by becoming what one is capable of becoming.

Maslow called actions to achieve a goal or meet a need *"motivation."* A person acts to meet a need until that need is satisfied. Then the person acts to achieve a higher-level need. Effort is exerted to maintain achievement of the lower level need but that is no longer a driving force. An individual, however, can have more than one set of needs operating at the same time. There is no definite line dividing them.

External circumstances can also influence what needs are paramount or can frustrate or facilitate the meeting of needs. Hard times can make safety needs more important or the individual may decide to be satisfied with less safety and remain unaffected by the hard times. External circumstances influence, but the final decision rests with the individual.

The lower-level needs (physiological, safety, and belonging), in Maslow's Hierarchy can be related to Herzberg's Hygiene Factors (dissatisfiers). Like Hygiene, they are more susceptible to external manipulation. Herzberg's Satisfiers (recognition, responsibility, achievement and growth) tie in to Maslow's esteem and self-actualization categories. This group of needs is less susceptible to external manipulation and even more strongly determined by internal drives and desires of the individual.

Theory X and Theory Y

Douglas McGregor, Professor of Industrial Management at MIT at the time of his death, described two sets of assumptions about the nature of people at work. He labeled these assumptions (beliefs or values) Theory X and Theory Y. McGregor inferred his *Theory X assumptions from research and observations on the behavior of working managers.* Theory X assumptions or beliefs are:

- People dislike work and will avoid it if they can.
- People must be coerced, controlled, or threatened with punishment to work hard toward organizational objectives.
- Most people want to be controlled or directed from the outside, to avoid responsibility, to have job security above all else.

McGregor's *Theory X assumptions about human nature are based on behavioral science research.* Theory Y assumptions or beliefs about human nature are:

- Work is as natural an activity as rest or play.
- If people are committed to objectives, they will work to achieve them without the threat of punishment.
- Average people learn, under proper conditions, to seek responsibility.
- Most people are capable of considerable creativity and imagination in solving organizational problems.

Theory X and Theory Y describe assumptions or beliefs that can be translated to group workers in a group setting. Specific situations influence how the worker's assumptions or beliefs are translated into action. Workers cannot be clearly labeled "all Y" or "all X." However, the Theory X worker can be described as primarily concerned with imposing external controls on group members because the worker feels this is the only way to get hard work. The Theory Y group worker is more likely to work to encourage development of internal control within the members through building an atmosphere of trust, respect, and commitment to common goal.

A worker with Theory X assumptions would probably try to achieve motivation by manipulating Hygiene factors and by emphasizing needs on the lower levels of Maslow's Hierarchy. Job Enrichment would probably not make sense to that worker.

McGregor's Theory Y assumptions relate to Herzberg's Satisfiers and to Maslow's esteem or self-actualization categories. A worker with Theory Y assumptions about human nature would probably see Job Enrichment as a useful approach.

Pygmalion in Management

In the book *High Expectations,* J. Sterling Livingston stated that a manager's expectations are the key to a subordinate's performance and development. The manager's self-image influences what he or she believes about subordinates, what is expected of them, and how they are treated. If the manager is confident enough to develop and stimulate them to improved performance, they will expect much of them and will treat them with confidence that those expectations will be met.

You can relate "Pygmalion in Management" to McGregor's Theory X and Y by asking yourself, "How would a group worker with Theory X beliefs treat members?" That worker would be likely to act as if they thought members were lazy, not interested in responsibility, wished to be externally controlled. According to Livingston, the members would begin to behave that way because the worker expected it. If a worker is preoccupied with his or her own job security, that worker is likely to assume members are concerned only with safety needs (Maslow).

The Classical Theories

Sigmund Freud: It was Sigmund Freud, according to Saul Gellerman, who first called attention to the importance of unconscious motivation. He meant that people are not normally aware of everything that they want, that they will often have tastes, biases, or attitudes which strongly influence their behavior, but for which they cannot really account. Freud was convinced that only a small portion of peoples motivations could be recognized, whereas the greater part were hidden and blocked off from consciousness. (Not necessarily bad, since this made for an orderly flow of thoughts possible and prevented distraction by irrelevant or disturbing notions.) In the long run Freud stressed our life-preserving and comfort-seeking instincts in reviewing man's motivations.

Alfred Adler: Adler, a one-time associate of Freud's who eventually broke with him to establish his own school of thought, also had an important influence on the understanding of work motivation. Unlike Freud, who stressed the pleasure seeking and life-sustaining motives, Adler placed a great deal of emphasis on the power motive. By "power" he meant the ability to require others to behave in ways that suited one's purposes. In Adler's mind, this ability to manipulate other people was inherently pleasurable.

The Competence Motive

Robert W. White: White, of Harvard University, notes that one of the mainsprings of human motivation is an interest in getting to know what the world is like and in learning to get what one wants from it. Whereas, Freud stressed the life-preserving and comfort-seeking instincts and Adler, going a step further, stressed the drive for power over others, White maintains that people also want to understand and manipulate their physical and social environment as well. To be able to make things happen—to create events rather than to submit to them passively. White calls this desire for mastery "the competence motive."

The Affiliation Motive

Stanley Schachter: Psychologists have been reviewing the question of human motivation from many facets, including what makes some people social creatures, whereas others are happy to be "loners."

Schachter, of the University of Minnesota, has made some progress in such a study. Affiliation, according to him, can be:

- A simple expression of good fellowship.
- Or the symptom of a drastic loss of self-respect.
- Or a voluntary strategem for increasing the likelihood of obtaining certain advantages.

(Schachter had pointed out that his work was incomplete in the sense of not having weighed the effects of other motives, such as sheer joy, curiosity, or dominance, in affiliation.)

The most likely explanation of the non-affiliating tendency is that at least two types of people are predisposed to show it (something that the embryo group worker should note).

- Some people refrain from joining groups because they are suspicious or contemptuous of them.
- Others refrain from joining groups because they are secure enough to get along without the group.

The group itself is sometimes defensive in nature. It is a means of creating an artificial, miniature world in which the things that are sometimes lacking in the real work-day world—pride, importance and security—are reproduced on a smaller scale. This is very attractive to some people.

The Achievement Motive

David C. McClelland: Shortly after World War II a group of psychologists led by McClelland of Harvard University placed the achievement motive under intensive analysis. They found that the achievement motive played a very rigorous role in the lives of the people who were influenced by it.

Just about everyone has an achievement motive to some extent, but some people are consistently more oriented toward achievement than others. Perhaps, the most important aspect of a really strong achievement motive, according to Gellerman, is that it makes its possessor very susceptible to appeals to try harder to to quickly accept challenges. (This is important information for the group worker to establish—those members of the youth group who are achievement oriented should be given appropriate challenging assignments.)

The Prestige Motive

The prestige motive, as always, is very much in evidence today. A person's prestige is largely a matter of how they can expect to be treated, and it therefore has a definite effect on how comfortably, conveniently, and efficiently one can expect to get along in life.

The group worker, however, must keep in mind that prestige is conferred by society (in this case by members of the group), not elected by the individual to suit his tastes. High prestige must be a matter of low-status group members wanting to put some well-liked teenager member on a pedestal. Inequality of ability and motives is the basis of prestige. This becomes a negative force only when natural inequalities are blocked by caste or prejudice. Too often the group members might struggle for the material trappings of prestige, rather than for the personal excellence that commands prestige in a quiet way. The group worker should certainly be able to delineate between the two approaches.

The Security Motives

There are two forms of security motivation:

- conscious: – a routine concern with the ordinary hazards of life.
- unconscious: – people entering into unilateral "alliances" with others or organizations who seem to be able to guarantee such people a reasonably unruffled life. These would be patient, passive group members, with a willingness to accept whatever fate comes along. Another way in which unconscious security motivation may be manifested is through overprotective or overindulgent treatment during the group member's formative years—giving the latter a notion that the world is a benevolent, tolerant community, which obligingly accommodates itself to his needs.

Despite all the learned dissertations dealing with motivations, there is still a vast difference of opinion among managers and scholars as to what motivates people. Howard Smith,[13] president of Smith and Donahue Inc., a firm of psychologists to management, has prepared a handy laundry list of misconceptions about motivation, which has impresed the author. There follows 10 "truisms" about motivation—and Smith's interesting explanations of why all are false.

---

[13]Reprinted with permission from the March 1979 issue of TRAINING, The Magazine of Human Resources Development, Copyright Lakewood Publications, Minneapolis, Minnesota (612) 333-0471. All rights reserved.

● We can use a carrot or, failing that, a stick to motive people. By its very nature, motivation can be elicited neither by carrot not by stick. The carrot-or-stick approach may cause movement; *it does not create motivation.* The dictionary definition of motive—"that within the individual, rather than without, which incites him to action"—makes this point clear.

When we recognize that developing people is more akin to farming than to manufacturing, we will understand better that we cannot "motivate" a person by doing something "to" him or her. We can only elicit motivated behavior; and we can only do that by creating conditions that increase the probability of its occurrence, a challenging endeavor that calls for a thorough understanding of and a genuine interest in the potentialities of people.

● There are goals for motivating people, or theories of what motivates people, that have general applicability. Motives vary widely, even within the same organization. The research chemist is stimulated by conditions different from those which excite the salesperson; and what challenges the salesperson differs from what turns on the production manager or the financial analyst. *There are no universally applicable tools for motivating people.*

● By studying groups and group members, salespeople, engineers, accountants, workers, executives—we can learn more about motivating indivuduals. Studies to find differences among different occupational groups, unfortunately, there is also so much variability within any one group that *studies of groups are unreliable guides to the understanding of what motivates a particular individual.*

● We can provide a person with a motive. Discussion of the first item indicates why this statement is false. Nonetheless, most of us have known individuals who appear to have been "turned on" by something, almost as if they had indeed been provided with a motive. Dramatic changes in behavior do occur. Analysis of such behavior changes will generally reveal that it was a turn-around of some circumstance in the individual's environment that aroused him or her to motivated action. A new job, a new boss, a new spouse, or a sharpening of one's vocational goals may be such a stimulus. In short, *we cannot provide a person with a motive, but we can change factors in the environment that may trigger motivated behavior.*

● If you make the necessary information available, behavior will change. This statement rests on the fallacious premise that knowledge inevitably leads to action; that if I know what my problem is, I will change my behavior. Most of us know that telling a paranoid schizophrenic that those voices he hears are only in his head does not stop him from hearing them. Why then, do we think that telling a group member, "Be more aggressive!" will make him more aggressive? Indeed, *much of the reticence of unaggressive individuals may reflect the overload of information they have received about their problem."* It is their self-doubt that is being reinforced.

● The more we know about a person, the better able we are to motivate him or her. The opposite of this statement is just as valid. That is, *the more you know about a person, the more you may recognize the impossibility of arousing motivated behavior.* Yet, in a sense the statement is true. The more you know about a person, the better able you are to specify the conditions most likely to arouse that person's motivation. No one is really devoid of motivation.

In the work situation, the majority of those presumed to lack motivation fall into one of three categories: 1) those who lack confidence in themselves and won't risk the effort required because they fear failure; 2) those who are bored; 3) those who don't understand what is expected of them.

● Incentives and bonuses motivate people. Denying that incentives and bonuses motivate people appears to attack the very foundation of our free enterprise society.

● People cannot change their behavior unless they know what their problem is. At the level of specific skills, this is a true statement. Feedback on performance is an essential condition for learning. It is a necessity in teaching skills like driving a car, typing, skiing, or operating a machine. However, when one gets much beyond the level of specific skills to the area of personality traits, the statement lacks validity. Telling another person what that person's problem is will quite likely work against developing the desired behavior. For example, *urging an introverted person to "be more outgoing" may only accentuate that person's tendency to withdraw.*

We gain confidence by solving problems and achieving goals within our range of ability and experience. Confidence grows as we learn to master increasingly complex problems and to reach ever more challenging goals. Effective managers, teachers, and parents are those who provide opportunities for problem solving at appropriate levels of difficulty. This is what "developing people" is all about.

● Eliminating stress and conflict improves productivity. Rather than improve productivity, *the elimination of stress and conflict is far more likely to foster an unproductive, comfortable adjustment to the status quo.* It can lead to loss of the capacity to deal with real problems. Research shows that performance is enhanced when individuals experience a moderate degree of tension. It is impaired by a high level of tension.

The problem lies in making the avoidance of stress and conflict a goal in itself. Emphasis on stress avoidance establishes a new norm in the organization: agreement and conformity with what exists.

● Basically, people want to be liked and are motivated by praise. Not all people. The need to be liked does loom large in our society. *But for many people, real satisfaction comes from achievement, whether or not people like them more for it.*

Praise itself has varying effects; it is easily given, costs nothing to administer, and bathes the praiser in a warm glow. But the time-honored pat on the back can be disingenuous. It can distract from genuine achievement by encouraging the recipient to engage in "praiseworthy" behavior. Unfortunately, praise can be interpreted as condescension, establishing the superior position of the person who praises.

There is one sense in which praise has a meaningful tie-in to motivation. Praise is important as a form of feedback on performance and behavior. In cases where results are difficult to measure or are too long-term, praise as feedback on the quality of performance is important in sustaining motivation.

REFERENCES

Calhoon, R. P. *Personnel Management and Supervision.* Prentice-Hall Inc., 1967.

Dalton, G. W., P. R. Lawrence, and L. E. Greiner. *Organizational Change and Development.* Richard D. Irwin Inc. and The Dorsey Press, 1970.

Gellerman, S. W. *Motivation and Productivity.* American Management Association, Inc., 1963.

Hawley, R. C., and I. L. Hawley. *Human Values in the Classroom – A Handbook for Teachers.* Hart Publishing Co., Inc., 1975.

Smith, H. *Misconceptions About Motivation.* Training/HRD, Mar. 1979.

Chapter 11

Motivating Youth Group Members (Practical Applications)

The Bureau of Business Practice in Waterford, Connecticut, had issued an "Action Guide to Motivating People."[14] Although this guide is geared to the business scene, the author found much in the pamphlet that is applicable to youth groups and their members. As a result he adapted the guide for us by group workers in dealing with problem teenagers.

Problem type group members encompass a broad spectrum of anti-social and sometimes undisciplined behavior. These include the goldbricker, the wise-guy, the chronic grouch, the complainer, the meddlesome do-gooder, the weakling, the non-cooperator, the non-conformist, the dead-ender, the compulsive talker, the busybody, the taciturn person and many more. This chapter deals with how to relate to these types of individuals in order to make them more cooperative and goal-oriented for the benefit for the group or organization as a whole.

The author has also converted from the aforementioned Action Guide, and included herein, a motivational check-sheet to be used by group workers to measure their own motivational quotient in day to day dealings with members of their groups. This check-sheet can serve as a quick appraisal of self-measurement of the workers own influence in getting group members to motivate themselves.

Every youth group has its share of problem members. They tend to make a nuisance of themselves. They're often unpleasant to associate with. And they may even threaten the efficiency and productivity of their groups. As a result they're often encouraged to quit. But, properly motivated, they can become well-above average members. Here's how to go about increasing their motivation.

Reprinted and/or adapted from ACTION GUIDE TO MOTIVATING PEOPLE – The Bureau of Business Practice, Waterford, Connecticut (1980).

The Goldbricker

He has a powerful aversion to work, he sidesteps it by every trick known. Each time he fails to meet a goal or target, he offers a dozen legitimate excuss. He easily out-maneuvers the officers and workers while they grit their teeth. If they complain he takes too long to do an assignment, he explains he's merely following their instructions. (Officer: "You were told to do it right, not to make a big production out of a small job." Goldbricker: "Oh, I thought you meant just what you said.")

What to do.

- Probe for reasons behind a goldbricker's actions. Don't jump to the conclusion he's completely shiftless. It may be that the key reason behind his behavior is dissatisfaction of some sort—with his school work, role in the group, social life and the like.
- If his project is repetitious, he may be bored. Give him additional and different tasks to perform. Or, reschedule his project so he works in shorter stints.
- If lack of interesting assignments is the reason for goldbricking, the only answer is better planning and better scheduling. Note: Be sure to give the member legitimate work. "Made-work" jobs will only increase goldbricking. The only way to spark enthusiasm for the additional work is to stress its importance and your reliance on them doing it.
- If they merely lack ambition—and you hesitate to use discipline because you're sure their potential is good—your only problem is to keep one step ahead of them. Here's how: 1) Give plenty of legitimate work. Hold them to high standards. Check their progress regularly. 2) Give them additional duties. This will force them to work harder at a normal pace, to get the time they need to handle the extra tasks. 3) Be sure to spell out standards each time you give them a nonroutine job. Challenge them with a time limit. 4) Assign them to a hard-working committee, where every member is expected to pull their share, where members ride herd on each other. Their industrious co-workers will pressure them to do a fair day's work.

The Wise Guy

Frequently, they're likable and competent. Often their know-it-all attitude covers up a lack of ability, aptitude, training. They'll argue at the drop of a hat, have a quick comeback for everything that's said. They can disrupt meetings by getting off the beam, and staying off. Or they antagonize others with sarcastic remarks.

Sometimes they're quite articulate and express themselves well. In this fact alone, they show certain qualities that can be used to develop a valuable member. Correctly handled, they may help officers build competitive spirit and enthusiasm. Otherwise they'll oppose well-laid plans and succeed in confusing others in a working group.

What to do.

● Keep them on their toes. Give them plenty of work; make sure they do it well. Sometimes it pays not to be overly critical of the work they produce. Note: Don't give the impression they're being persecuted.

● Avoid arguments. Often they're more interested in showing they can think a little better than anyone else. Or they may have a sense of humor and be entertaining in their arguments. But if you convince them you know what you're talking about, they'll respect you. Once you gain their respect, you'll have unusually loyal and cooperative group members.

● Be firm. The wise guy is often the type who's inclined to grab a yard once he's given an inch. So, keep a firm hand in dealing with them. If it's necessary to improve discipline, make sure it is 1) carefully planned; 2) has no loopholes; 3) can be made to stick.

● Give them more responsibility. Explain to them, make sure they understand you really mean it. This may have a sobering effect on them—by giving them a constructive outlet for their latent abilities and enthusiasm.

The Chronic Grouch

Sometimes they are angry at everybody. Usually they are mad at only themselves. Keep this in mind in any attempt to undermine why they're so grouchy. It takes patient investigation to find the underlying causes of their antisocial attitude. If there's any intention to keep them active, the reason for their attitude must be found without delay—before they undermind the morale of the entire group.

What to do.

● Begin with their relations with the group. Get answers to these questions: What's the record? Does it show steady progress, or a series of ups and downs? How many failures? Is one able to keep up with their fellow members? Or do they lack appropriate ability and aptitudes? Is their grouchiness confined to the worker and members? Or do they show it to everyone? Did something occur in their relation with the group that might cause them to feel they've been treated unfair?

● Find out about their life outside the confines of the group. Are they happy with the family? Do they associate with other people?

● Often the reason for a grouchy attitude is deficient hearing or vision. Or they may have certain physical handicaps that prevent them participating in normal activities. So, a physical checkup is in order. If you have an agency doctor, workers should talk it over with him before they send the man for a checkup. Note: This should be handled tactfully, without seeming to invade their personal life.

● Keep the grouch occupied, help them succeed. If they have enough work to do and know how to do it, they are less likely to think about their misfortunes, whether they're real or imagined. Helping them to succeed might be the key to straightening them out. Showing friendly interest in their development may change their viewpoint.

The Complainer

They're always complaining. Everything and everybody are targets for their gripes—the agency, the worker, their associates. They often look for trouble. If none exists, they imagine it. Their antagonism irritates workers and members. It breeds dissatisfaction, leads to general discontent.

What to do.

● As with the grouch, the problem is to find out why a member complains so much. Reasons may be similar to those that cause another member to be grouchy. Follow the same order of investigation.

● One of the first things to do is to appeal to their sense of reason. Whenever they voice a complaint, talk it over with them. Try to pin it down. Once it can be proved their their complaints are groundless, they may change their attitudes.

● The complainer may be an introvert. They are overly sensitive to other people's attitudes and remarks. Often they feel they're being persecuted. The only way to overcome this attitude is to direct their interest into other things. Try to get them interested in special projects—in some special training course, in an outside activity or hobby. Note: worker should be watchful of any influence a complainer may have on other members. If they see signs of others taking a complaint seriously, it should be investigated without delay and settled to everybody's satisfaction. (See Chapter 12 for a detailed review on how to handle complaints.)

The Meddlesome Do-Gooder

They're the reformers. They keep themselves busy trying to improve things and helping people, whether they're needed or not. Often they are so occupied taking care of troubles other than their own, they have little or no time for their own assignments. Their intentions may be the best. Still they can be annoying to co-members.

What to do.

● Often they'll show a tendency to spend most of their time with the group worker. As a result, other members will think they are the favorites. Workers must put a stop to this right away. Caution: Any appearance of favoritism toward an unpopular member will only breed dissention and distrust.

The Weakling

They may have real aptitude and ability. Yet they can't do a good job. Problems stand in their way—lack of confidence, fearful personality, or a combination of physical weakness and emotional instability. Usually they depend upon others for instructions; show no initiative.

What to do.

- The problem is to help him gain self-confidence. They should be kept on jobs they can do fairly well, to the worker's satisfaction as well as their own. At the same time, avoid making his co-members carry a load that should be his.
- Whatever the assignment, group workers should make sure that the weaklings carry it through to successful completion. This is the only way to help them gain confidence in themselves. Let them realize they can succeed, even if successs is in small and simple jobs. Eventually, they will want to cooperate freely and willingly with their peers.

The Noncooperator

They are not the ones who do not want to work or do a good job. They are the employee who feels they are superior to the other members. Perhaps they're timid and do not mix well with people. In any event, they do not cooperate willingly and freely with their worker and fellow members.

What to do.

- Team them up with members who are friendly, members who get along with people. This may eventually break down their noncooperative attitude. Particularly if it's due to a feeling of not belonging to a group.
- Develop their team spirit by showing them how to participate in successful achievements of the group.
- Workers and officers should be sure to include them in any group discussions, or in any praise of a group. If they can help them share in cooperative success, they'll come to like it.
- Workers and officers should avoid the tendency of expecting noncooperation when they're aware of a noncooperative attitude. If they assume a member wants to cooperate, he's more likely to do so. But if they expect resistance, that's what they may possibly get.

The Nonconformist

This type always thinks of different ways to do things. But they want to do them differently, rather than do them better. Often their actions are due to a desire to stand out, to be an individualist. In itself, this is not a bad trait. But if it interferes with group goals, it can be annoying. Sometimes their need to be different leads to idiosyncrasies and habits that irritate people. When this occurs, something must be done quickly.

What to do.

● Workers and officers should assign the nonconformist to the projects they can do best. They should avoid encouraging them to be different. At the same time, they must not discourage any ability they might have in creative thinking. This can be put to good use.

● Put them on a project that will represent a real challenge to them—one with problems with which they are not too familiar. This will force them to follow standard practice. Also, they'll be made to realize that others can be right, that other opinions are worth as much as their own.

● Try to find a place for them where they can have opportunity for real achievement. If they make good, they can prove valuable to the group.

The Dead-Ender

Usually this is an above-average member. They have reached the top of their ability range.

The dead-ender can be a most difficult problem. Unless they are properly handled and motivated, they must easily become an inferior member, or a disrupting influence, it not a troublemaker. The problem is easy to define. How can officers and group workers make the best of their superior abilities? What's the best way to motivate them?

What to do.

● Give them recognition. That's the key word in motivating the dead-ender. Note: This means more than the traditional pat on the back for a job well done.

● Let them know they're making a valuable contribution to the project, the group and the agency.

● Ask for their advice. Treat them as experts on the job, which they sometimes really are. Let them know their opinions are highly valued.

● Give them recognition in forms other than usual. Here are some ways: 1) Show confidence in them by putting them on their own. 2) Let them know they do not need such close supervsion as might be required for others in that particular project. 3) Encourage them to make suggestions and improve the work to which they're assigned. Get them started with a list of things that need improving. When they do come up with a good idea, give them full credit for it.

The Compulsive Talker

They can out-talk anyone in the organization. They can keep even the most inconsequential conversation going for hours. One may not realize his incessant chitchat annoys people. Perhaps he gives long and not-to-the-point answers to short questions just to postpone his getting to his group assignment.

What to do.

● Give the compulsive talker so much work waiting to be done, they will have no time for idle chatter.

● Whenever one rambles and rambles, ask them how far along they are on a specific assignment or project.

● Put them in a situation where other people depend on their efforts.

● Count on their co-members to keep their mouth shut and nose to the grindstone.

The Busybody

They are the professional meddlers. They think they know everything. Almost always they are wrong. (Often they accuse other members of slowing up group progress.)

What to do.

● First, get the meddler alone in a corner. Then get them to be more specific about their accusations.

● But be sure not to act like a prosecutor dealing with a hostile witness.

● Instead or proving the meddler wrong, try to help them understand why they are wrong. Get them to see how whispered charges can hurt the whole organization–the accuser as well as the accused.

The Taciturn Member

This is the indifferent type, the lounger. But at the same time, they irritate people around them. Though they neither break rules nor cause observable trouble, they make it clear they are completely indifferent to others. They do only what is required, passively resist change, and reject all efforts to arouse their enthusiasm.

What to do.

● There must be something they like. Seek it out. Keep probing until you find their particular interest.

● Once you discover what they like, show your own interest in it. Ask them questions, get their comments. Make them feel important.

● This procedure not only enables you to get your hand on the first thread of a working relationship. You also give the member recognition–something they might feel they are not getting elsewhere.

● As you get closer to them, try to make them see your point of view about your objectives. Explain to them why other members show interest in their assignments. In time, they will begin to understand why they're enthusiastic and willing. Their interest will prove contagious.

Summary

In wrapping this up, I want to point out to group workers and leaders that motivation is possible . . . only when the member you are trying to motivate is satisfied.

The major point to remember is that you can't get dissatisfied members to motivate themselves. Before you can start any program aimed at motivating your group members, you must first make sure that you are aware of any areas of dissatisfaction and work from there.

Human motivation being such a complex subject, it's impossible to come up with a pat formula with which everyone agrees. Even if you asked your people what factors motivated them, each person would probably give you a different list.

But few would neglect mentioning how their abilities are being used. Few people, aside from out-and-out "goldbrickers" enjoy being underused, or like to see their talents wasted. With rare exception, people are more satisfied when they are given more responsibility, more challenge, and when they get more sense of achievement from a day's activity.

Individuals with little responsibility, challenge, or feeling of accomplishment are hard to motivate, perhaps impossible. When the assignment is sick, so is the member.

Who is capable of broader responsibility and how can they be given it?

How can repetitive chores be broken up to give people a more satisfying variety of tasks?

Quite often a lot can be done in this area if we give some time and thought. And where it can be done, it pays to do it.

There is something that is much scarcer, something finer by far, something rarer than ability. It is the ability to recognize ability.

Motivational Self-Check List for Group Workers:

Answer each question by putting circle around "yes" or "no."

1. Do you manage to keep calm and even-tempered under the inevitable pressures and strains of the job? YES NO
2. Do you make promises to group members when you know you can't keep them? YES NO
3. Do you ignore complaints, which appear insignificant to you? YES NO
4. Are you strict with some members and lenient with others? YES NO
5. Do you cooperate and get along well with other group workers? YES NO
6. Can you refuse a member's request without making him feel antagonistic toward you? YES NO

7. Do you think that when a worker gets too friendly with the group members they begin to lose respect for him? YES NO
8. Do you ever ask for members' opinions about group improvements? YES NO
9. Do you explain reasons for changes in policies and procedures? YES NO
10. Do you usually tell the members the reason behind a highly directive order? YES NO
11. Do you tend to be impatient? YES NO
12. Do you give credit where credit is due? YES NO
13. Do you praise good work as well as criticize poor work? YES NO
14. Do you tend to see the other fellow's point of view? YES NO
15. Do you refrain from making sarcastic remarks; from speaking in a loud and commanding voice? YES NO

Answers to Self-Check List:

When you have finished through these answers, you will have a better awareness of your ability to handle others, and can determine just where you need improvement. You will probably find that you are stronger in some habits and attitudes; weaker in others. Keep building upon your strong points. Launch a program for the development of those weak points which might be standing in your way.

1. YES. A group worker who cannot control himself can hardly hope to influence others. Self-control under all circumstances give you that poise and sureness which commands respect and loyalty.

2. NO. Promises should not be made lightly. They should always be made with a full grasp of whatever circumstances might arise that would make it impossible to keep them. Make those circumstances very clear to the group member at the time promises are made. A worker who feels that he can make promises and not keep them is making a bad mistake. He cannot be a good leader unless he shows integrity of thought and action, and earns the confidence of the group members and their belief in his word. When you promise anything, do everything you can to deliver.

3. NO. No complaint is insignificant to the person who is making it. Even if the gripe is unjustified, there's no denying the fact the member does not think so. What you might consider unimportant looms very large in his eyes. He remains a problem if his complaint is taken lightly. It is the worker's job to ease ill tempers, not to aggravate them by inattention.

4. NO. If you are, teamwork goes out the window. Avoid any possible criticism that you are playing favorites. When one member is allowed to get away with something and another is not, discipline suffers. Don't give special privileges unless a special situation warrants it and everyone understands it.

5. YES. Share your thoughts and experiences with other group workers. Talk to them about your problems as well as your successful methods and ideas. Keep them informed whenever trouble in your group will affect operations in theirs. Contact their members only through them.

6. YES. An abrupt "No" to a request is sure to arouse hostility. When a member is told why his request cannot be granted, he will accept that refusal without showing ill will. Refusing tactfully requires that you make the member feel your personal regret.

7. NO. A cold or indifferent attitude doesn't add to your stature. It is much more important to be firm and decisive at the right moment than to be aloof all the time. You can be friendly without losing authority. The worker who gets "real respect" is the one who is technically competent and has a sincere interest in the members. The seclusive worker, whether technically competent or not, is handicapped by his lack of social contact. And that attitude is fatal in anyone whose job is to influence people.

8. YES. Soliciting a members' suggestions has a two-fold objective. First, the members might be more familiar with his particular project than anybody else. He is often in the best position to give you ideas for improvements. Second, it gives you a chance to satisfy the member's desire for recognition. When you ask a person what he thinks, you plant in him the seeds of self-assurance and self-satisfaction.

9. YES. The "why" of certain policies may not be as obvious to members as it is to you. Talking about a change of policy does much to overcome resistance; it gains cooperation.

10. YES. When a group member knows the reason for doing a project a certain way, they feel that they have your confidence. That feeling is essential to good human relations.

11. NO. Patience is an essential quality in the handling of group members. Many people do not possess an alert and quick-grasping mind. Being impatient with them doesn't serve to speed things; crowds them so that they become less capable of completing the project; and often plants the seeds of resentment and a feeling of being unjustly rushed. Be patient in giving them instructions, in training them, in setting limits for work, in cultivating better work habits. The slower way around will often lead to your goal more quickly.

12. YES. Don't hog all the credit. If you do, you will be resented by the members. They will hold back on the initiative and cooperation. Give them the recognition they want, need, and deserve.

13. YES. It is somewhat natural for a group worker to think that there is no special need for praise. But every human craves credit and praise. A practice which is very aggravating to a member is always to be blamed for making a mistake, but not to be praised when a good job is done. Priase is an important psychological incentive to better work, and adds much to a person's satisfaction.

14. YES. It takes more than goodwill to see someone else's point of view. Involvement is not only a willingness to listen. Equally important is the readiness to dismiss temporarily one's own biases and look at the issue with a new pair of eyes—the other fellow's. This isn't easy. It requires, primarily, an attitude of objectivity toward one's own notions and ideas.

15. YES. It is easy to commit one or both of these errors when the occasion calls for reprimands or corrections of mistakes. But it is difficult to deal with the varied emotional reactions which such comments generate in the member involved. Sarcasm makes members feel inferior, produces resentment and invites angry rebellion. The worker who uses sarcasm as a way to influence the members is deficient in leadership ability.

REFERENCES

Action Guide to Motivating People. Bureau of Business Practice, 1968.

Lesser, B. *The Group Advisors Handbook.* Nealco Publishing Co., 1970.

Chapter 12

Dealing With Complaints

The group worker who does not encounter varying complaints from parents and the members during his tenure is indeed a rarity. The complaints are always a source of deep concern to the worker and to the sponsoring organization. Human nature being what it is, the worker should be armed with the objective realization that some parents are concerned first with personal familial benefit rather than the general viability of the group. Keeping this in mind, a vexatious and ambivalent attitude on the part of a portion of the adult community should be expected from time to time and dealt with as one of the necessary functions of the work.

It is normal to take offense at complaints, particularly when the worker and others have extended themselves to ensure a thriving group and have been diligently trying to see that no preventable cause for grievance is given. However, personal feelings in this regard must be set aside by the worker.

Whereas we must sometimes expect complaints as part of the cost of innovation and expansion, we dare not overlook them. The irrelevancy of a complaint, from the worker's point of view, should not be a license for treating such complaint in an offhand way. The grievance which often seems ridiculous to the worker, looms large in the eyes of the complaining parents. Rightly or wrongly, these parents are disturbed over something and must be taken seriously, even though in many cases, the injury or injustice is grossly exaggerated or imagined. Even if the grievance can be fully handled with a little verbal dexterity, it should never be made to appear petty.

On the other hand, though not apparent at the moment, a seemingly minor complaint may be an indiciator of potential trouble of a more serious nature. Therefore a reasonably thorough investigation and follow-through into the factors relating to the so-called minor complaint might serve to the advantage of the worker.

Before leaving the minor complaint, it is well to remember that careful handling of the small problem can often serve to help build future loyal parental support for the worker and the group.

The most effective way of handling complaint situations is by attempting to prevent, at the outset, as many as possible—set a climate wherein the parents have little grounds for justifiable cause of distress. The worker does this by communicating regularly with the parents. To the extent possible and within the framework of their work environment and program, they should generally find out what the parents' wants and expectations are vis a vis their children and the program itself. Subsequent dialogues in this area will often forestall grievances. In addition, by communication with parents, often via informal talks, the worker can sense parental dissatisfaction long before it reaches the complaint stage. Many industries and professions do this as a matter of course to ascertain changes in attitudes, habits, etc. – "keeping one's finger on the pulse of the community is an accepted and valuable technique for an entity dealing with "people."

What a parent notices most about a worker, is not their normal day to day efficiency, which is taken for granted. That "extra" touch which demonstrates the worker's understanding of the child, their genuine interest in the child's welfare and their willingness and ability to do what is best for the child goes a long way toward negating some forms of potential grievance.

The writer, here again, does not intend to regale the reader with an endless summary of rules in this area–however, the review of a few basic principles in the handling of complaints might have some worth.

● Be honest – If you have erred, calmly admit it. Be frank and discuss the facts openly, judiciously and without recourse to ambiguities and time worn cliches as protection. The parent does not care about obscurities; he wants to know what you are going to do about his complaint. A straightforward apology when justified is always in order–an expression of regret is not a sign of weakness. Above all, corrective action must be quickly and tactfully taken without grudging demeanor, for the key to the corrective action is to retain the parents' faith and support and to deepen it if at all possible.

● The worker should make it clear to the constituency; the parents, members and the community in general that complaints are generally welcomed and looked upon as a constructive service. In this regard:

- sympathy must be shown to person(s) making complaints.
- willingness to investigate and take corrective action immediately must be apparent.
- argument or hints that the complainant is fabricating his story is not tactful and serves no purpose.
- If the complaint is completely out of order, the situation must be explained in simple, forthright terms while attempting to enlist the parent(s) sense of justice.

Complaints must be analyzed. They must be broken down into particulars so that the worker can see things in their proper relationships and in perspective. Try to uncover any hidden content in the complaint, for it may well be a disguise for a more serious problem.

Next, the workers must take a hard look at themselves and the program. What contribution have they made toward the situation incubating the grievance? Has it grown in size and intensity because of unconcern, negligence or a laissez-faire attitude? Can the problem be corrected without additional irritation? Find a sound and equitable rememdy for all concerned.

During the interview it might be well to exhibit the following personal attributes:

- Be a good listener and reflect the complainant's point of view.
- Avoid, at all cost, being drawn into an argument for then the parent and worker become protagonists in an adversary type situation, where there generally has to be a winner and loser. Win, lose or draw the worker runs the risk of outrightly antagonizing the parent and forfeiting his future goodwill—too high for momentary self-satisfaction.

Look for avenues of possible reconciliation, conceding a point here and there, sacrificing details at times in order to keep the key matters always within the sphere of settlement to everybody's satisfaction. Alternative solutions, discussed in a fair and pleasant manner, should be brought into play when the discussion seems to reach an impasse.

Courtesy, tact and dignity tend to ease tensions in any complaint situation, notwithstanding occasional rudeness on the part of some parents. These attributes may not settle the complaint but will certainly help ease the path toward settlement.

The worker, in conclusion, must be "people" oriented and must extend their understanding and insight as to the personal motivations that spur people into making complaints. If they keep in mind that complaints in themselves, as well as the complaintants, can be utilized and converted into positive factors. The worker and the parents all can benefit and develop a healthy communal vitality.

No discourse on complaints can readily be considered complete unless we examine the type of complaints registered by the group members themselves. Such complaints may take on all manner, shape and hue of trivia. Then again, a specific complaint may have some import on group operations or on the personal life of the member involved. Here again, in order to discern the relative importance of the complaint, the worker must *again* call upon one of his most important assets—patient listening.

The very things that cause trepidation on the part of the parents, discussed above, may very well carry over or rub off on the child. In this way the youngster often acts as an extension of the parent in airing a grievance. If the worker can determine that this is so, they may have to counsel both the child and parents at different conferences.

The techniques used in parental complaint conferences, described earlier in this chapter can well be used with the teenager, particularly the admitting of error, should this be the case, in a forthright and honest manner.

What motivates a youngster into making a complaint deriding the group, when from outward appearance the group itself is functioning well with a high degree of participation, effective communication and meaningful and timely programming? The reasons are myriad, however, the worker might well look at the following areas and circumstances before attempting to counsel the aggrieved teenager:

- Breakdown in social interaction
- Behavior deviation
- Competition
- Effects of failure and frustration
- Suppression

The most important facet in social interaction, according to Francis E. Merrill in "Society and Culture," is its mutual or reciprocal character. The teenager, in our case, is intially made aware of not only his own expected behavior toward the group and individuals in the group, but is also clued to expected behavior of others toward him. His reaction then is oriented toward the expected behavior and action of the others. Suppose then that the behavior of the others doesn't quite conform with the image intially portrayed for him by the worker or group officers? Or perhaps his minds' eye envisioned a more specific type of rapport with the group than actually materialized. Whatever the collateral considerations, this youngster is unhappy. He has a choice of quitting, withdrawing into himself, pressing himself into the limelight or complaining (generally or specifically to the worker) that he had been misled. Merrill states that group expectations are not always uniform. In many forms of interactions, the expectations cover only the general form of reciprocal response and do not prescribe with exactitude what each teenager will do in a given situation. The worker's guidance will be tailored to this avenue of counseling if the problem is in point.

Past and current behavioral deviations may well be an indicator of the causal factor involving the chronic complainer. One of the factors noted in identifying behavioral change is the sudden emergency of a series of complaints, often unrelated, by one of the group members. Samuel A. Kirk in "Educating Exceptional Children," passes on the thought that although social maladjustment and emotional disturbance in children are not necessarily synonymous, there is considerable overlap between them. Social maladjustment refers to behavior which is not within the range of the culturally permissible. Teenagers falling into such category will generally also similarly react, and often cause difficulty, in other settings such as school, home, dances, etc. A wise worker will explore, if possible, the chronic complainer's behavioral pattern in these other settings in order to confirm his evaluation of the situation.

Inability of a youngster to compete successfuly with others in the group often brings out complaints of unfair tactics used by other members of the group. This can relate to almost any phase of group operation—typically inability to attain 'status' jobs such as chairmanships, prize parts in dramatic programs, selection to attend youth conclaves, etc. The youngster generally demands that the worker rectify this "inequitable" situation.

How should the worker view competition in general? He should have some definitive philosophy before he can counsel the less successful members or the less popular members. The average teenager is not unacquainted with the competitive drive. Comparisons with others in school, as in all walks of life, is inevitable. The teenager uses this in developing himself and gaining an insight as to what he is in comparison to others. All youngsters are thrown into healthy competition via street games, intramural and formalized athletics, attaining merit badges in the Scouts, etc.

Arthur T. Jersild in the *Psychology of Adolescence*[15] brings this problem into focus by pointing out that competition is not only a developmental phenomenon but also a pervasive cultural condition in the adolescent's world. The youngsters are surrounded by an adult society that is saturated with competition. People compete for attention, for possessions, for power, for prestige and also in the sphere of love and sex. Most teenagers tend to emulate the competitiveness that prevails in the adult world. Competition is most assuredly unhealthy, however, if it is used for ulterior purpose or is a symptom of an underlying hostility. The youngster who is forever trying to "prove" his worth by surpassing others is also an unhealthy competitor. The worker must ferret out the facts and the true set of circumstances. The teenager's complaint may not have validity regardless of whether or not healthy competition was involved. However, if the competition is such that unhealthy manifestations are definitely involved, the worker must take a hard look at the key people and determine how they attained their jobs and then reevaluate the group's elective and appointive modus operandi.

The worker must give more than passing thought to the possibility that failure and accompanying frustration might be the key factors underlying certain members' fault finding attitudes. Repeated failures in a youngster's personal life or in group activity may create an undesirable attitude on the part of the youngster in relation to himself, which manifests itself in a type of pseudo bravado wherein he becomes the torchbearer for the passive malcontents in the group. He thereby gains compensatory status and perhaps a feeling of attainment so sadly lacking in his other pursuits. Here again, a patient demeanor on the part of the worker, permitting the youngster to talk to his heart's content, will often provide the necessary footprints back to the underlying motivation for the latter's behavior. On occasion, after talking it out, the teenager may well recognize and/admit to the motivating causal factors in his own right. In a sense this evolves into an elementary cathartic exercise.

---

[15]THE PSYCHOLOGY OF ADOLESCENCE by Arthur J. Jersild (Copyright © 1963 by Macmillan Publishing Co., Inc.).

Teenagers, sensitive creatures that many of them are, are wont to conceal or disguise their true feelings. Again calling upon Jersild, we find that in order to understand we must not only observe the emotions he openly reveals but must also try to fathom emotions he has learned to conceal or to deny. When adolescents conceal their feelings, or falsify their expression of emotion, they may do so knowingly or unknowingly. The conscious suppression of an emotion, whether it be anger, disappointment, fear, concern—etc., could well erupt into a one-time safety-valve type of complaint, which will lessen in intensity and importance to the youngster with the passage of time and usually poses no lasting problem to the worker.

The neophyte group worker may well attempt to classify all teenage complaints to one or more of the categories described above. This of course should not be done, in that many complaints are superficial in nature, and can be handled adroitly and expeditiously with little or no probing. The author in citing the aforementioned categorical array of casual manifestations is concerned with the chronic complainer or with the complaint that has no discernible nor visible reason for being. These types of complaints could well highlight insecurities of teenagers vis a vis the group or themselves. The worker must be aware of such situations, but should take care not to overreact to each and every complaint nor go beyond what is prudent or essential on run-of-mill complaints.

One of the greatest challenges to the worker is the identification of the emotionally troubled teenager. The worker who dares not play the role of amateur psychiatrist or therapist, however, can spot indicators that point toward trouble, often emanating from a chronic complaint situation. How does the worker recognize the warning signs of emotional disturbance? As in many other facets of youth work there is no predetermined formula. In industry and government supervisory and management personnel look upon a change in a person's behavior—a personality change—as a sign most easily noticed as an indicator of possible emotional trouble.

This marked change in behavior may show up in many ways such as emotional outbursts, chronic irritability, phlegmatic and apethetic demeanor, excessive fatigue, continued violation of rules, atypical boasts of engaging in alcoholic excesses, repeated accidents, chronic inability to get along with others and myriads of other signs reflecting deviation from what had been considered a normal behavioral pattern. The teenager who suddenly evolves into a chronic complainer at group activities or at home may be in the throes of a personal problem with which they are having difficulty.

A teenager reflecting one or more of the above symptoms doesn't necessarily and immediately fall into an emotionally disturbed category. These are merely a sampling of symptoms which have been found to exist in known cases of disturbance.

If a group member specifically seeks the advice of the worker about a personal problem–the latter should be a good listener and try to isolate or clarify the problem. A group worker should never attempt a diagnosis but should limit his function, as indicated, to listening when the troubled youngster wants to talk about his problems. If professional or other assistance seems necessary, the parents must be contacted and all pertinent information passed on to them.

However, the worker, if he is to recognize both the obvious behavioral deviations mentioned above as well as the more subtle signs manifested by the troubled teenager, must understand the concept of anxiety. This concept often provides the necessary key to an understanding of the sometimes unusual and baffling conduct of the teenager.

Jersild covers this condition in his *The Psychology of Adolescence*. He points out that anxiety has many facets which cannot be encompassed in a single definition. However, anxiety prevails when a person is at odds with himself. It is a persisting, distressful psychological state arising from an inner conflict. The distress may be experienced as a feeling of vague uneasieness or foreboding, a feeling of being on edge, or as any of a variety of other feelings, such as fear, anger, restlessness, irritability, depression, etc.

The underlying conflict springs from a clash between incompatible impulses, desires or values. Jersild explains that such a conflict prevails when a person (in our case the teenager) for instance is angry but is afraid of giving offense. Likewise it exists when our teenager is eager to be popular but has strong scruples against doing what is necessary, in some quarters, to become popular.

Anxieties can exist in both conscious and subconscious states. The latter manifests itself when the anxious teenager does not recognize what is troubling him or realize why he feels as he does. The worker, by being an adroit listener, can from time to time identify the source of the anxiety or determine what is troubling the youngster. However, the writer, redundantly, again cautions the worker not to assume the role of therapist–contact the parents and pass along any observations that are of importance.

In the worker's search for better ways to communicate with complaining parents and group members, you can learn constructive techniques from Carl Rogers, the author of *Nondirective Counseling* and other works.

It is easier to communicate when things are running smoothly and people are objective, than when things go wrong and people become emotional. When you have to answer objections to a proposal or suggestion you have made, or when you find yourself "in the middle" of an argument, you can use nondirective techniques to reduce differences and reach an understanding.

No one "wins" an argument. In fact, the "winner" may lose the respect or friendship of the "loser." Yet group workers should defend their ideas. Here is an expansion of some ways to arbitrate or negotiate amicably:

- LISTEN first, so that you fully understand what the other person *means*, not just what he *says*. Do not interrupt, argue, or contradict the speaker. Do *not inject your own ideas into their statements. You have to train yourself* to learn the other person's thoughts and feelings. You want to encourage the speaker to talk freely and say what is on their mind. Probably you have already used this technique with an angry telephone caller.

- KEEP CALM. Show by your body and facial expression that you are interested. Maintain eye contact, look pleasant, and don't wrinkle your brow or purse your lips. When you speak, don't raise your voice. Modulate your tone.
- USE THE PAUSE INTELLIGENTLY by saying, "I see," or "So that's what happened," or even, "Uh-huh."
- REPEAT A KEY STATEMENT on which the speaker has stopped in order to get him to go on. Say, for example "You think the instructions are confusing." Or, "He didn't tell you in advance."
- ASK QUESTIONS to bring out the other person's feelings and thoughts on the matter, rather than make dogmatic statements yourself. For example, "Did you feel that the decision was unfair?" Or, "Were you hurt or just disappointed, Helen?" Or, "You seem to have pretty strong feelings on the issue, Bob." Remember that the speaker's ideas and feelings are from their own point of view, and you can best understand them if you interpret them in that light.
- ANALYZE THE BARRIERS that are causing differences – "Let's see, is the basic difference . . .?" Or, "Is something else causing your objection to this . . .?" Then try to resolve the differences.
- LOOK FOR AREAS OF AGREEMENT which can minimize controversial points. You may say, "Then we are agreed that . . .," or, "We agree, here, but you feel that this point should be changed . . .?"
- COOL IT for a while if necessary. After you have reached some points of agreement, it may be wise to say, "Let's think more about this and discuss it tomorrow morning." Set a specific time to follow up. If a cool-it period is not required, review the discussion as described in the point below.
- FOLLOW UP on your discussion. Review any barriers that remain and, more important, discuss the areas of agreement. State your position clearly but in an understanding manner. Support your points with reasoning, facts, and explanation.

The way you respond to a controversial point, objection, or difference can make the difference between mutual understanding and misunderstanding.

As you practice using the basic nondirective techniques, you will find that you will communicate better, you will understand others complaints, and that they will be more likely to relate to you as the group worker in a more intelligent and understanding manner.

REFERENCES

Jersild, A. T. *The Psychology of Adolescence*. The MacMillan Co., 1963.

Kirk, S. A. *Educating Exceptional Children*. Houghton Mifflin Co., 1962.

Lesser, B. *The Youth Advisor's Handbook*. Nealco Publishing Co., 1970.

Merrill, F. E. *Society and Culture: An Introduction to Sociology*. Prentice-Hall, Inc., 1969.

Chapter 13

How To Utilize Volunteers

Most youth groups, particularly those of substantial size, will have some difficulty in achieving its goals, unless the group worker is able to obtain volunteer help from other sources. In the past, the chief other sources were often the parents of the youth group members (some were effective and reliable, others were not). One prime factor, that sometimes mitigates against the use of parent volunteers, is the resentment and/or apathy reflected by the parents' own offspring. The teenagers frequently object to having their parents serve in an adjunctive role for the benefit of the group. For many varied and imagined reasons the teenagers feel that the presence of mom or dad will in some way inhibit their own actions.

A new and important source of aid is the student volunteer. The federal government, through ACTION's National Student Volunteer Program, has been a leader in offering resource data for the recruiting, training and utilizing student volunteers for community projects. Much of such information is contained in this chapter.

Every year thousands of high school, college and graduate students search for ways to be of service to the communities surrounding their campuses. Recently, educational institutions themselves have begun to recognize that work in the community could benefit the student's overall education and could help make the institution more responsive and relevant to student needs. (The group worker should be able to make use of these student resources as aides and/or special project managers.)

The result has been increased school support for student volunteers, the establishment of comprehensive school-based student volunteer programs and in some cases, the granting of academic credit to students for volunteer work done in the community. The student volunteer movement has made its mark. It is growing in numbers, sophistication, skills, and expectations.

This presents tremendous challenges to those in the community who are using or seeking to use student volunteers in their programs. They must find ways to use students effectively, to meet their personal and professional development needs, and to insure that the resulting projects and activities meet the needs of the organization, individual and community being served.

As can be seen, the student volunteer movement has come a long way in the last decade (the authors' last training manual for group workers was published in 1970–a time when there was an apparent marked shortage of properly trained volunteer workers).

The questions community leaders must ask themselves are – How can we find ways to use these student volunteers most effectively? How can we meet the student volunteers' personal and professional development needs, and to ensure that the organization's needs are constantly being met?

The ACTION manual for student volunteers supports the contention that the student volunteer is not a new phenomenon. Students of all ages have been involved in helping to meet community needs for generations. We know from experience and personal involvement that student volunteers have served in tutorial programs, as recreation aides and as companions to the sick, the young and the aged. What is new is their joining together in their schools to form volunteer councils and committees to coordinate their efforts in the community. The support that educational institutions are providing, the integration of the concept of learning through service into academic curricula, and the range of services being provided by students are also recent innovations.

This institutionalization of the student volunteer concept and the development of a full-fledged volunteer movement can provide a continuous source of staffing to communities and organizations.

The ACTION experience points out that with the growth of the volunteer movement, there has been a shift in student attitudes and expectations concerning such volunteer work. Tutoring programs have been supplemented by work with community groups in churches, synagogues, neighborhood centers, schools and housing projects. Students are and want to be directly involved in group work, social work, education, legal services, tax help, health clinics and correctional institutions. They can, according to the ACTION survey, provide direct service to individuals, among other things (e.g. counseling, tutoring, transportation, companionship) research and write publications, provide training and technical assistance, analyze legislation, help fulfill administrative or fund-raising functions and give guidance and direction to the myriad of youth groups sponsored by the many community and religious organizations.

Why Use Student Volunteers?

Whether you, the group worker, are considering using student volunteers for the first time or have been using them for years, you should articulate for yourself the advantages of student volunteer services.

Ask yourself why students volunteer. Why would anyone want to use them? What particular talents and interests could they bring to your organization? Are they a special kind of resource? What are the benefits to your organization? The answers to these questions not only provide a rationale for involving students, but also provide criteria against which you can measure the suitability of your volunteer roles for students.

The student volunteer, whether involved because of enrollment in an accredited college course or a high school service-learning project, or simply because of a desire to help or test out a profession, also provides community groups with a real role in the educational process. Staff members serve as teachers, helping to influence the development of the volunteer.

In addition, many people who have begun to work with student volunteers have found that the involvement has led to effective and enriching relationships with the high school or college faculty. These educators can bring still more resources and technical expertise to bear on community problems, and may be influenced by what they see, offering the community-based professional an additional chance to provide input into the educational process.

What Student Volunteers Bring

- Flexibility

People who have long worked with student volunteers—both high school and college—know that flexibility is one of their greatest assets. The student is likely to be willing to learn, to swap service for experience and learning and to be open to new approaches and feedback on his or her effectiveness. Student volunteers are generally willing to learn the ways of the organization, learn new skills, and adjust to new experiences.

Student volunteers have also shown particular skill in dealing with difficult clients. Each of us knows stories of the uncommunicative institutionalized person or the difficult delinquent, neither of whom made any progress until assigned a youthful volunteer. Students are willing to work with more demanding challenging clients. They can provide intensive, compassionate attention and help.

- Career Orientation

Many of these volunteers have a career-orientation, meaning they see their volunteer experience not as a hobby, but as a first work experience, the beginning of a profession. Their performance and behavior are appropriately serious. They are seeking serious involvement with your organization in ways that will effectively apply their talents in pre-professional roles.

- Resources

Students can also provide access to valuable resources. Not only can they tap large manpower pools for the special needs of your organization, but they can often bring the materials, equipment, and expertise available in their schools, to the work of your organization. They often can be effective in the community as well, securing resources that the organization members themselves were unable to locate.

Students can provide a rich pool for future hiring. Just as the student volunteer can test a career, so the sponsoring organization can test future staff members. The history of volunteer programs is rich with examples of student volunteers whose performance was so outstanding that they were hired as permanent staff members upon their graduation. What more could an organization wish than to have at its disposal a group of people who are willing to try a work role in the organization?

- Support

In addition, students represent a pool of citizen support for your organization's work. A volunteer of any age who has had a good experience with your organization is your greatest booster. Students are often forgotten in this regard. Organizations know that if they involve adult community leaders in their programs these leaders will be a valuable source of support in the future. Too often they forget that the student of today is the community leader of tomorrow.

In summary, students can provide a valuable resource for your organization because they are:

- Flexible
- Willing to work with difficult clients.
- Serious and interested in professional growth.
- A source of the extra manpower your organization may need at certain times.
- Able to draw upon the expertise, interest and resources of a faculty member, department, or educational institution.
- Often eventually available as a pool of trained professional personnel.
- A base of future citizen support
- Relatively easy to find and recruit.

In addition, student volunteers can bring to you personally the rewards of working with youth. You can share their successes, enthusiasm, willingness to try, and excitement about learning.

The impact of a student volunteer and of student volunteers on the community can be tremendous, but the effectiveness with which this potential is tapped depends on the ability and willingness of community organizations to use this talent.

The following is designed to provide you with many of the tools needed to develop and carry out student volunteer projects which can tap this potential.

Selecting Your Volunteer

The details of the process used to select volunteers are related to the types of jobs for which you are recruiting, the numbers of volunteers you need, the recruiting techniques you utilize, and the resources at your disposal.

Elements of a selection process may include:

- Application–identifying skills, interest and availability through some kind of written form or resume.
- Interview–a verbal exploration between applicant and organization.
- Screening–a review of volunteer's background for work experience, psychological stability, reliability, criminal record.
- Selecting–picking from among many applicants; or if there is only one candidate, deciding whether or not the individual is acceptable.
- Matching–placing the selected volunteer in the appropriate job and with an appropriate client.
- Notifying the volunteer–letting the volunteer know whether or not she or he was selected and why. Trying to provide alternatives if he or she was not chosen. If he or she was chosen, letting him or her know what happens next and what responsibilities are involved.

Make sure each step of the selection process has a rationale and make sure that rationale is made clear to the volunteers and to the staff. Keep in mind the importance of making the procedures as simple and efficient as possible. The following sections describe each of the elements in more detail.

Application

The application form should contain space for vital information such as phone number, address, schedule, past experience and current interest. These forms help the coordinator sort out prospective volunteers in planning a program and provide a working index on the volunteer force. Be explicit in titling this form. Is it an "Interest Form" a "Volunteer Application," a "Volunteer Record Card?" If all volunteers will be accepted and there is no real application process, don't call it an application form. Decide exactly what you need to know about a prospective volunteer. Try not to make the volunteer fill out several copies of the same form. Let the volunteer know how long it takes to process the form.

Interviewing

Interview methods vary. They can be one-to-one between volunteer coordinator and applicant, or between group worker and applicant; or they can be in groups involving several staff members or a few applicants and one or more staff members. They can be exploratory, where each decides whether or not there is interest in going further; or selective where the staff person will determine the merits of a prospective volunteer.

The interview as a selection method is often overused. Before you arrange for one, know why you are having it. Be sure to tell the volunteer what to expect and what, if any, special preparation is needed. Indicate what will happen as a result. Be ready to answer questions on how decisions are reached.

During the interview, make the volunteer as comfortable as possible. Provide ample opportunity for questions about your organization and his or her potential role. Before the interview begins, read the volunteer's application carefully so that you don't ask him to repeat information already furnished. Make yourself a check-list to use during the interview.

- Attitude and relevant experience.
- Reasons for volunteering.
- Expectations—are they realistic.
- Prior opportunities for exhibiting independent judgment.
- Willingness to seek advice.

Screening

Screening is a process used to eliminate certain applicants. Sometimes it is as simple as seeing if certain objective requirements are met—age, availability of car, ability to work three afternoons. Other times more complex factors are involved. Does the volunteer have any kind of court record? Has the volunteer been on drugs? Can the volunteer exercise appropriate independent judgment? What is the volunteer's record for living up to commitments? These are not questions that will be important in every situation, but if you are placing applicants in situations which demand certain skills, attitudes and experiences, you need to be able to find out about their background. Schools which once maintained detailed records on their students and shared them with people seeking information are today much more concerned about privacy. If you must have this data, collect it yourself through references or other contacts. But make sure you are asking only for information you really need and make sure the applicant knows what information you are seeking.

Selecting

If you are choosing among several applicants for the same job, you need to establish a process and set of criteria for making the final decisions. Once the applications are in, the interviews are over and the screening is done, who makes the decisions and how? Do you make the decisions yourself? Do supervising staff members select their own volunteers? Or, is there a selection committee? Either way, make sure you and your staff members know what the process is, understand your roles, and know the selection critera. Set a deadline so that the volunteers are not left waiting indefinitely.

Notifying the Volunteer

As long as the news is good, this is an easy step. You contact the volunteer, either by mail or phone, and say, "Congratulations, you have been selected . . ." Be sure and indicate what will happen next. Tell him what to do, or to wait until he hears from you on or before a specified date.

If the news is not good, notification will be more difficult. How do you turn down a volunteer? It is not easy. Keep in mind that this person has offered to give away a valuable commodity–time–and you are going to reject the offer. Keep in mind the potential damage a rejection could do to a volunteer, particularly one who is young and immature.

Tell the volunteer the decision immediately; do it in person, or by phone. Do not write him a letter.

Indicate to the volunteer why the decision went against him. Be truthful and fair. "We really felt that you haven't had enough experience working with the mentally retarded in an unsupervised situation." "We really wanted someone who could be with us at least one year, and you indicated you must leave after the semester." The truth is certainly not as scary as what is going through the volunteer's mind–things like "They don't like me. I'm such a loser that I can't even get a job that doesn't pay."

Indicate alternatives. Is there a specific skill or experience that the volunteer could gain that would qualify him for the position? Be truthful. Don't suggest this just to get the volunteer off your back. He'll be back in a year and this time with the skill. Is there another role in your organization more suited to the volunteer's skill level? Is the volunteer interested in that role? Do you know of another organization that might be able to use the volunteer effectively? Would the volunteer be interested in that organization? Is there a central clearinghouse to which you can refer the volunteer to a more appropriate placement?

Make sure that you handle rejections in a manner that affirms the volunteer's value. Indicate your appreciation of his willingness to give his time, and your own disappointment in not being able to use him effectively.

Supervision of Volunteers

Supervision is a process of defining and maintaining effective work relationships, and its effectiveness or ineffectiveness impacts upon the extent to which a program meets its objectives. Students do not necessarily need more or less supervision than any other kind of volunteer. The kind required depends on the individual's skills and the nature of the work. For example, each of the situations listed below contribute to the need for more consistent, skilled supervision.

- Volunteer needs to gain many skills on the job.
- Volunteer is individually placed and doesn't have others to work with or to question about rules, expectations and procedures.
- Volunteer is receiving academic credit, and the teacher expects detailed information on the student's progress; or the volunteer experience relates

to course-related skills requiring special supervision.

- Placement is important to the volunteer's professional future; a professional internship, part of a career planning program; or there is the expectation that you will have to evaluate the volunteer's performance when the volunteer applies for a future job.
- Job the volunteer is performing is highly unstructured, calling for much personal judgment and involving almost no regularized routine.
- Volunteer, for personal reasons or because of the nature of the job, needs consistent feedback on how he is doing.
- Volunteer is working in close contact with difficult client—one with physical or emotional problems—or in a particularly delicate setting.

Remember, supervision is not a one-way process. It must also provide feedback to the volunteer, indicating how he or she is progressing and is contributing to the work of the organization. Even if supervision is not particularly important from the view of the organization, it may be of paramount importance to the volunteer.

Contracts with Student Volunteer

This non-legal document articulates the expectations of both volunteer and supervisor. It is completed by the volunteer and the supervisor once the volunteer is selected, but prior to the volunteer's actual involvement on the job. It is often part of the orientation process. In many ways it reiterates the job description and might be seen as a final negotiation for that job.

The exact document format depends on your needs. It should, however, contain at a minimum the following items:

- Volunteer's name, phone number and address.
- Group worker's name, title, phone number and address.
- Schedule agreed upon by volunteer and supervisor (group worker).
- Duties to be performed by volunteer and the objectives to be met in the performance of those duties.
- Nature of supervision—weekly meetings, daily de-briefings, on-site.
- Nature and schedule of evaluations.
- Instructions regarding missed assignments on given days and general reasons for justified absence.
- An indication of the volunteer's commitment—how long he is expected to stay.

If the volunteer is receiving credit for volunteer work, the expectations of the appropriate faculty member need to be included in the contract. The faculty member should also get a copy of the contract.

Questions relating to the learning of the student might include:

- Learning Objectives—What will the student learn as a result of the experience?

- Academic Products–Will the student be expected to complete a paper, keep a journal, complete a reading list, etc.?
- Evaluation of the Student–Will the teacher expect a report from the supervisor on the volunteer's effectiveness? What form will that report take–verbal or written? When will it be needed? Will the faculty member plan to visit the volunteer at work as part of the academic evaluation?

The contract is an important step in the articulation of expectations on the part of the organization and the volunteer helping the student and worker formulate individual and realistic expectations. It also makes clear to the student the nature of the evaluation and the schedule of events leading to it. By giving the student, faculty, and worker a copy of this contract, there is little chance the parties involved will have grounds to disagree.

Supervisory Formats

Group Meetings. These are best started within the first week or two and then repeated at regular intervals through the time the volunteer is serving. Not all volunteers will take advantage of this opportunity to get together with the worker. They may be too busy. They may feel comfortable with the way things are progressing. Volunteers having difficulties however, will appreciate and take advantage of this chance to talk with the worker and other volunteers. For many, this kind of group supervision may be the single most important experience enabling them to make the most of their situation and stay involved. These meetings can also be used as regular training sessions, introducing new materials, techniques, and skills. This form of supervision works particularly well if the worker is not on-site, or if the volunteers are working on a one-to-one basis at a wide variety of sites and seldom see each other or their supervisory worker.

On-the-Spot Supervision. The staff worker is physically present as the volunteer works and provides feedback, instructions, and direction. This is the most time-consuming type of supervision and shouldn't be necessary in any but the most delicate and demanding placements.

Pre-work Meetings. The supervisory worker and the volunteer get together each day the volunteer is on-site, prior to the beginning of the volunteer's work, to compare notes on what is to be accomplished, to discuss obstacles, and to answer questions. This kind of supervision can be used effectively with individuals and groups. It can be combined effectively with post-work de-briefing.

Post-work De-briefing. The supervisory worker meets with the volunteer after the day's work is finished to provide feedback, answer questions, and help the volunteer appraise what has occurred. This is a particularly effective way to handle supervision, and it is equally effective with individuals or groups.

Daily Reports. This kind of supervision is effective with a phone call or regular meetings. The volunteer completes a written daily evaluation of experiences including his uncertainties, need for clarification or problems he foresees. The worker checks over this report and uses it as a basis for future discussions with the volunteer. It enables the volunteer to record his reactions while they are still fresh. Daily reports are often a valuable resource as the volunteer looks back over the experience and tries to see how far he has come.

Written Log. The volunteer keeps a log of experiences, feelings, and uncertainties, which the worker can review periodically with the volunteer. It can be a basis for sharing ideas, for more effective ways of handling difficult situations and letting the volunteer know when something was done particularly well.

Phone Calls. A supervisory worker not able to give personal supervision can call the volunteer the day after the assignment to give encouragement, and to find out how things went. The phone call, though not enough by itself, allows the worker to contact the volunteer immediately after the experience. It can be combined effectively with bi-weekly or monthly get-togethers with the volunteers.

Supervision by Student Requestion. This is where the volunteer operates independently and is provided direct supervision only on request. A volunteer teaching in a multi-service agency might ask the worker to come in and observe a class and help improve his approach. This, too, can be combined with other forms of supervision.

Crisis Intervention. This is not the most effective form of supervision but it is widely used. The worker shows up when there is a problem. Sometimes he comes at the volunteer's request, sometimes at his or her own initiative. The worker operates as a kind of counselor and trouble shooter when the volunteer gets into a situation that is too much for him to handle. In many organizations, because of lack of staff this form of supervision is a necessity. The dangers are that the volunteers may find themselves in difficult situations too often and drop out; or that the difficult situations have a damaging effect on the organization itself or the clients it serves.

Orienting and Training the Volunteers

Providing student volunteers with the orientation, training, and leadership development which will enable them to make a maximum contribution and at the same time gain the most from their experience is of paramount importance.

Although the nature of your program and level of your resoures may not require or enable you to deal with all three components, the program that includes them all is usually the more effective and the one more likely to keep its volunteers involved and excited. Orientation, training and leadership development all take some time but the investment is generally worth it.

The amount of time and your actual role in these three areas will depend upon the program. You may be in a situation in which you are solely responsible for everything, or you may be working with a group of student volunteers who wish to be fully involved in the development and execution of the orientation, training and leadership programs. The way you, the worker, handle this partnership depends on your situation; however, it will be up to you to help the students plan the events and to insure that the activities meet their needs and those of your organization.

The following sections describe the basic purpose of each component and suggest techniques you might want to use.

Orientation

Orientation is the preparation of the volunteers for their first day on the job or their first experience as a member of your staff. It is a means to insure that the volunteer has some idea of what to expect and how to function, and to avoid any major mistakes during the first few hours. It is the initial process or preparing students to make the most of their roles as volunteers. Orientations could provide:

- A clear idea of the purpose, goals and structure of the organization.
- A profile of the client(s) served.
- An outline of the general role of the volunteer within the institution.
- An idea of how some particular roles might operate.
- An idea of what will happen to the volunteer on the first day.
- A chance to answer some questions.
- A chance for volunteers to get to meet each other and the staff.

The orientation might take place individually or in a group. It might be part of a lengthy interview, or it might be a walk-through of the role. It might be the traditional meeting of new volunteers with their supervisory worker volunteer coordinator.

While the group meeting is well suited to students because they may feel comfortable with their friends for their orientation, some of the students may not be able to fit themselves into your schedule. Thus, you might want to have a back-up system—interview, hand-outs, a movie or slides—to provide those students with individual orientation and introductions.

Whether you are working with a group or with individuals, the steps below should lead to an effective orientation:

Assess the students' orientation needs. Find out what your prospective volunteers alredy know about your organization and what they think is important for them to know. If it is not possible to personally question the new volunteers, you might be able to study reports of past orientation sessions to get ideas.

It may also be useful to ask the students to list everything that they want to know before they start on their jobs. The answers will give you items for your orientation agenda. You might ask the same question of staff who will be supervising volunteers. The combined answers produce the priority items for your orientation. Sometimes this needs assessment can be included as part of the orientation itself. Having the group articulate their needs can insure that your orientation is on target.

Translate the information accumulated from the needs assessment into goals for the orientation. These goals might look something like this:

- "At the end of the orientation, all of the volunteers will have a clear idea of what might happen to them the first day on the job."
- "All the volunteers will know where and to whom they are to report."
- "All volunteers will be able to act in accordance with the published rules for volunteers."

These goals should then be rewritten as precise objectives which indicate the exact ends to be met. For example, a precise objective for the first goal might be that

- "The volunteers will have talked with an experienced volunteer to learn about their first day on the job, and will have voiced their expectations of their first day."

Making the goal into a precise objective enables you to see more clearly exactly what you wish the volunteer to be able to do as a result or orientation.

Determine methods for reaching the goals and objectives. Often we get locked into certain ways of orienting people. Generally we talk at them. A careful look at the objectives may suggest some new approaches. For instance, the goal of "knowing what to expect the first day" might be reached by presenting the volunteers with an essay on a volunteer's first day; by having the volunteers role-play their first day; by listing and discussing the five most likely and five least likely occurrences. You might physically walk the volunteers through the events of the first day. You may be able to come up with many creative and effective activities. Be sure to use varying techniques. A role play, for example, might be followed by a discussion and question and answer session. Variety assures interest.

Determine the schedule for orientation events. If the schedule of events is too long, consider using the different formats—written materials or self-examinations to be completed later.

Complete all the details for orientation. Select staff. Arrange for physical facilities, equipment and refreshments. Duplicate handouts. Make sure that all the people involved in the presentation of the orientation are aware of their roles and the objectives to be accomplished.

Invite the volunteers. Clearly indicate the purpose of the orientation and state what it will enable them to do. Tell them when and where it will be, as well as approximately how long it will last. Indicate any preparation needed.

Conduct the Orientation

Evaluate the orientation. An orientation, like all aspects of your student volunteer program, can be made more effective in the future if you have some idea of how effective it has been in the past. You might have the participants fill out a simple evaluation at the end of the session. Six months later, when they have had a chance to reflect on its real usefulness to them, you might have them complete a second evaluation.

Be sure that you involve as many of the pertinent people as possible in the planning and execution of the orientation. These should include student leaders in your project, experienced volunteers, staff, and clients. There should be as many people present as possible to meet the new volunteers and to share with them their perspective. Each should have something to contribute to the goals of the orientation.

Training

Training is imparting the specific job skills to the volunteers. It may take place before the volunteers begin service, or it may be an on-the-job process. The following steps are involved in the training process:

Assess the training needs of the volunteers. Make sure that you aren't training them in something they already know how to do and make sure they have the skills you think they do.

Set your goals for the training. In general terms determine what you want the volunteers to be able to do at the end of the training session. For example, one goal might be: The volunteers will be able to counsel over the telephone someone who is experiencing a personal crisis.

Translate your goals into specific learning objectives. For example, a learning objective might be: The volunteer will be able to role-play three telephone counseling techniques without the aid of notes and to the satisfaction of the trainer and other participants. This learning objective indicates what the volunteer will be able to do and how one will know when he has achieved the desired level of learning.

Select training methods that can accomplish the objectives. There are numerous books available on training techniques. You may have people on your staff with expertise in training, or the people at the school with whom you are working may be able to help you. Again, vary your approach. Consider role plays, buzz sessions, lectures and discussions. Videotape, if available, can be a very effective tool.

Set a realistic but flexible schedule for the training events.

Select the training staff. Make sure they understand the goals and objectives of the training and their roles. They should be prepared to answer questions which might arise.

Handle the logistics—physical facilities, equipment, handouts. Make sure the facilities are comfortable, the equipment is in working order and handouts are in ample supply.

Invite the participants. Notify them of time and place far enough in advance for them to adjust their schedule. Give instructions on how to get to the training site. Ask them to notify you if they cannot attend.

Conduct the Training

Evaluate the training. How many of the participants can actually do what you hoped as a result of the training? How well? Do they perceive that the objectives you set were important? If not, what would have been more appropriate objectives? How do the participants feel about the training experience?

Don't overtrain. Sometimes we are tempted to throw in a lot of sophisticated training for a relatively unsophisticated volunteer job. The training you provide sets up expectations on the volunteer's part as to the kind of a role he will play. If the training suggest that the volunteer will be operating as a para-medic, the volunteer will be most suprised if he is assigned to opening the door for people rolling in on stretchers. Make sure your training is appropriate to the volunteer role.

Don't assume that training sessions are the only answer to your volunteers' needs to learn. Consider the other alternatives including on-the-job training.

Student Leadership Development

Many student volunteer projects have student leaders who take much of the responsibility. As the person who is working with the students in the community, you can have impact on the development of new student leaders and can assist in their effective integration into your organization.

Student project leaders don't materialize out of the air. They are nurtured, developed, supported, and enabled to function by the people they work with in the community. The success in developing and keeping student leadership depends on you and your program.

Student leaders need a clear idea of your expectations for them, their responsibilities, their parameters, and the way you plan to share with them responsibility for the project. This means that the project leaders should have a job description and have plenty of access to you to learn whether they are meeting expectations and meshing their activities with yours.

Student leaders need a reasonable expectation that they will be able to do a good job and can succeed. You contribute to the chances that they will succeed by providing them open access to your office, feedback in their work, and letting them know what has worked in the past. You can also increase their chances for success by using an overlap system in student leadership where a new person works with an experienced student leader for a few weeks before taking over completely.

Student leaders need to be able to assume leadership gradually. You can help develop intermediary student leadership roles by the way you structure your project. You might consider building in several such roles leading up to that of project leader—sort of a career ladder for your student volunteer leaders.

Student leaders like other volunteers need to be recognized for their contributions. As a professional in your organization you represent an important person in the student's life. The attention you pay to the student leader, the time spent in chatting about the project, planning for its future, evaluating its effectiveness, are all a form of recognition of that student's importance and competence.

Student leaders may have available to them formal leadership training. For example, the schools with which you are working may have some form of leadership training that could increase the effectiveness of your project leaders. If there are no resources available, consider setting up an occasional workshop for the student leaders in your own project. This kind of training is a reward in itself because it increases their perception of their own competence.

Student leadership does not always emerge spontaneously. You have an important role in fostering it and nurturing it. Remember that the time spent in developing the leadership role and in supporting the work of your student leaders will result in a more effective project and in the long run reduce your work load.

Checklist

The following questions should be kept in mind when you enter into the planning stages of a volunteer project. The answers need not be written out or drawn into your "contract" with the student volunteers, but there should be at least a tacit understanding of how each component of a project will work.

The Initial Planning Stage

- Does the youth group project have a clearly defined set of goals?
- Does the project contain the means to reach these objectives?
- Have you projected a reasonable time schedule for meeting your goals?

Transportation

- Have you made adequate arrangements for transporting the volunteers?
- Are the vehicles in good repair?
- Do you anticipate difficulty getting enough drivers?
- If your program grows, can you provide additional transportation?

Funding

- Have you provided for adequate funding? For transportation? Program supplies? Publicity?

- Is there a contingency fund for emergency expenses? (car repairs, extra supplies, etc.)
- Who will cover the indirect costs and how?
- Who will provide insurance? Have you determined whether your coverage is adequate?

Publicity

- Have you checked with the students about on-campus publicity?
- Are there ways you can publicize the volunteer program within your own agency? In the community?
- Will your publicity be offensive to any of the people involved in the project? Should you insure anonymity? Is individual recognition of the volunteers advisable?

Program Supplies

- Do the volunteers have adequate supplies or program materials?
- Are the supplies being used effectively?
- Are the volunteers being reimbursed for out-of-pocket expenses?
- Are the volunteers paying for supplies out of their program budget or as individuals? Is this advisable?

Insurance

- Have you checked with your insurance agent about liability coverage? For the volunteers? For your staff or people?
- Does the University policy cover your program, and to what degree?
- Is there adequate insurance on the vehicles used in transportation of the students?
- Are you meeting the conditions of your insurance policies?

Relations with Group

- Are the volunteers relating well with youth group members?
- Are they being accepted by the group members?

Recruitment

- How many volunteers will you need for your youth group? Is it likely you will have enough volunteers?
- If you recruit too many volunteers, can you direct them to other projects?
- Can you recruit additional volunteers if you need them during the year?
- Do you have plans for replacing volunteers who drop out?

Orientation

- Does your orientation give the volunteers an understanding of what your agency is and how it operates?
- Do the volunteers know the people they will work with? The community? The neighborhood? The youth group.
- Do the volunteers understand how their project relates to your overall goals and objects?
- Is the orientation program too long?

Training

- Does your training program provide the skills that the volunteers will need to be effective?
- Will additional training be necessary once the project begins?
- Are there special characteristics of culture or religion that the volunteers should be aware of in working with your people? How are these needs addressed in your training program?
- What is the total amount of time devoted to training and orientation? Are the volunteers put to work quickly?

Supervision

- Does your method of supervision allow continuing feedback from the volunteers?
- Are you in touch with their questions and problems as they arise?
- Do the volunteers feel restricted by you? Do they have a sense of freedom?
- Do the volunteers feel that there is too much supervision? Or too little?
- Do you, the worker, relate well the volunteers?

Evaluation

- Is the project making satisfactory progress toward your goals?
- If the goals are not being attained, can they be defined in more realistic terms?
- Are there any technical problems that could hurt the project? Problems with transportation? Supplies? Buildings?
- Do the volunteers carry out their assignments? Do they follow instructions? Are they regular in attendance?
- Do the volunteers cooperate effectively with you and community people?
- Has the project helped you to perceive new goals or new ideas for using volunteers?
- Does the project contribute to the overall purpose of your agency? Is it meeting a basic need of the community and/or group?
- Does the project contribute to the lives of the students?

Feedback to Colleges

- Did you arrange for a formal evaluation to be prepared and sent back to the student volunteer's professor or department head? (Keep in mind that some portion of the student volunteers receive academic credit for their efforts, particularly if they are in a cooperative education endeavor.)

REFERENCES

ACTION. *It's Your Move: Working with Student Volunteers. A Manual for Community Organizations.* National Student Volunteer Program, 1979.

Lesser, B. *The Youth Advisor's Handbook.* Nealco Publishing Co., 1970.

Chapter 14

The Drug Culture – Background Data

For the past several decades there has been a growing concern with the increased and illicit use by our teenagers of a diffuse array of drugs. All manner of causal reasons were given by professionals and others as to why our young people were turning to drugs such as:

- Changing mores
- Boredom
- Rebellion
- The quest for authentic experiences
- New philosophies
- Escape
- Basic normal impulse
- Fads

In the 1960s and early 1970s regardless of the publicized basic reasons for so doing, it was accepted that a large portion of our youth sought drugs as a way to strike at the establishment. It was in every sense counter-culture.

What is evident to the author is that doing drugs today is not counter-culture anymore. Today it is culture. Often to be "in" and "accepted" you must do drugs.

The magazine "New Dawn" ran an interesting article in the spring of 1979, citing the fact that a modest cache of drugs is today (among some adults) what a well-stocked bar was 20 years ago. There are many misinformed adults who actually think that the abuse of drugs is a thing of the past, and others who are accepting it as a way of life and/or a stage in growing up.

This attitude on the part of the community makes the job of the group worker that much tougher. The worker must arm him/herself with as much information as possible in the composition, use and effect of drugs to wit:

- Narcotics
- Depressants
- Stimulants
- Hallucinogens
- Cannabis

The next five chapters will contain a reasonably full description of the various categories of the drugs that are abused, including legal and illegal uses, impact and behavioral implications. A sixth chapter will include ready reference charts relating to the uses and effects of the various drugs and a glossary of slang terms for drugs. Most of this material is based on updated data developed by the Drug Enforcement Administration of the U.S. Department of Justice. The list of references and additional readings will be found at the rear of Chapter 20.

Patterns of Drug Use

The patterns of drug use may not have changed substantially over the years. The categories of drug users extant ten years ago, albeit the popularity of certain drugs have changed, is pretty much what they are today.

According to a 1969 edition of "A Time Guide to Drugs and the Young,"[16] almost everyone is a drug user at one time or another. Coffee, beer and hard liquor are drugs; so is aspirin. These drugs too have their "addicts," people who abuse themselves with the chemicals. The majority of adult drug takers, of course, only use the substances, and the distinction between abuse and use is equally important when discussing the drugs that young people take. Youthful drug users fall into at least four categories:

The Experimenter tries a drug from one to ten times, finds it either distasteful or unmeaningful (many neophytes derive no effects from a first try), and then quits, probably for good. Experimenters form the largest class of young drug users.

The Dabbler usually smokes pot but shuns other drugs, does not go out of his way to obtain the drug when it is hard to get, and is not psychologically or physiologically dependent on what he takes. He may smoke no more than once or twice per week. Increasing numbers of adults are in this category. By no sretch of the imagination do they resemble "dope fiends," and they typically have many other hobbies, diversions, and interests. Most are not on the road to addiction. Some youthful examples of this type, however, especially in high school or junior high, may move on to more serious use.

The Social Smoker uses marijuana roughly the same way most people use alcohol; he may occasionally use other drugs as well. Young people sometimes refer to him as a "head," the shortened, more respectable form of "acid head" or "pot head." For him, drug use is not an adventure but a way of life. Often he comes from a markedly advantaged background and is very intelligent. In most cases, he manages to stay in school or handle a job without becoming a dropout; he seems stable enough—or lucky enough—to keep some control of drug use.

The Pan-Drug User gobbles drugs not only constantly, but indiscriminately. He is most likely to be an adolescent who does not know the differences

---

[16]A TIME GUIDE TO DRUGS AND THE YOUNG, published by TIME Education Program, edited by Brian J. Brown (1969).

between drugs and is anxious to take so-called "guided tours" of all of them. He usually varies his diet of marijuana with occasional LSD, but may also get started on a regimen of pep-up diet pills proffered by friends without the supervision of doctor, and then need barbiturate tranquilizers to get to sleep.

The Abuser's use of marijuana, hashish, amphetamines, LSD and perhaps other drugs is chronic and regular. He spends most of his time turned on or talking about it. He is called a "speed freak," "acid freak," or "pot freak," connoting how deeply and irretrievably he has become involved with drugs. Forsaking the "straight" world and its attendant values of ambition, achievement and order, he is not likely to stay in school or hold a job for long.

Control Mechanisms

The legal foundation for the federal strategy of reducing the consumption of illicit drugs is the Comprehensive Drug Abuse Prevention and Control Act of 1970, Title II of which is more familiarly known as the Controlled Substances Act.

This article summarizes four fundamental parts of the federal law insofar as it governs control and enforcement: 1) the mechanisms for reducing the availability of controlled substances; 2) the procedures for bringing a substance under control; 3) the criteria for determining control requirements; and 4) the obligations incurred by international treaty arrangements.

The Drug Enforcement Administration (DEA) of the Department of Justice is responsible for enforcing the provisions of the Controlled Substances Act.

There are nine major control mechanisms imposed on the manufacturing, purchasing, and distributing of substances listed under the Act: 1) registration of handlers; 2) record-keeping requirements; 3) quotas on manufacturing; 4) restrictions on distribution; 5) restrictions on dispensing; 6) limitations on imports and exports; 7) conditions for storage of drugs; 8) reports of transactions to the government; and 9) criminal, civil, and administrative penalties for illegal acts. Some controls are equally applicable to substances listed in every schedule; the others vary, depending upon the schedule involved.

Registration

Any person who handles or intends to handle controlled substances must obtain a registration issued by DEA. A unique number is assigned to each legitimate handler of controlled drugs: importer, exporter, manufacturer, wholesaler, hospital, pharmacy, physician, and researcher. This number must be made available to the supplier by the customer prior to the purchase of a controlled substance. Thus the opportunity for unauthorized transactions is greatly diminished. The registration system also provides a means of expeditiously excluding persons who have been found participating in the diversion of drugs.

Drug Scheduling – Criteria

The Controlled Substances Act sets forth the findings which must be made to put a substance in any of the five schedules. These are as follows (Section 202(b)):

Schedule I

- The drug or other substance has a high potential for abuse.
- The drug or other substance has no currently accepted medical use in treatment in the United States.
- There is a lack of accepted safety for use of the drug or other substance under medical supervision.

Schedule II

- The drug or other substance has a high potential for abuse.
- The drug or other substance has a currently accepted medical use in treatment in the United States or a currently accepted medical use with severe restrictions.
- Abuse of the drug or other substances may lead to severe psychological or physical dependence.

Schedule III

- The drug or other substance has a potential for abuse less than the drugs or other substances in Schedules I and II.
- The drug or other substance has a currently accepted medical use in treatment in the United States.
- Abuse of the drug or other substance may lead to moderate or low physical dependence or high psychological dependence.

Schedule IV

- The drug or other substance has a low potential for abuse relative to the drugs or other substances in Schedule III.
- The drug or other substance has a currently accepted medical use in treatment in the United States.
- Abuse of the drug or other substance may lead to limited physical dependence or psychological dependence relative to the drugs or other substances in Schedule III.

Schedule V

- The drug or other substance has a low potential for abuse relative to the drugs or other substances in Schedule IV.
- The drug or other substance has a currently accepted medical use in treatment in the United States.
- Abuse of the drug or other substance may lead to limited physical dependence or psychological dependence relative to the drugs or other substances in Schedule IV.

In making these findings, DEA and HEW are directed to consider eight specific factors (Section 201 (C)):

1) Its actual or relative potential for abuse;
2) Scientific evidence of its pharmacological effect, if known;
3) The state or current scientific knowledge regarding the drug or other substance;
4) Its history and current pattern of abuse;
5) The scope, duration, and significance of abuse;
6) What, if any, risk there is to the public health;
7) Its psychic or physiological dependence liability;
8) Whether the substance is an immediate precursor of a substance already controlled under this title.

Aside from the criterion of actual or relative potential for abuse, subsections (c) of Section 201 lists seven other criteria, already referred to above, which must be considered in determining whether a substance meets the specific requirements specified in Section 202 (b) for inclusion in particular schedules and accordingly should be designated a controlled substance under a given schedule (including transfer from any other schedule) or removed entirely from the schedules. A brief discussion of each of these criteria follows.

Scientific evidence of its pharmacological effects. The state of knowledge with respect to the effects of uses of a specific drug is, of course, a major consideration, e.g. it is vital to know whether or not a drug has a hallucinogenic effect if it is to be controlled because of that. The best available knowledge of the pharmacological properties of a drug should be considered.

The state of current scientific knowledge regarding the substance. Criteria (1) and (2) are closely related. Howver, (1) is primarily concerned with pharmacological effects, and (2) deals with all scientific knowledge with respect to the substance.

Its history and current pattern of abuse. To determine whether or not a drug should be controlled, it is important to know the pattern of abuse of the substance, including the social, economic, and ecological characteristics of the segments of the population involved in such abuse.

The scope, duration, and significance of abuse. In evaluating existing abuse, the Attorney General must know not only the pattern of abuse but whether the abuse is widespread. He must also know whether it is a passing fad or a significant chronic abuse problem like heroin addiction. In reaching his decision, the Attorney General should consider the economics of regulation and enforcement attendant to such a decision. In addition, he should be aware of the social significance and impact of such a decision upon those people, especially the young, that would be affected by it.

What, if any, risk there is to the public health. If a drug creates no danger to the public health, it would be inappropriate to control the drug under this bill.

Its psychic or physiological dependence liability. There must be an assessment of the extent to which a drug is physically addictive or psychologically habit-forming, if such information is known.

Whether the substance is an immediate precursor of a substance already controlled. The bill allows inclusion of immediate precursors on this basis alone into the appropriate schedule and thus safeguards against possibilities of clandestine manufacture.

It should be noted that the above-mentioned factors do not require specific findings to be made with respect to control under, or removal from, schedules, but rather are factors to be considered in making the special findings required under Section 202 (b) for control under such schedules.

International Implications

The CSA further provides that if control of any drug is required by obligations of the United States under international treaty arrangements, the drug shall be placed under the schedule deemed most appropriate to carry out these obligations. As cited in the CSA, the United States is a party to the Single Convention on Narcotic Drugs of 1961, designed to establish effective control over international and domestic traffic in narcotics, including within the legal definition coca leaf, cocaine, and cannabis. A second treaty, the Convention on Psychotropic Substances of 1971, which entered into force in 1976, is designed to establish comparable control over such drugs as LSD, the amphetamines, certain barbiturates, and other depressants. Legislation has been passed by the Congress authorizing the United States to become a signatory to this treaty, and ratification is expected.

Most of the youngsters of youth group age are totally unaware that the Federal Government today can mete out relatively stiff penalties for simple possession of a controlled substance let alone trafficking in such items.

The group worker should be armed with knowledge as to penalties (federal) in existence for trafficking—information that might have a sobering impact on a large segment of the kids.

Federal Trafficking Penalties

		First Offense		
CSA Schedule	**Type of Drug**	**Max. Impris.**	**Max. Fine**	**Min. Parole**
I	Narcotic	15 yrs	$25,000	3 yrs
	Non-Narcotic	5 yrs	15,000	2 yrs

(Continued)

CSA Schedule	Type of Drug	Max. Impris.	Max. Fine	Min. Parole
II	Narcotic	15 yrs	$25,000	3 yrs
	Non-Narcotic	5 yrs	15,000	2 yrs
III	Narcotic	5 yrs	$15,000	2 yrs
	Non-Narcotic	5 yrs	15,000	2 yrs
IV	Narcotic	3 yrs	$10,000	1 yr
	Non-Narcotic	3 yrs	10,000	1 yr
V	Narcotic	1 yr	$ 5,000	0
	Non-Narcotic	1 yr	5,000	0

Second Offense

CSA Schedule	Type of Drug	Max. Impris.	Max. Fine	Min. Parole
I	Narcotic	30 yrs	$50,000	6 yrs
	Non-Narcotic	10 yrs	30,000	4 yrs
II	Narcotic	30 yrs	$50,000	6 yrs
	Non-Narcotic	10 yrs	30,000	4 yrs
III	Narcotic	10 yrs	$30,000	4 yrs
	Non-Narcotic	10 yrs	30,000	4 yrs
IV	Narcotic	6 yrs	$20,000	2 yrs
	Non-Narcotic	6 yrs	20,000	2 yrs
V	Narcotic	2 yrs	$10,000	0
	Non-Narcotic	2 yrs	10,000	0

For *simple possession* of any controlled substance, first offenders may receive up to one year, $5,000 fine, or both, and if under 21, may receive up to one year probation and thereafter motion court for expungement of all records. Second offenders may receive up to 2 years, $10,000 fine, or both.

Chapter 15

Drugs of Abuse – Narcotics

The term narcotic in its medical meaning refers to opium and opium derivatives or synthetic substitutes.*

Narcotics are indispensable in the practice of medicine: They are the most effective agents known for the relief of intense pain. They are also used as cough suppressants as well as a remedy centuries old for diarrhea.

Under medical supervision narcotics are administered orally or by intramuscular injection. As drugs of abuse, however, they may be sniffed, smoked, or self-administered by the more direct routes of subcultaneous ("skin-popping") and intravenous ("mainlining") injection.

The relief of suffering, whether of physical or psychological origin, may result in a short-lived state of euphoria. The initial effects, however, are often unpleasant, leading many to conclude that those who persist in their illicit use may have latent personality disturbances. Narcotics tend to induce pinpoint pupils and reduced vision, together with drowsiness, apathy, decreased physical activity, and constipation. A larger dose may induce sleep but there is an increasing possibility of nausea, vomiting, and respiratory depression–the major toxic effect of the opiates. Except in cases of acute intoxication, there is no loss of motor coordination of slurred speech as in the case of the depressants.

To the extent that the response may be felt to be pleasurable, its intensity may be expected to increase with the amount of the dose administered. Repeated use, however, will result in increasing tolerance: The user must admininister progressively larger doses to attain the desired effect, thereby reinforcing the compulsive behavior known as drug dependence.

Physical dependence refers to an alteration of the normal functions of the body that necessitates the continued presence of a drug in order to prevent the withdrawal or abstinence syndrome, which is characteristic of each class of addictive drugs. The intensity of physical symptoms experienced during the withdrawal period is related to the amount of narcotic used each day. Deprivation of an addictive drug causes increased excitability of those same bodily functions that have been depressed by its habitual use.

*Cocaine, ecgonine, and coca leaves, classified as narcotics under the CSA, are discussed in the section on Stimulants.

With the deprivation of narcotics, the first withdrawal signs are usually experienced shortly before the time of the next scheduled dose. Complaints, pleas, and demands by the addict are prominent, increasing in intensity and peaking from 36 to 72 hours after the last dose, then gradually subsiding. Symptoms such as watery eyes, runny nose, yawning, and perspiration appear about 8 to 12 hours after the last dose. Thereafter, the addict may fall into a restless sleep.

As the abstinence syndrome progresses, restlessness, irritability, loss of appetite, insomnia, goose flesh, tremors, and finally yawning and severe sneezing occur. These symptoms reach their peak at 48 to 72 hours. The patient is weak and depressed with nausea and vomiting. Stomach cramps and diarrhea are common. Heart rate and blood pressure are elevated. Chills alternating with flushing and excessive sweating, are also characteristic symptoms. Pains in the bones and muscles of the back and extremities occur as do muscle spasms and kicking movements which may be the source of the expression "kicking the habit." At this time an individual may become suicidal. Without treatment the syndrome eventually runs its course and most of the symptoms will disappear in 7 to 10 days. How long it takes to restore physiological and psychological equilibrium, however, is unpredictable. For a few weeks following withdrawal the addict will continue to think and talk about his use of drugs and be particularly susceptible to an urge to use them again.

The withdrawal syndrome may be avoided by reducing the dose of narcotic over a one-to-three-week period. Detoxification of an addict can be accomplished quite easily by substituting oral methadone for the illicit narcotic and gradually reducing the dose. Howver, the addict's entire pattern of life is built around drug taking and narcotic dependence is never entirely resolved by withdrawal alone.

Since addicts tend to become preoccupied with the daily round of obtaining and taking drugs, they often neglect themselves and may suffer from malnutrition, infections, and unattended diseases or injuries. Among the hazards of narcotic addiction are toxic reactions to contaminants, such as quinidine, sugars, and talcum powder, as well as unsterile needles and injection techniques, resulting in abscesses, blood poisoning, and hepatitis.

Since there is no simple way to determine the purity of a drug that is sold on the street, the potency is unpredictable. A person with a mild overdose may be stuporous or asleep. Larger doses may induce a coma with slow shallow respiration. The skin becomes clammy cold, the body limp, and the jaw relaxed; there is a danger that the tongue may fall back, blocking the air passageway. If the condition is sufficiently severe, convulsions may occur, followed by respiratory arrest and death. Specific antidotes for narcotic poisoning are available at hospitals.

Narcotics of Natural Origin

The poppy Papaver Somniferum is the main source of nonsynthetic narcotics. It was grown in the Mediterranean region as early as 300 B.C. and has since been cultivated in countries around the world, including Hungary, Yugoslavia, Turkey, India, Burma, China, and Mexico.

The milky fluid that oozes from incisions in the unripe seedpod has since ancient times been scraped by hand and air dried to produce opium gum. A more modern method of harvesting is by the industrial poppy straw process of extracting alkaloids from the mature dried plant. The extract may be in either liquid, solid, or powder form. Most poppy straw concentrate made available commercially is a fine brownish powder with a distinct odor.

More than 400 tons of opium or its equivalent in poppy straw concentrate are legally imported annually into the United States.

Opium

There were no legal restrictions on the importation or use of opium until the early 1900s. In those days patent medicines often contained opium without any warning label. Today there are state, federal, and international laws governing the production and distribution of narcotic substances, and there is little abuse of opium in the United States.

At least 25 alkaloids can be extracted from opium. These fall into two general categories, each producing markedly different effects. The first, known as the phenanthrene alkaloids represented by morphine and codeine, are used as analgesics and cough suppressants; the second, the isoquinoline alkaloids, represented by papaverine (an intestinal relaxant) and noncapine (a cough suppressant), have no significant influence on the central nervous system and are not regulated under the CSA.

Although a small amount of opium is used to make anti-diarrheal preparations such as paregoric, virtually all the opium imported into this country is broken down into its alkaloid constituents, principally morphine and codeine.

Morphine

The principal constituent of opium, ranging in concentration from 4 to 21 percent, morphine is one of the most effective drugs known for the relief of pain. It is marketed in the form of white crystals, hypodermic tablets, and injectable preparations. Its licit use is restricted primarily to hospitals. Morphine is odorless, tastes bitter, and darkens with age. It may be administered subcutaneously, intramuscularly or intravenously, the latter method being the one most frequently resorted to by addicts. Tolerance and dependence develop rapidly in the user.

Only a small part of the morphine obtained from opium is used medically. Most of it is converted to codeine and, secondarily to hydromorphone.

Codeine

This alkaloid is found in raw opium in concentrations ranging from 0.7 to 2.5 percent. It was first isolated in 1832 as an impurity in a batch of morphine. Although it occurs naturally, most codeine is produced from morphine. As compared with morphine, codeine produces less analgesia, sedation and respiratory depression. It is widely distributed in products of two general types. Codeine for the relief of moderate pain may consist of codeine tablets or be combined with other products such as aspirin or acetaminophen, manufactured to a lesser extent in injectable form for the relief of pain. It is by far the most widely used naturally occurring narcotic in medical treatment.

Thebaine

A minor constituent of opium, thebaine is the principal alkaloid present in another species of poppy, Papaver bracteatum, which has been grown experimentally in the United States as well as in other parts of the world. Although chemically similar to both codeine and morphine, it produces stimulant rather than depressant effects. Thebaine is not used in this country for medical purposes, but it is converted into a variety of medically important compounds, including codeine, hydrocodone, oxycodone, oxymorphone, nalbuphine, naloxone, and the Bentley compounds. It is controlled in Schedule II of the CSA as well as under international law.

Semi-Synthetic Narcotics

The following narcotics are among the more significant synthetic substances that have been derived by modification of the chemicals contained in opium.

Heroin

First synthesized from morphine in 1874, heroin was not extensively used in medicine until the beginning of this century. A German company first started commercial production of the new pain remedy in 1898. While it received widespread acceptance, the medical profession for years remained unaware of its potential for addiction. The first comprehensive control of heroin in the United States was established with the Harrison Narcotic Act of 1914.

Pure heroin is a white powder with a bitter taste. Illicit heroin may vary in color from white to dark brown because of impurities left from the manufacturing process or the presence of additives such as coloring, cocoa, or brown sugar. Pure heroin is rarely sold on the street. A "bag"—slang for a single dosage unit of heroin—may weight about 100 mg, usually containing less than 5 percent heroin. To increase the bulk of the material sold to the addict, diluents are mixed with the heroin in ratios ranging from 9 to 1 to as much as 99 to 1. Sugars, starch, powdered milk, and quinidine are among the diluents used.

Hydromorphone

Most commonly known as Dilaudid, hydromorphone is the second oldest semi-synthetic narcotic analgesic. Marketed both in tablet and injectable form, it is shorter acting and more sedative than morphine, but its potency is from two to eight times as great. It is therefore a highly abusable drug, much sought after by narcotic addicts, who usually obtain it through fraudulent prescription or theft. The tablets, stronger than available liquid forms, may be dissolved and injected.

Oxycodone

Oxycodone is synthesized from thebaine. It is similar to codeine, but more potent and with a higher dependence potential. It is effective orally and is marketed in combination with other drugs for the relief of pain. Addicts take it orally or dissolve tablets in water, filter out the insoluble material, and "mainline" the active drug.

Etorphine and Diprenorphine

Two of the Bentley compounds, these substances are both made from thebaine. Etorphine is more than a thousand times as potent as morphine in its analgesic, sedative and respiratory depressant effects. For human use its potency is a distinct disadvantage because of the danger of overdose. Etorphine hydrochloride (M99) is used by veterinarians to immobilize large wild animals. Diprenorphine hydrochloride (M5050), acting as an antagonist, counteracts the effects of etorphine. The manufacture and distribution of both substances are strictly regulated under the CSA.

Synthetic Narcotics

In contrast to pharmaceutical products derived directly or indirectly from narcotics of natural origin, synthetic narcotics are produced entirely within the laboratory. A continuing search for a product that will retain the analgesic properties of morphine without the consequent dangers of tolerance and dependence has yet to yield a drug that is not susceptible to abuse. The two that are most widely available are meperidine and methadone.

Meperidine (pethidine)

The first synthetic narcotic, produced originally a generation ago, meperidine is chemically dissimilar to morphine but resembles it in its analgesic potency. It is probably the most widely used drug for the relief of moderate to severe pain. Available in pure form as well as in products containing other medicinal ingredients, it is administered either orally or by injection, the latter method being the most widely abused. Tolerance and dependence develop with chronic use, and large doses can result in convulsions.

Methadone and Related Drugs

German scientists synthesized methadone during World War II because of a shortage of morphine. Although chemically unlike morphine or heroin, it produces many of the same effects. Introduced into the United States in 1947 as an analgesic and distributed under such names as Amidone, Dolophine, and Methadone, it became widely used in the 1960s in the treatment of narcotic addicts. The effects of methadone differ from morphine-based drugs in that they have a longer duration of action, lasting up to 24 hours, thereby permitting administration only once a day in heroin detoxification and maintenance programs. Moreover, methadone is almost as effective when administered orally as it is by injection. But tolerance and dependence may develop, and withdrawal symptoms, though they develop more slowly and are less severe, are more prolonged. Ironically, methadone, designed to control narcotic addiction, has emerged in some metropolitan areas as a major cause of overdose deaths.

Closely related chemically to methadone is the synthetic compound levo-alpha-acetylmethadol (LAAM), which has an even longer duration of action (from 48 to 72 hours), permitting a further reduction in clinic visits and the elimination of take-home medication, its potential in the treatment of narcotic addicts is now under investigation. Another close relative of methadone is propoxyphene, first marketed in 1957 for the relief of mild to moderate pain. Less dependence-producing than the opiates, its also less effective as an analgesic. Misuse of propoxyphene led to its placement in Schedule IV of the CSA in 1977.

Narcotic Antagonists

The deliberate effort to find an effective analgesic that is not dependence producing has led in recent years to the development of a class of compounds known as narcotic antagonists. These drugs, as the name implies, tend to block and reverse the effects of narcotics, and some of them may in the future prove useful in checking recidivist tendencies of former addicts who have undergone treatment. Nalorphine, introduced into clinical medicine in 1951 and now under

Schedule III, is called a partial antagonist. In a drug-free individual, it produces morphine-like effects; whereas in an individual under the influence of narcotics, it counteracts these effects.

Another partial antagonist is pentazocine. Introduced as an analgesic in 1967, it was determined to be an abusable drug and placed under Schedule IV in 1979. Relatively pure antagonists have also been developed. Naloxone having no morphine-like effects, was removed from the CSA when introduced as a specific antidote for narcotic poisoning in 1971. A number of "pure" antagonists have since been developed that are no longer lasting and effective when administered orally. One of them is Naltrexone, which was removed from control of the CSA in 1975, and which is now under evaluation to determine its utility in assisting post-narcotic addicts to remain drug free.

Chapter 16

Drugs of Abuse – Depressants

Substances regulated under the CSA as depressants have a high potential for abuse associated with both physical and psychological dependence.

Taken as prescribed by a physician, depressants may be beneficial for the relief of anxiety, irritability, and tension, and for the symptomatic treatment of insomnia. In excessive amounts, however, they produce a state of intoxication that is remarkably similar to that of alcohol.

As in the case of alcohol, these effects may vary not only from person to person but from time to time in the same individual. Low doses produce mild sedation. Higher doses, insofar as they relieve anxiety or stress, may produce a temporary sense of well-being; they may also produce mood depression and apathy. In marked contrast to the effects of narcotics, however, intoxicating doses invariably result in impaired judgment, slurred speech, and loss of motor coordination. In addition to the dangers of disorientation, resulting in a high incidence of highway accidents, recurrent users incur risks of long-term involvement with depressants.

Tolerance to the intoxicating effects develops rapidly, leading to a progressive narrowing of the margin of safety between an intoxicating and lethal dose. The person who is unaware of the dangers of increasing dependence will often increase the daily dose up to 10 or 20 times the recommended therapeutic level. The source of supply may be no further than the family medicine cabinet. Depressants are also frequently obtained by theft, illegal prescription, or purchase on the illicit market.

Members of the drug subculture often resort to the use of depressants as self-medication to soothe jangled nerves brought on by the use of stimulants, to quell the anxiety of "flashbacks" resulting from prior use of hallucinogens, or to ease their withdrawal from heroin. The dangers, it should be stressed, are compounded when depressants are used in combination with alcohol or other drugs. Chronic intoxication, though it affects every age group, is most common in middle age. The problem often remains unrecognized until the user exhibits recurrent confusion or an obvious inability to function. Depressants also serve as a means of suicide, a pattern particularly common among women.

As will be shown, the depressants vary with respect to their potential for overdose. Moderate depressant poisoning closely resembles alcoholic inebriation. The symptoms of severe depressant poisoning are coma, a cold clammy skin, a weak and rapid pulse, and a slow or rapid but shallow respiration. Death will follow if the reduced respiration and low blood pressure are not counteracted by proper medical treatment.

The abrupt cessation or reduction of high-dose depressant intake may result in a characteristic withdrawal syndrome, which should be recognized as a medical emergency more serious than that of any other drugs of abuse. An apparent improvement in the patient's condition may be the initial result of detoxification. Within 24 hours, however, minor withdrawal symptoms manifest themselves, among them anxiety and agitation, loss of appetite, nausea and vomiting, increased heart rate and excessive sweating, tremulousness and abdominal cramps.

The symptoms usually peak during the second or third day of abstinence from the short-acting barbiturates or meprobamate; they may not be reached until the seventh or eighth day of abstinence from the long-acting barbiturates or benzodiazepines. It is during the peak period that the major withdrawal symptoms usually occur. The patient may experience convulsions indistinguishable from those occurring in grand mal epilepsy. More than half of those who experience convulsions will go on to develop delirium, often resulting in a psychotic state identical to the delirium tremens associated with the alcohol withdrawal syndrome. Detoxification and treatment must therefore be carried out under close medical supervision. While treatment techniques vary to some extent, they share common objectives; stabilization of the drug-dependent state to allay withdrawal symptoms followed by gradual withdrawal to prevent their recurrence.

Among the depressants that give rise to the general conditions described are chloral hydrate, a broad array of barbiturates, glutethimide, methadqualone, meprobamate, and the benzodiazepines.

Chloral Hydrate

The oldest of the hypnotic (sleep inducing) drugs, chloral hydrate was first synthesized in 1862 and soon supplanted alcohol, opium and cannabis preparations for inducing sedation and sleep. Its popularity declined after the introduction of the barbiturates, but chloral hydrate is still widely used. It has a penetrating, slightly acrid odor, and a bitter caustic taste. Its depressant effects, as well as resulting tolerance and dependence, are comparable to those of alcohol, and withdrawal symptoms resemble delirium tremens.

Chloral hydrate is a liquid, marketed in the form of syrups and soft gelatin capsules. Cases of poisoning have occurred from mixing chloral hydrate with alcoholic drinks. Chloral hydrate is not a street drug of choice, its main misuse is by older adults.

Barbiturates

Among the drugs most frequently prescribed to induce sedation and sleep by both physicians and veterinarians are the barbiturates. About 2,500 derivatives of barbituric acid have been synthesized, but of these only about 15 remain in medical use. Small therapeutic doses tend to calm nervous conditions, and larger doses cause sleep 20 to 60 minutes after oral administration.

As in the case of alcohol, some individuals may experience a sense of excitement before sedation takes effect. If dosage is increased, however, the effects of the barbiturates may progress through successive stages of sedation, sleep, and coma to death from respiratory arrest and cardiovascular complications.

Barbiturates are classified as ultrashort, short, intermediate, and long-action. The ultrashort-acting barbiturates produce anesthesia within one minute after intravenous administration. The rapid onset and brief duration of action make them undesirable for purposes of abuse. Those in current medical use are hexobarbital (Evipal), methohexital (Brevital), thiamylal (Surital), andthipental (Pentothal).

Among the short-acting and intermediate-acting barbiturates are pentobarbital, secobarbital, and amobarbital; three of the drugs in the depressant category most sought after by abusers. The group also includes butabarbital, butalbital, allobarbital, aprobarbital, and vinbarbital. After oral administration the onset time of action is from 15 to 40 minutes and duration of action is up to 6 hours. Physicians prescribe short-acting barbiturates to induce sedation or sleep. Veterinarians use pentobarbital for anesthesia and euthanasia.

Long-acting barbiturates, which include barbital, phenobarbital, mephobarbital or methylphenobarbital, and metharbital, have onset times of up to one hour and durations of action up to 16 hours. They are used medicinally as sedatives, hypnotics, and anticonvulsants. Their slow onset of action discourages their use for episodic intoxication, and they are not ordinarily distributed on the illicit market except when sold as something else. It should be emphasized, however, that all barbiturates result in a buildup of tolerance, and dependence on them is widespread.

Glutethimide

When glutethimide was introduced in 1954 it was said to be a safe barbiturate substitute without an addiction potential. But experience has shown glutethimide to be another CNS depressant, having no particular advantage over the barbiturates and several important disadvantages. The sedative effects of glutethimide begin about 30 minutes after oral administration and last for 4 to 8 hours. Because the effects of this drug are of long duration it is exceptionally difficult to reverse overdoses, which often result in death.

Methaqualone

Methaqualone is a synthetic sedative chemically unrelated to the barbiturates, glutethimide, or chloral hydrate. It has been widely abused because it was once mistakenly thought to be non-addictive and effective as an aphrodisiac. Actually, methaqualone has caused many cases of serious poisoning. It is administered orally. Large doses cause coma, which may be accompanied by thrashing movements or convulsions. Continued heavy use of large doses leads to tolerance and dependence.

Meprobamate

Meprobamate, first synthesized in 1950, introduced the era of mild or "minor" tranquilizers. In the United States today more than 200 tons of meprobamate are distributed under its generic name as well as under brand names. Meprobamate is prescribed primarily for the relief of anxiety, tension, and associated muscle spasms. Its onset and duration of action are like those of the intermediate-acting barbiturates; it differs from them in that it is a muscle relaxant, does not produce sleep at therapeutic doses, and is relatively less toxic. Excessive use, however, can result in psychological and physical dependence. Mebutamate, a drug similar to meprobamate in its chemical makeup and effects, is also regulated under the CSA.

Benzodiazepines

The benzodiazepine family of depressants relieve anxiety, tension, and muscle spasms, produce sedation, and prevent convulsions. These substances are marketed as mild or minor tranquilizers, sedatives, hypnotics, or anticonvulsants. Their margin of safety is greater than that of other depressants.

These drugs have a relatively slow onset but long duration of action. Prolonged use of excessive doses may result in physical and psychological dependence. Withdrawal symptoms develop approximately one week to 10 days after continual high doses are abruptly discontinued. The delay in the appearance of the abstinence syndrome is due to the slow elimination of the drug from the body. When thes drugs are used to obtain a "high," they are usually taken in conjunction with another drug such as alcohol or marijuana.

Chapter 17

Drugs of Abuse – Stimulants

The two most prevalent stimulants are nicotine in tobacco products and caffeine, the active ingredient of coffee, tea, and some bottled beverages that are sold in every supermarket. When used in moderation, these stimulants tend to relieve fatigue and increase alertness. They are an accepted part of our culture.

There are, however, more potent stimulants that because of their dependence-producing potential are under the regulatory control of the CSA. These controlled stimulants are available on prescription for medical purposes; they are also clandestinely manufactured in vast quantities for distribution on the illicit market.

Users tend to rely on stimulants to feel stronger, more decisive, and self-possessed. Because of the cumulative effects of the drugs, chronic users often follow a pattern of taking "uppers" in the morning and "downers" such as alcohol or sleeping pills at night. Such chemical manipulation interferes with normal body processes and can lead to mental and physical illness.

Young people who resort to stimulants for their euphoric effects consume large doses sporadically, over weekends or at night, often going on to experiment with other drugs of abuse. The consumption of stimulants may result in a temporary sense of exhilaration, super-abundant energy, hyperactivity, extended wakefulness and a loss of appetite; it may also induce irritability, anxiety, and apprehension.

These effects are greatly intensified with administration by intravenous injection, which may produce a sudden sensation known as a "flash" or "rush." the protracted use of stimulants is followed, however, by a period of depression known as "crashing" that is invariably described as unpleasant. Since the depression can be easily counteracted by a further injection of stimulant, this abuse pattern becomes increasingly difficult to break. Heavy users may inject themselves every few hours, a process sometimes continued to the point of delirium, psychosis or physical exhaustion.

Tolerance develops rapidly to both the euphoric and appetite suppressant effects. Doses large enough to overcome the insensitivity that develops may cause various mental aberrations, the early signs of which include repetitive grinding of the teeth, touching and picking the face and extremities, performing the same task over and over, a preoccupation with one's own thought processes, suspiciousness and a sense of being watched.

Paranoia with auditory and visual hallucinations characterizes the toxic syndrome resulting from continued high doses. Dizziness, tremor, agitation, hostility, panic, headache, flushed skin, chest pain with palpitations, excessive sweating, vomiting, and abdominal cramps are among the symptoms of a sublethal overdose. In the absence of medical intervention, high fever, convulsions, and cardiovascular collapse may precede the onset of death.

It should be added that physical exertion increases the hazards of stimulant use since accidental death is due in part to their effects on the cardiovascular and body temperature regulating systems. Fatalities under conditions of extreme exertion have been reported among athletes who have taken stimulants in moderate amounts.

If withdrawn from stimulants, chronic high-dose users exhibit profound depression, apathy, fatigue, and disturbed sleep for up to 20 hours a day. The immediate withdrawal syndrome may last for several days. There may also be a lingering impairment of perception and thought processes. Anxiety, an incapacitating tenseness, and suicidal tendencies may persist for weeks or months. Many experts now interpret these symptoms as indicating that stimulant drugs are capable of producing physical dependence. Whether the withdrawal syndrome is physical or psychological in origins is in this instance academic since the stimulants are recognized as among the most potent agents of reward and reinforcement that underlie the problem of dependence.

Cocaine

The most potent stimulant of natural origin, cocaine is extracted from the leaves of the coca plant (Erythroxylon coca) which has been cultivated in the Andean highlands of South America since prehistoric times. The leaves of the plant are chewed in the region for refreshment and relief from fatigue, much as North Americans once chewed tobacco.

Pure cocaine, the principal psychactive ingredient, was first isolated in the 1880s. It was used as an anesthetic in eye surgery for which no previously known drug had been suitable; it became particularly useful in surgery of the nose and throat because of its ability to constrict blood vessels and thus limit bleeding.

Although many of its therapeutic applications are now obsolete, the legal use of cocaine in the United States has in recent years been increased by the introduction of a morphine-cocaine elixir designed to relieve the suffering associated with terminal illness. In England, where this mixture was developed at the Bromptom Chest Hospital, the use of cocaine in treatment of the terminally ill was largely abandoned after it was determined that it contributed to disquieting hallucinations and nightmares.

Illicit cocaine is distributed as a white crystalline powder, often adulterated to about half its volume by a variety of other ingredients, the most common of which are sugars such as lactose, inositol, mannitol, and local anesthetics such as lidocaine. Since the cost of illicit cocaine is high, there is a tendency to adulterate the product at each level of distribution. The drug is most commonly administered by being "snorted" through the nasal passages. Symptoms of repeated use in this manner may resemble the congested nose of a common cold. Less commonly, for heightened effect, the drug is injected directly into the bloodstream.

Unlike such drugs as LSD and heroin, cocaine is popularly accepted as a recreational drug, facilitating social interaction. It is erroneously reputed to be relatively safe from undesirable side effects. Because of the intensity of its pleasurable effects, cocaine has the potential for extraordinary dependency, which is all the more deceptive in view of its reputation as the recreational drug of choice.

Recurrent users may resort to larger doses at shorter intervals until their lives are largely committed to their habituation. Anxiety, restlessness, and extreme irritability may indicate the onset of a toxic psychosis similar to paranoid schizophrenia. Tactile hallucinations so afflict some chronic users that they injure themselves in attempting to remove imaginary insects from under the skin. Others are persecuted by fear of being watched and followed. Excessive doses of cocaine may cause seizures and death from respiratory failure.

Amphetamines

Amphetamine, dextroamphetamine, and methamphetamine are so similar in the effects they induce that they can be differentiated from one another only by laboratory analysis. Amphetamine was first used clinically in the mid-1930s to treat narcolepsy, a rare disorder resulting in an uncontrollable desire for sleep. After the introduction of the amphetamines into medical practice, the number of conditions for which they were prescribed multiplied as did the quantities made available. They were sold without prescription for a time in inhalers and over-the-counter preparations. Abuse of the inhalers became popular among teenagers and prisoners.

Housewives, students, and truck drivers were among those who used amphetamines orally in excessive amounts, and "speed freaks," who injected them, won notoriety in the drug culture for their bizarre and often violent behavior. Whereas a prescribed dose is between 2.5 and 15 mg per day, those on a "speed" binge have been known to inject as much as 1,000 mg every two or three hours. Recognition of the deleterious effects of these drugs and their limited therapeutic value has led to a marked reduction in their use by the medical profession.

The medical use of amphetamines is now limited to narcolepsy, hyperkinetic behavioral disorders in children, and certain cases of obesity—as a short-term adjunct to a restricted diet for patients refractory to other forms of therapy. Their illicit use closely parallels that of cocaine in the range of its short-term and long-term effects. Despite broad recognition of the risks, clandestine laboratories product vast quantities of amphetamines, particularly methamphetamine, for distribution on the illicit market.

Phenmetrazine and Methylphenidate

The medical indications, pattern of abuse, and adverse effect of phenmetrazine and methylphenidate compare closely with those of the other stimulants. Phenmetrazine is medically used only as an appetite suppressant and methylphenidate mainly for treatment of hyperkinetic behavioral disorders in children. They have been subject to abuse in countries where freely available and they are here in localities where medical practitioners write prescriptions on demand.

While the abuse of phenmetrazine involves both oral and intravenous use, most of that associated with methylphenidate results from injection after the drug in tablet form is dissolved in water. Complications arising from such use are common since the tablets contain insoluble materials which upon injection block small blood vessels and cause serious damage, especially in the lungs and retina of the eye.

Anorectic Drugs

In recent years a number of drugs have been manufactured and marketed to replace amphetamines as appetite suppressants. So-called anorectic drugs produce many of the effects of the amphetamines but are generally less potent. Abuse patterns of some of them have not yet been established, but all are controlled because of the similarity of their effects to those of the amphetamines.

Chapter 18

Drugs of Abuse – Hallucinogens

Hallucinogenic drugs, both natural and synthetic, are substances that distort the perception of objective reality. They induce a state of excitation of the central nervous system, manifested by alterations of mood, usually euphoric, but sometimes severely depressive. Under the influence of hallucinogens, the pupils dilate, and body temperature and blood pressure rise. The senses of direction, distance, and time become disoriented. A user may speak of "seeing" sounds and "hearing" colors. If taken in a large enough dose, the drug produces delusions and visual hallucinations.

Occasionally, depersonalization and depression are so severe that suicide is possible, but the most common danger is impaired judgment, leading to rash decisions and accidents. Persons in hallucinogenic states should therefore be closely supervised, and upset as little as possible, to keep them from harming themselves and others. Acute anxiety, restlessness, and sleeplessness are common until the drug wears off.

Long after hallucinogens are eliminated from the body, users may experience "flashbacks"–fragmentary recurrences of psychedelic effects–such as the intensification of a perceived color, the apparent motion of a fixed object or the mistaking of one object for another. Recurrent use produces tolerance, which tends to encourage resorting to greater amounts. Although no evidence of physical dependence is detectable when the drugs are withdrawn, recurrent use tends to produce psychic dependence, varying according to the drug, the dose, and the individual user. It should be stressed that the hallucinogens are unpredictable in their effects each time they are used.

The abuse of hallucinogens in the United States reached a peak of popularity in the late 1960s and a subsequent decline was attributed to broader awareness of their hazardous effects. Their abuse, however, re-emerged in the late 1970s.

Peyote and Mescaline

The primary active ingredient of the peyote cactus is the hallucinogen mescaline. It is derived from the fleshy parts or buttons of this plant which has been employed by indians in Northern Mexico from the earliest recorded time as a part of a traditional religious rite. The Native American Church, which uses peyote in religious ceremonies, has been exempted from certain provisions of the CSA. Peyote, or mescal buttons, and mescaline should not be confused with mescal, the colorless Mexican liquor distilled from the leaves of maguey plants. Usually ground into a powder, peyote is taken orally. Mescaline can also be produced synthetically. A dose of 350 to 500 mg of mescaline produces illusions and hallucinations lasting from 5 to 12 hours.

DOM, DOB, MDA, and MMDA

Many chemical variations of mescaline and amphetamine have been synthesized in the laboratory, certain of which at various times have won acceptance in the drug culture. DOM (4-methyl-2, 5-dimethoxyamphetamine), synthesized in 1963, was introduced in 1967 into the Haight-Asbury drug scene in San Francisco. At first named STP after a motor oil additive, the acronym was quickly reinterpreted to stand for "Serenity, Tranquility, and Peace." A host of related chemicals are illicitly manufactured, including DOB (4-bromo-2, 5-dimethoxyamphetamine), MDA (3, 4-methylenedioxyamphetamine), and MMDA (3-methoxy-4, 5-methylenedioxyamphetamine).

These drugs differ from one another in their speed of onset, duration of action, potency, and capacity to modify mood with or without producing hallucinations. They are usually taken orally, sometimes "snorted" and rarely injected intravenously. Because they are produced in clandestine laboratories, they are seldom pure, and the dose in a tablet, in a capsule, or on a square of impregnated paper may be expected to vary considerably. The names of these drugs are sometimes used to misrepresent other chemicals.

Psilocybin and Psilocyn

Like the peyote cactus, Psilocybe mushrooms have been used for centuries in traditional Indian rites. When they are eaten, these "sacred" or "magic" mushrooms affect mood and perception in a manner similar to mescaline and LSD. Their active ingredients, psilocybin, and psilocyn, are chemically related to LSD. They can now be made synthetically, but much of what is sold under these names on the illicit market consists of other chemical compounds.

LSD (LSD-25, lysergide)

LSD is an abbreviation of the German expression for lysergic acid diethylamide. It is produced from lysergic acid, a substance derived from the ergot fungus which grows on rye or from lysergic acide amide, a chemical found in morning glory seeds; both of these precursor chemicals are in Schedule III of the ICSA. It was first synthesized in 1938. Its psychotomimetic effects were discovered in 1943 when a chemist accidentally took some LSD. As he began to experience the effects now known as a "trip," he was aware of vertigo and an intensification of light; closing his eyes, he saw a stream of fantastic images of extraordinary vividness accompanied by a kaleidoscopic play of colors. This condition lasted for about two hours.

Because of the extremely high potency of LSD, its structural relationship to a chemical which is present in the brain, and its similarity in effects to certain aspects of psychosis, LSD was used as a tool of research to study the mechanism of mental illness. It was later adopted by the drug culture. Although its popularity declined after the 1960s, there are indications that its illicit use is once again increasing.

LSD is usually sold in the form of tablets, thin squares of gelatin ("window panes"), or impregnated paper ("blotter acid"). The average effective oral dose is from 30 to 50 micrograms, but the amount per dosage unit varies greatly. The effects of higher doses persist for 10 to 12 hours. Tolerance develops rapidly.

Phencyclidine (PCP) and Related Drugs

According to a consensus of drug treatment professionals, phencyclidine now poses greater risks to the user than any other drugs of abuse.

Phencyclidine was investigated in the 1950s as a human anesthetic, but because of side effects of confusion and delerium its development for human use was discontinued. It became commercially available for use in veterinary medicine in the 1960s under the trade name Sernylan. In 1978, however, the manufacturer stopped production. That same year phencyclidine was transferred from Schedule III to Schedule II of the CSA, together with two previously unscheduled precursor chemicals. Most if not all phencyclidine on the U.S. illicit market is produced in clandestine laboratories.

The drug is as variable in its effects as it is in its appearance. A moderate amount often produces in the user a sense of detachment, distance, and estrangement from his surroundings. Numbness, slurred or blocked speech, and a loss of coordination may be accompanied by a sense of strength and invulnerability. A blank stare, rapid and involuntary eye movements, and an exaggerated gait are among the more common observable effects.

Auditory hallucinations, image distortion as in a fun-house mirror, and severe mood disorders may also occur, producing in some acute anxiety and a feeling of impending doom, in others paranoia and violent hostility. PCP is unique among popular drugs of abuse in its power to produce psychoses indistinguishable from schizophrenia. Although such extreme psychic reactions are usually associated with repeated use of the drug, they have been known to occur in some cases after only one dose and to last or recur intermittently, long after the drug has left the body.

Modification of the manufacturing process may further yield chemically related analogs, capable of producing, so far as is known, similar psychic effects. Three of these analogs have so far been encountered on the U.S. illicit market, where they have been sold as PCP.

In view of the severe behavioral toxicity of phencyclidine and its analogs, the Congress in November 1978 passed legislation imposing penalties for the manufacture of these chemicals, or possession with intent to distribute them, more severe than for any other non-narcotic violation under the CSA. (For a first offense, a term of imprisonment of up to 10 years, a fine up to $25,000, or both; for a second offense, imprisonment up to 20 years, a fine of $50,000, or both.) Legislation was also passed which makes it mandatory to report all sales of the common precursor chemical piperidine, its salts, and acyl derivatives to the Drug Enforcement Administration.

Chapter 19

Drugs of Abuse – Cannabis (Marijuana, Hashish, Hashish Oil)

Cannabis sativa L., the hemp plant, grows wild throughout most of the tropic and temperate regions of the world, it is a single species. This plant has long been cultivated for the tough fiber of the stem, the seed used in feed mixtures, and the oil as an ingredient of paint, as well as for its biologically active substances most highly concentrated in the leaves and resinous flowering tops.

The plant material has been used as a drug for centuries. In 1839 it entered the annals of western medicine with the publication of an article surveying its therapeutic potential, including possible uses as an analgesic and anticonvulsant agent. It was alleged to be effective in treating a wide range of physical and mental ailments during the remainder of the 19th century. With the introduction of many new synthetic drugs in the 20th century, interest in it as a medication waned.

The controls imposed with the passage of the Marijuana Tax Act of 1937 further curtailed its use in treatment, and by 1941 it had been deleted from the U.S. Pharmacopoeia and the National Formulary, the official compendia of drugs. But advances continued to be made in the chemistry of cannabis. Among the many cannabinoids synthesized by the plant are cannabinol, cannabidiol, cannabinolidic acids, cannabigeral, cannabichromene, and several isomers of tetrahydrocannabinol, one of which is believed responsible for most of its characteristic psychoactive effects. This is delta-9-telrahydrocannabinol (THC), one of 61 cannabinoids, which are unique chemicals found only in cannabis.

Cannabis products are usually smoked in the form of loosely rolled cigarettes ("Joints"). They may be used alone or in combination with other substances. They may also be administrated orally, but are reported to be about three times more potent when smoked. The effects are felt within minutes, reach their peak in 10 to 30 minutes, and may linger for two or three hours. A condensed description of these effects is apt to be inadequate or even misleading, so much depends upon the experience and expectations of the individual as well as the activity of the drug itself. Low doses tend to induce restlessness and an increasing sense of well-being, followed by a dreamy state of relaxation and, frequently hunger, especially a craving for sweets. Changes of sensory perception—a more vivid sense of sight, smell, touch, taste, and hearing—may be accompanied by subtle alterations in thought formation and expression. Stronger doses intensify these reactions.

The individual may experience shifting sensory imagery, rapidly fluctuating emotions, and fragmentary thoughts with disturbed associations; an altered sense of self-identity; impaired memory, and a dulling of attention despite an illusion of heightened insight. This state of intoxication may not be noticeable to an observer. High doses may result in image distortions, a loss of personal identity, fantasies and hallucinations, and very high doses in a toxic psychosis.

During the past ten years there has been a resurgence in the scientific study of cannabis, one goal of which has been to develop therapeutic agents which, if used as directed in medical treatment, will not produce harmful side effects. While THC can now by synthesized in the laboratory, it is a liquid insoluble in water, and it decomposes on exposure to air and light, so that it is difficult to prepare stable dosage units.

Two of the most active areas of research are for the control of nausea and vomiting caused by chemotherapeutic agents used in the treatment of cancer and for decreasing intraocular pressure in the treatment of glaucoma. None of the synthetic cannabinoids have so far been detected in the drug traffic.

Three types of drugs that come from cannabis are currently distributed on the U.S. illicit market. Having no currently accepted medical use in treatment in the United States, they remain under Schedule I of the CSA. (Some states have approved its medical use recently.)

Marijuana

The term marijuana is used in this country to refer to the cannabis plant and to any part or extract of it that produces somatic or psychic changes in man. A tobacco like substance produced by drying the leaves and flowering tops of the plant, marijuana varies significantly in its potency, depending on the source and selectivity of plant materials used. Most wild U.S. cannabis is considered inferior because of a low concentration of THC, usually less than 0.5 percent. Jamaican, Colombia, and Mexican varieties range between 0.5 and 4 percent.

The most selective product is reputed to be Sinsemilla (Spanish, sin semilla; without seed), prepared from the unpollenated female cannabis plant, samples of which have been found to contain up to 6 percent THC. Southeast Asian "Thai sticks," consisting of marijuana buds bound onto short sections of bamboo, are also encountered infrequently on the U.S. illicit market.

Hashish

The Middle East is the main source of hashish. It consists of the drug-rich resinous secretions of the cannabis plant, which are collected, dried, and then compressed into a variety of forms, such as balls, cakes, or cookie-like sheets. Hashish in the United States varies in potency as in appearance, ranging in THC content from trace amounts up to 10 percent. The average is reported to be 1.8 percent.

Hashish Oil

The name comes from the drug culture and is a misnomer in suggesting any resemblance to hashish other than its objective of further concentration. Hashish oil is produced by a process of repeated extraction of cannabis plant materials to yield a dark viscous liquid, current samples of which average about 20 percent THC. In terms of its psychoactive effect, a drop or two of this liquid on a cigarette is equal to a single "joint" of marijuana.

The laws relative to marijuana use may on a state by state basis (or even federally) be decriminalized. Law authorities may be less interested in young people carrying around a few grams in their pockets. The group worker must keep in mind that this does not represent condoning or approval of government of marijuana. Nor does this imply that marijuana is not a harmful drug.

Graften Publications of New York, in a short but very informative pamphlet, "Marijuana,"[17] points out that government officials are worried about the wrong ideas some people may draw from decriminalization. They are concerned about the unintended message that seems to go along with recent changes in the law. Dr. Robert DuPont, director of the National Institute on Drug Abuse, has been reported to be concerned about the "surplus meaning" of decriminalization—about the danger of giving people a false message of permissiveness.

For there are still a lot of problems about marijuana—none of which has anything to do with decriminalization. A recent California survey shows that 22 percent of drivers stopped for drunken driving had marijuana in their bloodstreams. Decriminalization won't change that by one percentage point. All that decriminalization says is that some states are tired of spending up to $13,000 a year per person to keep basically law-abiding young people in jail because they were carrying some marijuana. That doesn't say that pot is useful, like toothpaste, or harmless, like hair tonic.

In other words, don't skip the decision-making process because some government units have decided to decriminalize marijuana. The decision as to whether to use marijuana or not to use it is a serious and important decision.

---

[17]Reprinted with permission of Graften Publications, New York, N.Y., Samuel Graften, editor.

The Graften pamphlet goes on to say that marijuana is not to be equated with alcohol—

> It was argued a few years ago that marijuana was "the young people's alcohol." It turns out that comparing alcohol and marijuana is comparing two things that have little to do with each other—like comparing horses and umbrellas. Marijuana, for instance, can cause almost immediate hallucinations, while alcohol does not produce hallucinations until the drinking disease is far advanced—as has recently been pointed out by Dr. Nicholas A. Pace, head of the New York City affiliate of the National Council on Alcoholism. (We are not arguing in favor of alcohol here, and certainly Dr. Pace wasn't—we are just pointing out differences.)

The Addiction and Substance Abuse report, August 1979, a service of Graften Publications, Inc., reported that marijuana *received far less than a clean bill of health* on July 19, 1974, when Dr. William Pollin, director of the National Institute on Drug Abuse, appeared before the Select Committee on Narcotic Abuse and Control of the House of Representatives.

"We are very concerned about the health hazards of marijuana use," Dr. Pollin began his statement. He went on to declare: "Mr. Chairman, presently available evidence clearly indicates that *marijuana is not a 'safe' substance* . . . I would like to briefly indicate to the Committee what the hazards of marijuana use are for adolescents and to various organs and systems of the human body . . ."

Under the heading: "Acute Intoxication Impairs Learning, Memory and Intellectual Performance," Dr. Pollin testified:

> Virtually all of the many studies which have been done of performance while 'high' converge toward the conclusion that marijuana interferes with immediate memory and intellectual performance in ways that impair thinking, reading comprehension, verbal and arithmetic problem solving. Less familiar, more difficult tasks are interfered with more than well-learned performance, and the effect depends on the amount used and the tolerance for the effect.

On the key issue of safe driving, Dr. Pollin testified (under the title "Marijuana Intoxication Impairs Driving and Other Skilled Performance"):

> Evidence strongly suggests that being 'high' interferes with driving, flying and other complex psycho-motor performance at usual levels of social usage . . . there is reason for believing that more marijuana users drive today while 'high' than was true in the past. As use becomes increasingly common and socially acceptable, as the risk of arrest for simple possession decreases, still more people are likely to risk driving while 'high.' In limited

> surveys from 60 percent to 80 percent of marijuana users questioned indicated that they sometimes drive while high . . .

A point to note is that some of the "performance decrements" resulting from marijuana use may persist for some time, "possibly several hours," said Dr. Pollin, beyond the "period of subjective intoxication." In other words, *the marijuana smoker's driving may be impaired even after he feels he is no longer under the influence,* and no longer feels 'high.'

Chapter 20

Drugs of Abuse – Ready Reference Indicators

This chapter is devoted to a series of tables, relating to data that a group worker can use for "on the spot" information relative to slang terms for drugs, as well as the uses and effects of controlled substances.

Table I
Glossary of Slang Terms for Drugs

Amphetamines

Beans, Bennies, Black Beauties, Black Mollies, Copilots, Crank, Crossroads, Crystal, Dexies, Double Cross, Meth, Minibennies, Pep Pills, Speed, Rosas, Roses, Thrusters, Truck Drivers, Uppers, Wake-ups, Whites.

Barbiturates

Barbs, Blockbusters, Bluebirds, Blue Devils, Blues, Christmas Trees, Downers, Green Dragons, Mexican Reds, Nebbies, Nimbies, Pajaro Rojo, Pink Ladies, Rainbows, Red and Blues, Redbirds, Red Devils, Reds, Sleeping Pills, Stumblers, Yellow Jackets, Yellows.

Cocaine

Blow, C, Coca, Coke, Flake, Girl, Heaven Dust, Lady, Mujer, Nose Candy, Paradise, Perico, Polvo Blanco, Rock, Snow, White.

Hashish

Goma de Mota, Hash, Soles.

Heroin

Big H, Boy, Brown, Brown Sugar, Cabalio, Chiva, Crap, Estuffa, H. Heroina, Hombre, Horse, Junk, Mexican Mud, Polvo, Scag, Smack, Stuff, Thing.

LSD

Acid, Blotter Acid, California Sunshine, Haze, Microdots, Paper Acid, Purple Haze, Sunshine, Wedges, Window Panes.

(Continued)

Table I

Marijuana

Acapulco Gold, Cannabis, Colombia, Ganga, Grass, Griffa, Hemp, Herb, J, Jay, Joint, Mary Jane, Mota, Mutah, Panama Red, Pot, Reefer, Sativa, Smoke, Stick, Tea, Weed, Yerba.

Peyote

Buttons, Cactus, Mesc, Mescal, Mescal Buttons.

Methaqualone

Quaalude, Quads, Quas, Soapers, Sopes, Sopor.

Morphine

Cube, First Line, Goma, Morf, Morfina, Morpho, Morphy, Mud.

Phencyclidine

Angel Dust, Crystal, Cyclone, Hog, PCP, Peace Pill, Rocket Fuel, Supergrass, TIC TAC.

(Concluded)

Table II
Schedule Designation and Medical Uses

Drugs	**Schedule**	**Medical Uses**
Narcotics		
Opium	II, III, V	Analgesic, antidiarrheal
Morphine	II, III	Analgesic, anti-tussive
Codeine	II, III, V	Analgesic, anti-tussive
Heroin	I	Under investigation
Hydromorphone		Analgesic
Meperidine (Pethidine)		Analgesic
Methadone	II	Analgesic heroin substitute
Other Narcotics	I, II, III, IV, V	Analgesic, anti-diarrheal, anti-tussive
Depressants		
Chloral Hydrate	IV	Hypnotic
Barbiturates	II, III, IV	Anesthetic, anti-convulsant, sedative hypnotic
Glutethimide	III	

(Continued)

Table II

Drugs	Schedule	Medical Uses
Methadqualone	II	Sedative, hypnotic
Benzodiazepines	IV	Anti-anxiety, anticonvulsant, sedative, hypnotic
Other Depressants	III, IV	Anti-anxiety, sedative, hypnotic
Stimulants		
Cocaine	II	Local anesthetic
Phenmetrazine	II, III	Hyperkinesis, Narcolepsy
Methylphenidate	II	Weight Control
Other Stimulants		
Hallucinogens		
LSD		
Mescaline & Peyote	I	None
Amphetamine Variants		
Phencyclidine	II	Veterinary anesthetic
Phencyclidine Analogs		
Other Hallucinogens	I	None
Cannabis		
Marijuana		
Tetrahydrocannabinol	I	Under investigation
Hashish		
Hashish Oil		None

Table 3
Dependence Factors, Tolerance, Duration of Effects

Drugs	Physical Dependence	Psychological Dependence	Tolerance	Duration of Effect (in hours)
Narcotics				
Opium	High	High	Yes	3-6
Morphine	High	High	Yes	3-6
Codeine	Moderate	Moderate	Yes	3-6
Heroin	High	High	Yes	3-6
Hydromorphine	High	High	Yes	3-6
Meperidine	High	High	Yes	3-6
Methadone	High	High	Yes	12-24
Depressants				
Chloral Hydrate	Moderate	Moderate	Possible	5-8
Barbiturates	High to Moderate	High to Moderate	Yes	1-16
Glutethimide	High	High	Yes	4-8
Methaqualone	High	High	Yes	4-8
Benzodiazepines	Low	Low	Yes	4-8
Stimulants				
Cocaine	Possible	High	Possible	1-2
Amphetamines	Possible	High	Yes	2-4
Phenmetrazine	Possible	High	Yes	2-4
Methylphenidate	Possible	High	Yes	2-4
Hallucinogens				
LSD	None	Degree Unknown	Yes	8-12
Mescaline & Peyote	None	Degree Unknown	Yes	8-12
Amphetamine Variants	Unknown	Degree Unknown	Yes	Up to Days
Phencyclidine	Unknown	High	Yes	Variable
Phencyclidine Analogs	Degree Unknown	Degree Unknown	Yes	Variable
Cannabis				
Marijuana	Degree Unknown	Moderate	Yes	2-4
Tetrahydro-cannabinol	Degree Unknown	Moderate	Yes	2-4
Hashish	Degree Unknown		Yes	2-4
Hashish Oil	Unknown	Moderate	Yes	2-4

Table IV
Usual Methods of Administration

Drugs	Usual Methods of Administration
Narcotics	
Opium	Oral, smoked
Morphine	Oral, injected, smoked
Codeine	Oral, injected
Heroin	Injected, sniffed, smoked
Hydromorphone	
Meperidine (Pethidine)	
Methadone	Oral, injected
Other Narcotics	
Depressants	
Chloral Hydrate	
Barbiturates	
Glutethimide	
Methaqualone	Oral, injected
Benzodiazepines	
Other Depressants	
Stimulants	
Cocaine	Sniffed, injected
Amphetamines	
Phenmetrazine	Oral, injected
Methylphenidate	
Other Stimulants	Oral
Hallucinogens	
LSD	Oral
Mescaline and Peyote	Oral, injected
Amphetamine Variants	
Phencyclidine	
Phencyclidine Acids	Smoked, oral, injected
Cannabis	
Marijuana	
Tetrahydrocannabinol	
Hashish	Smoked, oral
Hashish Oil	

Table V
Possible Effects, Effects of Overdose, Withdrawal Syndrome

Possible Effects	Effects of Overdose	Withdrawal Syndrome
Narcotics		
Euphoria, drowsiness, respiratory depression, constricted pupils, nausea	Slow and shallow breathing, clammy skin, convulsions, coma, possible death	Watery eyes, runny noses, yawning, loss of appetite irritability, tremors, panic, chills and sweating, cramps, nausea
Depressants		
Slurred speech, disorientation, drunken behavior without odor of alcohol	Shallow respiration, cold and clammy skin, dilated pupils, weak and rapid pulse, coma, possible death	Anxiety, insomnia, tremors, delirium, convulsions, possible death
Stimulants		
Increased alertness, excitation, euphoria, increased pulse rate and blood pressure, insomnia, loss of appetite	Agitation, increase in body temperature, hallucinations, convulsions, possible death	Apathy, long periods of sleep, irritability, depression, disorientation
Hallucinogens		
Illusions and hallucinations, poor perception of time and distance	Longer, more intense "trip" episodes, psychosis, possible death	Withdrawal syndrome not reported
Cannabis		
Euphoria, relaxed inhibitions, increased appetite, disoriented behavior	Fatigue, paranoia, possible psychosis	Insomnia, hyperactivity, and decreased appetite occasionally reported

REFERENCES

Department of Justice, *Drug Enforcement.* Drug Enforcement Administration, July 1979.

Graften Publications, Inc. *Marijuana,* 1977.

Lesser, B. The Youth Advisors Handbook. Nealco Publishing Co., 1970.

New Dawn Magazine. "A Young Woman's Guide to Drugs." Spring, 1979.

Chapter 21

Teenage Alcoholism

Alcohol use among teenagers has been increasing. Dr. Thomas C. Harford[8] of the National Institute of Alcohol Abuse and Alcoholism estimated, as far back as in July 1976, that approximately 39% of the in-school adolescent population of the U.S. are at least moderate drinkers and that 28% may be problem drinkers. It then becomes incumbent for the group worker to become acquainted with and to recognize the signs that portend alcohol problem manifestations among the group members. If the group worker is to make a contribution toward even a modicum of intervention (leading to treatment) they must gain some knowledges of the parental drinking models, peer structure and other aspects of the social network supporting teenage alcohol use.

Numerous surveys of adolescent populations, mostly high school students, have shown that a substantial proportion of teenagers consume alcoholic beverages at least occasionally. It has been estimated that between 70% and 90% of teenagers have tried alcohol. These estimates are not surprising in view of the fact that the majority of adults consume alcohol. Adolescence is the period of transition from an abstinence culture of children to a drinking culture of adults. For the majority of teenagers, drinking is an integral aspect of adolescent development.

The nearly universal use of alcohol by teenagers is not as troubling as the high rate of alcohol abuse which accompanies it. In a 1974 national survey, 30% of high school students reported that they had been "pretty drunk" at least once during the previous month, and 7% said they had been drunk four or five more times.

Another indicator of alcohol abuse by young people was provided by the Department of Justice Uniform Crime Report for 1973, which covers the period of 1960 through 1973. Arrests of persons under age 18 for alcohol-related offenses (i.e., driving while intoxicated, liquor law violations, and drunkenness) increased 135% during this 13 year period. Arrests for driving while intoxicated increased in this age group more than 400%.

---

[8]Adapted from "Post Graduate Magazine," July 1976 issue, by T.C. Harford. Permission granted by Daniel M. Kelley, Publishers, Minneapolis, Minnesota.

The Research Triangle Institute of North Carolina, under contract to the National Institute on Alcohol Abuse and Alcoholism, recently conducted a national survey to determine alcohol use among junior and senior high school students in the United States. This survey provides the most recent and comprehensive data on the extent and nature of adolescent alcohol use in this country.

Five drinking classifications, weighted for the national adolescent (in-school) population, were derived from the reports of adolescents on the frequency and quantity of their own alcohol use. The percentage in each classification follows.

- Abstainers (those who do not drink or who do so less than once a year) – 27%.
- Infrequent-to-light drinkers (those who drink once a month at most) – 33%; within this category, 16% consume one drink per typical setting and 16% consume medium amounts, 2 to 4 drinks, per typical setting.
- Moderate drinkers (those who drink at least once a week with small amounts per occasion or those who drink three or four times a month with medium amounts, 2 to 4 drinks, per setting) – 15%.
- Moderate-to-heavy drinkers (those who drink at least once a week with medium amounts, 2 to 4 drinks, per typical setting or those who drink three or four times a month with large amounts, 5 to 12 drinks, per occasion) – 14%.
- Heavy drinkers (those who drink at least once a week with large amounts, 5 to 12 drinks, per occasion) – 11%.

Regarding frequency of alcohol use, this survey indicated that 33.8% of U.S. junior and senior high school students drink once a month at most, 17.3% drink three or four times per month, and 21.6% drink at least once per week. Approximately 39% can be classified as at least moderate drinkers.

The study included demographic characteristics of the adolescents surveyed. Age and sex distributions are consistent with those of previous surveys; results indicate that more boys than girls drink and that amount and frequency of drinking increase with age. The amount of drinking among girls, however, is not low (approximately 18% are at least moderate-to-heavy drinkers) and reflects an increased proportion of girls who drink in 1974 compared with survey findings over the past decade.

The age distributions are also consistent with reports that increased numbers of younger teenagers have become alcohol consumers. Approximately 24% of adolescents age 13 and under are classified as at least moderate drinkers.

Some very interesting facts relating to teenage drinking has been published by the National Institute on Alcohol Abuse and Alcoholism to wit:

The *Second Special Report to the U.S. Congress on Alcohol and Health from the Secretary of Health, Education, and Welfare,* reporting on the 1974 survey, states that a significant proportion of the young alcohol users showed signs of problem drinking.

The number of regular drinkers, the quantity of alcohol consumed and the frequency of use increase proportionately with age among the school population, the national survey revealed. Among other major findings were these:

1) Two-thirds of teenage drinkers use alcohol primarily without parental supervision.
2) More boys than girls drink.
3) Boys generally consume larger quantities of alcohol than girls.

Drinking Contexts

Young people drink for a variety of reasons, but the most potent influences on drinking behavior seem to derive from parents and peers. Surveys indicate that over the last ten years, parental attitudes have changed, becoming more permissive of alcohol use by their children. In addition, young people themselves are more tolerant of drinking among their peers than were the youth of ten years ago.

For many adolescents, alcohol use seems to be an integral part of growing up in America. Drinking is one of several behaviors which resesarchers have identified as markers in the transition from adolescent to adult status.

Who are the teenage drinkers? They "represent all levels of scholastic achievement and aspiration—53 percent expect to go through college and beyond," according to another survey of young people conducted for the National Highway Safety Traffic Administration (NHSTA) in 1974. Those who drink "report the same range of sports and extracurricular activities as the students who are not involved in social drinking" the survey said.

Problem Drinkers

While most young people who drink do not use alcohol in a destructive way, there are as many as 1.1 million young people who can be considered problem drinkers. Five percent of the students in grades 7 through 12 polled in the NIAAA national survey reported getting "high" or "tight" at least once a week, and could on this basis be considered problem drinkers. On a less conservative criterion of problem drinking—getting drunk four or more times a year—approximately 23 percent of the students surveyed showed a potential for problem drinking.

Figures on youthful alcohol abuse and problem drinking may be low since most surveys do not include young people who are not in school. Studies indicate that among school dropouts and institutionalized delinquents there is a higher proportion of drinkers, and pathological drinkers, than among their peers who remain in school.

It is interesting to note that of a national sample of adults, the 18-20 year old group had the largest proportion of persons who had experienced some problem with drinking (27 percent).

Young people who have drinking problems often suffer from a variety of related adjustment or personality problems, exhibiting such characteristics as physical aggression, earlier and more sexual activity, greater use of other drugs, and parental defiance. Children of alcoholic parents are considered an especially high risk group in terms of developing alcoholism. Research strongly indicates that these young people are more likely than their peers to experience alcohol-related and other problems both during adolescence and later in life.

Adolescence is a turbulent period of physical and emotional changes and, for some young people, abusing alcohol is a way of acting out the negative feelings and fears that often accompany such changes. Many adolescents who misuse alcohol will outgrow the habit as they mature, but the eventuality that alcohol abuse may be outgrown makes its possible consequences no less serious, according to NIAAA officials. Alcohol abuse can lead (persons of any age group) into a variety of problems, with friends, family and even the law. For instance, a survey of teenage drinking practices noted that "there is an alarming amount of drinking and driving taking place among a large, mainstream group of U.S. youth." It seems, according to various studies, that the combination of inexperience behind the wheel and inexperience in drinking is a potentially deadly one.

The culprit in this scenario is alcohol. But how many of our youth group workers and aides have even a rudimentary knowledge of the nature of alcohol and alcohol beverages? The author guesses that only a limited number would answer in the affirmative. Therefore the following exposition developed by the New Jersey Department of Health should be of some help.

The term "alcohol" can refer generally to any one of a family of intoxicating chemicals. The alcohol of particular interest to use here because it is the chief ingredient of alcoholic beverages is known to chemists as ethyl alcohol or ethanol. For convenience, however, we shall refer to ethyl alcohol simply as "alcohol."

In its pure form alcohol is a colorless, almost odorless liquid with a sharp burning taste. It is produced naturally by fermentation, a chemical process set in motion when a tiny plant, called yeast, is allowed to grow in a solution of sugar. You may have noticed that sweet cider, for example, or grape juice start to change after standing too long. This happens because yeast is widely distributed in nature. It floats in the air, ready to drop into any suitable materials and go to work. During fermentation, yeast converts sugar into alcohol and a gas called carbon dioxide.

This fermentation process, by the way, is the same as that of raising bread with yeast. In baking, the carbon dioxide gas is caught and held as bubbles in the dough, giving it a porous texture, while most of the alcohol which is formed is driven out by the heat. The reverse is true in the production of alcoholic beverages: the carbon dioxide is allowed to escape into the air (except in the production of "sparkling" wines) and the alcohol is retained.

Unless interrupted, the process of fermentation continues until all of the sugar is converted to alcohol, or until so much alcohol is produced that it stops the yeast from working. This latter happens when the alcohol content reaches about 14%. But as soon as the action of the yeast is over, another process is ready to start unless it is controlled. Also abundant in the air are even tinier organisms, bacteria. One particular variety of bacteria can change the alcohol into another chemical called acetic acid, which we know as vinegar. This is why wine that is permitted to stand exposed to air for some time turns sour.

Distilled Spirits

In addition to wines and beers, there is a large class of liquors called distilled spirits. This family of beverages includes whiskey (scotch, bourbon, rye), brandy gin, and vodka, as well as a variety of cordials and liqueurs. Though these liquors are very different from one another, they are grouped together because the process of distillation is a necessary step in their production.

Distilling is a way of producing a beverage with a high alcoholic content. It is based on the principle that alcohol boils and vaporizes (turns into steam) at a lower temperature than water. Thus, when a fermented brew is heated, alcohol vapors are given off first. These vapors are directed through a cooling tube into a separate container, and condensed back into a liquid. The resulting fluid, the distilled spirits, has a high alcohol content.

Distilled spirits, then, contain no solids, minerals, or vitamins, but only water, alcohol, and small amounts of flavoring materials from the original brew which give to each kind of beverage its characteristic taste and aroma. Whiskey is distilled from fermented cereals or grains such as rye, corn, or barley; brandy derives from the distillates of fruit; and rum is distilled from fermented molasses. Gin is alcohol steeped in juniper berries, and cordials and liquers are alcoholic distillates to which herbs, syrups, or other flavorings have been added.

Distilled spirits are often 40% to 50% alcohol. The exact alcohol strength of distilled liquors is represented on each bottle in terms of "proof." The "proof" of a particular beverage is exactly twice its alcoholic content. Thus a 100 proof liquor is 50% alcohol, an 86% proof whiskey is 43% alcohol, and so forth.

Since the alcoholic content of liquors is one of the most significant factors in their physical effect it might be useful to keep in mind a simple equation: 1 1/2 ounces of unfortified wine, and one 12 ounce bottle of beer each contain approximately one-half ounce of pure alcohol.

We can now see that an alcoholic beverage can be considered a food only in a very limited technical sense. It does supply calories, or units of heat-energy, much as sugar does. But the vitamin and mineral content of beer and wines is extremely minimal, and that of distilled spirits negligible.

As one can see, people who drink one glass of wine, one can of beer, or one shot of hard liquor are all having about the same amount of alcohol. Many people think that someone who has a drink of hard liquor is taking a "stronger" drink—one with more alcohol in it—than a person who drinks a can of beer or a glass of wine. As we can see, this isn't true.

However, many people put more than one shot of hard liquor in their glass. Often they make mixed drinks (hard liquor mixed with juice or soda) which have two or three shots of hard liquor in them. As a result, many mixed drinks have two or three times as much alcohol as a can of beer or glass of wine. Martinis and Manhattans ("cocktails") for example, are made by adding hard liquor to wine. As a result, they usually have two or three times as much alcohol as a glass of wine or can of beer. The amount of alcohol in a mixed drink depends on how much hard liquor it was made with.

A simplistic resume as to how the alcohol passes through the body follows:

- **Mouth.** Alcohol is drunk.
- **Stomach.** Alcohol goes right into the stomach. A little of the alcohol goes through the wall of the stomach and into the bloodstream. But most of the alcohol goes down into the small intestine.
- **Small intestines.** Alcohol goes from the stomach into the small intestines. Most of the alcohol then goes through the wall of the intestine and into the bloodstream.
- **Bloodstream.** The bloodstream then carries the alcohol to all parts of the body, such as the brain, heart and liver.
- **Liver.** As the bloodstream carries the alcohol around the body, it carries it through the liver, too. The liver changes the alcohol to water, carbon dioxide, and energy. This process is called oxidation. The liver can oxidize (change into water, carbon dioxide, and energy) only about one-half ounce of alcohol an hour. This means that until the liver has time to oxidize all of the alcohol, the alcohol keeps on passing through all parts of the body, including the brain.
- **Brain.** Alcohol goes to the brain almost as soon as it is drunk. The bloodstream carries it there. Alcohol keeps passing through the brain until the liver has had tme to change (oxidize) all the alcohol into carbon dioxide, water, and energy.

Alcohol's Effects on Teenagers

Drinking often has a stronger effect on teenagers than it does on older people. There are three reasons for this.

- First, most teenagers weigh less than older people. As we've seen, the less people weigh, the more effect alcohol has on them.
- Drinking also can have a greater effect on teenagers because they have not yet learned to compensate or make up for what alcohol does to them. It

takes years for baseball outfielders to learn how to compensate for the wind when a fly ball is hit their way. Just as outfielders have to tell themselves, "slow down because the wind is going to hold up the ball" so people who get clumsy after two or three drinks have to learn to say to themselves, "Don't grab for the salt; reach very slowly." This ability to compensate for alcohol's effects, we noted, is called psychological tolerance.

● Finally, teenagers, often have more stresses than older people. The teen years for most people are a difficult time of life. Many new things happen to them which are often both exciting and frightening–for example, independence, a paying job, sex, a car, travel and so on. When alcohol is added to something which we're not used to and which is also very exciting or somewhat frightening, it can make it harder for us to control how we feel and what we do while drinking.

Who are Problem Drinkers and Alcoholics?
– General Population

What do we really mean when we say somebody drinks too much? What's too much? To some people, it's any alcohol at all. To others, its getting drunk. To some people, drinking two cocktails every evening or during lunch is too much.

Of course, we would all agree that getting drunk every day is too much. We would also agree that someone who doesn't drink any alcohol is certainly not drinking too much. But except for obvious examples like these, one has to decide for himself what is "too much."

One way to decide is to see whether someone's drinking is causing any problems. If so, that person is drinking too much. The problem may be with friends, at work,in school, at home, or with driving a car. The problem may be obvious, like a drunk-driving accident. Or the problem may be hidden, like damage to the liver.

There are two kinds of people who drink too much: *problem drinkers and alcoholics.* Both kinds have problems because they drink too much. But in other respects they differ.

Problem drinkers: First of all, problem drinkers may not drink very often. For example, the person who gets high while bowling or playing cards only on Friday evenings and then drives home, has a drinking problem even if she or he doesn't touch alcohol for the rest of the week. Such a person is risking a serious traffic accident 52 times a year. A person with a serious ulcer may set a limit of one martini a day before dinner. However, since alcohol in concentrated doses irritates the stomach this person too, may have a drinking problem.

Most problem drinkers not only drink less often than alcoholics, they can also control their drinking if they want to. If ordered by a doctor to stop or reduce their drinking, they probably could do so. Problem drinkers can also drink socially—that is, not get high or drunk if they feel the situation calls for staying sober.

Alcoholics: There are, however, people who cannot control drinking at all or only with great difficulty and for short periods of time. Such people are called alcoholics. Usually, alcoholics spend at least part of every day not just drinking, but getting high or drunk. And they can't drink socially: if they take one drink, they keep right on drinking until they're drunk.

However, some alcoholics can go through the major part of an entire day—every day—without drinking. But as soon as they get off work or as soon as the weekend arrives, they drink until they get drunk. Unlike the problem drinker, they must get drunk those evenings or weekends.

Because some alcoholics seem to be able to control their drinking, it is often difficult to tell the difference between problem drinkers and alcoholics. In addition, a problem drinker may simply be an alcoholic in an early stage of his or her distress.

There may be as many as ten million alcoholics in America today and several million more problem drinkers. While we hear a lot about how many teenagers "get into trouble" with "drugs," many more youths have problems with the drug alcohol than with all other drugs combined. In a recent survey of 13,000 junior and senior high school students across the country, nearly one in ten indicated he or she had problems connected with alcohol during the past year.

Some people think that the poor have most of the drinking problems, but in fact, people from every social class and ethnic group have drinking problems. And while more men have drinking problems than women, there may be as many as two million women alcoholics in America. Women alcoholics tend to hide their drinking more than men because "it doesn't look nice" for women to be seen drunk and because many alcoholic housewives drink only at home.

Behavior Reactions to Alcohol

The "Do It Now Foundation," Institute for Chemical Survival, has printed a handy pamphlet relating to the use of alcohol while performing other activity such as driving an automobile.

The alcohol-automobile combination is so spectacular that it even eclipses some of alcohol's achievements in other fields. Recent studies indicate alcohol may also be a factor in almost half of all drownings. Forty to sixty percent of all bone fractures involve alcohol. One-third of the general aviation pilots killed recently had a measurable blood-alcohol concentration in their bodies. One-half of all murders and fifty to sixty percent of all drug overdoses involve alcohol.

Alcohol can be counted on to be involved in more than its share on almost any accident statistic sheet. And you don't have to be dead drunk to incresae your chances of being added to a statistic sheet. A single mixed drink or a couple of beers noticeably affect judgment and coordination in controlled tests. Commercial pilots aren't allowed to drink any alcoholic beverages at all within 24 hours of flight time.

The laws of most states say when your blood-alcohol concentration reaches .10 percent you are too intoxicated to drive. Your own personal limit however, may be well below that. Increased accident causation is noticeable at 0.04 percent, and the probability is at least six times as great at 0.10 percent. The 0.05 to 0.10 range is critical. Somewhere in that range you've had too much to perform activities that require any degree or coordination or judgment. In particular, you're too intoxicated to drive. On the highway you're risking people besides yourself.

The concentration of alcohol attained in the blood depends on several things:

- The amount of alcohol (number and strength of drinks)
- Time elapsed since drinking began
- Body weight
- Quantity and kind of food in the stomach (this does not decrease alcohol's absorption into the blood stream, but only slows it).

Let's say you weight 160 pounds, and you drink five or six ounces of 86 proof liquor in a little more than an hour's time. You're at that critical 0.10 percent blood-alcohol mark. Since your body gets rid of alcohol at about 0.018 percent an hour, you have at least four hours to go before you can think about functioning with the same ability you have when sober.

Black coffee, cold showers, fresh air or other folklore remedies will not speed up the burning of alcohol. They may make you a wide-awake drunk, but you're still just as impaired. It might be better to go to sleep.

Some General Facts About Alcoholism

Alcoholism is the most neglected health problem in the United States today. It ranks with cancer and heart disease as a major threat to the nation's health. Deaths from cirrhosis of the liver, one of the many known physical conditions which are part of alcoholism, have increased 67% in the last 20 years.

Alcoholism is a complex, progressive disease in which use of alcohol interferes with health, social and ethnic functioning. Untreated, alcoholism results in physical incapacity, permanent mental damage and/or permanent death. The onset of the disease varies widely and may develop from the first to the twentieth year of drinking.

Some 100 million persons over the age of 15 in this country are consumers of alcohol. Of these, there are an estimated 10 million suffering from the disease of alcoholism.

There is no "typical" person with alcoholism. Among men, drinking problems occur most frequently in their early 20s, and among women most frequently in their 30s and 40s. Each year, about 100,000 drinkers develop alcoholism. The number of known women alcoholics has doubled since World War II. Less than 3% of the people with alcoholism are found on Skid Row.

Between six and ten percent of employees suffer from alcoholism. The total cost to the nation is 25 billion dollars a year due to absenteeism, health and welfare services, property damage and medical expenses. Lost work time alone, because of alcoholism, has been computed to 9.35 billion dollars annually. The human loss to individuals, families and communities is incalculable.

Of all fatal accidents occurring on the roads today, 50% involve alcohol. Two-thirds of these fatal accidents involve an alcoholic. Fifty-three percent of fire deaths, 45% of drownings, 22% of home accidents, 36% of pedestrian accidents, 55% of arrests are linked to misuse of alcohol. Alcoholism accounts for 37.4% of admissions to state and county mental hospitals.

Violent behavior attributed to alcohol misuse accounts for 64% of murders, 41% of assaults, 34% of rapes, 29% of other sex crimes, 30% of suicides, 56% of fights or assaults in the home and 60% of child abuse. When alcoholism is treated, associated violent behavior is known to decrease.

Alcoholism is treatable. Effective business and industry employee alcoholism programs show recovery rates of 65-80%. Air Force and Navy rehabilitation programs report 70-80% recovery rates. Leading clinical therapists report recovery rates of 50-70%.

Alcoholics Anonymous has an estimated 900,000 world membership. Seventy-nine percent of the people sober between one and five years will remain in the AA fellowship. Of the people sober more than five years, 91% will not drink and will remain in the fellowship.

Education, early detection, research efforts and community treatment facilities are the greatest forces operating today for the prevention, control and reduction of alcoholism.

We have gone through the background data and the "how." The unanswered question is "Why"? Why have so many teenagers turned to drink? Jules Saltman in the "New Alcoholics: Teenagers" gives us much to think about.

He asks the question—"Why do youngsters drink and, especially why do some drink heavily? Is it chemistry, alienation, defiance of parents, overwhelming emotional and personality problems, or just the manners and customs of their society." Saltman goes on to reply that teenage drinking seems clearly related to all those factors—and, even more clearly, to the fact that drinking is widely accepted and practiced by adults.

When questioned about their first drink, many youngsters say that it was taken at home with the approval of their parents. Others are started by their friends, generally also with adult knowledge and, often, permission.

In many social, national, and religious groups, the drinking of alcohol is an accepted practice for young and old alike. Among Jews, for example, wine-drinking has a religious connotation on several occasions in the year. People of French of Italian background generally have wine on the table at mealtimes for all ages. In other social groups, beer is a general beverage. In some families, drinking parents even permit their youngsters hard liquor.

The freedom to drink established by ethnic drinking habits does not always have similar results. Jews, Chinese, and Italians, who habitually drink a good deal, have a low ratio of alcoholics.

Among Kentucky mountain people, another group in which drinking is an accepted practice, half the junior high and high school students polled in a survey of seven counties considered themselves "drinkers." And their drinking was unusually heavy, reckless (it included Sterno and paint thinner) and led to trouble. A large number admitted to drinking several times a week, 45.2 percent had gotten into fights or destroyed property while drinking, and 28.3 percent had been injured or arrested because of their behavior while drinking.

The difference between those groups that have problems with drinking and those that do not seems to lie not so much in the extent of their drinking as in how and why they drink.

Search for Adulthood

In an atmosphere in which alcohol is taken for granted, young people start drinking for relatively uncomplicated and largely social reasons. Scientists George L. Maddox and Bevode C. McCall of Duke University, after surveying thousands of youngsters, decided that many teenagers began to drink as part of their normal efforts to take on the role of adults. Since adults approve of drinking and practice it freely in their presence, young people came to regard drinking as a badge of adulthood, and among boys as an evidence of virility. In addition, youngsters point out that the legal drinking age is going down in many states, the armed forces permit young servicemen to drink, and alcohol is widely praised in advertising. Therefore,they say, it must be both desirable and harmless

Asked why they thought adults drank, teenagers told Drs. Maddox and McCall that it was mainly for sociability and self-expression and to bring down their feelings of anxiety. Asked the same with regard to themselves, the youngsters again stressed sociability and self-expression, making little mention of reducing anxieties. Some, but not many, said they drank because their friends expected them to.

Much teenage drinking, however, does seem to be due to pressure from friends. In one region of North Carolina, many people, including the young drinkers themselves, believe that drinking is wrong. In a recent survey, of those youngsters whose parents opposed drinking and whose friends abstained, only a little more than one out of ten drank. However, almost nine out of ten of those whose parents condoned drinking and whose two best friends drank, were drinkers. Even among young people who abstained completely, almost three-quarters of those who had drinking friends confessed to having been pressured into tasting alcohol at least once.

Problems

On the whole, a social atmosphere of permissiveness and even of encouragement of teenage drinking—or simply the availability of alcohol—does not of itself lead to a large number of drinking problems. In a study of close to 3,400 high school boys in Boston, nine out of ten had had "a drinking experience" and more than half were regular light to moderate drinkers. About one-fifth drank heavily, though they suffered few adverse consequences, and only 2 percent were considered problem drinkers.

Often, of course, the apparent absence of problems may only mean a particular social group does not recognize "problems" in commonplace drinking behavior. Nor does it apply the pressure that would create difficulties. One observer of a group of middle-class high school boys in Canada found that many drink at parties (65 percent of those age 15 and over) and many had done so to the point of feeling "high," but difficulties were few. "Drinking occurs typically in a spirit of sociability and fun," says Dr. E. W. Vaz, "and in circumstances in accord with legitimate activities of the middle-class youth culture." Dr. Vaz suggests that such "middle-class delinquency (of which drinking is one measure) does not appear malicious in motive or violent in character. It causes little damage, rarely attracts police attention, and is not likely to be discovered or taken seriously by adults."

Disapproval

The story is different when the social atmosphere is one of disapproval of drinking, one in which most adults abstain. Here proportionately fewer young people drink, but those who do are disobeying their parents and the precepts of their society. Their drinking is an emblem of active rebellion—and they have more trouble as a result of it.

In one community in rural Mississippi, where drinking is frowned upon, only 27 percent of the youngsters studied were classified as "drinkers," but their drinking was often uncontrolled. Aside from not having parental permission, most of these drinkers belonged to churches that condemn alcohol on moral grounds, had to get their alcohol illegally from bootleggers, and tended to drink in secret with their drinking friends. Under these high-pressure conditions almost half the drinkers (42 percent) drank frequently; 28 percent drank "excessively," admittedly in an attempt to relieve their tensions; and 64 percent experienced social and personal complications because of their drinking.

Why Problem Drinkers?

There are many reasons why young people drink. The big question is why so many of them have problems with their drinking.

Of course, all teenagers are going through a period of particular stress and uncertainty. Generally speaking, they are less likely than adults to exercise judgment and restraint. These may be major reasons why for so many of them drinking results in damage. "The impact of adolescence is often more than a teenager can handle on an even keel," says writer Jean Libman Block. "Add alcohol to that precarious balance and the results may be disastrous."

For a few problem drinkers, it may be simply a matter of chemistry, though that has not been apparent to investigators. The chemistry theory of alcoholism—the theory that in some people a metabolic susceptibility will inevitably result in alcoholism after a few drinks have established the allergy—is not widely held as it once was.

Metababolic changes do take place in a heavy drinker, but it is no longer considered certain that thereafter one drink will lead inescapably to a drunken episode. Members of Alcoholics Anonymous do hold, however, that for an alcoholic one drink is likely to be followed by others and will lead to a return to dependence on alcohol. While there is some evidence of a connection between alcoholism and heredity, not many youngsters who are well balanced and self-controlled seem to become problem drinkers solely because of their body chemistry.

Personality Factors

One likely explanation for alcoholism that seems preordained, once drinking starts, is a personality factor, even in every young children, or perhaps a psychological aberration. Youngsters who beame alcoholics, Dr. M. M. Glatt of Great Britain believes, have a clear maladjustment of personality and even psychopathology (mental illness) before they start. For such youngsters, it seems not to matter when they have their first drink. Even if it is after they have grown up, they very likely will develop alcoholism.

"Young alcoholics are emotionally much more disturbed than the average adult alcoholic," Dr. Glatt says. "The early signs of dependence on alcohol develop very rapidly; alcohol releases hostility with which the young alcoholics seem to have great difficulty in coping. Frequent amnesias, morning and solitary drinking, and prolonged drunkenness at an early age suggest some psychopathological factors in the make-up of such individuals."

Such youngsters are different from those who drink socially. "The young alcoholic is distinguished from normal adolescent drinkers," Dr. Glatt observes, "by early use of alcohol for its effect, and often in solitude, rather than as an aid to social acceptance. The ensuring abnormal drinking patterns seem to be an attempt to short-cut to an adult role, supplying a false feeling of omnipotence to the disturbed personality acting out his inadequacy."

This is putting it strongly, and perhaps most observers would not agree to classifying many young drinkers as mentally ill. But there is no doubt that personality factors and emotional maladjustments of various kinds are involved.

Clearly, the same struggle with problems—emotional, social, psychological, and personal—that causes other youthful difficulties causes some teenagers to become drinkers. In any survey of delinquent versus nondelinquent youngsters, many more of the delinquents are heavy drinkers. Drinking "several times a week" was reported by 29 of 100 state school inmates in a Utah survey, but by only 5 of 100 senior high school students. (Incidentally, the seniors took their first drink, on the average, at fourteen; for the state school inmates the average age at first drink was eleven.)

Children who will become drinkers in later life can be identified by their personality traits in junior high school, says research associate Mary Cover Jones of the University of California at Berkeley. In data collected over 37 years, boys who became problem drinkers showed very heavy emphasis on masculinity, perhaps because of their concern about the male role. Their behavior was likely to be unstable, unpredictable, and impulsive. Women who drank too much tended, as teenagers to be depressed, self-negating, and distrustful.

Many experts see the roots of drinking problems in a complex interaction of physiological, psychological, and social factors.

Rebellion

As demonstrated in social atmospheres where drinking is condemned, teenager over-drinking is often related to defiance of the authority of parents and society. In a group of North Carolina high school boys, all of whose fathers were opposed to alcohol, drinking was greatest among youths who were in conflict with their fathers, in contrast with the behavior of those friendly to their fathers. "The rejection of parental authority," says Dr. C. N. Alexander Jr., "was associated with frequent drinking, excessive drinking leading to extreme intoxication, and drinking for psychological benefits rather than for social reasons."

But all sorts of personal and family problems may be involved, aside from parent-child disagreements. An extreme example of what may be found is presented by a small group of problem drinkers, aged 13 to 18, treated at the Peter Brent Brigham Hospital in Boston. Many had come to the hospital from training schools for delinquent children. All had become alcoholics even before adolescence, some having had their first drink at age five. "Family life had been marked by gross personal and economic deprivation," says Dr. J.R. MacKay. "Almost all the fathers and some of the mothers were alcoholics. In most cases the father had deserted the family permanently, leaving it in desperate financial straits. In every case the outstanding personality attributes (of the youngsters) were hostility, depression, impulsiveness, and sexual confusion. Self-destructive and homosexual tendencies were apparent in many."

The National Council of Alcoholism has developed a questionnaire[17] which group workers might utilize in making an assessment of individual members' alcohol use.

Teen-Age Alcohol Questionnaire[17]

- Do you lose time from school due to drinking? YES NO
- Do you drink because you are shy with other people? YES NO
- Do you drink to build up your self-confidence? YES NO
- Do you drink alone? YES NO
- Is drinking affecting your reputation—and do you care? YES NO
- Do you drink to escape from study or home worries? YES NO
- Do you feel guilty after drinking? YES NO
- Does it bother you if someone says you drink too much? YES NO
- Do you have to take a drink when you go out on a date? YES NO
- Do you make out generally better when you have a drink? YES NO
- Do you get into financial troubles over buying liquor? YES NO
- Do you feel a sense of power when you drink? YES NO
- Have you lost friends since you started drinking? YES NO
- Have you started hanging out with a crowd where the stuff is easy to get? YES NO
- Do your friends drink less than you do? YES NO
- Do you drink until the bottle is done? YES NO
- Have you ever been to a hospital or been "busted" (arrested) for drunk driving? YES NO
- Have you ever had a complete loss of memory from drinking? YES NO
- Do you "turn off" to any studies or lectures about drinking? YES NO
- Do you think you have a problem with liquor? YES NO

A "yes" to two or more of the above questions ought to be a warning that the respondent is on shaky ground. Alcoholism? Possibly. These are some of the early warning signs.

Glossary of Alcohol-Related Definitions

- **Absorption:** How alcohol goes from the stomach and small intestine into the bloodstream.

---

[17]Adapted from material provided by the National Council of Alcoholism—North Jersey Area Inc., Montclair, N.J.

- **Abstainer:** A person who doesn't drink alcohol.
- **Alcoholic:** A person whose drinking causes problems. The person usually drinks often, drinks until he gets drunk, and cannot control his or her drinking.
- **Alcoholics Anonymous (AA):** A worldwide organization of recovering alcoholics. There are local groups in many towns. Members meet to discuss their problems related to alcohol so they can continue not to drink and to help others with drinking problems.
- **Al-Anon:** A worldwide organization of wives and husbands of alcoholics. There are local groups in many towns. Members meet to discuss how to deal with their alcoholic husbands and wives.
- **Alateen:** An organization for teenagers whose mothers or fathers are alcoholics. There are local groups in many towns. Members meet to discuss how to deal with their parent(s).
- **Blackout:** Being unable to remember at all what happened (what one said and did) when drunk.
- **Blood Alcohol Content (BAC):** The percentage of alcohol in a person'a blood. In most states, a driver with a BAC of .10% is presumed to be driving while intoxicated (DWI).
- **Delirium Tremens (DTs):** Hallucinations, shaking, nausea and other symptoms when one suddenly stops drinking for several hours.
- **Distillation:** When wine or beer is heated, the alcohol becomes a gas. This gas is then cooled and becomes liquid alcohol. This is how hard liquor (whiskey, etc.) is made.
- **Drug:** Anything which people put on their skin or swallow which can have an effect on how their mind or body works.
- **Drunk:** The way people feel and act when they have had a lot of alcohol. "Drunk" usually means the person has lost all or a great deal of control of their actions and thoughts. Same as intoxicated.
- **DWI:** Also called DUIL. Driving while intoxicated or under the influence of alcohol. In most states, a driver whose Blood Alcohol Content (BAC) is .10% or higher is presumed to be DWI (DUIL).
- **Ethyl Alcohol:** The only kind of alcohol which is safe to drink. It is made from fruit or cereals.
- **Fermentation:** When yeast acts on the sugar in fruit juices or cereals to produce alcohol which can be used to make wine or beer.
- **Hangover:** The sick feeling (headache, upset stomach, etc.) some people feel several hours after having been drunk or high. People get hangovers after all the alcohol has left their body and they are sober again. Only time makes a hangover go away.
- **High**: The way people feel when they have had enough alcohol to feel

good, but not so much that they have lost significant control over what they say and do.

- **Intoxicated:** See DRUNK.
- **Methyl Alcohol:** A type of alcohol which is poisonous if drunk. It is found in anti-freeze, paint thinner, and fuels. It is made from wood and is sometimes called "wood alcohol."
- **Minor:** A person who is not legally an adult. Every state has its own law saying at what age a person becomes an adult (usually 18). Minors cannot vote or buy alcohol.
- **Oxidation:** The addition of oxygen to another chemical. The liver adds oxygen to alcohol to produce carbon dioxide, water, and energy.
- **Peer:** A person of your own standing and usually age. "Peer pressure" occurs when people with no special authority or power try to get other people like them to do (or not to do) something.
- **Problem Drinker:** A person whose drinking causes them a problem for other people. Problem drinkers have more control over their drinking than ALCOHOLICS do.
- **Proof:** The word used to describe the amount of alcohol in hard liquor. The proof number is always double the percentage of alcohol. One hundred proof whiskey is half or 50% alcohol.
- **Psychological Tolerance:** People's ability over a long period of time to learn what effects drinking has on them and to train themselves to prevent these effects from causing trouble.
- **Skid Row:** The part of a town where "bums" live. Most skid row "bums" are not alcoholics. Most alcoholics are not skid row "bums", either.
- **Tolerance:** The body's resistance to alcohol (or to any drug) because of repeated use. As a result of this tolerance, the person must drink more and more alcohol to get the same effects as earlier.

Glossary of Alcoholism Service Terms

- **Detoxification Service**

The provision of short-term (2 to 7 days) residential care and service for the reception and observation of intoxicated persons; the detoxification of intoxicated persons; the counseling of alcoholics to motivate their further treatment, and the referral of detoxified persons to appropriate treatment programs for continued care.

- **Residential Treatment Facility**

The provision of an intermediate term (28 days average) therapeutic residential program of comprehensive, structured alcoholism treatment services, medical support and a wide range of supportive services for detoxified individuals.

- **Extended Treatment Facility (Shelter)**

The provision of long-term (60 days or more) room, board and personal care services for chronically debilitated alcoholics with impaired self-maintenance capabilities and who need guidance, assistance and minimal medical observation in order to maintain sobriety and stable personal health.

- **Outpatient Service**

The provision of scheduled or non-scheduled, non-residential diagnostic and primary alcoholism treatment services by a detoxification, residential treatment center or a hospital.

- **Day Care/Evening Care Services**

The provision of intensive, scheduled, non-residential alcoholism services three or more times per week for not less than twenty (20) hours to individuals who are in need of but unable to participate in the traditional residential treatment program.

- **A.L.I.A.A.**

Aid to low income alcohol abusers (outpatient counseling, didactic lectures, lunch, individual and group counseling and transportation to A.A.).

- **Halfway House (Supportive Residence)**

The provision from one (1) to six (6) months or more, of room and board with supportive services, vocational, social and recreational activities for detoxified alcoholics to assist their adjustment to regular patterns of living and their engagement in occupational training, gainful employment and independent self-maintenance.

- **Information and Referral Service**

The provision of alcoholism information to individuals, groups, agencies and the community-at-large, together with specific assistance to individuals who seek to enter the alcoholism service delivery system.

- **Alcohol Awareness School**

The provision of alcoholism education, evaluating and reports to the referring criminal justice agency concerning individuals charged with alcohol-related offenses. Similar education is also available to families of offenders.

- **Service Force**

The provision of first-aid, general assistance and/or transportation to or from a treatment center or place of residence for alcoholic and/or intoxicated individuals by an "authorized person."

- **Court Liaison**

Detection, evaluation, counseling and follow-up services to cooperation with the courts for persons with alcohol-related problems.

- **Counselor/Coordinator**

A Certified Alcoholism Counselor whose functions include counseling-referral with clients as well as developing policies, procedures and inservice training in hospitals, community mental health centers and other public health and human service agencies.

- **Comprehensive Alcoholism Program**

The provision or access to the following components: Detoxification, Outpatient, Residential Treatment, Halfway House, Extended Care, Offender School, Service Force, Information and Referral Services and a local planning board.

REFERENCES

Harford, T. C. "Teenage Alcohol Use." *Postgraduate Medicine,* July 1976.

H.E.W. *Kids and Alcohol.* Developed by Abt Associates, Inc., 1976.

H.E.W. *Alcohol: Pleasure and Problems.* Developed by Abt Associates, 1976.

National Council on Alcoholism. *Facts on Alcoholism.* North Jersey Area Inc.

National Institute of Alcohol Abuse and Alcoholism. *Alcohol Topics in Brief.* 1974.

New Jersey State Department of Health. "Alcoholism." *Our Health,* Spring 1974.

Saltman, J. *The New Alcoholics: Teenagers.* Public Affairs Pamphlet No. 499, The Public Affairs Committee, 1973.

Chapter 22

Drug and Alcohol – Behaviors, Attitudes and Trends

No training text for youth group workers would be complete without some comment on national surveys conducted with adolescent subjects relative to drug and alcohol use. Of prime interest as well is the gathering of data which points towards the trends being established among the group workers' constituents, the teenagers, in the areas of drug and alcohol abuse.

Much data, in this regard, has been developed by surveys undertaken by the University of Michigan Institute for Social Research and a Social Research Group at the George Washington University. The ultimate survey findings were prepared for the National Institute on Drug Abuse by the aforementioned research teams and published by HEW's Alcohol Drug Abuse and Mental Health Administration.

The author is of the opinion that certain conclusions and findings by the survey teams will be most helpful to the youth group worker in assessing the potential problem areas of their group. Such excerpts are included herein.

Trends – Use of Marijuana and Stronger Drugs (National Survey – 1977)

In sharp contrast to the patterns of drug use in 1977, illicit drug use was an uncommon occurrence in the United States as recently as fifteen years ago. The rapid pace at which drug use spread has raised a host of questions concerning the specific nature of this increase: What segments of the population began using illicit drugs first? What drugs did they use? What changes have occurred in drug use by demographic subpopulations across time? Although the first survey in this series was conducted in 1971, it was possible to reconstruct trends in lifetime experience for at least fifteen years based on the age at which people reported first using an illicit drug.

Prior to 1962 lifetime experience with any illicit drug was limited to 2% or less of the population in most areas of the country and among most large population subgroups. At that time, the prevalence of marijuana use was slightly above average (about 5%) among males and racial minorities and people living in the

Western region of the country. Between 1962 and 1967 greater numbers of youth and young adults began marijuana use, primarily those in regions of the country other than the South, in metropolitan areas and in normal neighborhoods; although use increased slightly in many groups, males and minorities continued to have higher use rates than females and whites. Throughout this period use of stronger drugs remained at a very low level in all large demographic categories, including males and minority groups.

Between 1967 and 1972 dramatic changes occurred in the use of both marijuana and stronger drugs. Lifetime experience with drugs among young adults and youth, males and females in all regions of the country doubled and, among some groups, more than doubled. Exceptions to this pattern were certain groups in which social change is traditionally slower; adults over 26 years old and people living in southern, nonmetropolitan or rural areas. Use of marijuana grew at a greater rate among whites than other races, eradicating the racial differences observed for earlier years. While the use of all illicit drugs expanded rapidly between 1967 and 1972, it should be pointed out that experience with stronger drugs remained substantially less prevalent than marijuana experience. For example, in 1972 the reconstructed data indicated that approximately 20% of the males had used marijuana compared to about 7% who had used a stronger drug.

Among women, this difference between the drug categories also applied despite lower lifetime rates for women in general: In 1972, the reconstructed data indicated that about 11% of women had used marijuana and about 4% had used a stronger drug. Examination of trends in the use of stronger drugs showed that between 1967 and 1972 the greatest increase took place among young adults, whose rate of lifetime experience jumped from about 5% to over 15%; a *substantial increase also occurred among youth,* but almost no increase could be detected for older adults. *Among youth, the PCP "ever-use" rate rose from about 3% to 6%;* among young adults, from approximately 10% to almost 14%. Very little change in levels of heroin use has occurred since 1972 in any age group of the household population studied here.

Thus, the upward trends in lifetime experience with marijuana and other illicit drugs, which began in the late sixties, continue, as marijuana use spreads through a larger and more varied portion of the population—a pattern which may partially reflect the changing opportunity structure and social climate of illicit drug use in our society.

An important question is whether or not the increases in lifetime experience discussed above have been accompanied by similar rises in current use rates. Again, the answer is to be related to the age of the user and type of drug. Current (past-month) use of marijuana has maintained a relatively consistent pattern in relation to prevalence from 1971 to 1977: During these years, roughly half of the youth or young adults who had ever used marijuana reported using it in the month prior to the interview. Among youth who have ever used, there is some indication that the proportion who are currently using is growing.

Among several large subgroups of youth, for example, those living in large metropolitan areas or older youth 16 and 17 years of age, approximately 60% of those with marijuana experience reported using in the prior month. The continuing exceptions to this pattern are youth and young adults living in the South where only about one-third of the "ever-users" reported use in the past month. An even smaller proportion (approximately one-fifth) of the older adults who had ever used marijuana reported current use in any year; however, in 1977 one-fourth of the adult users between the ages of 26 and 34 reported using marijuana in the month prior to interview, suggesting that the current use rate for older adults may increase gradually in future years as this age group matures.

In all age groups, considerably smaller proportions of persons with stronger drug experience report using one of these drugs in the month prior to the interview: About one-third of the youth and one-fifth of the young adults who have used one of these drugs (and only about one-tenth of all older "ever-users") can be considered current users. The only significant trend in current use of stronger drugs is the increase in young adults who reported using cocaine in the month before the interview.

Individuals born in different decades (i.e., 10-year "birth control") show great diversity in their drug histories. The two older birth cohorts (persons born between 1930 and 1939 or between 1920 and 1929 are now over 37 years old; few of these older persons (less than 5%) used marijuana as youth or young adults. Very few of those persons born between 1940 and 1949 (now 28 to 37 years old) first used marijuana as youth; those who have used began in their twenties. The experiences of the youngest 10-year cohort (born between 1950 and 1959 and now aged 18 to 27) are quite different; about one-third of this group first used during their teens. Thus, adults just 10 years apart in age have had dramatically different drug experiences, illustrating the rapid pace with which this extensive change has occurred.

To summarize the drug use trends discussed in this section, noticeable changes in the prevalence of illegal drug use began in the mid-sixties with increased marijuana use among youth and young adults, particularly males and those living in metropolitan areas and outside the south. This trend continued in the late sixties accompanied by increases of a lesser magnitude in the use of stronger drugs. During recent years drug use has become more prevalent not only within those groups in which drug use increases were initially seen, but also among groups who demonstrated relatively low use rates in the sixties.

Recent Changes in Drug Use

Detailed analyses of recent changes in marijuana use reveal that previously low-use groups are "catching up" to high-use groups. Differences in drug use rates across demographic subgroups are less significant today than in former years. This observation, coupled with the rate and the extent of change in drug use, particularly over the past ten years, raises the issue of whether or not drug use, at least marijuana use, may be in the process of becoming a part of the general culture.

Trends in illegal drug use have occurred during an era of extensive social change. During the past two decades, the role of women and the position of minorities have undergone major modifications, as have sexual mores and attitudes about individual rights. Increased drug use can therefore be seen as but one manifestation of the changing character of American society.

The following sections summarize the levels of drug use reported by the high school class of 1978. Data are included for lifetime use, use during the past year, use during the past month, and daily use. There is also a comparison of key subgroups in the population (based on sex, college plans, region of the country, and population density or urbanism).

Lifetime, Monthly, and Annual Prevalence

- Between six and seven in every ten seniors (64.1%) report illicit drug use at some time in their lives. However, a substantial proportion of them have used only marijuana (27.6% of the sample or 43% of all illicit users).
- Over one-third of the seniors (36.5%) report using an illicit drug other than marijuana at some time.
- Marijuana is by far the most widely used ilicit drug with 59% reporting some use in their lifetime, 50% reporting some use in the past year, and 37% use in the past month.
- The most widely used of the other illicit drugs are stimulants (23% lifetime prevalence) followed by two other classes of psychotherapeutic drugs: tranquilizers (17% lifetime prevalence) and sedatives (16% lifetime prevalence).
- Next come hallucinogens (such as LSD, THC, PCP, mescaline, peyote) which have been used by about one in every seven students (14% lifetime prevalence).
- About one in every seven or eight students has used cocaine, and about one in every eight or nine has used inhalants. Opiates other than heroin have been used by one in ten (10%).
- Only 1.6% of the sample admitted to ever using any heroin, the most infrequently used drug.
- Use of either of the two major licit drugs, alcohol and cigarettes, is still more widespread than use of any of the illicit drugs. Nearly all students have tried alcohol (93%).
- Some 75% report having tried cigarettes at some time, and 37% smoked at least some in the past month.

Daily Prevalence

- Frequent use of these drugs is of great concern from a health and safety viewpoint. For all drugs, respondents are considered daily users if they indicate that they had used the drug on twenty or more occasions in the preceding 30 days.
- A particularly important finding is that marijuana is now used daily by a substantial fraction of the age group (10.7%). The proportion using alcohol daily stands at 5.7%.
- Less than 1% of the respondents report daily use of any of the illicit drugs other than marijuana. Still, .5% report unsupervised daily use of amphetamines, and the comparable figure for sedatives is .2%, for tranquilizers .1%, and for opiates other than heroin .1%. While very low, these figures are not inconsequential considering that 1% of each high school class represents about 30,000 individuals.
- Not surprisingly, given the strength and duration of their effects, hallucinogens are used on a daily basis by only about .1% of the sample. Cocaine also is used daily by only .1% of the sample, as are inhalants.
- Virtually no respondents (less than .05%) report daily use of heroin in senior year. However, in the opinion of the investigators heroin is the drug most likely to be under-reported in surveys, so the absolute prevalence figures may be somewhat understated.

Prevalence Comparisons for Important Subgroups

Sex Differences

- In general, higher proportions of males than females are involved in drug use, especially heavy drug use.
- Overall marijuana use is somewhat higher among males, and daily use of marijuana is substantially higher among males (14.2% vs. 7.1% for females in 1978).
- On most other illicit drugs males have considerably higher prevalance rates. The annual prevalence for inhalants, cocaine, and heroin tends to be two to three times as high among males as among females. Males also have slightly higher rates of use for hallucinogens, opiates other than heroin, and sedatives. Further, males account for a disproportionate number of the heavy users of these drugs.
- Annual prevalence for the use of stimulants is about equal for both sexes, though more of the frequent users are female than male. Slightly more females than males also are using tranquilizers, but frequent use occurs about equally for both sexes.
- Despite the fact that most illicit drugs are used by more males than

females, nearly equal proportions of both sexes report at least *some* illicit use of drugs other than marijuana during the last year. If one thinks of going beyond marijuana as an important threshold point in the sequence of illicit drug use, then nearly equal proportions of both sexes (28% for females) were willing to cross that threshold at least once during the year. However, the female "users" take fewer drugs and with less frequency.

- Greater than occasional use of alcohol tends to be disproportionately concentrated among males. Daily use, for example, is reported by 8.3% of the males but by only 3.2% of the females.
- Finally, for cigarettes, there is practically no sex difference in the prevalence of smoking a half-a-pack or more daily (18.9% for males vs. 18.0% for females), although among these regular smokers males appear to consume a somewhat higher quantity of cigarettes.

Differences Related to College Bound Students

- Overall, seniors who are expecting to complete four years of college (referred to here as the "college-bound") have lower rates of illicit drug use than those who are not.
- Annual marijuana use is reported by 47% of the college-bound vs. 52% of the noncollege-bound.
- There is substantial difference in the proportion of these two groups using illicit drugs other than marijuana. In 1978 only 23% of the college-bound reported any such behavior in the prior year vs. 30% of the noncollege-bound.
- For all of the specific illicit drugs, annual prevalence is lower for the college-bound: In fact, the prevalence rates tend to be about a quarter to half again as large for the noncollege-bound as for the college-bound on all illicit drugs except marijuana.
- Frequent use of all of the illicit drugs is even more disproportionately concentrated among students not planning four years of college.
- Frequent alcohol use is also more prevalent among the noncollege-bound. For example, drinking on a daily basis is nearly twice as common at 7.3% for the noncollege-bound. On the other hand, there are practically no differences between the groups in annual or monthly prevalence; 88% of both groups used alcohol at least once during the past year and 73% of the noncollege-bound vs. 72% of the college-bound used it at least once in the past month.
- The largest difference of all between the college plans groups involves daily smoking. Only 11% of the college-bound smoke a half-a-pack or more daily, compared with 26% of the noncollege-bound.

Regional Differences

- In general, there are not very great regional differences in 1978 in rates of illicit drug use among high school seniors. The highest rate is in the northeast, where 62% say they have used a drug ilicitly in the past year, followed by North Central with 55%, the West with 53%, and the South with 48%.
- There is even less regional variation in terms of the percent using some illicit drug other than marijuana in the past year: 31% in the Northeast, 27% in the North Central, 29% in the West, and 24% in the South.
- The Northeast shows the highest annual rate (or close to the highest rate) on all drugs, licit and illicit, except heroin. The North Central shows the highest rate on inhalants. The West shows a high annual prevalence for cocaine use, while the South shows the lowest for marijuana, hallucinogens, cocaine, other opiates, and stimulants. However, these findings should be interpreted cautiously, since a number of the regional differences are quite small.
- Alcohol use tends to be somewhat lower in the South and West than it is in the Northeast and North Central.
- The largest regional differences occur for regular cigarette smoking. In the Northeast 24% say they smoke half-a-pack or more per day of cigarettes compared with 20% in the North Central, 17% in the South, and only 12% in the West.

Recent Trends – Four Year Comparative Data, All High School Seniors

This section summarizes trends in drug use, comparing the classes of 1975, 1976, 1977, and 1978. As in the previous sections, the data include lifetime use, use during the past year, use during the past month, daily use, and comparisons of key subgroups.

Trends in Lifetime, Annual, and Monthly Prevalence

- The past three years have witnessed an appreciable rise in marijuana use without any concomitant increase in the proportion using other illicit substances. While 47% of the class of 1975 used marijuana at least once during their lifetime, fully 59% of the class of 1978 had done so. The corresponding trend in annual marijuana prevalence is from 40% to 50%.
- There has been practically no increase in the proportion who are users of illicit drugs other than marijuana. This proportion has remained steady over the last three years at about 36% for lifetime prevalence and between 25% and 27% for annual prevalence.

- Because of the increase in marijuana use, the overall proportion of seniors involved in illicit drug use has been increasing. About 64% of the class of 1978 report having used some illicit drug at least once during their lifetime, compared with 55% of the class of 1975. Annual prevalance figures have risen from 45% to 54% over the same interval.
- Although the proportion using other illicit drugs has remained relatively unchanged over the last three years, some interesting changes have been occurring for specific drugs within the class.
- The decline in hallucinogen use over the previous two-year interval (from 11% in 1975 to 9% in 1977 for annual prevalence), appears to have halted. The 1978 figure is 9.6%. The number of frequent users had also been declining steadily. In 1975, 1.0% reported use on 20 or more occasions per year vs. .7% in 1976 and .5% in 1977; but in 1978 the number was .6%.
- Cocaine, on the other hand, has exhibited an accelerating increase in popularity, with annual prevalence going from 5.6% in the class of 1975 to 9.0% in the class of 1978. While the majority of these seniors use cocaine only once or twice during the year, there is now getting to be a detectable number of frequent users.
- The use of opiates other than heroin, which had been increasing since 1975 (when 5.7% admitted use during the year, compared with 6.4% in 1977) is no longer increasing. Annual prevalence in 1978 was 6.0%.
- The popularity of sedatives appears to be declining very gradually among seniors. Annual use dropped steadily from 11.7% in 1975 to 9.9% in 1978, and for the first time this year tranquilizer use has shown some indications of declining.
- Heroin lifetime prevalence also appears to be dropping very gradually (from 2.2% in 1975 to 1.6% in 1978), though findings about heroin must be viewed with considerable caution. Annual prevalence, however, has been steady for two years.
- The use of stimulants has remained essentially unchanged across the last four classes.
- Trend data on inhalant use exist only over the past two-year interval, since this class of drugs was included for the first time in 1976. There has been some increase in prevalence over that year. Annual prevalence rose from 3.0% to 4.1%–a small, but still statistically significant, change.
- Thus, while the proportion using any illicit drugs other than marijuana has remained remarkably constant, the mix of drugs they have been using has been changing somewhat.
- Turning to the licit drugs, between 1975 and 1978 there has been a gradual but steady upward shift in the prevalence of alcohol use among seniors. To illustrate, the annual prevalence rate rose from 85% in 1975 to 88% in 1978.

- Over the past year there was virtually no change in lifetime prevalence of cigarette use, but a statistically significant drop (for the first time) in monthly prevalence.
- Tranquilizer use on a daily basis increased significantly between 1975 and 1977 (from .1% to .3%) but dropped significantly this year back to .1%.
- In contrast, marijuana has shown a marked increase in the proportion using it (and/or hashish) daily. The proportion reporting daily use in the class of 1975 (6.0%) came as a surprise to many. However, since then the number has risen considerably, so that now one in every nine high school seniors (10.7%) indicates that he or she uses the drug on a daily or nearly daily basis.
- Alcohol has not shown a comparable rise in use during the same time period. Daily use has remained steady between 5.7% and 6.1%. It is currently at 5.7%, exactly where it was in 1975.

Trend Comparisons for Important Subgroups

Sex Differences in Trends

- Most of the sex differences mentioned earlier have remained relatively unchanged over the past three years—that is, any trends in overall use have occurred about equally among males and females. There is, however, one important exception.

Trend Differences Related to College Bound Students

- Both the college-bound and the noncollege-bound have been showing parallel trends in overall illicit drug use over the last two years; that is, both showed a rising proportion using marijuana only, and a steady (or only slightly increasing) proportion using illicit drugs other than marijuana.

Regional Differences in Trends

- Between 1975 and 1978 the proportion of seniors using illicit drugs other than marijuana has remained relatively steady in all regions except the Northeast, where there has been an increase from 26% to 31%. Much of the increase in the Northeast may be due specifically to cocaine use, which has increased more there than elsewhere.
- The proportion using marijuana only has been steadily increasing in all regions, though in the West, the size of the increase has been only about half what it has been in the three other regions.

A good working tool for the group worker, is the *Handbook on Drug Abuse* issued by the National Institute on Drug Abuse and printed in January 1979. This book is available for purchase from the Superintendent of Documents, U.S. Printing Office. It is a compilation of recent research findings written in a style understandable to planners, clinicians and policymakers. Some 40 authors well known and respected in their fields, write on major developments of recent years and their implications for treatment and research.

For instance, Richard Blum and Louise Richards had written a very informative piece for the Handbook titled "Youthful Drug Use" which gives one an idea as drug use prevalence, trends, preferences, criminality, religiosity, taste as well as recommendations for treatment and prevention. They refer to D. B. Kandel's developmental findings, which in a review and integration from a selected group of longitudinal studies, extracted the following 20 principles and 10 accompanying qualifying comments in illicut drug use: (Some, very surprising in terms of general beliefs.)

- The period for risk of initiation into illicit drug use is usually over by the mid-twenties.
- A high proportion of youths who have tried marijuana will usually go on to experiment with other illicit drugs.
- Later age of onset is usually associated with lesser involvement and greater probability of stopping.
- There are usually clear-cut developmental steps and sequences in drug behavior; use of one of the legal drugs almost always precedes use of the illegal drugs.
- Addiction to heroin is not usually a permanent state.
- Occasional use of heroin does not necessarily lead to addiction.
- The dysfunctional attributes of drug users usually appear to precede rather than to derive from drug use.
- Different factors are usually involved in the transitions into different stages of drug use.
- Personality factors indicative of maladjustment usually precede the use of marijuana and of other illicit drugs.
- Poor school performance is usually a common antecedent of initiation into illicit drugs.
- Delinquent and deviant activities usually precede involvement in illicit drugs.
- A constellation of attitudes and values favorable to deviance usually precedes involvement in illicit drugs.
- There is a process of anticipatory socialization wherein youths who will initiate the use of drugs usually develop attitudes favorable to the use of legal and illegal drugs prior to initiation.
- Drug behavior and drug-related attitudes of peers are usually among the most potent predicators of drug involvement.
- Parental behaviors, parental attitudes, and parental closeness to their

children usually have differential importance at different stages of involvement in drugs.

- Sociodemographic variables usually hold little predictive power for initiation into marijuana.
- Time of onset of drug use usually declines as degree of deviance proneness increases.
- A social setting favorable to drug use usually reinforces and increases individual predisposition to use.
- Nonaddictive illicit drug use usually does not by itself lead to increased criminality.
- Cannabis use usually does not appear to lead to the "amotivational" syndrome.

By definition, principles are probability statements that ignore small deviations. To assure that the exceptions are recognized, Kandel added qualifying comments to the above:

- Some parents are initiated into illicit drug use by their youngsters.
- Amphetamines may sometimes be the initial illicit drug rather than marijuana. (In fact, underage smoking and drinking are the usual illicit antecedents to use of the unlawful compounds.)
- Later age of onset also is associated with better treatment outcomes.
- Addiction is as much a role as a state. Physical dependence, the pharmacological condition, is intermittent and often terminated. The addict role requires intention, effort, and learning, whereas physical dependency, to be produced, requires repeated doses.
- Drug use can lead to bad outcomes, either acute or chronic, and repetitive use may further limit coping judgment, and maturation.
- Maladjustment and pathological traits will not discriminate between users and nonusers when use is or becomes conventional in a population. Even then, though, some initial use will be triggered by individual psychodynamics as will be varieties of response.
- Peer influence dominates especially when families suffer or create conditions for it or reduce control. Although parental influence has different impact at different stages of drug involvement, there is some impact at any age.
- Age is a powerful predictor of marijuana (and most other drug) use. At the present time other sociodemographic characteristics do not distinguish strongly.
- Drug use may not inevitably create the amotivational syndrome, but acute effects of drugs easily impair judgment and motor coordination; and intensive use of some substances is incompatible with adequate social performance.

Observations and conceptions to date do offer insights, as well as descriptive statistics. One may not be satisfied that one "really knows why" youngsters use drugs, but there are sufficient data to provide understanding within the limits of present general knowledge in the fields of child development, psychopathology, social psychology, psychopharmacology, delinquency, etc.

Inhalants

The author is confident that many group workers do not recognize that there are many substances, such as commercial solvents, that serve as an intoxication vehicle, via inhalation, for the young. Sidney Cohen of the Neuropsychiatric Institute at UCLA tells us about inhalants in the *Handbook on Drug Abuse* to wit:

A large series of commercially available volatile solvents have the capability to intoxicate those who deliberately inhale them. They range from model airplane glue, fingernail polish remover, gasoline, paint thinner, liquid shoe polish, plastic cement, cleaning fluid, and wax strippers to a variety of aerosols. Literally hundreds of intoxicating volatile products are available in the home and in the marketplace. They are more available to young people than alcohol, and they can be found in very remote areas where alcoholic beverages cannot be obtained.

Many studies have shown that solvents are the intoxicants of the very young, and more often of males than of females. However, shifts in this pattern are taking place with increasing numbers of persons over 21 years old and of females participating in inhalant sniffing.

Middle-class youngsters are likely to experiment with these substances but are less likely to become chronic users. Within any community the distribution may be spotty with high-use neighborhoods scattered among districts where little use can be identified.

Often solvents are the first drugs of abuse, alcohol or tobacco being the only substances that may antedate them. Solvent sniffing diminishes when adulthood is achieved and the legal purchase of alcoholic beverages becomes possible. Rural adolescents sometimes have a higher level of usage than their urban counterparts. Inhalants are the only class of drugs that may be more frequently used in grade or junior high school than in high school or college. It would be encouraging if this "maturing out" process were unaccompanied by an overinvolvement with other intoxicants. Unfortunately, this is not so; the consistent solvent user tends to move on to alcohol, sedatives, and other drug classes.

School surveys will underreport the extent of solvent abuse. Many survey instruments do not even inquire into solvent use, and since many users are truants or dropouts, they are not ordinarily captured.

Causation

The intentional inhalation of volatile agents is often a peer-originated and peer-perpetuated activity. In poor communities much of the learned behavior occurs on the street. Mimicking the behavioral displays of the leader or of other peers not only instigates a practice like sniffing, but also dictates what kind and brand of solvent will be inhaled.

Unsuccessful and unrewarding school experiences have been mentioned as precipitating factors. Whether these are causes or effects of consistent solvent use is difficult to sort out. Personality deficiencies are reported to be important predisposing factors in confirmed inhalant abusers.

Social disorganization within the community also contributes to the practice. Growing up in an environment of hopelessness, one that provides little in constructive alternative activities, is an obvious etiologic factor in the flight to inhalants. Familial disorganization has been reported to be a contributing factor in certain instances.

It is evident that none of the causative elements mentioned acts to the exclusion of the others. It is disorganized existence, whether internal or external, and usually both, that is conductive to heavy, sustained inhalant use.

Consequences

Mental: The acute state resembles alcoholic intoxication except for its briefer duration. The period of relative stimulation and of disinhibited behavior is also similar to alcohol's. This can result in accidental injury or death and the releasing of aggressive impulses against one's self or others. It is because of such behaviors that the inhalant abuser becomes more visible in the criminal justice system than in the educational system. New evidence is accumulating that confirms older clinical impressions that a chronic brain deficit occurs with extensive solvent abuse. From 40 to 60 percent of chronic sniffers were rated as brain impaired on the Halstead-Reitan Neuropsychology Battery. Whether this impairment is reversible remains to be determined. Chronic solventism is a disorganizing experience for one's self and one's family. Psychological maturation is arrested, and aberrant behavior is not uncommon. The user may "turn on" his younger siblings. School failure is a normal consequence of solvent abuse. Shoplifting and other delinquent activities become a way of life.

Physical: Some of the volatile solvents are know poisons. Carbon tetrachloride is so toxic that it has been removed from commercial trade, and benzene's use is limited for the same reasons. Hexane and leaded gasoline can cause a serious polyneuritis, and the latter is capable of producing an encephalopathy. Toluene is one of the safer and more widely used solvents, but it has been involved in instances of kidney, nervous system, and bone marrow disorders. Metallic spray paints and other aerosols may have dangers caused by secondary ingredients rather than by the solvents themselves.

Sudden sniffing death has been described by a number of authors (Bass 1970; Taylor and Harris 1972; Flowers et al. 1972). It consists of the inhalation of a solvent or aerosol propellant usually associated with strenuous activity or a reduced oxygen content of the blood. Ventricular fibrillation or some other arrhythmia occurs, and the person dies abruptly. Another mode of death is suffocation due to the inhalation of the solvent in a closed space—a plastic garment bag, for example.

Angel Dust (PCP)

Angel Dust (PCP) is perhaps the most popular recent entry of psychoactive drugs with a potential for abuse. S. M. Pittel and M. C. Oppedahl of the Pacific Institute for Research and Evaluation, writing for the *Handbook on Drug Abuse* tell us that.

Among all of the varied patterns of drug use and abuse that collectively define the contemporary drug scene, it is unlikely that any phenomenon can be considered so strange as the emergence of PCP—phencyclidine—as a widespread drug of choice. PCP is an enigma! Neither the drug itself nor its apparently growing popularity in the drug culture can be understood easily in terms of the paradigms of conventional science or drug lore:

- The pharmacology and clinical syndrome of PCP are atypical; PCP cannot be classified easily among other psychotropic drugs.
- The subjective effects of PCP are highly varied; users do not describe the PCP "high" as being similar to that of other drugs.
- The reported pleasures and benefits of PCP use are few, and even confirmed users agree that it is a risky drug. Motives for the use of PCP are more obscure than those for using other drugs.
- Patterns of PCP use and its recent spread to communities throughout the United States do not appear to correspond to what is known about the use and spread of other drugs.

In the present context of growing fears about the potential dangers of PCP, there exists a pressing need for information upon which sane and realistic intervention, treatment, and control strategies can be based. Yet in almost all regards, questions about PCP far outnumber answers available through empirical evidence. Much of the extant literature bears tenously, if at all, on critical issues of policy, and a substantial majority of the most important questions that might be asked about PCP have yet to be addressed systematically.

The Menace of PCP: Based largely on increases in adverse medical and psychiatric effects attributed to PCP since 1973, and so on its spread through the United States from a few locales of concentrated use. PCP is fast gaining notoriety as the drug menace of the late 1970s.

Cases of PCP poisoning have been reported with increasing frequency in the medical literature and a score of deaths have been attributed to both its pharmacological and behavioral effects, i.e., deaths from drowning, fire, falls, and automobile accidents. Users are reported to exhibit bizarre, unpredictable, and aggressive behavior, combined with a severely confused and agitated state of mind while acutely intoxicated. Some users also experience a prolonged recovery period characterized by psychotic-like symptoms; particularly after high dose oral ingestions. Chronic PCP users report experiencing continuing problems with perception, speech, memory, and cognitive processes even during a period of drug abstinence, as well as psychological dependence and tolerance to behavioral effects.

Due in part to the unusually great variability among street samples of PCP, relatively little is known about its dose-response relationships. Low doses apparently give rise either to euphoria and disinhibition or to perceptual distortion, irritability, and paranoia. As dosage increases, sedation, catelepsy, and convulsions may occur, and in high doses PCP is known to be toxic, though what constitutes a toxic dose will vary both with route of administration and individual factors (National Clearing House for Drug Abuse Information, 1978).

Yet, as the evidence of adverse and dire consequences mounts, so, too do speculations that PCP is becoming a drug of choice; that at least some users are no longer victims of deception, but are voluntary seekers of PCP.

In sum, the history of PCP seems as enigmatic as the drug itself. From research with animals it was determined that PCP was highly potent but relatively nontoxic even when administered intravenously. Based on work with medical patients and volunteers, we learned that PCP was a uniquely potent psychotomimetic drug, even in low doses, and that it has been given to thousands who became neither violent nor seiously disturbed, and who suffered no immediate or long-term harm. Reports from the hippie era suggested that accustomed users of other psychotropic drugs so eschewed the effects of PCP that they had to be tricked into using it. Finally, we now learn that the use of PCP is spreading and that it may become a drug of choice, although its effects are even more profound and potentially harmful than was ever suspected or observed heretofore.

With cumulative emphasis, the history of PCP makes it painfully obvious that research findings cannot be generalized easily across different subject populations or from one to another context of drug use. At the very least, the history of PCP demonstrates that we have much to learn about this drug before a final verdict can be made.

REFERENCES

HEW. *Highlights From the National Survey on Drug Abuse: 1977.* Alcohol, Drug Abuse and Mental

Health Administration, P.H.S. (Prepared by the Social Research Group of the George Washington University, I. Cisin, J. D. Miller, A. V. Harrell, with the assistance of the Response Analysis Corp., Princeton, N.J.)

HEW. *Highlights From Drugs and the Class of '78:* Behaviors, Attitudes and Recent National Trends. Alcohol, Drug Abuse and Mental Health Administration, P.H.S. (Prepared by the University of Michigan Institute for Social Research, L. D. Johnston, J. G. Bachman, P. M. O'Malley.)

HEW. Ed. R. I. Dupont, A. Goldstein, J. O'Donnel. *Handbook on Drug Abuse.* National Institute on Drug Abuse, Office of Drug Abuse Policy, Executive Office of the President. 1979.

Chapter 23

Teenage Sexual Mores (Parenthood)

One constantly hears of the increase in sexual permissiveness among young people. An article by Dr. Aaron Hass titled "Teenage Sexuality"[19] was given excerpted coverage in *Penthouse* Magazine. The group worker might want to explore Dr. Hass's work in greater depth. However, the following data, exerpted by *Penthouse*, would seem to be highly supportive of those who maintain that there has been expanded and earlier sexual activity among teenagers today.

Age of First Experience

Historically, there has been a steady decline in the age at which teenagers have experienced sexual intercourse for the first time. In the late 1940s and early 1950s, Kinsey reported that 3 percent of the women and 10 percent of the men in his survey had lost their virginity by the age of 16. By the age of 19, those figures were 20 percent for females and 72 percent for males. In 1973 Sorenson reported that 30 percent of the females and 44 percent of the males who were interviewed in his sample had engaged in sexual intercourse before the age of 16.

Teenagers who participated in this youth survey were asked, "How old were you (if ever) when you had sexual intercourse for the first time?"

- Fifty-seven percent of the younger boys, ages 15-16, and 44 percent of the older boys, ages 17-18, had never experienced sexual intercourse.
- Forty-three percent of the younger group of boys had sexual intercourse by the age of 16 and 18 percent by the age of 13.
- Forty-two percent of the older group of boys had sexual intercourse by the age of 16 and 7 percent by the age of 13.
- Sixty-nine percent of the younger girls, ages 15-16, and 56 percent of the older girls, ages 17-18, had never experienced sexual intercourse.
- Thirty-one percent of the younger group of girls had sexual intercourse by the age of 16 and 7 percent by the age of 13.

---

[19]TEENAGE SEXUALITY by Aaron Hass, MacMillan Publishing Co. Inc., New York, N.Y. Including data from R. Sorenson: ADOLESCENT SEXUALITY IN CONTEMPORARY AMERICA (New York: World Publishing, 1973) Sorenson Survey (Cleveland, Ohio: Collins-world).

It is not the purpose of the author to develop an extensive profile on teenage sexual activity. However, he does feel that the youth group worker should be somewhat knowledgeable regarding two byproducts of such activity, teenage parenthood and venereal disease.

Teenage Parenthood

Charlotte MacDonald, writing in "Human Behavior"[20] points up the fact that the current staggering rate of pregnancies and births among U.S. teenagers has become a matter of official alarm and concern. The Planned Parenthood Federation termed the problem as "epidemic," whereas, a former Secretary of HEW called it one of the most serious, challenges facing the nation today. Although the overall U.S. birthrate has dropped since the early 1960s, the proportion of births to teenagers is soaring and now accounts for about 20% of the live births each year.

Much has been written about the dire effects early childbearing will have on the teenagers' lives. Among the documented consequences: serious health hazards for mother and child, a bleak educational future, a stunted career, a very good chance of living in poverty and a strong likelihood of more babies before the young woman turns 20.

MacDonald continues–In contrast, so little has been said about the impact of early parenthood on males that one might well assume that the experience leaves them untouched. Not so. MacDonald, in turn,cites the experiences of Dr. Josephine J. Card, of the American Institute for Research, Palo Alto, Cal. In a recent study, one of the first to explore the long-term impact of adolescent childbearing for males along with females, Card found the following: That for both sexes, early parenthood had a greater negative impact on future educational and occupational attainment than the factors of race, social or economic status, academic aptitude or early ambition.

MacDonald continues to review Dr. Card's findings to wit:

"As might be guessed," says Dr. Card, "the negative consequences were more pronounced for females, but the differences were there for males, also. These consequences were, in fact, most striking for those "advantaged" subgroups of teenage parents who were white, bright, rich or all three–the kids who might well have gone farther had they not become parents."

Card's study (funded by the National Institute for Child Health and Human Development) was based on data from Project TALENT, AIR's long-term study of 400,000 Americans who were in the ninth through 12th grades in 1960 and are now in their early to middle 30s. The original TALENT data were collected in

[20]"The Stunted World of Teenage Parents" by Charlotte MacDonald in Jan. 1979 issue of HUMAN BEHAVIOR. Permission granted by publisher, Manson Western Corp., Los Angeles, California.

1960, when students in more than 1,000 school districts across the country took a day's worth of aptitude, achievement and personality tests and answered a second day-long battery of questions about their family backgrounds, activities, interests and personal ambitions.

TALENT later sent these same students detailed followup questionnaires at intervals of one, five and eleven years after the graduation of their high school classes—when they were approximately 19, 23, and 29 years old. At each of these followups, TALENT researchers took considerable pain to track down a representative portion of the nonrespondents, either by telephone or in person. As a result, TALENT now has a remarkably comprehensive bank of data that can be used to compare a nationally representative sample of people who become teenage parents with a group who did not.

Those who came to parenthood early tended to fit several popular stereotypes. Their families proved less affluent, and they were somewhat less academically gifted than were their classmates in the nationwide TALENT sample. They also tended to come from smaller communities and were more likely to be black. As a group, the teenager parents had lower grades, fewer academic interests and lower educational goals than their peers. "Personalitywise," the girls in the group were different from their classmates even before they became mothers. On self-ratings made during ninth grade, the girls who later became teenage mothers were more likely to judge themselves more impulsive, less calm, less mature, less "cultured" and less leadership oriented than their comparison-group classmates. (Card found no such personality trademarks for the group of boys who later became teenage fathers.)

This apparent link between personality and teenage motherhood led Card to speculate—again in keeping with traditional notions—that its the more impulsive, less mature, perhaps less assertive girl who gets pregnant, while the boy who helps her to get that way could be anybody."

Not only did the young parents in Card's study start out "different" from their classmates, but they became different, over the years, in a number of important ways that Card attributes directly to the fact of their early parenthood.

Education proved to be a bellwether difference. Previous studied cited by the Alan Guttmacher Institute indicate that 80 percent of the women who become mothers at 17 or younger never finish high school. Card's study suggests that this "dropout effect" is not limited to women, but that teenage parents of both sexes receive far less education their classmates. In Card's TALENT sample, only about 40 percent (among boys and girls who were ninth graders in 1960) of those who had children before 18 had made it through high school by the time they turned 29. Older teenage parents did somewhat better, with 60 percent of the 18-year-old parents and 80 percent of the 19-year-olds earning their diplomas by age 29. In contrast, virtually all (over 95 percent) of the young parents' TALENT classmates were high school graduates by the time of the last followup.

At the college level, these educational differences became even greater, with only 12 percent of the teenage parents—again, this includes both sexes—earning degrees by age 29, as compared with more than 50 percent of their classmates who were college graduates at age 23.

Teenage parents—particularly the females—also fared worse than their classmates in the work world, where they earned less money, held lower-prestige jobs and experienced less job satisfaction. Although young fathers tended to enter the work force earlier and were earning more money than their classmates at ages 19 and 23, by age 29 the classmates had begun to catch up in salary and held higher-prestige jobs—presumably because of their earlier investment in education.

Teenage mothers, on the other hand, had significantly lower incomes and lower-prestige jobs than their classmates at ages 23 and 29. Five years out of high school, less than half of the young mothers were employed, as compared with more than 80 percent of their female classmates who deferred childbearing until age 25 or later. By the time of the 11-year followup, however, many women in the comparison group had dropped out of the job market (presumably to raise families) while large numbers of former teenage mothers had gone to work—a quarter of them in rock-bottom jobs such as domestic servant or nurse's aide. (By contrast, only 3 percent of the women in the comparison group held jobs at this category.)

Not surprisingly, the former teenage mothers expressed a *significantly lower degree of satisfaction with their work* than did women in the comparison group. For males, however, Card found no significant relationship between teenage fatherhood and later job satisfaction.

On the family front, teenage parents, who tended to marry earlier than their classmates, *had a higher rate of divorce and remarriage.* "The younger the teenager at the birth of the first child, the higher his or her chances of subsequent separation or divorce," reports Card. Despite the relative instability of their marriages, the teenage parents tended to have more children than their classmates. They also had—and expected to have—more children than they themselves considered an "ideal" number. Again, Card found a relationship between the parent's age at first childbirth and the total number of children he or she would later produce.

At the time of conception and birth of the first child, the teenage parents were far more likely to be single than were their classmates who had children at age 20 or older. This was especially true of the males. "Evidently the father's age is a strong determinant of marriage—either preceding or following a pregnancy," says Card. "When the father is very young, a marriage is unlikely, either because the mother is as young or younger, or because the father is perceived—rightly or wrongly—as incapable of being a breadwinner."

Those teenage mothers who were married at—or close to—the time of their first childbirth tended to have more stable marital futures and a higher level of education and career attainment. The mother who returned to school after teenage childbearing tended to go farther in their carers, but slightly more of them were divorced or separated, says Card.

Many of the early marriages among teenage parents were spouses of what Card calls "low educational and occupational potential." This point is worth noting, since Card also found that the married couples tended to parallel one another in their future educational and occupational attainment.

Some of the most revealing of Card's findings are the most subjective ones. When asked, at the five- and eleven-year followups, "What things would you do differently in the light of what you know now?" the teenage parents expressed significantly more educational and marital regrets than their classmates did. Teenage mothers who hadn't graduated from high school wished that they had. Teenage parents of both sexes who made it through high school regretted not graduating from college. Teenage mothers, especially, wished they had taken vocational programs, combined work with school or taken additional training after high school. Teenage fathers wished they had taken different vocational programs.

Both males and females—but especially the females—said they wished they had married at a different time in their lives. This was an age-related regret, according to Card. The younger the girl when her first child was born, the more likely she was to regret the timing of her marriage, regardless of whether it took place before or after the birth.

Counseling the Teenage Parents

How does the group worker, often unsophisticated in his/her own right, counsel the teenage parents? It would seem to the author, that in addition to encouraging the teenagers to seek professional guidance, all efforts should be directed toward keeping the young lady in school.

The State of Pennsylvania, for one, has worked out a desirable program aimed at retaining teenage parents in school.

The law in Pennsylvania reads as follows:

> All persons residing in the Commonwealth between the ages of six and twenty-one years are entitled to a free and full education in the Commonwealth public schools. This right extends to migratory children and pregnant or married students.

Section 12:1 (a) Chapter 12, Students, Regulations and Guidelines on Student Rights and Responsibilities.

The legal requirements are explained:

The fundamental public policy expressed in the Pennsylvania Constitution and school laws is to provide equal educational opportunity and a thorough and

and efficient system of education to all the children of the Commonwealth. This policy is stated in Section 1327 of the School Code, which requires compulsory attendance, and Sections 1301 and 1302, which grants all residents of each school district a right to free school privileges. In its regulations on students' rights and responsibilities, the State Board has restated the public policy in relation to school-age parents:

A student may not be excluded from public schools nor from extracurricular activites because of being married or pregnant.

It is obvious from the judicial interpretations of the school laws and the State Board regulations that a school district has a duty to provide an education to school-age parents and to encourage these students to remain in school by assuring access to available support services. If extracurricular activities are offered by the district, the school-age parents shall not be excluded from them simply because of their marital or parental status.

In the case of a pregnant student, the school districts first obligation would be to keep the woman in school. This is required by the compulsory attendance laws. It should be noted that the exceptions to compulsory school attendance do not include pregnancy. The mere status of being a school-age parent should not be viewed as an automatic physical or mental disability, nor as an "urgent reason."

Nor can the status of being a school age parent qualify the student as handicapped for purposes of homebound instruction unless the student has shown an exceptional physical or mental condition as certified by a physician.

In short, a physically healthy, pregnant girl or an expectant father should be kept in school and given counseling and other services so they will remain. If it is determined that continued attendance would endanger either the physical or mental health of the student, they may be exempted from attendance. It is extremely important, however, for school districts to realize that pregnancy by itself is not a sufficient excuse for nonattendance. If there are complicating factors, it is not unreasonable for the school district to require that a doctor certify the effects of continued attendance on the student. The same would be true for a school-age parent who wishes to remain at home to care for their child.

The duty of care required of a school district towards school-age parents is the care that a reasonably prudent person would exercise towards a pregnant woman or expectant father. Basically the duty owed to school-age parents by school personnel is the same as the duty owed to all other students—to act as a responsible and reasonable person in light of each student's particular condition.

If the parent cannot continue their education in school, the school has options discussed below. Although none of the options are mandatory, a reasonable effort to educate school-age parents is legally required. In the past, some school districts have ignored their obligation to educate school-age parents. In light of the clear mandates of state law, the Department of Education cannot ignore its responsibility to insure that school districts educate this segment of the student population.

Placement Alternatives

In Pennsylvania, a pregnant student or teenage parent must be given the opportunity to participate in the most appropriate educational program. Any placement must be based on the unique needs of the student as identifeid through counseling services of the school.

The first and most desirable alternative is keeping the student in the regular program with support services. This alternative insures a complete educational program with minimal disruption to the student. In Pennsylvania, they recognize, however, that maintaining school-age parents in a regular program may necessitate adaptive measures such as:

- Counseling.
- Special Schedule and Activities.
- Adaptive Physical Education.
- Individualized Assignments.

Guiding and counseling services should be readily available to enable the students to cope with problems which would interfere with regular school attendance and participation in the total school program. The special needs of each school-age parent should be identified by school counselors with, if possible, appropriate input from the youth group worker and resource persons from various community agencies.

Again borrowing from the program in Pennsylvania, teenage parents should be counseled as follows:

- Assurance of the right to continue to attend school and the provision of information about alternative school placement.
- Assistance to students in coping with their new roles as school-age parents.
- Assistance in coping with the responsibilities of parenthood by providing courses in parenting education and helping the student find adequate infant care. The school should have an organized means of providing students information through referrals, mini-classes provided by community agencies and written information about community services.
- Guidance to promote those attitudes and behaviors that will prevent any unwanted pregnancies.
- Consultation, at the initiation of the student or of school personnel, on personal problems to assure the development of a healthy self-concept.
- Assistance in developing the skills, knowledge and attitudes necessary for a school-age parent to function as a student, parent, husband or wife, and adult.

- Information about all available support services.
- Education for parenthood in the area of child growth and development.

References and Additional Readings

References dealing with teenage mores and parenthood will be found at the close of Chapter 24, interspersed with venereal disease readings.

Chapter 24

Venereal Disease and the Teenager

Because of the apparent increase in teenage sexual activity, we could reasonably expect an increase in venereal disease among the young people and this has actually happened. The group worker, therefore, must again become knowledgeable in this all important area. Not only for noting the symptoms, but in order to establish, where necessary, a viable education program dealing with V.D. diagnosis and complications.

The two most common venereal diseases in the United States are syphilis and gonorrhea. These diseases are transmitted via sexual intercourse. In very rare instances syphilis may be spread by kissing. The disease germs which cause syphilis and gonorrhea are very fragile. They can live outside the body for only a few seconds. Therefore, according to the New Jersey State Department of Health, there is no danger of anyone catching either syphilis or gonorrhea from public toilets, doorknobs, drinking cups, or eating utensils.

- Young persons under 20 years of age are responsible for one out of every four reported cases of venereal disease. Venereal disease strikes 430 teenagers per day or one every three minutes.
- More cases of syphilis and gonorrhea are reported each year than the combined number of cases reported for – infectious hepatitis, malaria, whooping cough, polio, rubella (German measles), streptococcal sore throat, scarlet fever, and tuberculosis.
- It is estimated that at least two million cases of gonorrhea and as many as 75,000 cases of syphilis occur each year. Some 510,000 persons need treatment for syphilis and do not know it.
- The direct cost of maintenance of patients with syphilitic psychoses in mental hospitals is estimated to be $41 million a year.

Syphilis and Gonorrhea

The following resumes of syphilis and gonorrhea are contained in data issued by the Public Health Service.

Syphilis:

Syphilis affects men and women very much the same way. Usually the syphilis germ enters the body through the skin in or around the sex parts.

The first sign of syphilis may be a sore. This probably will show up sometime between 10 and 90 days. This sore usually appears at the place where the germ enters the body; but it may appear on fingers, lips, or breasts. When a person has such a sore, he or she is said to have syphilis in its primary stage.

Sometimes, such a sore does not show up at all; or it may be so small that it goes unnoticed. Or it may be hidden deep inside a woman's sex organs where it cannot be seen. At any rate, it does not hurt.

Chancre May Look Like a Pimple

This first sore is called a chancre (pronounced "shanker"). It may look like a pimple, a blister, or an open sore. When a person has such a sore, he or she is very dangerous to other persons. The sore is full of germs, and the disease may be passed along very easily.

Soon after the first signs of syphilis show up, the germs begin to spread through the body and a blood test will show positive.

If a person has such a sore and does not take any treatment or does not put anything on it, the sore will go away by itself. But this does not mean that the syhphilis is gone.The germs still are hiding inside the body, increasing in number, and spreading through the whole body.

Rash After 3 to 6 Weeks

From 3 to 6 weeks later a rash will show up. This rash may look like a food rash or a heat rash or even hives. It may cover the body, or it may be just on the hands and feet.Sores may appear in the mouth. Sore throat, fever, or headache may develop. Hair may fall out in patches. This is called the secondary stage of syphilis.

In this stage, the disease may be passed on by kissing if there are mouth sores. In this stage also, the disease can imitate many other diseases. Because of this, many persons have syphilis in this dangerous stage and don't even know they have it. Of course, a blood test will tell.

Like the primary signs of syphilis, the secondary ones also will disappear in time without any treatment.

By this time, the disease is strong inside the body and, if it is not treated, it now begins to attack the heart and brain and spinal cord. After all the outward signs have disappeared, the syphilis is said to be latent or quiet.

May Feel Fine

A person may feel fine. He may go along for years thinking he is healthy. But sometime he may become blind, or insane, or crippled in other ways. He may die of heart trouble.

Even in the later stages of syphilis, one could be treated and cured of the disease. But the damage to the body could never be repaired.

Syphilis and Babies

Most state laws say that people who want to get married must have a blood test first to make sure they do not have syphilis. One reason for this is to protect their unborn children. Of course, syphilis may be caught after marriage if either husband or wife has intercourse with a third person who has syphilis.

A father with syphilis cannot pass his disease on to his unborn child directly, but he can pass it to the mother. Then, if she is not treated, she can pass the disease to her baby before it is born.

If a baby gets syphilis this way, it is said to have "congenital syphilis." Such a baby may be born too soon. It may be born dead. If born alive, it may have "snuffles," be very weak and sickly. Or it may have sores or rashes from which syphilis may spread to other people. Sometimes the child may be born deformed. Or it may be born with hidden syphilis which later can cause it to become blind, deaf, paralyzed, or insane, or even to die.

The best way to avoid such a tragedy is for every expectant mother to have a blood test as soon as possible after she knows she is expecting.

If a pregnant woman is found to have syphilis, she should get treated at once. If she gets treated before her fifth month of pregnancy, her child almost certainly will be born without syphilis. But a mother with syphilis who does not get treated has only one chance in six of having a healthy baby.

How To Tell If Its Syphilis

In the early stages of syphilis – primary and secondary – a doctor can take scrapings from the sores. He can look at these under a special microscope and actually see the syphilis germ.After the sores have gone away, the only way to tell is by having a blood test. So it is important to have a blood test at least once or twice a year, just to be sure.

Gonorrhea:

If a man has sex relations with someone who has gonorrhea, in a few days or a week he probably will start to notice a burning pain when he urinates. Then he may notice a discharge or "tear drop" of pus from his sex organ.

On the other hand, a woman almost never notices any pain or other signs when she has gonorrhea. So she can pass the disease on to any men with whom she has sex relations and not realize what she is doing.

A woman with gonorrhea does not feel sick and there is no sign of the disease until it spreads up through her womb and into her tubes. Then she has great pain and may have to go to the hospital for treatment. She may even have to have an operation, and after that she may not be able to have any babies.

It never is easy to tell if a woman has gonorrhea. Sometimes the germ may show at once in the "drop" from a man, because the pus is thick with germs. But in a woman, the germs may be few and far between, and so they must be grown and studied in a laboratory to decide whether they are the germs of gonorrhea.

Gonorrhea from a mother can get into a baby's eyes, either while he is being born or afterwards. This can make him blind. This is why drops are put into the baby's eyes when he is born, just to make sure, even if his mother is not known to have gonorrhea.

If a man has gonorrhea and does not get treated, it may spread to his glands and organs, and he may not be able to produce offspring.

If gonorrhea is not treated, it can also cause heart trouble and arthritis, blindness, and sometimes even death.

How To Tell If Its Gonorrhea

If a person thinks he or she has gonorrhea, it is best to go to the doctor or public health clinic at once. The doctor will take a small smear of the pus from the sex parts with a cotton swab and put it on a special dish. This dish will be kept in the laboratory for a few days until the germs grow thickly enough so that they may be found.They will then be stained and examined under a microscope. Then the doctor will be able to tell for sure if it is gonorrhea. Sometimes, this test is not necessary for men, because the germs grow so thickly in the man's organ that often they may be easily found and examined at once.

Herpes – The Incurable Disease:

Much less publicized, but growing fast, with 300,000 to 500,000 new cases a year, is the disease called herpes. There is as yet no cure for it (although it can be controlled), and once the person has the virus it never goes away. The sores and symptoms may recur at intervals of two weeks to several years. Herpes has been linked to cervical cancer as well as to birth defects. At this writing, one of the key people leading the attack on this virus is Dr. Paul Weissner,[21] director of the V.D.

[21]Reprinted from Oct. 1, 1979 issue of People Weekly, Time Inc. Text by Judy Kessler.

division of the federal control in Atlanta. Dr. Weissner was interviewed on the subject by *People* Magazine's Judy Kessler. The interview questions and answers appeared in *People* Magazine on October 1, 1979, and follows in order.

What is genital herpes like?

It is similar to a cold sore on the lips. Everybody knows what they are. In fact, the common cold sore is caused by a similar virus.

What types of herpes are you studying?

There are two. Herpes type 1 is most common on the lips. Herpes type 2 is most common in the genital area. However, each can occur in either location. This can be caused by oral-genital sex or by an individual's transferring the virus from one part of the body to another by touch. This is called auto-transmission.

Is sexual activity the only way herpes type 2 can be contracted?

That's clearly the odds-on favorite, except for auto-transmission. By and large, genital herpes is a sexually transmitted disease. When I see patients who have it, I don't have to talk about toilet seats and so forth because they know where they got it.

Can anything be done to cure herpes?

No, but there are things you can do to prevent getting it. You can choose to be either celibate or monogamous – but neither of those choices is extremely popular. Real prevention depends on communication between sexual partners. The virus is not infectious all the time, although we're not precisely sure when it isn't. We do know that when the patient has a sore or blister, the disease is most infectious. Many male and female patients feel a burning sensation on the lips or genitals before the blisters appear. Some women say it always happens to them during the menstrual period or during a time of stress. If someone can predict when a blister is about to occur, then he or she can prevent transmitting herpes to somebody else – either by avoiding sex or having the male partner wear a condom.

How long does an average attack of herpes last?

It depends on whether it is the first episode or a recurrence, and upon the sex of the patient. The incubation time is usually the same; very short, one to two days. For women the first episode is usually a three week period with sores and a high degree of suffering. They have fever, flu-like symptoms, headaches and severe vaginal discomfort. Then it goes into a latent phase. The recurrence is usually of shorter duration, 7 to 14 days, and the time between attacks varies with the individual.

Is it less bothersome for men?

Yes, the first episode tends to be shorter in duration – maybe only two weeks – and there is nowhere near the kind of pain and discomfort. Then the recurrences tend to be very brief – three to five days. Actually, part of the problem is that genital sores in men may not really inhibit their sexual activity that much. Men also don't have to worry about cervical cancer. Almost across the board, sexually transmitted infections are not "equal opportunity" infections. Women suffer the burden.

Are some people immune to herpes?

Undoubtedly. There are people who are exposed to it but never seem to acquire it. A few have what we call subclinical infection – they may not have the real blisters but may be infected just enough to develop an immunity. Some people believe that having lip herpes protects you from genital herpes, but this is uncertain.

Why is it so difficult to develop a herpes vaccine?

Its difficult to develop any vaccine, first. Then, this is a dangerous area. The herpes virus increases the risk of cervical cancer, but it may not just be the virus. It may be the virus plus some body reaction to it on the cells in the womb. We may be inducing that reaction in some way with a vaccine.

What is known about the connection between herpes and cervical cancer?

There are many suspected links but we cannot definitely say herpes causes cervical cancer. We can say if a young woman has herpes today she has a five-to-seven-fold increased risk of developing cancer.

Can anything be done to prevent cervical cancer?

There is action a woman can take – like having yearly Pap smears on an absolutely religious basis. Cervical cancer is a disease that can be prevented by early detection of precancerous changes in the cervix.

What is the danger from herpes to the newborn?

The danger is from a mother who has an active case at the time of her delivery. In at least half the cases infants will be infected, and of those that are infected half will die. The virus goes throughout their bodies, into their brains, their livers – all their organs. Of those that survive at least half will be left with some mental deficiency. So its a serious infection, but it is relatively rare; and it is preventable with Caesarean section, because the infant does not come through the infected birth canal.

Is there a test to detect the presence of herpes?

Yes. There is a culture test, but it will be positive only at the moment the virus is present in the area of the body being sampled. Unfortunately, in the dormant stage the virus could still exist somewhere else in the body but would not show up in the test. If a woman has had herpes, even in the distant past, she should tell her gynecologist so a sample can be taken during pregnancy. This kind of correction prevention is not spoken about enough.

What can a couple do if one has herpes?

They can avoid transmission through periodic abstinence. The one good thing about herpes is that most of the transmission of infection occurs within a fairly defined period of time. But nothing is foolproof.

Is any treatment effective?

None that removes the infectious virus. The history of herpes treatments is very long, but each supposed cure has fallen by the wayside. However, there are now some drugs that look very promising when they are tested on laboratory animals. One of these drugs is taken orally and is reported to decrease the duration of the sores and diminish the recurrence rate. It seems inevitable that somewhere along the line there will be a breakthrough.

Can you predict when there might be a cure?

No. But there is more hope now than a year or two ago. More funds are being invested by the private and public sectors to deal with herpes. People said we couldn't do anything about gonorrhea, either – it had been increasing for 10 years at an average rate of 12 percent a year. There has been no further increase in the last three years. There is similar cause for optimism about herpes.

New Herpes Treatment

The VD Newsletter, put out by the American Council for Healthful Living (new name for the Venereal Disease Service Organization) reported that a natural food ingredient, lysine, is proving successful in treating herpes infections. While no cure was claimed, trials have shown that lysine provided fast relief for pain and prevented recurrence of outbreaks of blisters and sores. Researchers found lysine inhibits the growth of the virus in the body. So far no harmful side effects have been noted.

Sterility – Gonorrhea

The aforementioned Dr. Paul Weissner, in an article contained in the Venereal Disease Service Organization Newsletter noted that an estimated 60,000 to 100,000 young women are made sterile each year as a result of gonorrhea.

This phenomenon is being called a "sterility epidemic." Women who have contracted gonorrhea frequently have no symptoms. Therefore, many do not find out they are infected until after permanent damage has occurred. Fifteen to twenty percent of women who contract gonorrhea develop PID (pelvi inflammatory disease) which frequently results in sterility.

A nationwide V.D. screening program, sponsored by CSC, identified 188,200 cases of gonorrhea in 4,294,044 women tested over a six month period. These positive cases represent an infection rate of 4.4% of the population tested. The screenings were conducted in a variety of health care facilities ranging from student health care centers to V.D. clinics.

This screening program, begun in 1972, has tested 8.5 to 9 million women. The objective of the program, Weisner said, was to aid women with the disease before it did permanent damage. Despite t screening program gonorrhea has continued to rise.

VDSO suggests that women can better protect themselvves from gonorrhea by being aware of the risks, using V.D. preventive measures and having regular gonorrhea checkups.

Fiction & Facts About V.D.

- You can catch venereal diseases from contact with a toilet seat, doorknob, shaking hands, etc.

FALSE
- Fortunately not. Venereal diseases are transmitted through sexual intercourse.
- You can't get a veneral disease again once you've had it.

FALSE
- There is no immunity to the venereal diseases – you can have a venereal disease any number of times.

- Gonorrhea or "clap" is caused by strain, as in lifting a heavy object.

FALSE • Lifting and straining have nothing to do with gonorrhea.

- You can tell by looking at a person whether or not he or she has a venereal disease.

FALSE • Venereal diseases can be detected only through medical examinations and laboratory tests.

- Syphilis is hereditary.

FALSE • Syphilis CANNOT be inherited. An expectant mother who has syphilis can transmit the disease to her unborn child, but this has nothing to do with the factors responsible for inheritance.

- A quick cure for these diseases can be purchased in a drugstore.

FALSE • Only a licensed physician is qualified to treat a venereal disease. Anyone who suspects he has a venereal disease should visit a physician or the health department venereal disease clinic – at once.

Table I[22]
Glossary of Other Terms By Which Venereal Diseases Are Known

- Syphilis may be called:
  Pox, Lues, Bad Blood, Syph, Hair-Cut, Old Joe.
- Gonorrhea may be called:
  Drip, Clap, Strain, Gleet, Morning Drop, A Dose, The Whites.
- Non-Specific Urethritis may be called:
  NGU, NSU.
- Herpes Simplex II may be called:
  Herpes
- Trichomonas Vaginalis may be called:
  Trich, TV, Vaginitis.
- Monilial Vaginitis may be called:
  Moniliasis, Vaginal Thrush, Yeast, Candidiasis.
- Venereal Warts may be called:
  Genital Warts, Condylomata Acuminata.
- Pediculosis Pubis may be called:
  Crabs, Cooties.
- Scabies may be called:
  Itch Mite.

Table II[22]
Veneral Disease Symptoms
(From American Council for Healthful Living)

Disease	First Symptoms Usually Appear	Usual Symptoms
Gonorrhea Cause: bacterial	2-10 days (up to 30 days)	White or yellow discharge from genitals or anus. Pain on urination or defacation. Pharyngeal infections are usually without symptoms. WOMEN: Low abdominal pain especially after period. May have no symptoms. MEN: May have no symptoms.
Syphilis Cause: spirochete	10-90 days (usually 3 weeks)	1st STAGE: Chancre (painless pimple, blister or sore) where germs entered body—i.e. genitals, anus, lips, breast, etc. 2nd STAGE: Rash or mucous patches (most are highly infectious) spotty hair loss, sore throat, swollen glands. Symptoms may reoccur for up to 2 years.
Herpes Simplex II Cause: viral	Highly variable	Cluster of tender, painful, blisters in the genital area. Painful urination. Swollen glands and fever.
Non-Specific Urethritis Cause: bacterial chlamydia	1-3 weeks	Slight white, yellow or clear discharge from genitals, often only noticed in the morning. WOMEN: Usually no symptoms. MEN: Mild discomfort upon urination.
Trichomonas Vaginalis Cause: protozoan	1-4 weeks	WOMEN: Heavy, frothy discharge, intense itching, burning and redness of genitals. MEN: Slight, clear discharge from genitals and itching after urination. Usually no symptoms.

(Continued)

Table II

Disease	First Symptoms Usually Appear	Usual Symptoms
Monilial Vaginitis Cause: fungal	Varies	WOMEN: Thick, cheesy discharge and intense itching of genitals, also skin irritation. MEN: Usually no symptoms.
Venereal Warts Cause: viral	1-3 months	Local irritation, itching and wart-like growths usually on the genitals, anus or throat.
Pediculosis Pubis Cause: 6 legged louse	4-5 weeks	Intense itching, pin-head blood spots on underwear, nits in hair.
Scabies Cause: itch mite	4-6 weeks	Severe itching at night, raised gray lines on skin where mites burrow—hands, genitals, breast, stomach, buttocks.

Table III[22]
Venereal Disease Transmission, Diagnosis and Complications
(From American Council for Healthful Living)

Disease	Transmission	Diagnosis	Complications
Gonorrhea	Direct contact of infected mucous membrane with the urethra, cervix, anus, throat or eyes.	Women: Culture Men: Smear or culture.	Sterility, arthritis, endocarditis perihepatitis, meningitis, blindness. Women: Pelvic inflammatory disease. Men: Urethral stricture, erection problems. Newborn: Blindness.
Syphilis	Direct contact with infectious sores, rashes or mucous patches.	VDRL blood test or microscopic examination of organisms from sores.	Brain damage, insanity, paralysis, heart disease, death. Also, damage to skin, bones, eyes, teeth and liver of the fetus and newborn.

(Continued)

Table III[22]

Disease	Transmission	Diagnosis	Complications
Herpes Simplex II	Direct contact with blisters or open sores.	Pap smear, culture taken when blisters or sores are present.	Has been linked with cervical cancer; severe central nervous system damage or death in infants infected during birth.
Non-Specific Urethritis	Direct contact with infectious area.	Smear or culture usually to rule out gonorrhea.	Women: Pelvic inflammatory disease. Newborn: Pneumonia and conjunctivitis.
Trichomonas Vaginalis	Direct contact with infectious area.	Pap smear, microscopic identification.	Women: Gland infection. Men: Urethral stricture.
Monilial Vaginitis	The organism is frequently present in the mouth, vagina and rectum without symptoms. Active infection may follow antibiotic therapy or direct contact with infectious person.	Microscopic identification.	Women: Secondary infections by bacteria. Newborn: Mouth and throat infections.
Venereal Warts	Direct contact with warts.	Examination	Highly contagious; can spread enough to block vaginal, rectal or throat openings.
Pediculosis Pubis	Direct contact with infested area or clothes and bedding which contain lice or nits.	Examination	Secondary infections as a result of scratching.
Scabies	Direct contact with infested area or clothes and bedding containing mites.	Examination	Secondary infections as a result of scratching.

REFERENCES

American Council for Healthful Living. *9 Common Sexually Transmitted Diseases.* American Council for Healthful Living, 1979.

"New Herpes Treatment." *ACHL Newsletter,* May-June, 1979.

Hass, A. *Teenage Sexuality.* Macmillan Publishing Co., 1979.

H.E.W. *About Syphilis and Gonorrhea.* U.S. Department of Health, Education and Welfare – Public Health Service (Pub. 410).

Macdonald, C. "The Stunted World of Teen Parents." *Human Behavior,* Jan. 1979.

New Jersey State Department of Health, *Strictly for Teenagers – some facts about venereal disease.*

Pennsylvania Department of Education. *School-age Parents and Their Education.* Bureau of Instructional Support Services, 1979.

Venereal Disease Service Organization. "Sterility Epidemic." *VDSO Newsletter,* March-April 1979.

Weisner, P. "On Hiw Own Words (An Incurable V.D. Called Herpes is Sweeping the Country)." An interview by Judy Kessler for *People Magazine,* 10/1/79.

---

[22]Tables I, II, III, contained in this chapter, developed from material reflected in "9 Common Sexually Transmitted Diseases" by American Council for Healthful Living, Orange, N.J.

Chapter 25

General Health Concerns Relative to the Teenager

Food: Needs of Teenage Girls

The author never ceases to be amazed at the number of teenage girls, who rigidly adhere to self or family induced diets (most of the time without medical advice or guidance). The New Jersey State Department of Health points out that food via a good diet is important for the teenage girls—the woman of tomorrow by affecting her:

- Appearance – Through its influence upon her complexion, skin, fingernails, teeth, hair, posture and body size.
- Personality – As shown by her pep, energy, self-confidence, poise, cheerfulness, interest in others, emotional stability and emotion.
- Efficiency – Through its influence on her physical fitness and mental activity.
- Future – A good diet protects her health and helps her prepare for a healthy, happy future.

The nutrition experts of the aforementioned New Jersey State Department of Health make the following recommendations relative to proper eating. This is supplemented by a chart of needs by food group, sources of vitamins and minerals and why the minerals and vitamins are needed.

- Be wise – Teenage girls should eat properly to have the get-up-and-go they need for school activities and social life. When they do not use the energy provided in food (measured as calories) excess energy is stored as fat.
- Be smart – Our teenagers should eat breakfast. It takes careful planning to make up for a skipped meal and supply their bodies with the nutrient they need each day.
- Be sensible – The group workers should caution the teenagers not to fall for fad diets. Whether they are too fat, too thin, or "just right" depends primarily upon what they eat, how much they eat and how much exercise they take. If a teenager has a weight problem or a skin disorder, it should be discussed with their physician.

What Does the Teenage Girl Need?

Food Group	Sources Of	Why?
Milk (Milk, cheese, ice cream) 4 or more glasses, 1 serving = 8 oz milk; 1 oz cheese	CALCIUM	Calcium is important for that winning smile. Not enough calcium in your diet results in poor teeth, poor posture.
Meat, fish, poultry, eggs; with dried beans, peas, nuts as alternatives.	PROTEIN Meat, fish, poultry and eggs. Milk and cheese, dried beans and peas. Peanut butter and nuts.	Protein is an important beauty aid—you can't be without it. With a severe shortage nails become brittle, muscles flabby.
Vegetables & fruits, 5 servings. Include 1 serving of dark green or yellow vege- citrus fruits or tomatoes (1 serving = 1 med. orange, ½ cup orange or grapefruit juice; 2/3 cup strawberries, ½ cup broccoli; 2 tomatoes; 1 cup tomato juice) 1 serving = 1 raw, 1/3 cup cooked carrots, ½ cup cooked greens, ½ cup winter squash, ½ med. sweet potato, ½ med. cantaloupe	IRON, B VITAMINS VITAMIN C VITAMIN A	This group contains vitamins and minerals. Vitamin A keeps the skin soft and smooth; Vitamin C helps maintain firm healthy gums. This group is an answer to a maiden's prayer for "that sparkle" from head to toe.
Bread and cereal (whole grain) enriched or restored.	Enriched or whole grain bread and cereal. Dried beans and peas.	This group has been enriched with iron and three B vitamins, thiamin (B) riboflavin (B) and niacin for health protection.
6 servings, 1 serving = 1 slice bread; 3/4 cup ready-to-eat cereal; ½ to 3/4 cup cooked cereal, including macaroni, spaghetti, noodles, rice.	Milk, cheese, meat, especially liver are good sources of riboflavin.	If your supply of these vitamins is too low you will feel tired, cross, weak and run down.

Athletic Prowess and the Proper Food for Teenage Boys and Girls

Most youth groups have many youngsters, boys and girls, that are involved in organized athletics at the school, community or group levels. Their performance is often impacted by the nature and amount of food intake. June Roth of the Newark, New Jersey *Star Ledger* gives some very heady advice in this area to wit:

Food can affect athletic performance in a positive or negative way, either by reinforcing endurance or by depleting the muscles of stored glycogen. A recent conference on athletic performance and nutrition, presented by the Rutgers College of Medicine and Dentistry of New Jersey, heightened the awareness of athletes, coaches, and sports nutritionists to the kind of menu choices that are best suited to rigorous physical activities.

David Castill, Ph.D., director the Human Performance Laboratory at Ball State University, Muncie, Ind., stated that athletes should eat a normal diet with a good balance of protein, carbohydrates, and fats. They should add extra carbohydrates in proportion to the anticipated amount of calories that will be burned off by the activity. For competitive sports, such as football and track meets, a high carbohydrate diet the day before the event will help to build up the necessary glycogen. This helps to keep the blood glucose levels at normal and prevents the occurrence of hypoglycemia. It is wise to eat a pre-competition meal about three hours beforehand, to prevent the ill effects of exercising on a full stomach.

Its also important to try to prevent dehydration during the sporting activity by sipping plain water, or slightly sugared water. Pick the right liquid because the more particles of sugar in the solution, the longer it will take to enter the intestine for absorption. All the speakers recommended cutting a prepared drink for athletes in half with water before they drink during competition breaks. The ideal liquid solution takes 15 to 20 minutes to get into the blood stream – hyperthermia (overheating) can occur in 30 minutes unless cool liquid is imbibed to offset the problem.

Foods that are high in carbohydrates include potatoes, pasta, bread, fruit, and cereal. Since the body loses a great deal of potassium in the process of sweating, its a good idea to eat high potassium foods the day before and in the meal preceding the athletic event. Foods that are high in potassium are bananas, fresh or dried apricots, dates, raisins, cantaloupe, watermelon, orange, grapefruit, prune juice, tomato, Brussels sprouts, beef and turkey.

Vitamins

Marcella Katz, the nutrition director of the Health Insurance Plan of Greater New York, advises in Public Affairs Pamphlet, *Vitamins,* Food and Your Health, that the amounts of each type of food to be eaten daily should be individually determined (generally larger amounts for *active* people such as adolescents). The author has underlined the word active – keeping in mind the cautions directed toward teenage girls earlier in this chapter.

According to Katz, vitamins are essential components of many enzyme systems, which act like spark plugs, initiating and giving impetus to the body's functioning. Though only very small quantities of vitamins are needed, humans and animals suffer disaster without them. The 13 essential vitamins are a mixed group of chemical compounds found in small quantities in food. They can also be reproduced in the laboratory. For group workers interested, Katz's article lists the nutrients needed, why they are needed, symptoms of deficiency, food sources and losses in food preparation.[23]

Fiber Diets

Much as been said and written recently about the advantages of a fiber diet and how it induces weight loss and helps prevent certain illnesses. Lawrence Galton[24] has written an interesting and to-the-point article in the December 30, 1979 issue of *Parade Magazine,* which addresses itself to the subject. The author feels that every sophisticated group worker might want to store this information for use when needed.

What is a Good High-Fiber Diet?

In the minds of many people, fiber is bran, and bran is fiber.

Not so. While bran is rich in fiber, there are numerous other sources.To get maximum nutritional value from fiber, experts recommend a variety of whole-grain products, fruits and vegetables, including:

Cereals such as old-fashioned, slow-cooking (not instant) oatmeal; shredded wheat; cereals labeled as being all-bran or largely made up of bran.

Bread, cakes, muffins, pastries made with whole-meal flour (whole wheat or whole rye).

Seeds, including whole sesame seeds and sunflower seeds; and seed-filled berries, such as raspberries and blackberries.

Vegetables and other fruits in this order; mango, carrot, apple, brussels sprout, eggplant, spring cabbage, corn, orange, pear, green bean, lettuce, winter cabbage, pea, onion, celery, cucumber, broad bean, tomato, cauliflower, banana, rhubarb, old potato, new potato, turnip.

---

[23]This is the kind of day to day information that can be passed on by the group worker to the group members in an informed way or could be made subject of special programs/projects (particularly those working with disadvantaged or poverty level kids).

[24]Reprinted from Parade Magazine, issue 12/30/79 – "How Fiber Diet Cuts Disease" by Lawrence Dalton. Permission granted by Mr. Dalton.

When the Surgeon General's Report on Health Promotion and Disease Prevention, in the summer of 1979, called for efforts to produce a "public health revolution," one recommendation was more consumption by Americans of foods rich in fiber – whole grains, cereals, fruits and vegetables.

In October, 1979, in testimony before the Senate's Nutrition Subcommittee, Dr. Arthur Upton, director of the National Cancer Institute, also urged "generous" intake of dietary fiber as a measure that might help reduce the risk of colon cancer.

Now scientific studies have also pointed to the importance of dietary fiber for people prone to atherosclerotic artery disease, for diabetics, weight watchers, those with a tendency to gallstone formation, and sufferers from other common gastrointestinal complaints.

Because of our low-fiber diets, many Westerners are constipated, with stools that are small, hard, pebbly and slow-moving. But fiber, once in the intestinal tract, absorbs water and swells. This makes stools soft and large, and it reduces "transit time," the interval between intake of food and elimination of waste. For example, transit time among African villagers – who eat far more fiber than we do – averages only 35 hours, compared to 90 hours for many in the West.

Constipation, rare among the African villagers, is more than a nuisance. It leads to straining, which raises pressure in the colon, pushing on the colon wall and causing the outpouchings of diverticular disease. Straining also raises pressure within the abdomen and may push the stomach up through the diaphragm, producing hiatus hernia and heartburn, regurgitation, and burning back-of-breastbone pain.

Raised pressure in the abdomen also can be transmitted elsewhere – to leg veins, dilating them into varicose veins; and to anal region veins, dilating them into hemorrhoids.

Colon cancer is believed to result from cancer-causing (carcinogenic) chemicals produced by bacteria in the bowel. With small, hard, slow-moving stools, the bacteria have more time to act; similarly, the carcinogens they produce are more concentrated in small stools, are retained longer, and can act for longer periods n the colon lining.

Establishing clear proof of fiber's good effects takes years. The evidence, however, is very clear about fiber's value in overcoming constipation and diverticular disease. With the latter, fiber's benefits are so striking – relieving it, often eliminating need for surgery – that so-called "bulk," once banned for diverticular patients, is now prescribed for them.

Recently, evidence has also been accumulating about fiber's values in other areas.

Weight loss. Several years ago at Britain's University of Bristol, Dr. Kenneth Heaton, a pioneer in fiber studies, noted that when he, his wife and some collegues increased fiber in their diet by using whole-meal bread instead of refined white bread, they lost weight. Not dramatically, but gradually, smoothly. The losses went as high as 15 pounds – and without any attention to calories or attempts to restrict the amount eaten.

In a study in Denmark, 25 healthy nurses took a little less than an ounce (24 grams) of wheat bran daily for five weeks. Their food intake remained constant, yet they lost weight.

Heart and blood-vessel diseases. Fiber may also help reduce elevated blood-fat levels, which are believed to be involved in atherosclerotic artery disease, heart attacks and strokes.

In one study, for example, fiber-rich rolled oats reduced cholesterol levels in three weeks. In another, when high-fat diets were fed to healthy men, their cholesterol levels shot up, but when one form of fiber, Bengal gram, was combined in these feedings, cholesterol increases was inhibited. In other studies, guar gum and pectin – other forms of fiber – have reduced cholesterol levels.

Diabetes. In 1975, a study showed a decline in insulin requirements in diabetic patients who ate increased amounts of fiber-rich foods. Since then, other studies have shown drops in blood-sugar levels and in the need for insulin or oral antidiabetes drugs, sometimes within two weeks after high-fiber diets are begun.

Gallstones. Stones in the gallbladder are comonly believed to be formed from excess cholesterol in the bile. Now studies indicate that adding fiber to the diet reduces bile cholesterol. A Unviersity of Bristol study found bile cholesterol reduced in 80 percent of patients.

Bowel irritation. Victims of this most common and troublesome of human afflictions have no organic disease, yet they suffer chronically from distention and cramps, often with heartburn, belching, nausea, weakness, headaches and faintness.

Several years ago, Dr. J. L. Piepmeyer of the Beaufort (N.C.) Naval Hospital reported improvement in 88 percent of irritable bowel patients placed on a high-fiber diet. Other studies have since substantiated these findings – to the point where in England and other European countries it is now standard practice to treat irritable bowel with high fiber.

Care of Teeth

Many teenagers keep a regular schedule of visits to their dentist. Yet what happens between visits – even in the first 24 hours after an appointment – can lead to trouble if the patient himself doesn't follow instructions for daily home care as outlined by the dentist or his hygienist.

● Consider these statistics.

Of every 100 Americans, fewer than five go through life without tooth decay. According to U.S. Department of Health, Education and Welfare, by the time school age is reached the average child has three decayed teeth. And, of children over fourteen, 75 to 80 percent have some form of gum disease. Other reliable sources point out that, in addition to gum disease, 4 out of 5 in this age group also have an average of 11 cavities. By the time they reach middle age, 2 out of 3 people will have serious gum problems and may be well on the way to losing all of their teeth.

● A clean, healthy mouth: its your responsibility, too!

Your dentist sees you only so often in any given year. He can do whatever work is currently necessary and advise you how to protect your precious teeth and gums between visits. The rest is up to you.

● The new "third rule."

We were all brought up with the two rules for good dental care: "Brush your teeth twice a day; see your dentist twice a year." Dental scientists have added a most important third rule: "Remove the plaque from your teeth at least once every 24 hours."

Tooth plaque . . . a prime cause of tooth decay and gum disease.

● What is plaque?

Plaque (pronounced plak) is a sticky, almost invisible film that clings to tooth surfaces. It is composed of saliva, cells from the tissues of the mouth and living bacteria always present in the mouth.

Even when you have just cleaned your teeth and have eaten no food, plaque continues to form because saliva is continually bathing the teeth and gums. Your mouth produces approximately 1½ quarts of saliva a day, which washes the plaque and its bacteria into every tiny, minute crevice of teeth and gums – just where it can do the most harm.

When you eat food containing carbohydrates (such as sugar and starches) the bacteria in the plaque can produce acid. And while tooth enamel is the hardest substance in the body, this acid can actually dissolve the enamel and cause decay.

● The 24-hour protective period.

If plaque is not removed daily, it can harden between teeth and at the gum line into a substance called tartar or calculus which can eventually contribute to periodontal (gum) disease – the main cause of tooth loss in adults. Plaque can build up to significant levels within 24 hours. Once the hardening process takes place and calculus builds up, a visit to the dentist will be required to remove it.

● Can plaque be controlled?

Yes, it can. You can control the plaque that deposits on your teeth, especially at the gum line, by carefully brushing and the use of dental floss. The procedure may seem a bit involved at first, but it will soon become a simple routine. And you will be rewarded with a cleaner, healthier mouth – with greatly reduced chances of tooth decay and gum disease.

- Your weapons against plaque.

The equipment you will need is easily obtained and quite inexpensive – much less costly in time, discomfort and professional fees than the destruction to which plaque can lead.

- The right toothbrush.

A soft nylon brush with double-rounded bristles is recommended. The head of the brush should be small enough so that you can reach safely all accessible surfaces of the teeth – especially at the gum line – as well as the cramped molar areas where most cavities occur. A gently rounded brush head also helps.

Mental Health

Richard Christner in *A Positive Apprach to Mental Health*[25] states, as we know, that there are a number of different types of mental illness, each with distinguishing characteristics of its own. As far as the layman is concerned, the individual names and symptoms are confusing. What the group worker needs to know, is what manifestations among the group members point towards *good* mental health. How does the teenager, who is enjoying good mental health, think and act? Here are some of the characteristics recited in *A Positive Approach to Mental Health:*

- He has emotions, like anyone else, but they don't explode for little or no cause. When he gets mad, his anger is in proportion to what caused it. He doesn't fly off the handle for odd or slight reasons.
- He experiences fear, love, hate, jealousy, guilt and worry – but he isn't overcome by any of them.
- He gets satisfaction from simple, every-day pleasures.
- He gets disappointed, but not so crushed by disappointment that he can't pick himself up and start over again.
- He doesn't underestimate his own abilities. He feels able to deal with most situations that come his way.
- On the other hand, he knows he has shortcomings and can accept them without getting upset. He knows how to laugh at himself.
- He expects to like and trust other people and assumes that they will like him.
- He is tolerant of others' shortcomings just as he is of his own. He doesn't expect them to be perfect, either.
- He doesn't try to push other people around and doesn't expect to be pushed around himself.
- He is capable of loving other people and thinking about their interest and well-being. He has friendships that are satisfying and lasting.

---

[25]Reprinted with permission of The Economics Press, Fairfield, N.J.

- He can identify himself with a group, feel that he is part of it, and has a sense of responsibility to his neighbors and fellow men.
- He handles problems as they come up. If he can't change something he doesn't like, he adjusts to it. He plans for tomorrow without being afraid of what's coming.
- He's open-minded about new experiences and new ideas.
- He tries for goals he thinks he can achieve through his own abilities; he doesn't want the moon on a silver platter.
- He does whatever he tackles to the best of his ability.

If the result is not perfect, he doesn't fret about it, just tries to do better the next time. He enjoys life, school.

Cigarette Smoking

Much has been written about the dangers of smoking. The author therefore will not go into an in-depth review of such dangers. He will, however, cover some comments made by Nancy C. Doyle, in the Public Affairs Pamphlet, *Smoking – A Habit That Should Be Broken.* Doyle is a staff member of the American Lung Association and a freelance writer on health and mental health.

- The teenage years are critical years, especially in the life of a cigarette smoker. When a teenager starts to smoke, the prospects are that they may be smokers for years to come: Three-quarters of adults who smoke took up the habit before age 21. That is why it is so disturbing to find young people starting to smoke at earlier ages than ever before.
- One hundred thousand children under the age of 13 are smokers. What's more, a government survey for 1979 showed there are 1.7 million teenage girls and 1.6 million boys who are regular smokers. This is the first time in the nation's history that smoking among females – in any major age group – has exceeded smoking among males.
- From 1968 to 1974 there was a steep rise in the rate of smoking among 12 to 18 year olds. But subsequently, during the period of 1974 to 1979, there was a heartening decline: Overall, their rate of smoking went from 15.6 percent to 11.7 percent – just about the same as 1968. It was, however, disheartening to see smoking among 17- and 18-year old girls contiue an upward climb, while smoking among boys the same age declined sharply. In fact, except for 15- and 16-year olds, the percentage of smokers among girls in 1979 was higher than among boys.

Why Teenagers Smoke: The big question is: Why do 3.3 million teenagers smoke at all? It is not that young people are unaware of the hazards of smoking. Government surveys show that 87 percent of all teenagers – including the overwhelming majority of teenage smokers themselves – believe smoking can harm their health.

When the parents of these teenagers began to smoke – most of them in their teens – the evidence of the devastating effects of smoking on health was not conclusively documented. Decades of research have since shown that, in most disease categories, there are significantly higher rates of premature death among adults who started smoking at a young age. There is also evidence that the health effects of smoking start to develop early and evolve over a lifetime. Even young smokers are affected adversely, whether or not symptoms are obvious.

There are other factors that lead to encouragement of teenage factors such as peer initiation, advertising and the like. The costs of smoking and the premature death rate among smokers are statistics that the group worker has at his disposal in dealing with the teenage smoking syndrome.

Cost of smoking: The health damage from cigarette smoking, says the 1979 Surgeon General's report, cost the nation $27 billion a year in medical care, absenteeism, decreased work productivity and accidents. Of this huge amount, direct medical expenses for smoking-caused illness account for $5 to $8 billion. A large percentage of the cost is born by the public through health insurance, disability payments, and other private and taxpayer-supported programs.

Smoking has been called "public health enemy no. 1" because its terrible toll is entirely preventable. The public health problem of smoking, however, is very different from that posed by most other environmental hazards because it cannot be curbed simply through the usual public health measures and massive public and private expenditures. It is a personal habit and it calls for personal action, a change in behavior.

Each year almost 350,000 Americans die earlier than they would have if they had never smoked. Below are the figures for premature deaths each year due to conditions caused by smoking.

Premature Deaths From Conditions Caused by Smoking –

number of deaths	cause of death
80,000	lung cancer
22,000	other cancers (oral, larynx, esophagus, urinary, bladder, kidney, pancreas)
225,000	cardiovascular disease
19,000	chronic pulmonary disease

Tuberculosis

Many group workers have the opinion that TB is now a rare disease. This is not so. In 1969 there were over 38,000 new cases of active tuberculosis reported, and more than 5,000 persons died from it. Moreover, there are an estimated 20,000,000 Americans who have been infected by the germ that causes tuberculosis, and as a result are at special risk of having this infection progress to active disease.

This has special significance for teenagers in groups, which work and interact at close range, in their normal environments.

Briefly, here is the pattern that the disease usually takes. A person with active tuberculosis coughs or sneezes into the air tiny, moist droplets – each containing one or two tubercle bracilli. These droplets dry out and become small flecks called "droplet nuclei"–light enough to remain floating about in the air similar to the way smoke moves.

The typical setting for infection is a closed room with poor ventilation. If the germs float out into sunlight, they are quickly killed. In a closed room, another person can breathe in these tiny droplet nuclei. But the body has many natural traps for catching such foreign elements. To infect a person, a droplet nucleu must ride the air deep into the lungs without being stopped. There it becomes imbedded and the germ begins to multiply very slowly.

Even though the germ starts to multiply, the body immediately sets up a defense. Usually it is strong enough to stop this growth. At this point the person has a primary infection. After most primary infections the disease is stopped right there for the rest of the person's life. This fact is possible because the germ is content just to infect and then to hibernate without ever developing into disease. Strangely enough, the damage done seldom has any effect on the person's physical wellbeing. Sometimes, though, either the body defenses are not strong enough or the germ is too strong, and disease develops soon after a person becomes infected. This does not occur often, so the greatest danger is the long-term threat of tuberculous infection. Progression of infection to active disease may occur in periods of stress caused by other illnesses or physical or emotional hardship. But often there is no explanation for why sleeping germs of a primary infection from years earlier suddenly spurt into action, causing disease.

Antituberculosis Medication

Antituberculosis medicines now available make it possible for all patients to recover. Cure takes 18 months to two years of taking medicine because these medicines are only able to kill the germs that are reproducing. When active tuberculosis is present, many germs are multiplying, but others are present in a resting phase. These resting germs make it necessary for treatment to be continued many months to handle the resting germs when they start to multiply.

Treatment with several medicines is the rule for tuberculosis patients because some germs may be resistant. Isoniazid, streptomycin, para-aminosalicyclic acid (PAS) and ethambutol are the four primary medicines used in the treatment of tuberculosis.

Studies have shown that most patients stop spreading tuberculosis soon after they start treatment. As a result, few patients need extended periods of hospitalization, and some don't have to spend any time in the hospital. Because of this important change in the treatment of tuberculosis, health departments are expanding and improving out-patient services so more TB patients can be treated at home.

Tuberculosis treatment is no longer limited to persons who have the disease in its active stage. Treatment with isoniazid for one year is recommended for infected persons to prevent their infection from progressing to active disease.

Things to Remember:

- TB can be cured – but the earlier the better.
- A person can have TB and feel well.
- TB is not inherited.
- Special climate, rest and food are not important in treatment.
- TB is a communicable, airborne disease.
- Local health services are available for help with personal or family problems.

REFERENCES

A Healthier Mouth Is Up to You. Block Drug Co., 1975.

Christner, R. *A Positive Approach to Mental Health.* The Economics Press.

Doyle, N. C. "Smoking – A Habit That Should Be Broken." *Public Affairs Pamphlet No. 573,* 1979.

Galton, L. "How Fiber Diet Cuts Disease." *Parade Magazine,* December 30, 1979.

HEW. *Tuberculosis.* Public Health Service – Health Information Series 33, 1970.

Katz, M. "Vitamins, Food, and Your Health." *Public Affairs Pamphlet No. 465,* 1975.

New Jersey State Department of Health. *Food.* Nutrition Department.

Roth, J. "Athletic Prowess and the Proper Food." Newark *Star Ledger,* 12/9/79.

Chapter 26

"Alternative" Services For Teenage Runaways and Others With Emotional Problems

The typical group workers will not be exposed to a runaway situation very frequently, if at all, during their careers. However, as in suicide episodes, a responsible and respected member of the community such as the group worker, can intervene in some situations to prevent such actions. A knowledge of the causal factors and remedial facilities and avenues in the community would be most helpful to the group worker, on an ongoing basis, should they ever be confronted with the problem.

Frances A. Koestler, a writer and editor specializing in the social, behavioral and health sciences, prepared an interesting pamphlet for the Public Affairs Committee titled *Runaway Teenagers*. She tells us who the runaways are and what makes them run. Much of the following data is taken from her pamphlet.

There is much in this chapter dealing with alternative services for the like of teenage runaways and others beset with a variety of emotional problems. The group worker might consider serving in such alternative service organizations, as runaway houses or group foster homes, at some juncture in their career. The author felt it incumbent to relay some data on the structure of such organizations (contained in the latter pages of this chapter).

Who Are Today's Runaways?

The simplest definition of a runaway is "a juvenile who has left home without parental permission." Legally, this constitutes a "status offense"—an act that is against the law only if committed by a person under a given age. But who is a "juvenile"? In more than half the states, a juvenile is a boy or girl under the age of 18; in the remainder, under the age of 16 or 17. State, county, and local ordinances introduce still other inconsistencies—such as how long a juvenile must be away from home to be considered a runaway—which complicate matters for young people and those trying to help them.

Estimates of the number of runaways have ranged from 500,000 to a million or more each year. A survey made by the Opinion Research Corporation for the Department of Health, Education, and Welfare, put the number for 1975 at

733,000. Its findings that 53 percent of the runaways were male contradicted a longheld belief that more girls than boys run away from home. The misconception was apparently due to the fact that girls are more likely to be reported as missing persons, more likely to be spotted by police, more likely to apply somewhere for help.

Eighty percent of the 1975 runaways were between the ages of 15 and 17. Seven out of ten runaways were gone less than a week; four out of ten, no longer than a day. In more than half the cases, the distance traveled was less than ten miles; in two out of ten instances, less than one mile.

According to the survey, runaways were "significantly more likely" to come from single-parent households or households where both parents worked. They had low academic aspirations, did poorly in school, were often truant, and felt that their teachers had a low opinion of them.

What Makes Them Run?

In the considerable literature on the runaway phenomenon, there are many attempts to explain its causes. At one extreme, the act of running away has been said to result from severe emotional disturbance. At the other, it has been viewed as a positive and natural step in growing maturity. In the late 1970's, the trend was to attribute the causes of most runaway episodes to external circumstances rather than internal psychological factors. This is unmistakably so for the group known as "throwaways" or "pushouts"—youths whose families have overtly or covertly spurred their departure.

While most parents feel hurt and rejected when a child runs away, some refuse to take the episode seriously, as if to deny the reality of it. In telephone conversations with parents of runaways the Opinion Research team heard comments like these:

- "He was just mad at us. We figured he'd be back."
- "We thought she had been picked up and someone had taken her."
- "They always come back."

Some comments clearly pointed to a pushout situation:

- "He had an argument with his father and his father told him to get out."
- "It was a mutual agreement. The best thing at the time."
- "We told him when he thought he could make it on his own without our help, he could leave. So he did."

Saddest and most revealing of all was what one parent said:

- "He had gone away before, but unfortunately he came back."

What do the runaways themselves say? Hear their voices:

- Michael, 14: "My parents hassle me all the time. Everything is always my fault."

- Larry, 17: "I'll never make it to college like my brothers. My mother and father are disappointed in me. They don't even try to understand."
- Linda, 14: "The other girls in my class don't have curfews. Why do I have to be the only one who must be home by 10:00, even on Saturday nights?"
- Carol, 16: "My folks didn't like the idea of my going steady with John. His parents also thought we were too young, so the both of us took off."
- Jerry, 15: "My father beat the hell out of me for smoking grass. But he never lays a finger on my kid brother, no matter what."
- Debby, 15: "My father drinks and my mother takes pills. They're too stoned to listen when I try to talk to them."
- Tom, 16: "I hate school. Tried to get a job pumping gas but the man knows my aunt and she told him I'm underage. Someplace where they don't know me, I might be able to swing a job, be on my own."
- Judy, 13: "I'm just getting even with my folks for being so mean."
- Barbara, 15: "My folks would just die if they knew I was pregnant. I heard there are places where you can get an abortion without too many questions."
- Peter, 16: "I've been busted for ripping off a sporting goods store. Now I'm on probation, and supposed to be in school every day, but I can't hack it."
- Jennifer, 12: "My stepfather raped me, then said he'd kill me if I ever told. I was afraid to stay there another minute."
- Don, 17: "There's got to be more to life than just hanging around that dumb old neighborhood. I'm heading for where the action is."

The "Alternative Services"

Until the creation of runaway programs, the only alternative to life on the streets for teenagers in flight was to aply to "establishment" resources such as the police, public welfare bureaus, traditional social agencies—all symbolic of the "straight" world many runaways were trying to escape. The traditional social, medical, and mental health facilities, young people felt, were disapproving and judgmental in their attitudes, unresponsive to youth's needs, bureaucratic in structure, arbitrary in policies, inflexible in procedures. Nine-to-five office hours, long waiting lists, appointments scheduled weeks in advance were not only unacceptable to young people in flux but unsuited to the emergency nature of their needs. Particularly objectionable to runaways was the practice followed by many social agencies of automatically contacting parents without waiting for the youth's consent.

The "alternative services," developed in the late 1960s, offered a third option in the form of a variety of unofficial helping agencies: free medical and drug clinics, hotlines, storefront drop-in centers, therapeutic communities, runaway houses, and the like.

The distinguishing characteristics of an "alternative service" were profiled in a 1975 report published jointly by the American Psychiatric Association and the National Association for Mental Health:

- Its service is readily available, with no strings attached. It sets no conditions of eligibility.
- It provides anonymity, not requiring that the young person give his last name or other identifying information. It pledges absolute protection of confidentiality—from parents, from schools, from the police, from everybody.
- It charges no fees except in unusual situations or for particular procedures.
- It is not usually located in a vast, dehumanizing building, but probably in an old house. Such furniture as there is will likely be ramshackle, and the walls covered with psychedelic posters.
- Its mostly young staff all have good "vibes" with young people and like them and enjoy them. The staff resist any impulse to impose their own value systems on a client. They usually do not have desks to sit behind. Mostly they wear blue jeans while they work.

The pioneer runaway houses fit this profile, as do many currently in operation. But there have been changes in the years since the first runaway service, Huckleberry House in San Francisco, was launched in 1967. Today's runaway programs are financially more secure, and are more professional in structure and in program than than was the case in the late 1960s.

During the last ten years the needs and demands of some young people have begun to be met and articulated by new helpers and new institutions. These people and their projects owe their origins to a "youth culture" and a "counterculture" which are themselves both influences on and heirs to powerful political and social forces: the civil rights movement of the late 1950s and 60s, the antiwar movement, and the women's movement. These workers in "alternative services" affirm the experience of young people in its autonomous integrity, not as a promise of future achievement or reflection of parental or societal ideals.

Among the first of the services they created were runaway houses, refuges for some of the estimated 600,000 to 1,000,000 young people who each year left their homes or the institutions to which they had been confined. Runaway houses offered young people a protected alternative to a street life which made them vulnerable to exploitation as well as to arrest and involuntary return home. Since 1967 their numbers have grown from a handful in large cities to well over one hundred in communities of every size.

The people who founded the early runaway houses were more likely to be the natural helpers of the "hip" community—ministers, organizers, street people—than those certified by schools of social work, psychology, or criminology. As sympathizers with, if not participants in, both radical politics and the counterculture, they tended to see running away not as a symptom of individual psychopathology or as evidence of criminality, but as a sign of familial disorder and of a society in turmoil. They believed that in a supportive context, running away could become running toward, an act of hope rather than a festure of petulance or despair.

Once in a runaway house, young people were automatically given the kind of respect that they rarely experienced in the adult world or from its institutions or professional helpers. The workers in the house believed that the young runaways were capable of making the decisions that affected their lives. They tried to listen to the young people, to sympathize without labeling or coercing or trying to "do things for (their) own good."

For these young people whose homes were confusing and disturbing but not intolerable, a few days at a runaway house and some individual and family counseling could provide the support necessary to weather a crisis or understand a particular dilemma; for those who were already all but independent, it was a reassuring way station. But significant numbers of young people left runaway houses after a few days or weeks to return home, only to become embroiled in the same futile destructiveness which had originally forced them to leave. Others, written off by their parents, left home to bum around or live on the street, only until they were picked up by the police–to be committed, or recommitted, to mental or penal institutions.

The latter young people returned over and over to runaway houses, often leaving in their wake legal, social service, and mental health agencies, which had made attempts at institutional and foster placement, at counseling and therapy. Between their periodic flights to runaway houses some wrote plaintive letters: "Can I stay at Runaway House for good?" "Isn't there any place I can go?"

Over the last several years, workers in some runaway houses have created group foster homes to answer these dilemmas and needs, to provide more or less permanent places for young people who could or would not stay elsewhere. But in making use of the structure and financing of the group foster homes, workers in alternative services have tried to transfor the homes' spirit. They have been trying to create real alternatives to institutions and to conventional "agency operated" group homes, as well as to the family situations to which the young people can't or won't return–that is, they are trying to create communal households which will respect the rights of young people to run their own lives, extended families in which power can be democratically distributed and decisions collectively made.

Dr. James S. Gordon, Research Psychiatrist and Consultant on Alternative Forms of Service for the Center for Studies of Child and Family Mental Health, NIMH, has had much experience in the area of foster homes, hot lines and crisis intervention centers–places where young people, who rarely felt comfortable elsewhere, could find shelter, food, affection, respect, and the kind of direct but sympathetic counseling that older siblings might offer younger ones. These organizations were often run by nonprofessionals and subsisted on a shoestring, particularly in the early days. Dr. Gordon recounts his experiences in a group of essays published by the HEW's Public Health Service, titled *Caring for Youth—Essays on Alternative Services.* His observations on the group foster home are worth repeating.

The Group Foster Home: An Alternative to Mental Hospitalization for Adolescents

Each year over 100,000 adolescents are hospitalized for "mental illness." Many of these young people could successfully grow to adulthood in the context of a cooperative household rather than as patients in a hospital or "residential treatment centers." What follows is a brief account of the way that one group foster home for adolescents, Frye House, served four young people who were diagnosed as "psychotic" or "borderline psychotic." Each of the young people had been referred for institutionalization or continued institutionalization at the time of their entry into the group home.

The Young People

- Sixteen-year old Tom came from a working-class Irish-Catholic family. A tall, thin, long-haired young man, he arrived at Frye House in a state of considerable agitation. In the previous two years he had been a truant from high school and a heavy user of LSD. During the last year he had run several times from a home where he had "always felt weird": "My mother was all over me and I hated that. I just couldn't deal with it." He shouted at his mother, cursed her, and spent increasing amounts of time away from home. He stayed with friends and in vacant buildings. Apprehended by the police, he ran again. For more than a year Tom had been experiencing auditory hallucinations, ideas of reference and particularly vivid fantasies of homosexual attacks. He believed that the television and the radio had "special messages for him" and that he had been born on another planet. Psychiatrists who examined before and during his stay at Frye diagnosed him as "schizophrenic" and recommended "long-term residential treatment."
- Clyde, a taciturn, serious, stiff-limbed working-class black youth came to Frye House a year after Tom. He had just been released from a training school where he had been sent for 7 months after striking his mother. He denied any problems—"nothing wrong with me that I know of"—but reports from the psychologist at the training school focused on a "long-standing phobia, dating to latency age"; on Clyde's absent father and his ambivalent attachment to his alcoholic and capricious mother; on his moroseness, reclusiveness, and sudden inexplicable fits of anger. Residential treatment was recommended and a diagnosis of "borderline psychosis" was made.

● Karen was almost 16 when she came to Frye. A bright and talkative middle-class young woman, she had spent the better part of the previous 3 years in two private mental hospitals. At 12 she had begun to be involved in protracted and violent arguments with her mother over her relationships with older boys. Within a year her parents had had her committed to a mental hospital, citing frequent episodes of running away, drug use, and Karen's anxiety as well as her promiscuity. During her hospitalizations Karen made numerous suicide attempts and gestures. She was diagnosed "schizophrenic" and was maintained for 2 years on phenothiazines. The hospital psychiatrist released her reluctantly, believing that further "residential care" was needed. He suspected that the improvement in her behavior—she was cooperative and affable—was simply a ploy to gain her release, a mask for severe underlying psychopathology.

● Lisa, the 17-year-old daughter of an Army noncommissioned officer, arrived at Frye House, in flight from her parents, and the psychiatrists to whom they had brought her. She wanted, she said, to live at home, but she couldn't obey the rules; she loved her parents "as people" but hated their "hypocrisy" and racism, their lack of love." In examining her at a mental health center, one physician had found "autistic preoccupations, loose associations, and marked ambivalence. He had diagnosed her as "schizophrenic" and recommended that Lisa be sent to a State hospital. Only 9 months before, she had been released from a private psychiatric hospital to which she had been committed for prolonged and heavy drug use and delinquent behavior—sexual liaisons, frequent episodes of running away—that her parents could neither curb nor understand. During her 2 years in the hospital she had been treated with moderate to heavy doses of phenothiazines.

All four of these young people 1) bore ominous (borderline or psychotic) psychiatric diagnoses; 2) remained for 1½ to 3½ years in Frye House; and 3) have now been living outside of it for at least 2 years. They represent approximately one-quarter of the young people who stayed in the House during a period of 3 years and one-half of those who had been hospitalized (the others were diagnosed as having "adolescent adjustment reactions" or "acting out disorders of adolescence") and the total of those who were diagnosed as borderline or psychotic.

The Group Foster Home

Frye House was opened in 1970 by the staff of a nearby runaway house, to provide long-term residential care for young people who, in spite of individual and family counseling, were unable to live with their parents. Frye House was both an extension of the communal philosophy of the runaway house and a version of the group foster home, a living situation which has generally been thought to be particularly appropriate to adolescents. The founders of Frye

House shared the therapeutic ideals of child guidance workers who tried "to identify with the child despite his behavior; and the political activism of the youth movement of the 1960s. The teenagers who lived with them were to be full participating members of their household, as entitled to make policy decision about their program and their lives as they were to receive therapeutic care and concern.

Each of the young people was placed in Frye House by a local court. In addition to their psychiatric diagnosis some were labelled "delinquent," others, "in need of supervision," and still others, "dependent and neglected." For keeping each young person, Frye House received between $350 and $650 a month (depending on the jurisdiction in which the teenagers' parents lived). With a total of six young people in the house at any one time, this provided a working budget of between $25,000 and $30,000 a year. Out of this budget House expenses (including food, rent, and clothing for the young people) and the salaries of two nonprofessional counselors were paid.

During its first year Frye House philosophy and practice oscillated between an informal living situation and a highly structured therapeutic community. As members of the emerging counterculture and youth advocates, the counselors were inclined to live in and provide the young people with a loosely structured commune. confronted with an array of disturbed and disturbing behaviors they briefly adopted the model of a closely structured therapeutic community based on transactional analysis and "re-parenting."

In the fall of 1971, in its second year of operation, Gordon began as part of his research into "alternative services for young people" (runaway houses, telephone hotlines, group foster homes) to consult with the House. His interest in working with Frye House grew out of previous experiences as chief resident and ward administrator on a psychiatric inpatient service. LIke its early proponents, he had learned to value the healing potential of a therapeutic community. Like more recent critics of conventional ward psychiatry, he tended to focus his initial therapeutic efforts on institutional and attitudinal barriers to personal change—on arbitrary and mystified authority. Frye seemed like a place where he could help the staff to drop these barriers and work sensitively and respectfully with the young people with whom they lived.

He began to meet once a week for 2 or 3 hours with all members of the House. In these meetings they talked about whatever came up—house rules, interpersonal and family problems, drug use, sex, etc. As a consultant his initial emphasis was on helping all House members to be, and understand themselves as, members of a functioning living community; to view their behavior as in some ways responsive to the exigencies of that community. Later on, the focus of these meetings sometimes shifted to understanding interpersonal dynamics, and later still, when it seemed both necessary and acceptable, to examining intrapsychic motivation. Thoughts and behaviors were always viewed in the context of current life in the House and of the way each person felt about them, never labelled and isolated as "sick" or pathological. He met separately with the counselors (also once a week) to discuss the interpersonal problems which came up between them.

He consulted with Frye House for 20 months; during the final 1½ years of the period covered by this paper a psychiatric social worker and social psychologist (with whom he continued to confer) took his place.

Gordon focuses on those characteristics which seemed to make the House particularly useful to the four young people described above. All of these represent goals and ideals, states of being, and attitudes which developed during the course of the young people's stay in the House. They took time and much effort to achieve, were precariously maintained, and continually subject to attack, erosion, and compromise.

- A deep affection for the young people who came to live in the House and an abiding concern for their welfare.
- Counselors who have this kind of feeling and commitment can weather a great many interpersonal and organizational problems and move beyond many of their own personal limitations. It is the indispensable precondition for the success of a place like Frye House; without it, all of the radical reforms listed below can become parodies of themselves.
- A refusal to exclude or include any one on the basis of any previous behavior, psychiatric treatment or diagnostic label.
- Prior to admission, each young person was interviewed by all the House members, young people as well as counselors. A dinner meeting and overnight stay (or in doubtful cases a stay of several days) followed. Decisions about admission were then made on the basis of how House members felt about the new person. The most important considerations were, in approximate order, how desperate the new person's situation was (the fewer alternatives the young person had, the more likely he or she was to be accepted); how much they liked him or her; and how they felt he or she would "fit in." Only the most obviously violent and aggressively antisocial young people were turned down.
- Respect for the right and ability of each young person to work out his or her destiny.
- Counselors encouraged all young people to talk over any major decisions, problems, or aspirations with them. They were likewise committed to helping the young people get what they needed—whether that meant teaching them how to cook and clean, helping them find an appropriate school or apprenticeship program, or locating and then taking them to appointments with a psychotherapist. But it was up to the young people to decide to go to school or work, to enter therapy, or to stay home. They were not restricted as to curfew or activities outside the house. Their

decisions respected, the young people were allowed to make their own mistakes and encouraged, in group and individual discussions, to learn from them.

- An insistence that the house be run according to principles of participatory democracy.
- Just as counselors wanted to govern the conditions of their own work, so they felt that they and the young people should jointly run the House. They believed that, given this power, the young people would feel a responsibility for a House which was truly theirs. Accordingly, all young people in the House had, from their first day, a full say in making and enforcing House rules; deciding budgets; hiring new counselors; regulating overnight visits, etc. Together, they and their counselors tok account of what was necessary for the House's survival in its neighborhood (no loud music late at night, restrictions on numbers of people who could hang out in front, yard cleanup, etc.); satisfactory to the probation officers who placed young people there (no drug use or sexual activity in the House); and adequate to insure the mutual comfort of all House residents (no physical violence, rotating schedules of House chores, etc.).
- A willingness on the part of counselors to be rigorously self-critical and scrupulously attentive to derelictions from mutually decided-on rules.
- In a House where consensual decision making had replaced hierarchic rule making, counselors were tempted to evade commitments they had already made. Counselors had to assert again (to themselves as well as to the young people) that they were coresidents, friends (and sometimes guides), not parents and custodians; that adherence to agreements or House cleanliness was important to them as people sharing a living situation, not as "authorities" who wanted to enforce rules.
- The presence of a consultant (or consultants) who helped shape (or shared) the above values.

The consultant's work was a) to provide a source of emotional support for all members of the House as a group and as individuals; b) to provide, at House meetings, an "outside perspective" on the way people were getting along with one another; and c) to remind all House members of their values (participatory democracy, mutual respect, etc.) when, under the pressure of particularly disturbed or disturbing behavior, they were tempted to label, ignore, or extrude one or more of the young people; d) to convey a sense of confidence that even the most peculiar or troublesome behavior and thoughts could be understood, dealt with, and learned from.

- The presence of a supportive community outside the House.

In the case of Frye House, this consisted, most immediately, of the counselors and young people who worked and lived in the larger organization (a collective of several social service projects, a runaway house, and a second group foster home) of which Frye was a part. These people met House members at organization-wide meetings, dropped by to visit, and were available to help out in a time of crisis. In addition, Frye House was located in a neighborhood of many other counterculture projects (including a number of "antiprofit" businesses) all of which encouraged "youth rights" and practiced participatory democracy.

- The possibility of a relationship between young people and their counselors and consultants which could continue after any or all of them left the House.

New Roads to Mental Health

Dr. Gordon points out that recent surveys reveal that 2 out of 10 Americans are in "serious need" of mental health services. Each year almost 1 percent of our population is admitted to mental hospitals. Millions of people are addicted–to barbiturates, heroin, methadone and alcohol. Psychosomatic disease is endemic.

In searching for answers to the problems of mental health, we tend to forget that they often have roots in the particular conditions of our society. Of course, we know that poverty predisposes people to psychosis and hospitalization; that fragmenting community structures and confused family relations promote depression, alcoholism and even "schizophrenia"; that pressured and alienating working conditions precipitate psychosomatic illness and drug use; that lack of employment opportunities and a narrow social vision make young people disturbed and disturbing; that isolation and institutionalization depress older people.

Yet we ignore all this and focus therapeutic attentions and our "economic resorces on individual sufferers. We call them "mentally ill" and all too often–as if their problems were simply analogous to a physical illness–treat them with drugs and electroshock treatment. When they do not get "better," we lock them up in mental hospitals.

During the last several decades the mental health establishment had adopted two major approaches to the American people's problems in living; biomedical research and the establishment of local mental health facilities. Neither has lived up to expectations. Both have been flawed by the pervasive and narrowing influence of the "medical model of mental illness."

Biomedical researchers, ignoring whole people in families and communities, work places and cities, have searched for the specific physiological and biochemical cuases of schizophrenia, manic depressive psychosis, depression and anxiety. They have experimented with medical and surgical cures–the right drug or the right operation, the right place in the brain to stimulate or depress—just as they might with treatments for diabetes or cancer of the lung.

When the phenothiazine group of tranquilizers—Thorazine is one—were introduced in 1954, they were heralded as the "cure" for schizophrenia. An immediate exodus from state and county hospitals was followed over the years by a leveling off process. Twenty-two years later, the percentage of the overall population in mental hospitals had decreased somewhat, as has the average length of stay, but the overall numbers of patients had remained the same.

Some of those "maintained" on phenothiazines, or more potent drugs developed later, seemed to function well outside the hospital. But many have come to feel as constricted, as robbed of their full potential, by the supefying and numbing effects of the chemicals as they had been by the hospitals walls. And many who felt satisfied with the emotional level maintained by their medication have found themselves experiencing severe physical "side effects"—impotence, disabling tremors, extreme sensitivity to sunlight, chronic skin rashes, easy tiring, obesity.

The passage of the Community Mental Health Centers Act in 1963 was hailed as a "bold new approach" by John F. Kennedy. It signaled a modification of the medical model, a growing sensitivity to the effects of poverty and social stress on the creation of "mental illness," an increasing awareness of the possibilities of helping people by working with them, their families and their communities to change their social situation.

The facilities which the act has helped create have indeed brought mental health services to millions of people. They have not, however, resolved the contradiction between a social and a medical definition of "mental illness." Too many community mental health centers simply perpetuate the medical model and, in so doing, provide inappropriate services.

In outpatient clinics that are little more than an aggregation of private therapists' offices, the center staffs insist that people fit into one or another diagnostic category and predetermined therapeutic experience. Instead of providing the services—economic and educational, residential, vocational and counseling—necessary to help seriously disturbed people live successfully at home and in their community, they tend to hospitalize them or to obliterate anxiety about these problems with maintenance doses of drugs. The consultation and education they provide is often directed at strengthening the skills of other professionals—teachers, guidance counselors, etc.—rather than, say, changing the classroom conditions which frustrate students, teachers and guidance counselors alike. Rarely do they provide services to people who, though needy, are unwilling to define and stigmatize themselves as mentally ill. Still more rarely do staff members spend a substantial amount of time outside their clinic doors, in the community they are supposed to serve.

A Profile of Alternative Services

Though there are many differences among "alternative" services, they share certain assumptions, attitudes and practices which make them particularly useful and responsive to the people they serve. Among the most significant, Dr. Gordon has found in five years of work with alternative services, are these:

- They respond to people's problems as those problems are experienced.
- A woman whose husband is beating her is regarded as a victim not scrutinized as a masochist; a child who leaves his home is seen, housed and fed as a runaway, not described as an "acting out disorder" or judged as a "status offender."
- They provide services that are immediately accessible, with a minimum of waiting and bureaucratic restriction.
- Hotlines, shelters for battered women, runaway houses and many drop-in centers are open 24 hours a day to anyone who calls or comes in off the street. If they cannot provide help, they regard it as their responsibility to find someone or some agency that can.
- They emphasize the strengths of those who seek help and their capacity for self-help.
- A 13-year-old girl, instead of being labeled a patient and dragged to a psychiatrist, is encouraged to bring her whole family to counseling sessions.
- They reach out to help the individual change the social situation—job, family school, workplace—in which he or she is feeling distressed.
- This may mean helping a young person to talk to her parents, providing legal services to a tenant who wishes to challenge a landlord, guiding a welfare mother through a bureaucratic maze.
- They are willing to change, to expand their services as the community's needs dictate and their increasing skills permit.
- As phone aides become aware that young people would not go to traditional mental health facilities, one suburban hotline expanded its services from information and referral to phone counseling and crisis intervention. Workers at an urban runaway house opened a job cooperative to assist young people looking for employment and a free high school for those who could not fit into their assigned schools.
- They are actively involved in educating the larger community about individual needs and in helping that community to participate in meeting these needs.
- Staff members give frequent talks at local schools, churches and civic groups—about drugs, sexuality, venereal disease and problems between parents and children.
- They actively encourage those they have helped to become helpers and reduce feelings of loneliness and uselessness by doing useful work with others.
- They rely to a large degree on nonprofessional workers.

In many alternative services more than half the paid staff are nonprofessionals. Mental health professionals who work with them do so on a cooperative or consultative basis, and often as volunteers rather than full-time paid staff. The professionals are there to share their skills with nonprofessionals, not to run the program.

- They are committed to using volunteers from their own community.
- Some programs use nonprofessional volunteers as an important adjunct to paid staff. Others are staffed and run almost entirely by volunteers—students, housewives, old people, businessmen and women.
- They generally operate under some form of participatory democracy or consensus decision making.
- In this context it is possible to change policies to meet the rapidly changing needs of clients, to provide with a sense of pride in and control over what they do.
- They function as mini-communities or extended families.
- This provides staff with a sense of warmth and security; they grow and change to meet personal as well as work-related needs.
- They are far more economical than traditional mental health facilities.
- An hour of counseling at a drop-in center costs a sixth to a third as much as an hour of therapy at a community mental health center. The price per day of staying at a runaway house is about one-eighth to one-fifth the cost of that of a general hospital psychiatric ward.

Building on Experience

Dr. Gordon continues: In the early years, alternative service workers believed they would always remain responsive to those who needed their help. Time, enlarging programs, increased funding needs and the attendant compromises, and above all the recession have all taken a toll. At a recent conference, runaway house counselors and administrators spoke sadly of their impending bureaucratization; or difficulties in meeting long-term needs for jobs, housing and specialized schooling, and of certain people—the violent, the seriously suicidal and the one retarded—who they simply did not have the time or skills to deal with.

Still, alternative services are successfully reaching several million people and shaping their lives. Any attempt to make mental health services more responsive to people's needs logically should take account of the kinds of innovations alternative services have made and the spirit pervading them.

To begin with, the facilities direct their services primarily to the residents of specific communities and neighborhoods, rather than to the amorphous and sometimes sprawling catchment areas and counties which now define their borders. The buildings themselves should be small—ordinary houses have served alternative services well—and as inviting as present facilities are forbidding. These places should be open 24 hours a day and provide phone and walk-in contact and crisis intervention with a minimum of formality and delay.

The people working in these centers should be encouraged to develop more skills and take on more responsibility. Staff roles would be flexible and those expert in a given area—psychiatry or administration—would be expected to teach each other. To keep all workers more sensitive to the problems of their fellows and their community, clerical, administrative and supervisory personnel would be expected to on-the-line work with clients. To make sure that all participate in governing the center, these programs would be staffed largely by nonprofessionals who live in the community; policies and operations would be formulated and overseen jointly by center workers and community representatives. The professionals involved would neither automatically control policy nor receive disproportionately high wages.

As a reflection of change in approach, such places might best be called "human service centers" or "community centers" or simply "centers." The names, designed to indicate a responsiveness to people's needs, would avoid creating the feelings of depreciation of inevitably associated with defining oneself as "mentally ill."

A center staff, instead of defining problems in mental health terminology, would help people to define their problems in their own terms. If a woman with five children is suicidally depressed because of the inadequacy of her welfare payments, the dreariness of her home and the rats that threaten her family, the center's crisis team would , first of all, on those realities, help her deal with the welfare department, assist her with child care and bring in an exterminator. Instead of involving her in long-term psychotherapy or drug treatment, they might help her become part of a group of parents in simlar situations; here, she could begin to find alternatives to her situation. In the context of this supportive group she might, at some point, feel free to talk about the "personal problems" which so many mental health professionals would insist on "attacking" first.

For people who need them, places to stay would be available. Thus, a person experiencing the personality disintegration and overwhelming anxiety that often signal an acute psychotic episode would be able to go to "crisis house," where he could be guided and protected by especially patient and skillful staff. There symptoms would not be suppressed by drugs; instead, the psychotic episode could become the kind of a natural healing process that exists in some traditional societies and in such modern experimental communities as London's Kingsley Hall and California's Soteria.

Similarly, young runaways, battered wives or those suffering the traumas of divorce, death or separation could shelter in residences and there rest, gain perspective, share problems. Though a dangerous and uncontrollable few would continue to require institutionalization, the vast majority of those who need longer-term care could be kept in their own communities—in ordinary houses, easily accessible to their friends and relatives.

The Opinion Research Corporation screened more than 60,000 households to locate some 14,000 households with youths in the appropriate age bracket. Among the most important findings were:

- Between 519,500 and 635,000 youths ran away during 1975. This comprises 1.7% of youths aged 10-17 and 3% of households with youths.
- Nine out of ten runaways ran only once during 1975.
- The West and North Central states tend to have a higher incidence of households with runaway youths than the Northeast or South.
- Most runaways were between the ages of 15 to 17; the most frequent age of a runaway youth was 16.
- Fifty-three point two percent of all runaways were male.
- Children of blue collar and white collar workers were equally prone to run away.
- More Hispanic youths (4.6%) ran away than whites (2.9%) or blacks (3.2%).
- More than half of the runaways (52.5%) traveled less than ten miles from home, while two out of ten traveled less than one mile.
- The majority of youth, seven in ten, returned home in less than a week.

The above findings and the following material can be found in the National Youth Work Alliance's National Directory of Runaway Programs.[26]

The Opinion Resesarch Corporation, in an extensive questionnaire, collected information from the samples of youth and their parents: 1) "returned youth" were youths who had returned home following the runaway incident; 2) "comparison youth" were young people of similar age from the same neighborhood who had *never* run away; 3) nonreturns were shelter residents or street people without a permanent place to live. The major findings were:

Family Stress:

- The single most important reason for running was not getting along with parents.
- Runaways were significantly more likely to come from single-parent homes, or, if both parents were available, where the mother was more likely to work.
- Runaways more often perceived parental rejection and felt themselves more often punished.

When compared with siblings, runaways felt they received less positive treatment and support.

School Stress:

- Academically, the runaways did significantly less well than the comparison group of nonrunners.
- Runaways were truant twice as often as nonrunners.

[26]Reprinted with permission of National Youth Work Alliance, Washington, D.C.

- Runaways felt their teachers perceived them as more "troublesome," "bad," more likely to break rules, and to lose their tempers.
- Both academic aspirations (what they expect to achieve) were significantly lower among runaways.

Peer relations:

- Only about 10% of runaways felt themselves to be excluded from peer relationships. However, runaways were significantly less likely to be included in peer activities.
- Significantly less runaways belonged to community organizations.
- Delinquency was significantly more often associated with being a runaway.

National Runaway Hotlines

National Runaway Switchboard, (800) 621-4000. Provides counseling and referral services on a 24-hour, free, confidential basis. Also allows a runaway to make long distance calls home at no charge. (HEW sponsored).

Peace of Mind, (800) 231-6946. Provides confidential relay of messages from youth to parents without revealing location.

Much more detail in terms of specific addresses and phone numbers of runaway houses and other alternative services and references will be found in the National Directory of Runaway Programs put out by the National Youth Work Alliance, Washington, D.C.

REFERENCES

HEW. "Caring for Youth – Essays on Alternative Services." *Public Health Service.* Alcohol, Drug Abuse, and Mental Health Administration, 1978.

Koestler, F. A. "Runaway Teenagers." *Public Affairs Pamphlet No. 552,* 1977.

National Youth Work Alliance. *National Directory of Runaway Programs,* 1979.

Chapter 27

Adolescent Suicides

The National Institute of Mental Health Task Force on Suicide defined the terms used in this field in 1970. This is something the group worker should fine most helpful, particularly in intervention activity. This definition and much other pertinent data is contained in a Public Affairs Pamphlet, *Adolescent Suicide: Mental Health Challenge,* by Arthur S. Freese, who has written extensively for medical journals.

In addition, a very informative pamphlet has been issued by the Public Health Service of the U.S. Department of Health, Education, and Welfare titled *Self Destructive Behavior Among Younger Age Groups,*[27] and was written by Dr. Calvin J. Frederick, chief of the Disaster and Emergency Mental Health Section of the NIMH. (The article contained in the pamphlet is a reprint of one that Dr. Frederick originally wrote for *Keynote* magazine and the Boys Club of America (now known as Connections Magazine).

Completed suicide "includes all the situations in which the circumstances surrounding the death lead to the conclusion that the individual took a positive action with the primary purpose of ending his (or her) life." This would include what is ordinarily meant when we speak of "suicide" or "committing suicide."

Suicide attempts "include those situations in which a person performs a life-threatening behavior with the intent of jeopardizing his life or (giving) the appearance of such an intent." This describes the behavior of a 12-year-old who, following her parents' divorce, repeatedly overdosed herself with pills, tried to jump off a bridge, and tried stepping in front of cars.

Suicide ideas "include behaviors which might be directly observed or inferred and which are concerned with or more in the direction of a possible threat to the individual's life. However, the potentially lethal act is not actually performed." This category includes those who make the actual preparations for suicide (get a rope and make a noose, get a knife, or accumulate lethal pills) but then go no further. It also includes those who suggest thoughts of suicide by letter, for example, or by obviously false denials when questioned about any thoughts or plans for suicide.

---

[27]This article is adapted and reprinted from material published by The Public Health Service and which in turn was reprinted from *Keytone* Magazine, of the Boys Club of America.

Obviously, in their direct research, suicidologists are limited to those who attempt suicide. The attempters are the ones from whom researchers seek to learn the reasons behind self-destructive behavior as well as the most effective preventive treatment of suicide. Studying people with suicide ideas may also give some insight into the reasons for self-destruction.

Generally, adolescence is a period of rapid growth and development in all aspects of life—physically, sexually, emotionally, and socially. For some adolescents it is a time of particularly intense turmoil, rebellion, confusion, and disturbance. This explains why teenagers can be so difficult to deal with—and why many adolescents have so much difficulty in dealing with themselves as well.

In a relatively few years, these young people must become adjusted to a new and much larger body, establish their sexual identity, become free and independent, learn adult responsibility and how to deal with authority, choose vocations, develop feelings of adequacy and self-esteem, develop standards and value systems, and gain self-control—in short, they must mature. And for young people today, such vast personal change takes place in a society that is itself changing at a very fast rate.

Not surprisingly, adolescents are particularly susceptible to depression, to feelings of hopelessness and helplessness. Normally, adolescents swing from one emotional extreme to the other, provoke and test parents and society, are irrational and impulsive. They are very susceptible to peer pressure and are likely to imitate their friends and classmates.

Though when faced with internal and environmental pressures many teenagers have turned to suicide, experts at The National Institute of Mental Health point out that actual completed "suicides (among them) are not as common as they are among older persons." It is, as they explain, important to understand that "very often when adolescents use a suicide gesture it is an unconscious cry for help in solving some problem that appears urgent and hopeless to them."

Dr. Calvin J. Frederick, chief of the Disaster and Emergency Mental Health Section, NIMH, discussed methods of recognizing and responding to behavior that can culminate in suicide in *Trends in Mental Health.* He points out that various forms of self-destructive behavior among youth, including suicide, have continued on an alarming course in recent years. The suicide rate has almost dou bled among young males in the younger age groups over the last decade. The figures have risen from 6.3 to 11.0 per 100,000 population for males of all races in the 15-19 year age group.

Sex Differences

Historically, males have been regarded as committers of suicide, while females have been viewed as attempters. The facts continue to bear out this belief, as a general rule. Nevertheless, both sexes can and do attempt the act for a variety of reasons, such as impulsivity, feelings of personal rejection, hurt and anger, the desire to get back at someone else by making him sorry, misguided martyrdom, loss of face, fear of disgrace, and the like.

Profiles

A typical profile for the young suicidal male is one in which the father has died or been separated before the boy is 16 years of age. The father is often a successful professional or business man. There has been a characteristic lack of close father-son relationship which brings on feelings of rejection, anxiety, sleeplessness, and heavy smoking.

By contrast, the young suicidal female is the product of a self-centered mother and an ineffectual father. After feeling rejection by her family and/or boyfriend, she frequently attempts to take her life. Thus, fathers are particularly important figures with both sexes. In the past, the mother has been regarded as the prime parent of the child and has unfortunately received the bulk of the blame for childhood misbehavior and the subsequent emotional and mental problems. Many serious and emotional problems, especially those with boys, can be laid squarely at the doorsteps of the father. If the father takes an active part in the child rearing process, young boys especially are likely to reap the benefits in a most constructive way.

Types of Self-Destructive Behavior

Three terms are frequently used to characterize acts of a self-destructive nature. Self-assaultive behavior suggests an attack or assault upon the self. Such an act may not be clearly suicidal. It is not uncommon for children to threaten injury to themselves or others. They may verbalize the fact by warning a parent or parental surrogate that they intend to hurt themselves. Persons experiencing repeated injuries are called "accident prone." These acts are often aimed at gaining love and sympathy which are not felt through other avenues. This may stem from sibling rivalry in an effort to draw attention away from the rival at almost any cost.

The term self-destructive behavior ordinarily connotes more serious cases than those in the self-assaultive range. There are varying degrees of intensity, and clearly self-destructive acts blend unmistakably with overt suicide. "Psychological equivalents" of suicide or self-destruction may be difficult to recognize because they can rest beneath the level of consciousness. As an illustration, we might cite the youngster who has a physical infirmity such as diabetes and fails to take insulin properly, even after having been carefully instructed about the importance of the procedure. Different degrees of understanding may exist, regarding death, even among older teenagers. Some youngsters live in a virtual dream world and feel as though they will be saved at the last moment and nothing will happen to them no matter what they do. On the other hand, they may feel the risk is worth taking just one time, especially if there is a need to meet with some peer-group approval.

There is some doubt about the exact age at which a youngster really understands the concept of death, particularly suicidal death. Most youngsters seldom appreciate suicidal death before the age of seven or eight years. Some authors believe suicide is not fully understood before the age of 9 or 10. The age at which youngsters can comprehend the nature of their actions regarding death will vary with cultural background, relationship to parents, presence of older siblings, intelligence, and exposure to violence, both within and outside of the home setting.

Suicidal behavior, per se, can be viewed as less equivocal than the other two categories. It may be defined as any willful act designed to bring about one's own death. A person may injure or destroy a part of himself without actually taking his own life, of course. This is the reason why self-assaultive or self-destructive behavior are useful dimensions on the continuum of behavior. A finality exists in suicide which sets it apart, at least in principle, from the others, even though the difference may be a matter of degree.

Intervention Roles

A number of persons who come in contact regularly with youngsters may provide first-line intervention, both in terms of spotting the difficulty during its incipiency and in rendering intial "psychological first-aid." Such persons may be club leaders, teachers, high school counselors, scout leaders, church group leaders, and the like. Youngsters who are in difficulty emotionally are often likely to talk to another adult, rather tan to their own parents. It is important for a youngster to have a leader or counselor who can establish the image of a stable and trustworthy friend. Because of the lack of such a relationship with adults, youngsters often turn to peers for support, many of whom are not capable of providing it or may be harmful influences in and of themselves.

Identification of Potential Suicides

Numerous contributing factors are apparent in self-destructive behavior, but the experience of personal losses continues to be a pervasive theme. These losses include those which are internal, such as loss of self-esteem, loss of confidence, or loss of face, resulting in humiliation. Then, there are external losses which are especially traumatic, such as loss of a job, loss of standing in school, or loss of a loved friend or relative. Many precipitating events which seem miniscule and insignificant to adults are viewed as monstrous to a young person.

Behavioral clues that may aid in suicidal identification may be either overt or covert. Overt behavioral clues include actions such as purchasing a rope, guns, or pills. Covert behavioral clues are shown by loss of appetite, loss of weight, insomnia, disturbed sleep patterns, fatigue or loss of energy, isolated behavior, changes in mood, and increased irritability. Signs of deterioration are often revealed by a sudden change of behavior, which may not be flagrantly rebellious enough to include rule breaking and legal violations.

Symptoms of depression are not always strikingly apparent, especially among youth. When these signs often do appear, the youngster may not have all the classical signs, such as loss of appetite and weight. It is a mistake to feel that an individual will not take his life unless he is clinically depressed. Adult depression and youthful depression may not be synonymous. Behavior patterns the worker should look for in potentially self-destructive youth include the following:

- Adolescents contemplating suicide are apt to have little solid verbal communication with their parents. In fact, this is part of the problem. They are more likely to communicate with a peer or another interested individual in whom they have some faith and trust. Thus, if it is apparent that a youth cannot talk to his parents, the listener should be alert to the nuances of a serious problem.
- A prized possession may be given away with the comment that it will not be needed any longer.
- The individual is apt to be more morose and isolated than usual.
- Young males are likely to have experienced the loss of a father or a close male figure through death or divorce before the age of 16 years.
- Girls who attempt suicide are likely to show much difficulty with their mothers, especially in the presence of an inadequate father figure.
- Adolescents are apt to smoke heavily, suggesting the presence of severe tension or anxiety.
- General efficiency and school work performance may decline markedly.
- Drug and alcohol use have increased in recent times, accompanied by anxiety, depression, and irritability.
- Even though apparently "accidental," one should be alert to instances or prior self-poisoning behavior, if known.
- The same youngster who tries to kill himself frequently has a history of self-poisoning, often requiring medical treatment. Ultimately, this behavior will result in self-destruction.
- Homes in which the professional suspects child-abuse, or finds the so-called "battered child" syndrome, are cause for serious concern, since there is mounting clinical evidence to indicate that future violence, including suicide, may evolve from abuse in childhood. If the youngster

feels openly rejected by his parents, this feeling should be noted, even if severe physical punishment is absent.

- It may be helpful to look for verbal or behavioral signs which suggest a desire to get even with parents. A prominent component in suicidal behavior is the wish to make those left behind sorry that they did not treat the victim better when he was alive.

Subtle verbal clues may take three forms: 1) talking about another individual's suicidal thoughts; 2) inquiring about the hereafter, usually referring to a third person; and 3) discussing legal matters like the disposal of personal property, or the handling of documents such as insurance policies or wills.

Psychological First-Aid:
(Not to be Mistaken for Professional Therapy)

The following are temporary preventive steps for the mature group worker dealing with the suicidal youngsters:

Step 1: Listen

The first thing a person in a mental crisis needs is someone who will listen and really hear what he is saying. Every effort should be made to understand the feelings behind the words.

Step 2: Evaluate the seriousness of the youngster's thoughts and feelings.

If the person has made a clear self-destructive plan, however, the problem is apt to be more acute than when his thinking is less definite.

Step 3: Evaluate the intensity or severity of the emotional disturbance.

It is possible that the youngster may be extremely upset but not suicidal. If a person has been depressed and then becomes agitated and moves about restlessly, it is usually cause for alarm.

Step 4: Take every complaint and feeling the patient expresses seriously.

Do not dismiss or undervalue what the person is saying. In some instances, the person may express his difficulty in a low key, but beneath his seeming calm may be profoundly distressed feelings. All suicidal talk should be taken seriously.

Step 5: At times it may be in order to ask directly if the individual has entertained thoughts of suicide.

Suicide may be suggested but not openly mentioned in the crisis period. We are told that harm is rarely done by inquiring directly into such thoughts at an appropriate time. We are told further than the individual frequently welcomes the query and is glad to have the opportunity to open up and bring it out. (Guidance from a professional therapist, as to the wisdom of this approach on all cases, should be sought.)

Step 6: Do not be misled by the youngster's comments that he is past emotional crisis.

Often the youth will feel initial relief after talking of suicide, but the same thinking will recur later. Followup is crucial to insure a good treatment effort.

Step 7: Be affirmative but supportive.

Strong, stable guideposts are essential in the life of a distressed individual. Provide emotional strength by giving the impression that you know what you are doing, and that everything possible will be done to prevent the young person from taking his life.

Step 8: Evaluate the resources available.

The individual may have both inner psychological resources, including various mechanisms for rationalization and intellectualization which can be strengthened and supported, and outer resources in the environment, such as ministers, relatives, and friends whom one can contact. If these are absent, the problem is much more serious. Continuing observation and suport are vital.

Step 9: Act specifically.

Do something tangible; that is, give the youngster something definite to hang onto, such as arranging to see him later or subsequently contacting another person. Nothing is more frustrating to the person than to feel as though he has received nothing from the meeting.

Step 10: Do not avoid asking for assistance and consultation.

Call upon whomever is needed. The skills of the professional community is generally essential. Do not try to handle everything alone. Convey an attitude of firmness and composure to the person so that he will feel something realistic and appropriate is being done to help him.

Additional preventative techniques for dealing with persons in a suicide crisis may require the following:

- Arrange for a receptive individual to stay with the youth during the acute crisis.
- Do not treat the youngster with horror or deny his thinking.
- Make the environment as safe and provocation-free as possible.
- Never challenge the individual in an attempt to shock him out of his ideas.
- Do not try to win arguments about suicide. They cannot be won.
- Offer and supply emotional support for life.
- Give reassurance that depressed feelings are temporary and will pass.
- Mention that if the choice is to die, the decsion can never be reversed.
- Point out that, while life exists, there is always a chance for help and resolution of the problems, but that death is final.
- Call in family and friends to help establish a lifeline.
- Allow the youngster to ventilate his feelings.
- Do not leave the individual isolated or unobserved for any appreciable time if he is acutely distressed.

These procedures can help restore feelings of personal worth and dignity, which are equally as important to the young person as to the adult. In so doing, the adult helping agent can make the difference between life and death. A future potentially productive young citizen will survive. The author reiterates that this is merely temporary psychological first-aid. Appropriate professionals must be in some way contacted in order to deal with the causal implications. The youth group worker generally does not have the skills or experience to deal with the suicidal youngster on an extended basis.

REFERENCES

HEW. "Self Destructive Behavior Among Younger Age Groups." *Trends in Mental Health,* Public Health Service; Alcohol, Drug Abuse and Mental Health Administration.

Freese, A. S. "Adolescent Suicide: Mental Health Challenge." *Public Affairs Pamphlet No. 569,* 1979.

Chapter 28

Guidance For Careers and Vocations, Job Interviews and College Preparation

How can the group worker contribute in the areas of vocational, career and college guidance? At first blush it would seem that the group worker, unless they have some special training and background in this specialty, would be advised to stay away from primary counseling. However, there are any number of related and tangental contributions the worker *can* make.

At the outset the worker can keep their pulse on the labor market by subscribing to the U.S. Department of Labor's *Occupational Outlook Quarterly*. This periodical helps young people, employment planners and guidance counselors keep abreast of current occupational and employment developments. The *Quarterly*, written in nontechnical language and illustrated in color, contains articles on new occupations, training opportunities, salary trends, career counseling programs, and the results of new studies from the Bureau of Labor Statistics. Some recent articles have covered these topics:

- Jobs working with animals.
- Job prospects for college graduates.
- How to look for a job.
- Training programs for professional chefs.

The Bureau of Labor Statistics (BLS) of the U.S. Department of Labor conducts a continuing program to gather and disseminate information about occupation and employment trends. They publish books, bulletins and leaflets dealing with the job market and careers. For instance, the *Occupational Outlook Handbook* is a mammouth 840 page "encyclopedia of careers" covering several hundred occupations and 35 major industries. For each major job discussed, information is included on:

- What the work is like.
- Job prospects to 1985.
- Personal qualifications, training and educational requirements.
- Working conditions.
- Earnings.
- Chances for advancement.
- Where to find additional information.

The BLS also publishes Education and Job leaflets. These are a series of five leaflets that list jobs that require specified education. Titles are jobs for which:

- High school education is preferred, but not essential.
- High school education is generally required.
- Apprenticeships are available.
- Junior college, technical institute or other specialized training is usually required.
- College education is usually required.

Careers

The BLS puts out a series of 11 leaflets on careers, called Motivational leaflets. These discuss the types of jobs that may be available to persons with an interest or proficiency in a particular academic subject or field—such as clerical jobs, ecology, English, foreign languages, health (without a college degree), liberal arts, math, mechanics, outdoors, science and social science.

This and other resource material such as film strips is available for distribution at the various BLS Regional Offices at a reasonable cost and in some instances at no cost.

The Summer 1979 *Quarterly* reported that the BLS has prepared projections of employment by industry through 1990. Information such as this is of value, as adjunct information, for the typical group worker.

Some Industries Will Grow Like Pumpkins

Overall, employment is expected to grow less rapidly than it did in the 1960s, but some industries will grow much faster.

The service industries, especially private medical care and miscellaneous business services, will lead the pack, if current trends continue.

These ten industries will have the highest rates of growth in employment:

Others Will Wither Like Prunes

Several industries are projected to employ fewer people in 1990 than they did in 1977. The largest cutback is among private household workers, a result of the decreasing supply in this group. Lower demand for some goods will cause employment drops in other industries.

These ten industries are projected to have fewer workers in 1990 than they did in 1977:

Employees Turn Over Like Flapjacks

The average firm hired about as many workers during the year as it employs at any one time, according to the first study ever made of total hiring in the private sector. In other words, a firm with 100 employees is likely to hire about 100 new ones during the year. New employees usually don't fill new positions, however. The need to replace workers who leave the company

- Medical services other than hospitals and doctors' and dentists' services;
- Miscellaneous transportation equipment, such as motor homes;
- Miscellaneous business services, such as mailing services;
- Synthetic fiber manufacturing;
- Computer and peripheral equipment manufacturing;
- Hospitals;
- Floor covering manufacturing;
- Transportating services;
- vices;
- Copper ore mining;
- Radio and Television broadcasting.
- Chemical and fertilizer mineral mining;
- Leather tanning and industrial leather manufacturing;
- Structural clay product manufacturing;
- Private households;
- Wooden container manufacturing;

Manufactured dairy products;
- Gas utilities;
- Agricultural, dairy and poultry products;
- Sawmills and planning mills; and
- Railroad transportation.

accounts for most of the hiring. The study, which was commissioned by the U.S. Employment Service, points out that the average is high because industries such as building construction, eating and drinking places, amusement and recreation establishments, and hotels and motels have hiring rates in excess of 220 percent. On the other hand, some industries, such as communications, public utilities, and air transportation have rates of less than 32 percent. Rates also vary widely by state, ranging from 200 percent in Wyoming to 48 percent in Pennsylvania and Michigan.

Job Interview Demeanor

Another positive contribution the group worker can make is to train the teenagers, via lecture and/or role playing, how to deport themselves during job interview sessions.

Factors to be Observed During Interview for Non-Supervisory Positions

Generally speaking employers will be looking for similar facts in interviews for the various types of positions filled. However, there are some significant differences in terms of emphasis as well as some basic differences in factors when interviewing for supervisory vs. non-supervisory positions. When conducting interviews for non-supervisory positions, employers look for:

Oral expression

- They look for three things when observing a candidate's ability in oral expression:
- Fluency in expressing thoughts.
- Appropriateness of language.
- Voice and delivery.

Candidates can possess varying degrees of proficiency in any combination of these three elements. Ideally, all three should be possessed to a high degree. Clarity, suitable language, and a convincing manner demonstrate these three items sought from an individual who is orally communicating thoughts and ideas.

Poise

- "Poise" might be defined as the outward indication of inner assurance. In observing the candidates on this factor, employers watch for indications of whether they are at ease (recognizing, of course, that the interview itself will create some tension). They notice whether the applicants seem to be in command of themselves and the situation. They will be especially interested in observing the candidate as the interview moves from a somewhat relaxed situation to one of greater stress and in observing mannerisms and bearing as the interview is concluded.

Initiative

- Initiative can be described as the ability to think and act on matters without being urged. Candidates are often asked questions relating to this factor which, when answered, will demonstrate willingness to seek a course of action related to work situations with little or no prodding from supervisors. In their areas of responsibility, they should clearly demonstrate that they have been willing to think and act on matters with relatively little instruction to do so.

Ability to communicate

- Probably one of the most important factors to consider, the ability to communicate brings most elements of a person's performance together. Employers look for a person's ability to transmit ideas in a coherent, easily understood manner of development, one which conveys all the salient points witout confusion and with full understanding.

Self-confidence

- This factor should not be confused with any subjective evaluation of what self-confidence should be in an individual. It should not be equated with aggressiveness, nor should it be contrasted with self-effacing behavior. Evaluation of self-confidence should be based on the assuredness with which an individual takes a position and the willingness to hold that position based on the knowledges which were used to arrive at the decision. Other individual personality factors should not affect an evaluation of a person's self-confidence.

Decision-making ability

● "Knowing where to go" is one way of describing decision-making ability. In non-supervisory positions, this is as important as in supervisory positions. What kind of information to obtain to resolve an issue, what to do with the information once received, where to go when faced with the unexpected—these are all decisions made by individuals in non-supervisory positions as part of their daily routine and should be demonstrated in an interview.

Judgment and analytical ability

●Before making a decision, an individual analyzes data, facts, other information and has to make judgments or have opinions about their value and their proper use. Also, in dealing with other individuals and in following a course of action, good judgment ought to clearly demonstrate understanding and good sense.

Factors Observed During Interview for Supervisory Positions

All of the above seven factors will be observed during an interview for a supervisory position. Special attention must be given to four of them.

Initiative

● As above, employers look for the ability to think and act on matters without being urged; however, application would be to situations appropriate to someone in a supervisory capacity.

Ability to communicate

● In addition to the description given to this factor above, other considerations become equally important in interviews for a supervisory position. Effective communication with subordinates as an element of this factor is a necessary ability for all supervisory candidates.

Decision-making ability

● For a supervisor, this factor enters into virtually every aspect of job performance. To demonstrate possession of this factor, a candidate should be able to decide between alternative courses of action with little vacillation, when presented with all of the relevant facts in a given situation.

Judgment

● Again, the description of this factor and what to look for applies equally to candidates for supervisory positions. Application is expanded, however, in terms of the types of situations in which it can be demonstrated, such as in work planning and supervision of employees.

Other Ways to Help

The group worker can be of aid to the membership in a number of other ways, such as helping them with the preparation of resumes, college applications and other types of correspondence.

For those going to college, it might be to their advantage if the group worker were to advise them of such work-study programs known as Cooperation Education. Many colleges feature such programs on a full or part-time basis.

The group worker could be of further aid to teenage job applicants by conducting mock interviews and asking a series of typical questions that might ordinarily be directed toward such applicants by prospective employers.

Economically Disadvantaged Individuals

Group workers involved with econimcally disadvantaged youths might get such young people placed with employers choosing to participate in a special program wherein the employers' receive entitlement for a special Federal Tax credit for hiring such youths.

For tax years ending after 1978, but before 1981, a new targeted jobs credit was allowed that replaced the previous new jobs tax credit. The targeted jobs credit was designed to provide an incentive to employers to hire certain persons from groups that have a particularly high unemployment rate, or that have other special employment needs. Youth workers should check into similar follow-up programs for subsequent years.

Targeted Groups

A person was considered a member of a targeted group if the person met the requirements of any of the groups listed in the next paragraph. To take the credit, the employer must first have hired the employee after September 2, 1978. If one hired the employee after that date but before 1979, the employee was treated as if he or she was hired on January 1, 1979. An exception to this rule applies to vocational rehabilitation referral employees on whom a jobs tax credit was taken in a tax year beginning in 1977 or 1978. These employees do not have to be first hired after September 26, 1978.

Members of targeted groups are persons who are:

- Vocation rehabilitation referrals;
- Economically disadvantaged youths;
- Economically disadvantaged Vietnam-era veterans;
- Supplemental Security Income (SSI) recipients;
- General assistance recipients;
- Youths participating in a cooperative education program; or
- Economically disadvantaged ex-convicts.

Certification. For an employer to claim the targeted jobs credit on the wages paid to an employee, that employee must have been certified as a member of a targeted group by the designated local agency. Designated agencies are generally local offices of the State Employment Security Agency (Jobs Service). In the case of a student participating in a qualified cooperative education program, the student is certified by the school.

Cooperative Education

Cooperative Education is an on-the-job training program directly related to the student's academic major and career interests. It provides an off-campus work assignment through which they earn degree credit and, in some situations, a salary as well. Its a concentrated period during which they develop professional skills and greater knowledge of the world of work, while still in college. With participation in Cooperative Education, they have the advantage of graduating with both academic preparation and practical experience.

While on the job they are usually supervised by professionals in the field and by members of the college faculty. They are expected to maintain high standards of accomplishment and performance equal to or better than their academic level. They earn a pass/fail grade and work under a "learning contract" developed jointly between the supervising faculty member, employer, and the student. Salaries which may be offered vary according to the nature of the particular work assignment.

Many commercial organizations and government agencies participate as partners in cooperative education endeavors. One example of a government agency, which has successfully operated a co-op program is the Internal Revenue Service.

The Internal Revenue Service began its Cooperative Education activities in 1966, with a program designed to develop undergraduate accounting majors for positions as Internal Revenue Agents and Internal Auditors. Since then, undergraduate programs have been expanded to include students with all academic backrounds, for positions as Revenue Officers, Tax Auditors, Special Agents, and Internal Security Inspectors. Today there are over 800 students participating annually in these programs, and co-op agreements have been negotiated with over 350 colleges and universities across the country.

The Internal Revenue Service believes that cooperative education performs a vital function for all concerned by integrating classroom theory and practical work experience.

The Co-op receives training and work assignments which supplement their studies. At the same time they acquire a marketable skill and eligibility for a position with IRS upon successful completion of the program. The Co-op program assists their school in its placement efforts and provides the IRS an input of trained, skilled men and women to help perform their mission.

Non-Graduates

Edwin Herr and Stanley Cramer in *Vocational Guidance and Development in the Schools* point out that all students to be placed will not be high school graduates. Therefore the group worker, if he is to do supplemental counseling, will need to know of jobs available for the school dropout as well. At the point of placement of school dropouts, the counselor (or the group worker) needs to reject the temptation to admonish about how much monetary difference exists between them and high school graduates or why this choice condemns them to a life-long position of unskilled or semiskilled work. Herr and Cramer feel that the appropriate course is to ensure that the teenager understands he is not foreclosed from continuing his education. Along with this should be the reassurance that if and when he is interested in resuming his high school program, he undoubtedly will be welcome to do so.

Herr and Cramer quote Bottoms and Matheny who have suggested that three sequential steps are necessary to a high school placement program:

- Preparation for entrance into the world of work which includes assessments on one's own desires, abilities, etc., and the acquisition of knowledge about occupations and what is expected of a person in a work setting.
- Locating and accepting a job, which includes making plans for moving from school to work and in implementing plans as well as contacting of potential employers.
- Follow-through personal contact and counseling for students once they are placed on a job to assist them in retaining the job and in establishing plans for moving up the job.

It is obvious that the group worker, with a myriad of other duties, cannot do full justice to the follow-through contact and counseling requirements along with the many other requisites that vest with the full-time vocational guidance professionals. The author, reiterates his stand that the group workers' involvement in this discipline remain peripheral and adjunctive, rather than primary in nature.

Preparation for College

The group worker should attempt to develop a mini library of various college catalogs and brochures as a reference point for young group members beginning to think in terms of college attendance. These catalogs are available by writing directly to the colleges.

In further helping the group member to prepare for college, the group worker could steer the members toward publications and aids such as the ARCO series. The latter company puts out a book called *2300 Steps to Word*

Power, which includes college board vocabulary practice. The group workers might also acquaint themselves with the various college board "prep" programs available in most communities, again for reference purposes.

There are many published "How To" or "Practice" aids available to help the youth group member get into college or to attain highly desirable employment. The "ARCO" books mentioned above specialize in this field and the author will mention a few, just to give the group worker an idea as to what is available.

Practice Materials

The books in this series are designed to give college-bound high school students thorough preparation and practice material in the subjects required by hundreds of coleges as part of the college entrance examination. Each book contains: 1) complete sample tests closely following in format and level of difficulty the actual test given in the specific subject; 2) every type of question appearing on the actual test; 3) answers and, where appropriate, full explanations of the correct answers. The authors and consultants are all specialists in their fields.

The following titles have been published:

- *Aptitude Tests*

Preparation for the Scholastic Aptitute Test, taken annually by over 800,000 students. Practice for the verbal and math parts are included as well as "College Board" vocabulary list, writing sample tips, and 2,000 SAT-type questions and answers. Sample SAT tests with answers are given.

- *How to Pass on the American College Testing Program Exams*

Book to assist the high school senior in entering the college of his choice where the American College Testing Program is the method of student selection. This book offers a sample examination for practice along with complete study sections in each phase of the exam.

Thousands of test-type questions are provided with complete answers for practice.

- *National Merit Scholarship Tests*

Book presents full details on all phases of the scholarship program; helps high school seniors to pass the screening and qualifying exams and win a college scholarship. Provides two realistic example exams plus hundreds of test-type questions and answers for intensive study and practice.

- *Scoring High on Reading Tests*

Easily understood material in this book is designed to help candidates pass high on one of the most difficult subjects that appears on exams. Includes question and answer study sections on reading comprehension, interpretation, paragraphs, sentence completion, literary materials, judgment and reasoning and a concise course for faster, more efficient reading and comprehension.

- *Nursing School Entrance Examination*

A book for those seeking admission to all types of professional nursing schools. It is designed to help applicants pass high on the National League for Nursing Pre-Nursing and Guidance Examination, or on the Psychological Corp. Entrance Examination for Schools of Professional Nursing. Over 2,000 nursing school entrance exam-type questions and answers on all phases of the examination as well as sample tests.

- *Vocabulary Building and Guide to Verbal Tests*

Material in this book is designed to help civil service candidates pass the test subjects that appear most frequently on exams. Includes etymology, vocabulary, verbal questions, analogies, antonyms, synonyms, spelling and grammar. Thousands of questions and answers.

Dictionary of Occupational Titles

Of utmost importance to any group worker providing adjunctive services in vocational guidance is access to the Department of Labor's *Dictionary of Occupational Titles.*

- Contains a review of contents and purpose
- Focuses on occupational classifications and definitions
- Includes standardized and comprehensive descriptions of job duties, related information for 20,000 occupations.
- Covers nearly all jobs in U.S. economy
- Groups occupations into systematic occupational classification structure based on interrelationships of job tasks and requirements.
- Designed as job placement tool to facilitate matching job requirements and worker skills.

Hard to Employ

Many of the group workers will be in contact with youths that for any number of reasons are hard to employ. The Committee for Economic Development, 477 Madison Avenue, N.Y.C., has published a number of publications and materials relating to jobs for the hard-to-employ including:

- *Training and Jobs Programs in Action: Case Studies in Private-Sector Initiatives for the Hard-to-Employ*

Presents the results of a CED survey of what over 60 companies and organizations are doing to develop training and jobs for the hard-to-employ.

- Review and Discussion Guide: *Jobs for the Hard-to-Employ*
- Digest: *Jobs for the Hard-to-Employ*
- Filmstrip: *Jobs for the Hard-to-Employ*

Resources — Job and Career Guidance

Many insurance companies, such as New York Life, engage in public service programs to help young people choose productive and satisfying careers. Some of the reference books and data mentioned herein are drawn from their booklets.

Libraries are invaluable resources when you're trying to dig out obscure information. Under the heading "Occupations" in Subject Guide to Books in Print, a librarian may find listed a book about the field the worker is interested in. The librarian may also be able to give on the name and address of a professional society, trade association, or labor union which has pamphlets or other material. Three directories which may be useful along this line are the Encyclopedia of Associations, the Directory of Trade and Professional Associations of the United States, and the Directory of Labor Unions.

Other books of a general nature which may be helpful:

Bibliography of Current Career Information.
Blue Book of Occupational Education.
Directory of Accredited Institutions.
Encyclopedia of Careers and Vocational Guidance.
How to Get The Right Job and Keep It.
Lovejoy's Career and Vocational School Guide.
Modern Vocational Trends Reference Handbook.
Occupational Outlook Handbook.
Who's Hiring Who ... The Journal of Jobs: How and Where To Get a Better Job

The following important reference works are in most cases too expensive for individual purchase. However, they should be available at college and public libraries.

- *Directory of Corporate Affiliations,* Skokie, Ill. National Register Publishing Co.

Lists 3,000 American companies with divisions and affiliates.

- *Million Dollar Directory,* New York, N.Y. Dun & Bradstreet.

Lists approximately 39,000 U.S. companies. Gives officers, directors, products or services, approximate sales, and employees. A companion volume. *Middle Market Directory* covers about 31,000 companies that have an indicated worth of from $500,000 to $999,999. *Reference Books of Corporate Managements* lists top executives arranged by company, gives date of birth, college attended, past and present employment. Dun and Bradstreet of Canada, Ltd, Toronto, annually publishes the *Canadian Key Business Directory.*

- *Standard & Poor's Register of Corporations, Directors and Executives,* New York, N.Y. Three volumes.

Listing of over 36,000 U.S. and Canadian companies. Gives officers, directors, products, or line of business, sales, and number of employees.

- *Standard Directory of Advertisers,* Skokie, Ill. National Register Publishing Co.

Directory of 17,000 companies that advertise nationally. Gives officers, products, agency, advertising appropriations (in some cases), media used.

- *Thomas Register of American Manufacturers and Thomas Register Catalog File,* New York, N.Y.

Listing of American manufacturing firms. Lists manufacturers by product, gives address, branch offices, subsidiaries, products, assets.

- *U.S. Industrial Directory,* Denver, Colo., Cahners Publishing Co., Four volumes.

Similar to *Thomas,* better known under its former title, *Conover Mast Purchasing Directory.*

Government Jobs

A most important source for employment is the Federal Government (and State Governments).

Jobs in the Federal Civil Service are filled under a merit system which is based on the principle that positions should be filled by the people best qualified to fill them—not on the basis of influence or being in a particular political party when a new president or congress is elected. The basic principles of the merit system are as follows:

- Equal and fair pay.
- Training employees as needed to assure high quality performance.
- Keeping employees on the basis of the adequacy of their performance and separating them when poor performance can't be corrected.
- Fair treatment of applicants and employees without regard to political affiliation, race, color, national origin, sex or religion, with respect for their privacy and constitutional rights as citizens.
- Protection of employees from coercion for purposes of party politics and, by the same token, prohibiting employees from using their official authority to influence the result of an election or nomination for office.

Most of the jobs you know about, and many you may never have heard of, exist in the Federal Civil Service.

The federal government needs all kinds of skills to serve a nation of over 200 million people, 24 hours a day, every day of the year. Government employees work in offices, shipyards, laboratories, national parks, hsopitals, military bases and many other settings across the country and around the world. (Only about 12 percent of the jobs are in Washington, D.C.)

Federal Job Information Centers

The Civil Service Commission maintains more than 200 Federal Job Information Centers across the country to provide local job information. They are listed under "U.S. Government" in metropolitan area phone directories. Information centers are open Monday through Friday, except on holidays.

Other Pamphlets

If a group worker has any questions concerning federal employment, the following publications may be of interest. Single copies are available at Federal Job Information Centers.

General	**Pamphlet No.**
Directory of Federal Job Information Centers	BRE-9
Returning Peace Corps and Vista Volunteers	BRE-11
Federal Jobs Overseas	BRE-18
Federal Employment of Non-citizens	BRE-27
List of Current Federal Salaries	AN-2500
Handicapped Disadvantaged	
Mentally Restored Persons in the Federal Service	BRE-6
Mentally Retarded Persons in the Federal Service	BRE-7
Physically Handicapped Persons in the Federal Service	BRE-8
Deaf Persons in the Federal Service	BRE-22
Blind Persons in the Federal Service	BRE-23
Rehabilitated Offenders in the Federal Service	BRE-29
Accent on Youth (Disadvantaged Youth)	BRE-19
Working for the U.S.A.	BRE-37
Occupational Fields	
Take a Giant Step (Typists, Stenographers, Office Jobs)	BRE-58
Law Enforcement and Related Jobs	BRE-38
Government '76 (College Graduates)	BRE-64
Beyond the BA (Graduate Students)	BRE-65
Veterans	
Vietnam Era Veterans	BRE-28
Opportunities in the Federal Service for Vets	BRE-48
Reemployment Rights for Federal Employees Who Perform Duties in the Armed Forces	FED FACTS 14
Retired Military Personnel in Federal Jobs	BRE-61
Veterans Readjustment Appointments—Questions and Answers	BRE-36

Miscellaneous Data

According to *Peterson's Annual Guides to Graduate Study,* published by Peterson's Guides of Princeton, N.J., there is a shortage of radiation specialists. These are persons who majored in radiological health or health physics and know something about the measurement, control and evaluation of radiation so as to minimize its harmful effects on people and their environment.

There are also many career opportunites—especially in petrochemical and pharmaceutical firms—for chemistry majors with a Master's or PhD.

At the Master's level, employment opportunites abound for meteorologists who specialize in areas related to air pollution.

However, there is more demand for petroleum engineers than for professionals in any other field in the U.S. Graduates with Master's degrees in petroleum engineering can command annual starting salaries of $25,000; PhD.'s start at $27,000. (Note: Updated figures may be different.)

The National Tool Die and Precision Machining Assocation says there is a chronic shortage of tool-and-die makers, even though the occupation ranks high in terms of lifetime earnings. The Association is working to increase the number of workers through pre-apprenticeship and pre-employment training programs, which have been offered since 1964. The programs have a 100 percent placement rate for those who complete them. *The Job Service* which is listed in the State government section of local telephone directores, can provide more information about the programs.

REFERENCES

Bottoms, J. K. and K. Matheny. "Occupational Guidance Counseling and Job Placement for Junior High and Secondary School Youth." Paper presented at the National Conference on Exemplary Programs and Projects Section of the Vocational Education Act, Amendments of 1968, at Atlanta, Ga., March, 1969.

Bureau of Labor Statistics. *Occupational Outlook Quarterly,* Summer 1979.

College Placement Annual – 1980. The College Placement Council, Inc., 1979.

Herr, E. L. and S. H. Cramer. *Vocational Guidance and Career Development in the Schools: Toward a Systems Approach.* Houghton Mifflin Co., 1972.

I.R.S. Publication 906: *Targeted-Jobs Tax Credit and Win Credit.* Department of the Treasury-Internal Revenue Service, 1979 Edition.

Resesarch and Policy Committee. *Jobs for the Hard To Employ.* Committee for Economic Development, Jan. 1978.

United States. *Working for the U.S.A.,* BRE-37.

U.S. Dept. of Labor. *Dictionary of Occupational Titles,* 1977.

Chapter 29

Youth Group Project Ideas Involving the Community

One of the critical concerns of most youth groups is how to maintain or sustain interest in group functions. A diversification of program areas geared to special interests will keep most of the young people coming to meetings on a fairly consistent basis (i.e. music, athletic, fund raising, community projects, drama, political, health issues and social programs each will attract specific types of youngsters, in their own right). Collectively, they provide for a fairly viable overall program. Group workers and members are constantly looking for new program and project ideas. It is not the author's purpose to write an all encompassing manual of project and program ideas—for this would entail the preparation of a complete, albeit collateral, book in addition to this text.

Group Projects

There are a number of projects that high school level youth groups can sponsor—generally on a service oriented or volunteer basis. Many of the project ideas contained herein are recommended by ACTION's National Student Volunteer Program.

Education

- Sesame Street

Using Sesame Street as a nucleus, the students improvise plays, puppet shows and other devices to enhance the effectiveness of the televised presentation.

- Teacher Aides

High school students volunteering as teacher aides in an elementary school serve as small group discussion leaders and researchers.

- Language Lab

As the "laboratory" portion of a language course, students teach English to Hispanic employees in local businesses. In turn, students benefit from the opportunity to converse in Spanish.

Health

- Project Turn-Off

A student-organized drug and education program informs parents how young people feel about drugs and teaches teenagers the dangers of drug abuse.

● Drug Drag

Students design and present a drug education program for elementary school children, including a play, puppet show, comic books, and mini-lectures.

● Hospital Aides

Visiting patients, helping run the gift shop, and assisting in children's ward are among the duties performed by student hospital aides.

● Hospital Interns

Working as interns in the various departments of a hospital—the kitchen, the laboratory, the physical therapy room—students assist hospital workers while learning health-related occupations.

● High School Red Cross

Under the auspices of the local Red Cross chapter, students volunteer in hospitals, disaster relief efforts, and blood drive registrations.

● 4-H Volunteer Corps

Organized through the high school's 4-H Club, this project develops and presents a nutritional education program for children from poor families, using puppets and other creative techniques.

Aging

● Benefits for the Aged

As part of a study of the Social Security program, a social science class works in conjunction with the local Social Security office to bring information about benefits to the elderly and shut-ins through neighborhood canvassing.

● Senior Summer Festival

An arts and crafts fair displaying the work of the elderly is organized by student volunteers.

● Adopt a Grandparent

Each volunteer adopts an elderly person. Telephone calls, letters, visits, and social activities all give the "grandparents" a sense of being wanted.

Children

● Library Aides

Assisting in the local public libraries, students hold story hours and help children select books.

● Neighborhood Paint-In

Students enrolled in art courses organize children to decorate interior and exterior walls of a community center building.

● Day Care Corps

Student volunteers act as recreation leaders and teacher aides at a day care center, allowing it to operate at substantial savings.

● Music Instruction

Music students and choir and orchestra members give free music lessons to underprivileged children.

- Nature Study Center

High School biology classes furnish guides, helpers, and animal handlers at a non-profit nature study center which provides free education programs and tours for inner-city children.

- Inner-City Football League

Coaches and team members from city high schools organize an inner-city football league for boys from 9 to 12 years of age, with a championship game to be played on the same day as the high school championship game.

Housing

- Project Reclaim

Student volunteers in the field section of an industrial arts course repair run-down dwellings in the community, using materials donated by local merchants and under the supervision of members of the local building trades unions.

- New Housing Aides

The city housing authority uses home economics students as aides to instruct new residents of housing developments in the use and care of household facilities.

Environment

- Environmental Action

In conjunction with local and national ecology groups, students campaign for neighborhood clean-up and trash collection; run pick-up centers for bottles, cans, and paper; and support environmental legislation.

- National Parks and Forests

Students volunteer to work on recreation projects, build camps and shelters, and create play areas in nearby parks.

Consumer Services

- Project Price Watch

Students survey food and drug stores in and around the community to establish the relative prices and quality of essential items. They issue a monthly listing of this information, which helps prevent inner-city stores from raising their prices above those found in surrounding suburban areas.

- Neighborhood Co-op

Students in an accounting class assist in running and staffing a cooperative food store and credit union.

- Quantity Buying Club

In conjunction with community residents, home and economics classes organize a quantity buying club in a ghetto area. Students take orders for food and clothing so as to enable residents to buy in large quantities at reduced prices.

Community Organization

- Vest-Pocket Parks

Working with a citizens' group and the city parks department, student volunteers help raise funds to turn vacant lots into miniature playgrounds. The students also assist in clearing the land, constructing play equipment, and supervising recreational activities once the parks are completed.

- Cross-Cultural Arts Fair

Organized by a language club, this project closes off a side street on Saturday for the exhibition and sale of arts and crafts, ethnic foods, and other homemade items. Dancing and costumes are also featured.

- Social Action News

Students from English and Journalism classes assist a community group in running its own newspaper.

- Community Libraries

Students organize a book drive to set up community libraries in inner-city community centers. They also staff the libraries.

- Volunteer Patrol

Students work in the office and patrol the streets with policemen in a project aimed at improving student understanding of the Police Department and increasing community support and participation in combatting crime.

Community Services

- Meals on Wheels

A volunteer group delivers hospital-prepared meals to people confined to their homes.

- Free Breakfasts

In a project sponsored by the school district, students use home economics facilities to prepare free breakfasts for elementary school children.

- Car Pool Corps

Working afternoon and early evening shifts, students supply transportation for the elderly, handicapped, and any others who need assistance in getting around.

- Cool-Line Committee

A clearinghouse for short-term volunteer requests from agencies and individuals (such as the clean-up campaigns, shopping for shut-ins), the Cool-Line Committee keeps a roster of students willing to serve on an "on call" basis.

- Senior-Student Service Corps

Students team up with senior citizens to volunteer at a local orphanage. The project gives the elderly a feeling of being needed, while introducing orphans to such activities as homemaking and arts and crafts.

- Sick Car Clinic

Students in the auto mechanics class at a vocational high school staff a sick car clinic where poor families can have their automobiles repaired in the school's automotive shop for the cost of materials only.

- Office Manpower

Advanced typing becomes a field course as students get on-the-job experience in agencies short on manpower and long on need.

Miscellaneous

- Tutorial Services

Adjunctive prepping in basic reading, English and math to keep deprived kids interested in staying in school.

- Religious Services for Hospital Patients

Performing religious services through hospital private TV channel for those patients who cannot get out of bed—according to the traditional time such services are ordinarily held in the particular denomination (Sunday morning, Saturday morning, etc.)

- Taping of Special Events

Electronically recording weddings, confirmations and other special events for retention by the families of the participants (this can also serve as a fund raiser).

The following projects can be sponsored by college level groups and in some cases by high school groups.

Children

- Camp on Wheels

Students use buses provided by the University to take neighborhood children on field trips and overnight camping trips. Museums and historical sites, sports events, concerts, and plays are also included on agenda. A variety of agencies or groups contribute to the expense.

- State Home for Boys

College students "adopt" a dormitory of pre-adolescent boys who have been referred to the state home by the courts. The students provide recreation, arts, and crafts. They supervise a short wave radio station and direct a drama group.

- Day Camp

Students act as counselors at a day camp for poverty children. Their work involves recreation, drama, art, music, field trips, camping, and visits to children's homes.

Community Health

- Neighborhood Health Clinic

Students help to set up health and hygiene programs. They assist nurses and doctors in patient write-ups and lab work.

- Family Planning Clinic

Has a training program which provides students with basic nursing skills, interview techniques, and a knowledge of supplies and equipment. Students work with nurses and doctors in the day-to-day operation of the clinic.

- Neuro-Psychiatric Care

Students serve as assistants in therapy, remedial education, and recreation. They spend several days in each division of a state hospital, and are integrated into the full range of hospital services.

Community Organization

- Social Action News

A student-run newspaper created after a meeting of agency representatives, students, and University personnel. The paper reports events of social and humanitarian interest. It helps to keep the community informed of activities sponsored by a variety of agencies and groups. Essentially an information network, it reports social service and action projects not covered in depth by the commercial news media.

- The Urban Workshop

Students from the Architecture and Urban Planning Department at a local university are asked to attend meetings of the City Council and other government and private agencies. They exchange their reactions during a weekly seminar, and each term they draw up a list of suggestions. Several ideas advocated by the students have been enacted by the city.

- Suburban Action Campaign

Grew out of a panel discussion organized by students at the request of a local church. Students were asked to speak on the urban problems of an inner-city neighborhood where they were involved in a volunteer program. Several of the panelists decided to continue as a separate group. They make themselves available to surburban service clubs, women's groups, churches, and schools to lead seminars on urban problems.

Correctional Institutions

- Prison Action Committee

Involves students as teachers in a prison school. Volunteers also collect data, information, and complaints from prisoners, and they act as advocates for prison reform. On occasion volunteers help to secure legal aid for individual inmates.

- Parole Assistants

Working through the Board of Parole, students are assigned to work as assistant parole officers. They work chiefly with juvenile offenders, helping them to find a job or return to school.

- Workhouse Aides

Students volunteer to work for a one-to-two year period in a state workhouse. They assist with group therapy and training sessions, job placement, and career development.

Economic Assistance

- Project Provide

A group of economics majors offers their services to community groups which need to raise capital or program money. The students help with funding requests, conventional financing, and special projects.

- The Consumer in Action (CIA)

Works with an urban Family Assistance program to research and publicize consumer information. Students produce a local shopping guide. They also provide information concerning wholesale and retail and discount stores.

- Income Tax Service

In operation January through April. Business students help disadvantaged citizens fill out and file income tax forms.

● Neighborhood Co-op

Students assist in running and staffing a cooperative food store and credit union.

● Business Education

Business students provide technical assistance to minority businessmen. Faculty members of the Economics and Business Department meet with the students to work out actual problems. Projects include: marketing feasibility studies, financial analysis and loan packages, development of management seminars, and government funding sources.

● Industries Unlimited

Students work with a consortium of private agencies to assist in setting up new industries. Problems in production, management, and marketing are worked out. New industries now produce furniture, candles, ceramics, glass and metal work.

Education

● Volunteers Cooperative

University students, experienced in volunteering, train prospective high school tutors and help to prepare them for work in elementary schools.

● Teacher's Aide Program

Designed to relieve a teacher shortage in an urban high school. College students act as gym instructors, assistant teachers, study-hall monitors. They have made it possible to lower the average class size significantly thorugh the school.

● Day Care

A center sponsored by a national women's organization. Students act as recreation leaders and assistant teachers. Their volunteer help makes it possible for the center to continue operating despite a serious program deficit.

● School of Skills (S.O.S.)

A church sponsored program. Academic tutoring by college students is offered along with instruction in the trades by electricians, carpenters, and other skilled workers. The auto mechanics course is always filled to capacity. A course in practical economics was also popular. No paternalistic image is possible since neighborhood people contribute on an equal basis with students.

Employment Training and Opportunites

● Computer Careers

Specific skills in computer programming are offered by students at a neighborhood center. The students also track down job opportunities in the area and act as a placement service for their "graduates."

● Job Training

Programs sponsored by government or private agencies use students as teachers in special assistance classes including: economics, accounting, engineering, computer programming, management training.

Environment and Ecology

● In cooperation with local or national ecology groups, students campaign for neighborhood clean-ups and trash collection; run pick-up centers for bottles, cans, and refuse, and support environmental legislation.

● National Parks and Forests

Students volunteer to work on recreation projects, build camps and shelters, and create play areas in nearby parks.

● Environmental Education

Students work in the planning and development of a degree-granting environmental university. They also help to edit an environmental magazine.

Housing

● Tenant's Association

Students work with neighborhood people to push for enforcement of housing codes, and to have more significant representation on the city Planning Board.

● Community Development

Students work with a private citizens group to design, finance, and build low-income housing for their neighborhood. The students secure the assistance of the Architecture Department at the University. They also organize recreation, arts and crafts, and remedial education for the neighborhood children.

Miscellaneous Services

● The Hot Line

Students work alongside volunteers from a variety of community organizations to man a 24-hour telephone answering service. Anyone in need of conversation with a sympathetic listener or specific emergency help may call in. Volunteers are trained to listen, and if necessary, to refer the caller to proper professional help.

● Television Workshop

University students use TV monitors and video recorders with teenage youths in a neighborhood center. The teenagers produce their own plays, new shows, and other material, some of which is broadcast on local television.

● Project Together

Students hold rap sessions with high school drop-outs, mentally handicapped citizens recently released from medical care, former drug addicts, parolees, and other individuals in transition to and from institutions of health and education. The purpose of these rap sessions is to share the experiences of readjustment, and to provide sympathetic feedback during a time of difficult change.

● Emergency Service Program (ESP)

A twelve-hour emergency service center deploys students to individuals or groups with emergency needs–i.e., child care for welfare mothers who are hospitalized, clothing drives for disaster victims, emergency transportation for the sick.

- Senior Service

Students recruit help from senior citizens and work with them in a variety of volunteer agencies. Retired white collar workers assist in job training; widows teach home-making; couples teach arts and crafts. Senior citizens team up with college students to adopt "little brothers" and "little sisters" at a nearby orphanage.

- Food and Clothing Bank

In cooperation with a local church, students maintain a supply of food and clothing to be distributed by a committee of neighborhood people to individuals and families with temporary emergency needs.

- Cross-Cultural Arts Fair

Organized by third world students and Spanish-American clubs in a large metropolis, a side street is closed off for an exhibition of arts and crafts, Spanish cooking, dancing, costumes.

REFERENCES

ACTION. *Its Your Move.* Working with Student Volunteers – a Manual for Community Organizations. The National Student Volunteer Program.

High School Student Volunteers. The National Student Programs.

Chapter 30

Youth Group Program and Project Ideas – An Inward Look

Many youth groups are so community oriented, that few programs and projects are geared inwardly, for the group members own benefit. There are a number of activities and exercises that can be used for group member maturation purposes. The author will cite and explore several examples.

Understanding the Federal Tax System

An approach aiding our youth group members' in learning how to assume good citizenship duties is to teach them how to prepare tax returns and to understand the tax system. This can be done as a group project with the group worker or a student volunteer acting as instructor.

The I.R.S. publishes several booklets relating to this subject, geared to high school civics and math classes, but which can be adopted for youth group use. *Understanding Taxes* along with the "Teachers Guide" for this publication is available from I.R.S. offices without cost.

Student Text Publication 21

In addition to sections on U.S. tax history and the U.S. budget, the general unit contained practical exercises in filing income tax returns progressing from the simplest form to more complicated tax situations.

Farm Supplement – Publication 22

The supplement contains instructions on how to fill out farm income tax returns and contains a farm tax problem. The supplement ends with a problem about a farm student who must file an income tax return to report the income earned from a 4-H project.

Teacher's Guide – Publication 19

Lesson plans corresponding to the chapters in the student texts had been included to help you teach the course. The lesson plans can be modified depending on the way you want to teach the material. This booklet also contains answers to questions and problems in the student texts. Blank tax forms are included in the back of this book that can be used to make transparencies or additional copies for the class. Some other visuals are also included that the worker may wish to use as transparencies.

Reference Books

A copy of Publication 17, *Your Federal Income Tax,* is sent to each instructor who orders the Understanding Taxes program material. The *Farmer's Tax Guide* is available free from your local Internal Revenue Service office, as are other free tax publications that can assist in teaching the course.

Film

The Understanding Taxes Program Coordinator at each IRS district has a film to supplement the Understanding Taxes program which may be borrowed free of charge on request. This 16 mm color film is entitled *Money Talks* and covers the history of taxation. The approximate running time for the film is 25 minutes.

NOTE: *Money Talks* is also available from the IRS coordinator on audio-visual cassette.

How to Order These Aids

You may order these material by letter or by a telephone call to the Understanding Taxes Coordinator in the Internal Revenue Service district office for each area. The correct mailing address and telephone number for each coordinator is listed in the booklet.

Crossword Puzzle on Tax Terms

To add interest in studying taxes, there is included a crossword puzzle on tax terms on the back of the student text. The worker may want to use this as a quiz. A completed puzzle was included for reference.

Program Objectives

Program objectives are included. Instructional objectives are listed at the beginning of each lesson plan.

Projects for Students

Teachers have found that one of the most successful and enjoyable ways to get students involved in the Understanding Taxes Program is to have them prepare their own Federal tax returns in class using their W-2 forms from their employers. If most of the students or members are not required to file a tax return, the worker may want to let them create what they think their tax situation will be in ten years from now, inventing their own gross income, itemized deductions, number of dependents, etc., for Form 1040. Other classes have set up assistance centers during free class periods for fellow students who need help filing Federal returns.

The following projects have been implemented quite successfully by many teachers in the past:

- Prepare a bulletin board display illustrating the variety of Federal taxes.
- Collect cartoons to use in making transparencies for the overhead projector illustrating or explaining such points as filing requirements, itemized deductions, etc.
- Check the library for the amount and kind of information available on Federal taxes. Tell the class or group what you found.
- Have the students or group members keep a notebook of any newspaper items about taxes that they see during the filing period.
- Select two teams of three "tax experts" from the class or group. Let the teams compete in quiz-program fashion to answer questions based on the Understanding Taxes unit.

Objectives

At the end of this lesson one should be able to:

- Describe the history of taxation in the United States.
- Describe the role of taxes in our society.
- Understand the rights and responsibilities as a taxpayer.
- Describe the Federal budget process.

Job Interview Program

In a prior chapter, the author suggested that the group worker role-play a job interview with the members of the group. This can serve as an excellent project pointing "inwardly" for the benefit of group members. Although the author in that chapter set forth some suggestions and aids, he would like to point out that an in-depth project of this sort requires extensive preparation on the part of the group worker.

An informative vehicle for so doing is a booklet published by the New York

Life Insurance Company titled *Making the Most of Your Job Interview.* Their suggestions include both preparing for the interview and the interview process itself.

Employment Interview Questions[28]

The following questions compiled at a major university's placement center are typical interview questions. The group member should familiarize himself with them thoroughly so that he can answer such questions briefly, fully, and, above all, persuasively.

What are your future vocational plans?

In what school activities have you participated? Why? Which did you enjoy the most?

In what type of position are you most interested?

What percentage of your college expenses did you earn? How?

How did you spend your vacations while in school?

What do you know about our company?

Do you feel that you have received a good general training?

What qualifications do you have that make you feel that you will be successful in your field?

What extracurricular offices have you held?

What are your ideas on salary?

If you were starting college all over again, what courses would you take?

How much money do you hope to earn at age 30? 35?

Do you think that your extracurricular activites were worth the time you devoted to them? Why?

What do you think determines a person's progress in a good company?

What personal characteristics are necessary for success in your chosen field?

Why do you think you would like this particular type of job?

Do you prefer working with others or by yourself?

What kind of boss do you prefer?

Are you primarily interested in making money or do you feel that service to humanity is your prime concern?

Can you take instructions without feeling upset?

How did previous employers treat you?

What have you learned from some of the jobs you have held?

Can you get recommendations from previous employers?

What interests you about our product or service?

---

[28]Contained in the Endicott Report "Trends in the Employment of University and College Graduates in Business and Industry". Printed with permission of Victor R. Lindquist, Associate Dean and Director of the Placement Center, Northwestern University, Evanston, Illinois.

Have you ever changed your major field of interest while in college? Why?
When did you choose your college major?
Do you feel you have done the best scholastic work of which you are capable?
How did you happen to go to college?
What do you know about opportunities in the field in which you are trained?
Which of your college years was the most difficult?
Did you enjoy your four years at college?
Do you like routine work?
Do you like regular hours?
What size city do you prefer?
What is your major weakness?
Define "cooperation."
Do you demand attention?
Do you have an analytical mind?
Are you eager to please?
What job in our company would you choose if you were entirely free to do so?
What types of books have you read?
Have you plans for graduate work?
What types of people seem to rub you the wrong way?
Have you ever tutored an underclassman?
What jobs have you enjoyed the most? The least? Why?
What are your own special abilities?
What job in our company do you want to work toward?
Would you prefer a large or small company? Why?
Do you like to travel?
How about overtime work?
What kind of work interests you?
What are the disadvantages of your chosen field?
Are you interested in research?
What have you done which shows initiative and willingness to work?

Note: If the applicant takes the time necessary to write out brief answers to each of the questions in the list, it can help him clarify his own thinking and establish ready answers. Bear in mind that positive, optimistic answers create the most favorable impression.

Typical Programs Dealing With Disadvantaged Group Members

A substantial number of group workers and their volunteer aides get to work with groups that are socially and economically disadvantaged. It will be of significant value if such workers get to know when, where and how to advise group members as to what domestic assistance programs are available for their personal and family benefit (this can be used as a community outreach program as well).

Some years ago the author came across and was impressed with a catalog published by the Office of Economic Opportunity titled *Catalog of Domestic Assistance.*

This catalog provided a comprehensive listing of 581 domestic assistance programs and activities administered by 47 federal departments and agencies. The purpose of the catalog was to aid potential beneficiaries in identifying types of assistance available, determining eligibility requirements for particular assistance being sought, and to provide guidance on how to apply for specific types of assistance.

The catalog included information on various forms of assistance available to State and local governments, public and private or quasi-public organizations and instructions, private business and industry, and individuals. The various types of assistance described in the catalog included:

- Financial aid in the form of grants, loans and advances, loan guarantees, and shared revenues.
- Provision of federal facilities, direct construction or goods and services.
- Donation or provision of surplus real and personal property.
- Technical assistance and counseling.
- Statistical and other information services.
- Service activities of regulatory agencies.

The catalog was compiled for the Executive Office of the President by the Information Center of the Office of Economic Opportunity. The information included in the catalog was the product of a joint effort of all federal departments and agencies. (Please check out updated adjustments and cut-backs that may obtain today.)

Guides to Using the Catalog

The summmary description for each program or activity in the catalog provided specific and useful information about the program, its nature and purpose, its availability, its authorizing legislation and the administering agency, and where additional information may be obtained.

Program descriptions were grouped in alphabetical order by departments, followed by independent agencies. Within the departments, programs are grouped by the primary subunit.

Many programs listed in the catalog provided several types of assistance. To aid the user an index offering alternative subject matter references provided an extensive cross-indexing of specific types of assistance available.

A listing of regional office addresses for various departments and agencies was also provided in the Appendix. These offices could be contacted, in addition to the headquarters office, for additional information on specific programs and activities administered by their agencies.

This type of information and availability of similar catalogs is a prime aid and resource for those working with disadvantaged youth.

CAUTION:

Group workers and their volunteer aides must update themselves as to which federal and state economic assistance programs are being phased out or are being significantly altered starting in 1981. I.e. the "CETA" program may well be eliminated in its entirety, qualifications for receipt of food stamps are being altered, etc., etc.

Those group workers working with disadvantaged (socially and economically) youth must keep abreast of all governmental adjustments to the assistance programs so that the workers can dispense updated and accurate information to the disadvantaged youth and their families.

REFERENCES

Internal Revenue Service. *Understanding Taxes,* 1979.

New York Life Insurance Co. "Making the Most of Your Job Interview." *Careers for a Changing World.*

Office of Economic Opportunity. Catalog of Federal Domestic Assistance, 1969.

Chapter 31

An Overview of Therapy

Throughout this text, the author has cautioned the group worker not to attempt primary therapy, on his own, with troubled teenagers, but rather to recommend referral to those with appropriate skills. The author will attempt in this chapter to give the group worker a condensed overview of some of the types and "schools" of therapy available. He will also delve into some of the lesser known therapies, such as Dance Therapy, Hypnosis, Psychodrama and Transactional Analysis, that might prove most interesting. However this is for information only, and does not represent an invitation to delve into experimentation.

At the outset, the author found a Therapy Chart, developed by Dr. Joyce D. Fleming, a freelance writer, psychologist and former editor of *Psychology Today*. She prepared the chart for the August 1979 issue of *Self Magazine* and contains the type, focus of attention, goals and methods used by six different "schools" of therapy to wit:

Therapy Chart[29]

Type	Focus of Attention	Goals	Methods
Behavioral Therapy (behavioral modification)	Personal habits	Alter and control behavior by changing reward systems	Measuring behavior, setting goals increasing motivation, changing rewards
Family Therapy	Relationships between individual and family	Alter subjective experiences of individual by changing family structure	Objective observations of family interactions, incorporating therapist into family, restructuring family relationships

(Continued)

[29]Copyright ©1981 by The Conde Nast Publications Inc. New York, N.Y. and reprinted with permission of author, Dr. Joyce D. Fleming, Santa Monica, California.

Therapy Chart

Type	Focus of Attention	Goals	Methods
Gestalt Therapy	Personal Integration	Unity personality elements with experiences by removing emotional blocks	Coordinating self with environment, recognizing and experiencing emotions, therapists, demonstrating behavior
Psychoanalytic Therapy (Freudian Therapy)	Conflicts between ego, id and superego	Understand role of unconscious in feelings, behavior and relationships	Analyzing dreams, exposing repressed experiences and emotions, identifying repeated patterns
Rational-Emotive Therapy	Irrational thoughts that underlie self defeating behaviors	Eliminate emotional problems by changing thought patterns	Recording thoughts, analyzing logic, recognizing consequences, developing rationality

Dance Therapy:

An unusual therapeutic vehicle is dance therapy. This mode of reaching troubled individuals has received a great deal of publicity in the press. As a result the author contacted a dance therapist friend of his, Shirley Weiner, for some background information on the history, methodology and goals of this therapy.

History

Dance is the oldest art—antedating architecture and has been the method whereby all of life's rites of passage have been celebrated or expressed. Havelock Ellis called life itself a dance—certainly the times of birth, development, puberty, courtship, creativity, illness, death—and the times of war, of victory and defeat—of Nature's bounty and catastrophe—the mystery of life itself—all of these have been marked in human history, in the lives of all peoples, by dance.

And if we expand our view of what dance is and take the concept "movement" we realize then that livingness itself is movement—common to us and the animal world. Death then is but the end of movement. So with the infant there is movement before speech or thought and with the dying there is the last flutter of a pulse after speech is no longer possible. We move outwardly as we move inwardly—our heart beats a rhythm, the blood courses along to a beat, time itself gives us the measure, and our patterns, habits, values from the choreography—each of our lives is a dance. Like all art dance is a thing in itself and at the same time a communication. It is symbolic or expressive of feelings—a reaching out for something or a drawing away to preserve something. It can be involuntary, immediate, mysterious—it can be designed, planned and executed with the greatest discipline man achieves—the control and direction of the body. It is the area where the dichotomy of mind/body can best be bridged—for through dance—at the moment of dance—we are one, integrated, united.

Dance therapy as a practicing discipline in mental hospitals is a more recent phenomenon. Marion Chace, a gifted modern dancer and dance teacher was invited to develop this field at St. Elizabeth Hospital in Washington, D.C. during the early 1940s, and she continued to practice and teach her method until her death in 1970. Dance as a calling has been known to all peoples in all times. Chace's pioneering work was to develop a technique suitable to a hospital setting of this modern age while finely attuned through experience of her art to its unique qualities as a communication and therapy.

Goals

The communication of the therapist and patient in the area of movement or dance establishes opportunities for understanding, trust, mutual respect, catharsis, change through self-awareness, self-sufficiency, physical well-being and mood uplift and in group dance therapy the additional qualities of being part of a whole that is larger than any one person, which in dance provides the ancient, ritualistic, creative, healing art.

The American Dance Therapy Association, 2000 Century Plaza, Columbia, Maryland 21044, was founded in 1966 to establish and maintain high standards of professional education and competence in the field. The Association holds an annual conference and publishes literature on dance therapy, such as *The American Journal of Dance Therapy,* monographs, conference proceedings and a newsletter.

The Association maintains a Registry of dance therapists who have met professional standards of education and clinical practice. Registered dance therapists are identified by the initials D.T.R. The Association considers D.T.R.'s to have attained a minimum level of competence to enable them to engage in private practice and train dance therapists.

Group workers should please note that a Speakers Bureau has been organized by the Association. Dance therapists are available to make presentations on the field to interested organizations, facilities and schools.

The American Dance Therapy Association explains the nature and applications of dance therapy in the following manner.

What is Dance Therapy?[30]

The use of dance and body movement in therapy is not a new phenomenon. The healing, integrative properties of dance have been recognized for centuries, and it has been used as a therapeutic and preventive modality in diverse cultures all over the world. Body movement and posture reflect people's feelings about themselves and their relationship to others. Psychological states are manifested in physiological counterparts such as muscle tension, breathing and movement. This knowledge is often applied both diagnostically and therapeutically.

Dance therapy is defined as the "psychotherapeutic use of movement as a process which furthers the emotional and physical integration of the individual." It espouses a holistic view of the individual, recognizing the complex interaction of psyche in sickness and health. Dance therapy is distinguished from other utilizations of dance (e.g., dance education) by its focus on the non-verbal aspects of behavior and its use of movement as the mode for intervention.

Adaptive, expressive and communicative behaviors are all considered in treatment, with the expressed goal of integrating these behaviors with psychological aspects of the individual. The dance therapist focuses on movement, posture, breathing and interaction, complementing the traditional therapeutic flow of words with a more immediate, less defended flow of movement. Personal imagery and symbols are made available to the individual, and movement themes and interactions are developed verbally and nonverbally to clarify their meanings. Expansion of the movement repertoire affords a greater range of adaptive response to the environment and can support change by providing alternatives to inappropriate coping behaviors.

Dance is the most fundamental of the arts, involving as it does one's body—one's self. It is an especially intimate powerful medium for therapy, and one that is universally applicable. It engages the total person and provides a vehicle for self-expression, understanding and growth for individuals of diverse needs. Examples of applications of dance therapy with several different populations are seen on the following pages.

Applications

Retarded. Mobility and physical coordination are often affected in the retarded, making simple tasks frustratingly difficult to master. Movement activities help to improve coordination and to develop motor skills necessary for self care and work. The concreteness and immediacy of movement make it an ideal medium for learning basic concepts. Focus and sustainment of attention, essential in

[30]Reprinted from material prepared by the American Dance Therapy Association, 2000 Century Plaza, Columbia, Maryland, 21044

developing cognitive potential, are developed through dance. When language deficiencies exist, social interactions are hampered and the ability for self expression become limited. Dance therapy provides a means through which the individual can express feelings through movement and can communicate them to others. Whether working in a residential facility, group home or special classroom setting, it is the goal of the dance therapist to provide an atmosphere that permits retarded persons to explore and develop their unique potential and to experience the joy of self expression.

Visually and hearing impaired. Blind or visually impaired persons often exhibit hesitant, restricted movement due to their uncertainty in moving through an unseen environment. Their posture is frequently out of alignment as a result of this tentative movement style creating additional tension. While exploring a safe and familiar space in the dance therapy session, the visually impaired person can learn to move with assertiveness and confidence. They can explore spatial and dynamic qualities of movement, enlarging the range of adaptive movement available to them in everyday living. Dance can play a key role in learning about the self, others and the environment as movement experiences develop the body image and spatial awareness. Deep feelings and fears can be expressed and worked through in movement and, as with other populations, the individual can draw strength and support from a group made cohesive through movement.

Hearing impaired persons, like the blind, often feel isolated because of their handicap. Dance therapy provides a means of expressing feelings, building a more positive self image and making satisfying contact with others in an atmosphere of sharing and trust. In addition, the expressive quality of dance makes it useful in language acquisition, often a problem for the deaf.

The Aged. Inactivity, social isolation and the loss of suppleness, fitness and mobility are problems common to most geriatric clients, whether they reside in the open community or in supervised facilities. Expanding the range of movement provides a sense of vitality and well-being in a supportive, congenial group environment. The dance therapy session fosters an atmosphere of physical and psychological safety in which the older person can regain a sense of self-worth through the accomplishment of simple movement achievements. A sense of group consciousness and feeling of belonging provide a forum for social interaction and for risk taking in a non-threatening setting. By actively stimulating the senses through touch, sound and movement, the dance therapist can support the sensory modalities that are still functioning, placing less stress on the person's limitations. In our society, the elderly individual often feels anger at being made to feel unproductive and being cast aside by children and other loved ones. The environment of the dance therapy group provides a unique medium in which the individual can find a way to deal with these feelings in the company of peers, experiencing the sense of renewal, relaxation and purpose that comes from feeling one's body in motion, in harmony with others.

Severe Mental Impairment. Feeling overwhelmed and unable to cope with real or imagined internal and external pressures, those suffering from various psychoses revert to earlier, simpler levels of functioning. The severe personality disorganization characteristic of schizophrenia is reflected in fragmented, disconnected movements and postures, whereas the depressed mental patient sinks into flaccidity and immobility. These atyical behaviors increasingly isolate such individuals because of their inability to communicate in normally acceptable ways.

The dance therapist may employ the organizing structure of the circle, connecting mechanisms of touch and rhythmic synchrony and supportive verbal imagery to provide psychotic clients with an experience of reintegration, contact, and mobilization. As a group moves in and out of meaningful effective gestures, giving non-verbal expression to fears and impulses frozen in rigid body postures, the terror and anxiety of psychosis can be momentarily relieved. Such repeated safe expression of highly charged emotions can, over a period of time, find verbal expression as the individual begins to reintegrate at a higher level of functioning. Communication in the dance therapy session can provide psychotic individuals with a positive experience, beginning the long-term process of healing their damaged self image. It can, at times, be the first move in the direction of mental health.

Anxieties. Anxiety is the hall mark of emotionally troubled persons, and most such individuals manifest this anxiety in muscular tensions and distorted postures. Dance therapy reduces tension and misalignment through relaxation, body awareness and corrective movement techniques. Improvement in physical function permits fuller respiration, increased energy and efficiency and a better emotional state, interrupting the vicious body/mind cycle with expresses and maintains the neurosis. However, this physical relief is ineffective unless the individual explores and resolves the meaning of tensions and postural distortions and the source of his or her anxiety. Movement experiences in the dance therapy session provide a means for eliciting repressed affect and personal imagery, which the individual can develop and explore. In group sessions the dance therapist may facilitate group and dyadic movement experiences to provide feedback for clients on the impact of their interactions on others. As clients become aware of their personal movement style and its significance, other movement dynamics may be introduced to expand the movement repertoire and provide the resources to develop alternate means of coping. Verbal processing of the movement experiences integrates thought, feeling and action, enabling the individual to assimilate cognitively as well as experientially the movement discovered through movement.

Autistic Children. Autistic children are characterized by their inability to form relationships or to interact with the environment in a meaningful manner. These children often engage in bizarre, repetitive movement behaviors, such as rocking, twirling and hand flapping. These movements draw their attention inward, away from the environment, and reinforce their isolation. The dance therapist uses body movement to make contact with these children on a non-verbal level. Characteristic elements of their movement are mirrored, creating a dance which is reassuring in its familiarity and implicit acceptance of the child. The establishment of a one to one relationship with the therapist is a primary objective. Movement parameters such as proximity and synchrony may be used to evaluate the evolution of this process. As the relationship develops, the dance therapist seeks to engage the child in meaningful exploration of the self, the environment and others and to enlarge the movement repertoire, providing the child with movement tools for constructive interaction with the environment. Through their interactive dance, the dance therapist meets the child on a primitive, non-verbal level and engages him or her in relationship which expands self-awareness and the ability to cope with the environment.

Learning Disabled. Children with learning disabilities frequently exhibit distorted, incomplete body images, perceptual problems, poor balance and coordination, and behavior problems. They often have extremely poor self concepts, due to their repeated failures at school. Dance therapy addresses each of these needs. Movement activities directly stimulate kinesthetic and tactile senses, developing the body image and helping the child to integrate sensory input and organize perceptions. Balance and coordination are developed through movement exploration. Children may experiment with generalized motor patterns and movement dynamics and learn to adapt them to a variety of situations. Movement activities set limits within which children can learn to focus and to sustain attention and to control impulsive behavior. The atmosphere of the dance therapy group facilitates self-expression and respect for individual differences and enhances self-esteem and sensitivity to peers.

About Dance Therapists

Dance therapists work with individuals and groups of all ages. They are employed in psychiatric in and out patient settings, in halfway houses, clinics, nursing homes, special schools and developmental centers. Dance therapists function as clinicians, as part of a treatment team or as primary therapists. They also act as consultants and engage in research. Professional training of dance therapists occurs on the graduate level. Studies include courses such as dance therapy theory and practice, psychopathology, human development, movement observation and research skills, and a supervised internship in a clinical setting. Extensive dance training and study of anatomy/kinesiology are prerequisites.

Government Recognition of Dance Therapy

Dance therapy is included as related service under PL 94.142, the Education for All Handicapped Act. Dance therapists can be hired with federal funds to improve educational opportunities of handicapped children. They are also eligible to be hired under the Comprehensive Employment and Training Act (CETA) in locally administered programs sponsored by government agencies or non-profit organizations. Some states identify dance therapists on civil service lists, while others are in the process of creating separate job lines.

In 1978 President's Commission on Mental Health recommended greater use of dance therapists in Federally assisted facilities, community mental health centers and programs reimbursed by third party payments. Representation of dance therapy on the arts task panel of the President's Mental Health Commission and at the proposed White House Conference on the Arts reflects the growing recognition of its importance in the field of mental health.

Transactional Analysis:[31]

This concept was originally developed by Dr. Eric Berne, a California psychiatrist around 1958.

Murial James and Dorothy Jongward capture the essense of T.A. in *Born to Win,* first published in 1971. James and Jongward stated that in transactional analysis people gain both emotional and intellectual insight, but the method focuses on the latter. It is a thinking process often analytical, in which the person frequently concludes, "So that's the way it is!"

According to Dr. Berne, his theories evolved as he observed behavioral changes occurring in a patient when a new stimulus, such as a word, gesture, or sound, entered his focus. These changes involved facial expressions, word intonations, sentence structure, body movements, gestures, tics, posture, and carriage. It was as though there were several different people inside the individual. At times one or the other of these inner different people seemed to be in control of his patient's total personality.

He observed that these various "selves" transacted with other people in different ways and that these transactions could not be analyzed. He saw that some of the transactions had ulterior motives; the individual used them as a means of manipulating others into psychological games and rackets. He also observed that people performed in predetermined ways—acting as if they were on stage and reading from a theatrical script. These observations led Berne to develop his unique theory.

[31]Much of the material contained in this section was adapted or reprinted from Morrison/O'Hearn, *Practical Transactional Analysis in Management,* ©1976, Addison-Wesley Publishing Co. Inc., Chap. 6, Pgs., 91-114, "You've Got To Motivate Them," reprinted with permission.

Originally, T.A. was developed as a method of psychotherapy. Transactional analysis is preferably used in groups. The group serves as a setting in which people can become more aware of themselves, the structure of their individual personality, how they transact with others, the games they play, and the scripts they act out. Such awareness enables persons to see themselves more clearly so that they can change what they want to change and strengthen what they want to strengthen.

Change begins with a bilateral contract between the therapist and client. A contract may be about the alleviation of symptoms such as blushing, frigidity, or headaches. It may be about gaining control over behavior such as excessive drinking, mistreating children, failing in school. It may focus on childhood experiences which underlie current specific symptoms and behavior, experiences in which the child was belittled, abandoned, overindulged, ignored, or brutalized. The contractual approach preserves the self-determination of a client. It also allows a client to know when the terms of the contract have been met.

Transactional analysis is not only a useful tool for those in psychotherapy, it also provides a thought-provoking perspective of human behavior that most people can understand and put to use. It encourages the use of words that are simple, direct, and often colloquial instead of psychological, scientific words. For example, the major parts of the personality are called the Parent, Adult, and Child ego states.

Transactional analysis is a rational approach to understanding behavior and is based on the assumption that all individuals can learn to trust themselves, think for themselves, make their own decisions, and express their feelings. Its principles can be applied on the job, in the home, in the classroom, in the neighborhood–wherever people deal with people.

Berne says an important goal of transactional analysis is "to establish the most open and authentic communication possible between the effective and intellectual components of the personality." When this happens, the person is able to use both emotions and intellect, not just one at the expense of the other.

One of T.A.'s greatest appeals is that it avoids traditional jargon.

The Advantages of T.A. for therapists, managers, and group workers are:

- The basics are simple to learn.
- It is readily demonstrable.
- It provides a means of reducing the amount of bad feelings experienced by an individual.
- It increases the efficient use of time.
- It can be used to improve the efficiency of communications.
- It is applicable at home as it is at work.
- It reinforces and complements other management-development activities, including training in communication, leadership, brainstorming, management by objectives, job enrichment, etc.

The Disadvantages of T.A. are:

- Few scientific studies of outcomes are available.
- Ego states, basic to understanding and utilizing T.A. are difficult to define (although seemingly easy to teach and demonstrate operationally).
- If inappropriately applied T.A. tends to encourage "amateur psychologizing."
- The proliferation of new theories and extensions of old ones outpace the scientific evidence to support them.
- The jargon may lead to more "cuteness" than insight into human encounter.
- It can be used as a put-down, or a discount, in interpersonal relations.

One of the more recent developments is the incorporation of T.A. into organizational and teamwork development activities. This has provided a welcome relief from earlier, sometimes disastrous, sensitivity training, which has been used in the past as a teamwork improvement method. Transactional analysis seems to provide the authenticity of a growth-oriented process that appeals as much to an individual's sense of personal growth ("It's good for me as a person") as to the individual's occupational skills ("It's good for the organization, too"). These two factors have become increasingly crucial to the acceptance and successful application of concepts conveyed by management training-and-development activities. Transactional analysis supplies both.

The T.A. esentials are ego states of the individual—an ego state is defined as a system of feelings accompanied by a related set of behavior patterns. More simply, "Ego states" refers to the chief ways that individuals demonstrate their states of being in the world—to wit:

1) Parent
2) Adult
3) Child

All three ego states are found in each individual and, although only one ego state at a time has power to act, the other two ego states may be observing; as an illustration, consider one's response when told a joke. He hears the joke in his adult state, then gets the point and laughs from the child ego states.

To illustrate the comparative states and how adults shift from one ego state to another, consider an instance in which a group worker is reviewing project performance with a volunteer, Joe.

If Joe responds with anger, yells and pounds the table, you would say Joe was acting like a child. In T.A. terms, Joe is in his *Child Ego State*. In this state he feels, thinks and acts like a child no older than 8 years old. He is *not imitating* a child; he is not role playing, at the moment, for all practical purposes, Joe *is* a child.

Joe's explosion may actually have been triggered by the group worker. If the group worker sounded critical or sarcastic, didn't recognize any of Joe's good points, and shook his index finger in Joe's face during their meeting, the worker would have been in a *Parent Ego State*. The child ego state in Joe responded as if he were being criticized by one of his own parents.

All parent states are not necessarily critical, any more than all actual parents are critical—parents nurture, nourish, comfort, etc., and stroke their children, so that children feel good a reasonable amount of time. Ditto for Ego State.

The adult ego state is in essence a data processor, almost devoid of feelings. If decisions are made entirely by the Adult, they will be based on factual information, not based on strong feelings.

Ego states can be reflected both by words and nonverbal as follows:

Parent:

Nonverbal – The pointing finger, shaking head, handwringing, arms folded across the chest, foot tapping, wrinkled brow, pursed lips, sighing, impatient snort, grunts.

A comforting touch, consoling sounds, holding and rocking, patting a person on the shoulder.

Verbal – Always, never, remember, you ought to know better, don't, now what, naughty, stupid, disgusting, how dare you, shocking, asinine, absurd, ridiculous, horrid.

Poor thing, dear, sonny, honey, there-there, cute, try again, don't worry.

(Unthinking evaluative reactions of all types.)

Adult:

Nonverbal – Lively facial expressions, listening, appropriate responses to what the other person is saying.

Concerned, interested appearance and posture.

Relaxed calm when appropriate, vigorous "body english" when appropriate.

Verbal – Why, what, where, when, who, how.

Alternatives, possible, probably, relatively.

Identification of opinion as an opinion (not fact).

Restating what the other person said and identifying it as a restatement to check understanding.

Child:

Nonverbal – Flirtatious behavior, giggling, teasing, squirming, bubbling.

Hand raised for permission to speak.

Tears, pouting, temper tantrums, whining tone, quivering lip.

No answer, biting lower lip, downcast eyes, nail biting, shrugging shoulder.

Verbal – Wow! Gee whiz! I love you, baby talk, didn't I do good?

Please help me, I wish, I want, I dunno, I'll try, I don't care.

Look at me, nobody loves me! MINE! Now!

Back biting *after* other person has left the room.

Can't, won't.

We can learn a great deal about ego states by watching people as they transact their daily business. The group worker is often in the position of using his or her parent ego state to control, criticize, regulate and lead. If the group worker leads entirely from the critical parent ego state, he is not likely to get much work done, since the ego state that matches the parent is another parent ego state or a child ego state.

Much work must be done from the adult. Adult behavior on the part of one person invites such behavior on the part of another.

An integral part of T.A. is a negative type of game playing. Although many people (including the author) do not feel there are any good games—they are played none-the-less. Transactional analysis games have three characteristics:

A bad payoff. T.A. games have a bad feeling payoff for at least one person.

An ulterior or hidden quality. Something other than what appears to be going on is going on.

Are usually played outside the adult ego states. The game initiator, and usually the person who is the object of the game, do not have adult-ego-state awareness that a game is being played. (You are either coming from a parent ego state or from a child ego state in gamemanship.)

Games Played from the Parent Ego State (samples)

P – A favorite with some manager is NIGYYSOB (now I've got you, you S.O.B.) – the person constantly coming to work late.

P – Blemish. That's nice, but did you notice the blemish. "If it weren't for *you* dumbbell," "we'd have made our quota." "I'm only trying to help you."

Games Played from the Child Ego State (samples)

V – *"Kick me"* – an individual repeatedly sets up situations so that he or she is caught, figuratively, kicked, as though a "kick me" sign was pinned on his or her back. (The person that continually sneaks a smoke—despite no smoking signs all over)

V – *Stupid.* The stupid player is usually a smart person who acts stupid when caught in "stupidity." The person may say "I don't know why I can't figure that out. I must be stupid, I guess."

V – *See what you made me do* – The secretary angrily pulling paper out of typewriter after mistake – if boss is near proximity – or husband doing paper work and wife asks question – blames her for error.

V – *See How Hard I Try* – Subordinate who stays late, reads self-help boks, etc.; much of his effort spent in looking hard at work rather than actually spent in efficiently working hard.

V – *Wooden Leg* – "How do you expect me to run this race with wooden leg."

V – *Love me no matter what I do* – players put out one "bait" after another – hair style or clothes style that are trendy or tardiness hoping manager will tell them to stop. Then will try to convince manager that he is an old-fashioned grump for not accepting them as they are.

V – Harried Executive – so busy with minute details that always seems harried – people tend to leave him alone – from above and below.

Key-Victim games – reinforce an "I'm not O.K." life position = V; Persecutor games – reinforce a "You're not O.K." life position = P; Rescue games – reinforce a "You're not O.K." life position = R.

Why Do People Play These Games?

A way to obtain familiar strokes. Even negative strokes are better than being ignored.

One way to spend time–more exciting than many work activities.

A game provides a familiar and predictable environment.

Most people want intimacy, but also have some uneasiness about it. Some people make halfhearted attempts at intimacy, then sabotage themselves by playing a game instead. Games do avoid intimacy. This happens in men-women relationships as well when a person sometimes instead of pursuing a situation from the adult level or state, resorts to child-like gamesmanship or cuteness.

Gestalt Therapy:

James and Jongeward, mentioned earlier relative to their expostion on T.A., also give us a meaningful overview of Gestalt therapy in their *Born to Win*.[32] We capture the essence of their analysis as follows:

Gestalt psychology is not new. Gestalt therapy is new. Dr. Frederick Perls, a Freudian analyst of many years, used some of the principles and discoveries of gestalt psychology to invent and develop gestalt therapy. "Gestalt" is a German word for which there is no exact English equivalent; it means, roughly, an organized whole.

Perls perceives many personalities as lacking wholeness, as being fragmented. He claims people are often aware of only parts of themselves rather than of the whole self. For example, a woman may not know or want to admit that sometimes she acts like her mother; a man may not know or want to admit that sometimes he wants to cry like a baby.

The aim of gestalt therapy is to help people become whole–to help them become aware of, admit to, reclaim, and integrate their fragmented parts. Inte-

---

[32]Reprinted from *Born to Win* by Murial James and Dorothy Jongeward, Copyright ©1971, by permission of Addison-Wesley Publishing Co., Reading Mass.

gration helps a person make the transposition from dependency to self-sufficiency; from authoritarian outer support to authentic inner support. Concretely, having inner support means that a person is self-reliant. Such a person is no longer compelled to depend on a spouse, academic degrees, job title, therapist, bank account, and so forth for support. Instead, he or she discovers that the needed capacities are internal and that they can be depended on. According to Perls, a person who refuses to do this is neurotic.

Some of the methods common in gestalt therapy are role-playing, exaggeration of symptoms or behavior, use of fantasy, the principle of staying with the immediate moment, which is the experience of "being in the now," the use of the word "I" rather than "it" as a way to assume responsibility for behavior, learning how to talk to rather than at someone, becoming aware of bodily sensors, and learning to "stay with feelings" until they are understood and integrated.

The most difficult method for many people to understand is Perls' specialized form of role-playing. Role-playing is not new to psychological practice. As early as 1908 Dr. Jacob Moreno was working on this method from which have emerged many forms of group encounter and treatment. He coined the word "psychodrama" in 1919 to describe how he directed people to take on the identities of others and to act out their problems from different points of view.

In contrast to Moreno, Perls rarely uses other people to role-play with his patients. He claims that these others would "bring in their own fantasies, their own interpretations." Therefore, Perls requires the patient to imagine and act out all the parts. He focuses on how the patient is acting now, not on the why of the patient's behavior.

Although many arrangements can be used for this kind of role-playing, the chair technique is uniquely Perls. His props are the "hotseat" a chair for the patient who chooses to "work," an empty chair facing the patient onto which the patient projects his or her many selves, and a box of tissues for runny noses and tearful eyes.

Sometimes people are aware of only one of their roles. Sometimes they may be aware of both and say, "I'm either as high as a kite or weighted down with depression," or "I'm either angry and aggressive, or afraid and full of doubt."

A person whose personality is fragmented by polarization operates in an either/or manner—either arrogant or worthless, helpless or tyrannical, wicked or righteous. A person who is stuck at the impasse of such opposing focuses is fighting an internalized war. By using Perls' role-playing technique these opposing forces can have it out with each other, forgive each other, compromise, or at least come to know each other.

Using the double chair technique, people can develop an awareness of their fragmented parts by starting a dialogue and by acting out various roles, switching chairs with each switch in role. The role players may be people—as they are now, or as children, or as a mother, father, spouse, or boss. The role played may also be physical symptoms—ulcers, headaches, backaches, sweaty palms, palpitating hearts. They may even be objects encountered in a dream, such as a piece of furniture, an animal, a window.

Psychodrama:

The author was exposed to Psychodrama in a training situation in England during the summer of 1979 and became enthralled with its possibilities. Dr. Jacob Moreno, mentioned under role-playing in the section on Gestalt Therapy, is the recognized founder and implementer of this concept. "Adam" Blatner, a west coast psychiatrist, with whom the author studied in England, is a foremost disciple of Moreno and an exponent of psychodrama. The following thumb-nail biography of Moreno, contained in Blatner's book, *Acting-In: Practical Applications of Psycho-dramatic Methods,*[33] will give the group worker an insight into the therapy and how it can be used.

The history of the development of psychodrama is essentially equivalent to the biography of one man, Moreno.

Jacob Levy Moreno was born on May 19, 1892, in Bucharest, Rumania, and five years later his family moved to Vienna. Moreno became a student of philosophy at the University of Vienna (1910-1912), and from his earliest years was interested in the theological and religious dimensions of creativity and spontaneity. In 1911, Moreno observed and began to catalyze the play of children in the Vienna Gardens. *Here was the germination of psychodrama and improvisatory dramatics.*

While in medical school, Moreno become involved with a form of social action: the challenge of helping the aliented class of prostitutes in Vienna. With other physicians, he initiated small self-help groups; this work marked the beginning of group psychotherapy, as well as being one of the earliest examples of practical community psychiatry.

After receiving his medical degree from the University of Vienna in 1917, he worked at a refugee camp in Mittendorf. There, he began to attempt some scientific research with the cultural group dynamics of the refugee population.

During the years 1914-1921, Moreno continued his creative activites in the realm of poetry, philosophy, theology, and literature. He edited a literary journal, *Daimon,* and associated with many of the intellectuals of Vienna at that time, such as Martin Buber and Max Scheler. However, his philosophy was closely related to interpersonal themes. Themes such as "here-and-now" and "encounter," so popular today in the human potential movement, were to be found as key ideas in Moreno's poetic writings of this early period. One of the best known of these works is his book, *The Words of the Father.*

[33]From Howard Blatner, *Acting-In Practical Applications of Psychodramatic Methods,* pp. 140-143. Copyright © 1973 by Springer Publishing Company, Inc., New York, N.Y. Used by Permission.

The years 1921-1923 saw the birth of "the Theater of Spontaneity." Issues of current events were subjects of the theater's activities at first, but later Moreno applied this improvisatory setting to the treatment of individuals, marriages, and small groups. It is of interest that the idea of psychodrama followed, rather than preceded, Moreno's work in religion group psychotherapy, and sociometry.

In 1925, Dr. Moreno moved to the United States in order to find a more fertile field for his explorations. He lived in New York City and applied his methods to the challenges of emotionally disturbed hospitalized children, prisons, and socio-political psychology ("the Impromptu Theater"). His use of recording devices in the process of evaluating psychotherapy method was, at that time, the first application of this technique. Later, when television was developed, Dr. Moreno was the first to note many of its therapeutic possibilities also.

During the next several years, Dr. Moreno developed his ideas in many directions. While working at residential treatment centers for adolescents, he further elaborated on the work that began at Mittendorf, culminating in his book *Who Shall Survive?* – Foundations of Sociometry, Group Psychotherapy, and Sociodrama, (Sociometry has become a major tool in sociology today). Moreno also emphasized the value of work with groups, and in 1932 coined the term group psychotherapy. He thus became a major force in the introduction of new ideas into the field of American psychiatry.

In 1936, the Moreno Sanitarium was established in Beacon, New York, and became a school, a hospital, and the first real theater of psychodrama, as well as his home. In 1937, he edited and published his first journal, *Sociometry.* Over the next several years he continued his work in many interdisciplinary fields: social psychology, psychotherapy, sociology, and philosophy, among others. Many of those who would later become prominent in various fields were associated with Dr. Moreno in this early period—Kurt Lewin, Garner Murphy, Ronald Lippitt, Leland Bradford, Kenneth Benne, Jack GIbb. (The last three were later to become founders of the "T-Group"—The National Training Laboratories [N.T.L.]—which, in turn, was to become a cornerstone of the human potential movement.)

During the Second World War, Dr. Moreno advised the military services in the applications of role-playing to personnel selection and management. He was influential in the growth of group psychotherapy as a treatment modality in military and veterans hospitals.

After the war, Moreno continued to publish monographs, books, and a number of articles. He married Zerka Toeman in 1949, and together they began a routine of international conferences and travels, lecture-demonstrations, and prolific writing, which has continued to the present time. Moreno's influence can be found in many of the innovations in psychiatry over the last generation: e.g., family therapy, therapeutic community, Gestalt therapy, and many others.

In summary, the development of psychodrama should be viewed as inextricably interwoven with Moreno's work in philosophy, group psychotherapy, sociology, personality theory, and social psychiatry. Some of the concepts which he emphasized fifty years ago have only recently become recognized as vitally relevant for the challenges of the modern world. Throughout his life, Dr. Moreno has not only maintained an energetic pace of work, but also has been a model of his belief in spontaneity and creativity as a way of life.

Some of the Themes and Concepts Which Moreno Emphasized in His Writings

- Play as an element in culture and the helping relationship.
- Catharsis—its place in history, drama, religion, and psychodrama.
- The place of warm-up everyday life—e.g., boxing, sexual activity, group process, psychotherapy.
- Imagination—the creative potential; applications of fantasy.
- Spontaneity and creativity as primary elements of human growth.
- The importance of nonverbal communication, body tone and movement, posture, position, territoriality, lightning, sound, music, colors, textures, body contact, laughter, and humor as elements in human relationships.
- The social network, family network, community and societal network, and interpersonal transaction (therapeutic milieu), and so forth.
- Here-and-now,—an essentially existential approach.
- Focus on process rather than content.
- Acting-out (in the service of the ego) as an expression of act-hunger, can be synthetic rather than dissociative phenomenon.
- The religious implications and applications of subjective, creative and spontaneous man in relation to a creative Cosmos.
- Utilization of wide variety of methods, techniques, and technologies to help the client explore the dimensions of his experience (rather than restriction to one technique), i.e., electicism.
- The applications of role-reversal to child-rearing, the teaching of empathy and interpersonal sensitivity.
- The use of therapy in-situ, (i.e., the intervention on-the-spot, exploring the problem in the context and social network from which it arose), now applied in milieu therapy, residential treatment centers for children and adolescents, and other contexts.

Hypnosis:

F. L. Marcuse, a Canadian, who spent most of his life in the United States, has attempted to paint an accurate and in-depth picture of hypnosis. His book

Hypnosis: Fact and Fiction[34] covers many interesting facets of this exciting and often maligned process.

Material for this book, whether it describes fact or fiction, has come from many sources: books, professional journals, magazines, lectures, newspaper articles, and personal experiences. Marcuse had also asked over a thousand persons what questions they would most like to see answered if they were to pick up a book dealing with hypnosis. That almost everyone has some interest in hypnosis is indicated by the fact that out of the thousand only five had no questions. Some of the questions asked were: "Why do they hypnotize people?", "Is it really possible to be hypnotized or is it just a trick?", "Define hypnosis very clearly," "Should you let people use you as a subject?", "What is the value of hypnosis for the average person?", "What are the modern and past uses of hypnotism?", "Will a hypnotic state wear off eventually?", "Is frequent hypnosis dangerous to the physical organism?", "Can a person really float in mid-air under hypnosis?", "Just how is a person hypnotized?", "Can hypnosis be performed without instruments such as pendulums?", "Is the power of hypnosis in the eyes or in an object?", "Can a person be hypnotized over the radio or by television?", "Does the same hypnotic method work for everybody?"

"How can you tell if someone is actually hypnotized or not?", "What are the different stages or degrees of hypnotism?", "Is hypnosis done completely through the power of suggestion?", "Are you more susceptible to hypnosis after being exposed a number of times?", "Does the person who has been hypnotized remember it afterwards?", "Can a hypnotist exact physical evidence on a person's body through hypnosis; that is, on telling a subject he is being burned with a poker and actually using a pencil eraser, would there be a blister?", "What are a person's feelings under hypnosis?" "What type of person do you have to be in order to be hypnotized?"

"What is the percentage of people who can be hypnotized?", "Why isn't it possible to hypnotize everybody?", "Are those who can be hypnotized stable-minded people or just those who can be talked into anything?", "Which is the easiest to hypnotize, an intelligent man or a relatively stupid man?", "Can a person under hypnosis actually recall events which occurred when he was one year old or even younger?", "Is it possible to take a person back before the time of his birth (reincarnation)?", "What kind of person must the hypnotist be?", "How can a person accomplish things he can never do in everyday situations?", "Can the bodily actions be influenced by hypnosis—can a person be made to run faster than he normally could?", "Can you hypnotize a person against his will?", "When the person is under the hypnosis, would he do anything that he would not do in an ordinary state?", "Are hypnotic states induced by drugs similar to those

[34]Extracts reprinted from chapters 5 and 6 of F. L. Marcuse: *Hypnosis: Fact and Fiction* (Pelican Books Ltd., London, England) Copyright © F. L. Marcuse, 1959. Reprinted with permission.

induced mechanically?", "Has hypnosis been of medical aid to civilization, such as in dentistry, childbirth, medicine, surgery, etc.?"

"Is there a therapeutic lasting effect—after hypnosis does the patient retain the effect desired?", "What about mental telepathy?", "Illustrate examples of phony hypnotizing as compared to correct and useful procedures," "Why should or should not the novice attempt hypnosis?", "What are the different classes of animals that can be hypnotized?", "Could it be used on criminal suspects to uncover lies?", "Can hypnotism be an aid in learning?" "How about self-hypnosis, is it possible?" "Is hypnosis at all comparable to sleep?", "What nerves are affected by hypnosis?", "How does the process affect the brain?", "How can be the person who wants hypnosis used on him go about getting it and being sure the hypnotizer is reliable and well trained?", etc., etc.

In addition, some dozen individuals well known and experienced in the field of hypnosis were asked what problems, if any, they considered were generally ignored and were therefore important to mention in this book. Mentioned were: the problem of attitudes both professional and nonprofessional, the question of dangers, the possible difficulty of dehypnotization, the tie-up with everyday experience, the risk invovled in self-hypnosis, the quacks in the field. Finally in regard to its use in a therapeutic (curative) setting, the President of the American Society for Clinical and Experimental Hypnosis stated: "Just as surgical conditions are treated not by anaesthesia but under anaesthesia, so psychiatric or psychological matters are treated not by hypnosis, but the process is aided and facilitated by means of hypnosis."

It was partly around such questions, raised by nonprofessionals and professionals alike, that the Marcuse book was written.

Marcuse gave us much pithy information in his book including some of the characteristics of tests by hypnosis, characteristics of susceptible and non-susceptible subjects, and some general commentary concerning the nature of therapy. The author of this text has screened Marcuse's material and recorded the following for the group worker's store of information and knowledge.

Nature of Hypnotic Scales

Measuring the depth of hypnosis has never been a simple matter. In the early days, when surgery had to be performed, tests included making loud sounds, plucking hairs in the beard, squeezing the testes, and so on. Contributing to the complexity of this problem is the fact that many people think of hypnotic susceptibility as being all or none, and often fail to realize that there exist degrees of susceptibility. Furthermore, hypnosis constitutes a type of behavior which is not well understood, and it is especially difficult to get agreement as to what behavioral phenomena are characteristic of hypnosis—especially in its lighter stages. Steps between forceful advertising, subtle persuasion, and light hypnosis are not always clear. We know that water usually becomes ice at 32°F, but we cannot say exactly when waking suggestion (no matter how defined) involves hypnosis.

Another difficulty lies in the failure to realize the fact that scales of hypnotic depth (to be described) may be of a hierarchical (ordered) nature. This would mean that if a subject passed test C, it could be assumed that he had also passed test A and test B. In similar fashion if he passed test D, it could be assumed that he had already passed tests A, B, and C. There are at present certain scales for measuring depth of hypnosis which make this kind of assumption (hierarchical) by which individuals reflect progressively increased depth of hypnosis as they pass successive tests. In these scales, the last test that an individual passes indicates his score or the depth of hypnosis obtained. There are other scales (non-hierarchical) that assume that any and all tests of hypnosis are approximately equal in value. In these scales the individual's score or the depth of hypnosis obtained is shown by the total number of tests passed. Considering our lack of knowledge, it may well be that this non-hierarchical scale which makes less assumptions is preferable. Both points of view or both scales, however, may in part be correct: that is, there may be something in both the hierarchical and in the non-hierarchical scales. Briefly, there may be a cluster of tests at one level in which each test at this particular level may be of equal value; but there may be other clusters of tests at a higher level, and at this new level each test may have the same value, but all have a greater value than the tests at the first level. The value of each test will be higher if the level is higher, and lower if the level is lower. Something approaching this idea is assumed in the following tests.

- *Paralysis of Minor Muscles* – response to sugestions of loss of use of minor muscles such as loss of control of the muscles which open and shut eyes (after eight minutes of experimental work or more than eight minutes of therapeutic work).
- *Paralysis of Major Muscles* – this test centers on the inability, per suggestion, to use the larger muscle groups, such as those employed in rising from a chair.
- *Analgesia* – this test, is presumed to reflect a deeper state of hypnosis than either of the first two. It involves a suggested lack of sensitivity to pain (analgesia) or generalized loss of sensitivity (anaestheia).
- *Hallucinations* – the test involves the hypnotized subject's perception of objects which either have a changed physical reality or no physical reality at all (positive hallucinations) as well as failure to perceive objects which do have physical reality (negative hallucinations).
- *Post Hypnotic Suggestion* – this test must be evaluated for its effectiveness after the subject has been dehypnotized. Post hypnotized suggestion is simply tested by giving the post-hypnotic signal and observing whether the suggested post-hypnotic behavior results.

- *Amnesia* – in order to evaluate the amnesia test (inability to recall) the subject after awakening from the hypnotic state is asked to write down or tell everything that happened during the hypnotic session.

One gets the impression that there are a lot of ands, ifs, and buts in evaluating the above tests. There are many corollary behavioral and external considerations that must be evaluated along with the basic clinical manifestations.

The author wants to warn the group worker not to experiment or permit experimentation by inexperienced people in putting on a hypnotism show for laughs. There may be some inherent dangers and emotional repercussions that may evolve from this "fooling around."

Characteristics of Susceptible and Non-susceptible Subjects

Are there any ways in which tests or pre-tests or hynotic susceptibility may be avoided? In effect, is there any way in which we can say, by observation of individuals, that A will make a good subject and will be susceptible to hypnosis, whereas B will not be susceptible and therefore a waste of time? Are there any specific personality aspects of the individual which indicate susceptibility? There are certain characteristics of the individual which indicate some relationship with susceptibility to hypnosis, although practical considerations frequently make it simpler to attempt actual hypnosis (especially group hypnosis) in determining who is and who is not susceptible. Although the results of these (completely non-hypnotic) tests may be of questionable value from a practical point of view, they are of value theoretically, for they say something about the characteristics of susceptible and non-susceptible individuals, and thus about the nature of hypnosis.

Concerning the question of determining by non-hypnotic means just who is and who is not susceptible to hypnosis, there exist many ideas—some held by the layman, some by the professional. Many such beliefs are fictitious. It is said that if one has low intelligence or is stupid, is suggestible or is submissive, has a small degree of will power, has poor emotional stability, or possess a low forehead—then he will be susceptible to hypnosis. While such beliefs may be widely held, few are true. The meaningless and the vague generalizations inherent in such beliefs are well illustrated by a magazine article in which it is stated that the most susceptible subjects are those who are either male or female! Let us examine some of these beliefs.

Intelligence. With regard to intelligence the relationship found is, if anything, contrary to that popularly expected. It would seem that of two groups of hypnotic volunteers, the group having the higher average of intelligence tends, though only slightly, to have the greater number of hypnotically susceptible individuals. This finding, however, is based on college students and dental patients, a select sample from the higher socio-economic group, and it is doubtful whether we can generalize. It may be safest to conclude that there has been no indication that the lower the intelligence the greater the susceptibility.

Suggestibility. A moment's reflection about the use of this term makes one pause. When is a man suggestible? Is he suggestible if he wears a tie or is this merely custom? Is he suggestible when duped by a salesman or is this merely what we call submission? Is he suggestible if during an experiment he detects an odor which actually is not present, or is this merely confidence in the experimenter? Is he suggestible if in the midst of studying he accepts a friend's invitation and goes to a movie or is it merely that he is bored? Is he suggestible when he attributes a liberal statement to a labor leader than to a conservative individual who has actually made the statement or is this merely the operation of intelligence? Is he equally suggestible in all areas such as business, health, sex? Is he suggestible if in word association (giving an immediate verbal response to another word) he replies with a word that is found to be frequent in the general population? Is he suggestible if he yawns when another does or when a yawn is vividly described? All the foregoing, as well as other instances, have been claimed at one time or another to be examples of suggestibility. Consideration shows that popularly and often professional the many different psychological processes involved in the term suggestibility are often confused and the word 'suggestion' is frequently nothing more than a wastepaper for vague and ambiguous concepts.

Suggestions and its problems were the subject of a typical chapter in the older textbooks of psychology. The ommission of this topic from current texts is not a sign that the problems have been solved but that they were and still are embarrassing. Difficult in defining the terms is probably due to the fact that there are many types of suggestion. As an example of the large number of terms describing suggestion, consider the following: direct vs. indirect, negative vs. positive, true vs. untrue, overt vs. convert, prestige vs. non-prestige, verbal vs. nonverbal, primary, secondary, and tertiary. Despite this multiplicity of types, there have been numerous attempts by many people at different times to define suggestion. It has been said that suggestion implies resistance, represents the influence of one person upon another without the latter's consent, reflects the role of impulse rather than of will, is present to a certain degree in everybody, reflects the implanting of an idea. Illustrates the submissive instinct, appeals to the unconscious, is indistinguishable from education, etc.

The definitions which have been proffered are varied, confusing, incomplete, and seem to reflect the old saying that to define is to limit. The complexity of the problem is further reflected by the fact that our culture plays a significant role in determining the individual's acceptance or rejection of suggestions. Thus, for example, if Marcuse were to attempt to modify the attitude that many people have towards homosexuality, he would immediately encounter the cultural suggestion (at least in some countries) that homosexuality represents a 'crime against nature' and is a perversion. Since there are many types of suggestion, it would be simpler to define each by what it stands for and by what it does.

It is also popularly thought that a hypnotically susceptible person must be suggestible in the sense of being gullible or easily taken in (in the waking state). Such a statement is ambiguous unless one specifies what kind of suggestion is meant. If this is done it is often found that the type of suggestion referred to has nothing whatsoever to do with gullibility. Popular opinion tends to think of suggestion as characterized by deceit and lying and the recipient as being a victim who has been taken in. In actual fact the type of suggestion (direct) found in hypnosis has no relation to the type of suggestion (indirect) which possesses these attributes. Hypnosis depends upon entirely different types of suggestion, one which is straightforward and obvious. It can even be questioned whether the term suggestion should be used at all with regard to hypnosis, inasmuch as the type of suggestion involved is so much different from what is popularly assumed to be suggestion. This confusion or ignorance probably accounts in part for the debatable status of hypnosis in professional circles today; the repeatedly encountered boast "I'll bet you can't hypnotize me," made by the person who glories in his so-called 'will power' and in his ability to resist being 'taken in'; and the suspicion and scorn with which highly hypnotizable subjects are regarded.

Scientists working with groups of patients have by mathematical means, which need not concern us now, separated out at least two and possibly more types of suggestion. The first type of suggestion that they found corresponds to direct suggestion and shows a positive relationship with hypnosis. In short, it can predict susceptibility. This type of suggestion, not commonly thought of as suggestion, is illustrated by the body-sway test. The second type of suggestion found is the indirect type and corresponds to what is usually thought of as suggestion. It shows no relationship whatsoever to hypnosis. This form of suggestion is illustrated by the odor test. In this test deception and misleading cues are used, and the subject is led to report smelling a substance that just is not there. For example, an instructor may walk into the classroom, announce that today he wishes to demonstrate the speed with which an odor is diffused throughout a room, proceed to uncork odorless colored water and ask students to raise their hands when they detect an odor. In this type of indirect suggestion, if one has seen it done to another person, read about it, or been told about it, the effect is destroyed. In the direct suggestion of hypnosis, on the other hand, all these things (watching, reading, or being told) may occur without destroying the effect. For example, it is often of value to have the subject actually see another person being hypnotized.

Some hypnotists, in their desire to differentiate between these two forms of suggestion being involved in hypnosis have advised other hypnotists to preface all challenges or tests by the words 'as if.' Thus, in the first test one might say that the eyes cannot be opened because it is as if they were glued down. In this way they believe that even the slightest appearance of deception, associated with indirect suggestion, can be avoided. It can be debated whether this terminological difference really makes a difference.

In the induction of hypnosis, elements of indirect suggestion may actually be present in other than the verbal pattern. It is customary in inducing hypnosis to tell the subject, who may be fixating an object some eight to twelve inches away and above the line of sight, that his eyes are tired and they will close—they usually are and do because of physiological rather than psychological reasons. Or, again, consider the hand-clasp test where the fingers of one hand are interlaced with those of the other. The statement is made that one cannot unclasp one's hands. Inability to do this has a physical explanation—the knuckles are larger than the bones of the fingers and make unclasping somewhat difficult. Other techniques involving the use of indirect suggestion are sometimes used to 'impress' the naive individual and to increase his confidence in the hypnotist and so make him more susceptible. In all probability both physiological and psychological factors are at work in the individual's reactions.

Submissiveness. It is also assumed by many that to be a hypnotically good subject is to be submissive. This belief probably stems from the previous idea that to be hypnotically susceptible you must be gullible (indirect suggestion), and probably adds the statement that to be gullible is to be submissive. Inasmuch as susceptibility to hypnosis is unrelated to indirect suggestion, it would be surprising, if hypnosis and submission were actually related. Such a relationship was only assumed to be present because of the confusion that exists between hypnosis and direct suggestion. The problem was, nevertheless, investigated, and tests of submission given to subjects who had been shown to be susceptible to hypnosis. The results showed no relation whatsoever between hypnotic susceptibility and submissiveness.

Triadic Hypothesis. This theory holds that three personality factors go together more often than would be expected by chance. These factors are: susceptibility to hypnosis, impunitiveness (avoiding aggressive behavior), and repression (excluding unacceptable ideas from consciousness). Individuals susceptible to hypnosis have been found to be impunitive; that is, in a situation involving conflict they blame neither themselves (intropunitive) nor others (extrapunitive), but find a logical reason for the occurrence of the particular act. They also use repression as a favorite method of defense when confronted with conflict. The theory holds that for too long we have sought for variations in susceptibility to hypnosis to be related to one personality factor, while all along we should have been looking for variations in susceptibility to be related to many personality factors.

How exactly, it may be asked, is the direction of punitiveness indicated or how is repression measured? An example from the former will indicate how this particular test is scored. A cartoon picture of a man walking on the pavement and being splashed by a passing car is shown. Above the man's head is an unoccupied 'balloon' which is to be filled in by the subject, who is so doing gives the man's (essentially his own) reaction to the situation. If the subject writes down that the man has said to the occupants of the car, 'Why don't you watch where you're going?', this is extrapunitive, for it directs the blame to the outside. If, on the other hand, the subject indicates the man to be saying that this will in effect teach him not to walk near the curb, such an answer is in the direction of being intropunitive. If, however, the subject indicates, in this empty balloon, that the driver had to do this to avoid running over a dog, this would be impunitive, for it neither blames the driver nor himself, but finds a legitimate reason for the occurrence of the splashing. Repression is measured by seeing which of twelve puzzles the subject remembers. He purposely (but this was not known to him) was made to succeed in six and fail in six. Predominance of remembering successful rather than failed puzzles is characteristic of repression.

Other Personality Factors. With regard to will, little can be said since the very concept itself is not clear or meaningful. In connection with emotional stability, there is no evidence that emotional stablity or instability makes one more or less susceptible to hypnosis. The idea that having a low forehead makes one more susceptible to hypnosis can only be said to be a remnant of the old-time physiognomy when it was said that a person's character could be read from the bumps on his head or by the gross shape of his body. Data concerning the influence of sex, age, and mental disease on the question of susceptibility to hypnosis are conflicting and unsatisfactory. In general, there appears to be a slightly greater tendency for women to be more susceptible than men. Such a finding, however, may be spurious. Eight years of age is said to be the most susceptible stage in life, and over fifty the least. An individual who is susceptible to hypnosis tends to give or project stories to stimulus cards with hypnosis as a theme and with the outcome of the hypnotic induction being successful. Confronted with a similar situation, the non-susceptible individual will either tend to give a story unrelated to the theme of hypnosis or, if hypnosis is involved, there will be a negative outcome for the attempted induction. Purported differences in susceptibility as related to nationality have never been satisfactorily shown. It is frequently said that sleep-walkers or sleep-talkers are susceptible to hypnosis. What little evidence there is does not support this notion. Other normal personality variables share this rather nebulous situation.

There is no good evidence that the psychotic is more or less susceptible to hypnosis than the mentally healthy person. In point of fact, a strait-jacket or some kind of restraint has sometimes been used on non-manageable psychotics to induce fatigue, whereupon hypnosis was achieved successfully. While there is at present a fair amount of agreement that psychotics can be hypnotized, the depth which they can reach is disputed. Some die-hards who maintain that psychotics cannot be hypnotized will, if they are successful in hypnotizing a psychotic, change their diagnosis of the individual from psychotic to neurotic! It is often stated that the mentally deficient or the feeble-minded cannot be hypnotized, but such a conclusion is reached in the absence rather than the presence of data.

The Non-susceptible. Are there any definitive factors which indicate a lack of susceptibility? If there are, they again are not clear. Before failure in induction can be considered final there must be considered of adequate time (in one case 300 hours was required), variety of hypnotic induction techniques used (different techniques may be required according to whether the subject is sick or well), and different hypnotists (an individual may be susceptible to hypnotist A but not to B). When such factors are taken into consideration, it is not surprising to find reports of success in the hypnotic induction of alcoholics, seniles, syphilictics, and psychotics of various kinds.

Even when all these precautions have been taken, there may still be resistance to hypnotic induction. Subjects may resist for various reasons: the procedure may elicit an emotional complex; hypnosis may be associated with letting go sexually; there may be fear of possible revelations; there may be unrecognized antagonism; or there may be reasons unknown to both subject and experimenter, patient and clinician. Such resistance may be shown by shivering, restlessness, actual sleep, coughing, or verbal depreciation of the effectiveness of hypnosis. If more were known about the various reasons for resisting hypnosis, we should at the same time know more about hypnosis. Partial resistance may show itself by a difficulty in dehypnotizing or by lighter depths of hypnosis.

General Comments

In addition to what has been said, some general points concerning the nature of therapy may briefly be made.

- Deep hypnosis is not always necessary for therapeutic effectiveness.
- Patients will often go to a physician for an infected toe or an upset stomach before they will see a clinician for an infected or upset mind.
- Patients often resort to hypnotherapy in a final frantic attempt, a last resort. Consequently, results for this type of patient as compared to patients who come early in the course of disease might well differ.
- Abrupt or even gradual break-through in hypnosis of a patient's defenses may give rise to anxiety. Paradoxically, it would seem that the patient wishes to be rid of a symptom yet at the same time appears to defend it by his resistance (forgetting, etc.). Consequent to this, the patient in therapy may give the impression at first of appearing to be worse when problems which bother him come to the surface.

- Confabulations (untruths) which may occur in hypnosis are thought to be important in the patient's life history if he, the patient, believes them.
- The mere induction of hypnosis without suggestion may produce improvement. The fact that the patient feels that finally someone is interested in him and that something is being done may be important. In addition to this, there may unwittingly be some self-suggestion during this 'pure' hypnosis.
- The main difference between psychotherapy and hypnotherapy is that the latter depends on hypnosis to obtain information. Hypnosis is said to lessen resistance, and thus make available to the clinician data which might otherwise not be accessible, or if accessible might take a long time to elicit. In this way time and money may be saved. One such method is the 'intensification of the mood of the movement.' Here the patient is told that whatever feelings he experiences at the moment will grow stronger and stronger until they are overwhelming. This technique is said to result in the production of data even in non-communicative patients—but it sometimes also produces physical aggression. A knowledge of the phsychodynamics of behavior in addition to a knowledge of hypnosis is mandatory.
- About one-half of non-hospitalized patients terminate therapy themselves. Some therapists make the gratuitous assumption that this indicates a lack of need for further therapy. While this assumption is nice for the therapist, such a conclusion may be debated. Lack of confidence in the therapist or lack of money might just as well be indicated.
- Fear of being hypnotized, which to some individuals symobolizes taking a submissive role or accepting authority, may be such that symptoms will sometimes be given up even before hypnotherapy has been attempted.
- Many widely different systems of therapy apear to have approximately the same percentage of cures. This would suggest that the important factor is not the system's theoretical formulation but rather the relationship between patient and clinician which is common to all systems of therapy. It has not been shown that the strength of the dependency relationship between patient and clinician is any greater in hypnotherapy than in other forms of therapy.
- The patient may often be able to talk of intimate matters in hypnosis, something he may not be able to do or may be uncomfortable in doing during the non-hypnotized state.
- Hypnosis may be thought of as a therapeutic agent in a number of distinct ways: its mere induction without suggestion, though rarely used, may have therapeutic benefits; obtaining of relevant facts may be directly elicited (direct therapy); it may be combined as an adjuvant with other therapeutic procedures (indirect therapy); or finally, it may be used to eliminate symptoms (symptom therapy). It is not always easy to differentiate these procedures, as more than one at a time may be involved.

To reiterate, the foregoing should not be considered as constituting in any way a survey of the fundamentals of therapy. What points have been made were advanced in order to allow the group worker to evaluate more properly the role of hypnosis.

Non-Directive Approach Vis a Vis the Directive Approach:

Most group workers knowledges of therapy, if at all, generally center on some form of directive approach, wherein the therapist explores, diagnoses and treats the youth's problems, provided the latter gives his active cooperation to the proceedings. The therapist or counselor accepts a major responsibility in solving the problem, according to this concept.

Carl R. Rodgers is an exponent of the non-directive approach which simplisticly articulated is centered on free expression on the part of the client with some gentle, infrequent inquiry and encouragement on the part of the therapist.

The non-directive approach avoids channeling the interview in specific directions. Instead, the therapist attempts to develop a very permissive atmosphere in which the respondent will feel free to express his feelings without fear of disapproval.

Rodgers, in his *Counselling and Psycho-therapy,* states that in effective counselling and psychotherapy, one of the major purposes of the counselor is to help the client to express freely the emotionalized attitudes which are basic to his adjustment problems and conflicts. In carrying out this purpose, the counselor adopts various methods which enable the client to release his feelings without inhibition. Primarily the counselor endeavors to respond to, and verbally recognize, the feeling content, rather than the intellectual content, of the client's expression. This principle holds, no matter what the type of emotionalized attitude—negative attitudes of hostility, discouragement, and fear, positive attitudes of affection and courage and self-confidence, or ambivalent and contradictory attitudes. This approach is sound whether the client's feelings are directed toward himself, toward others or toward the counselor and the counseling situation. In each case, the counselor aims to recognize and respond to the feeling expressed, openly accepting relationship. He avoids the verbal recognition of repressed attitudes which the client has not yet been able to express.

In this process the client finds emotional release from feelings heretofore repressed, increasing awareness of the basic elements in his own situation, and increased ability to recognize his own feelings openly and without fear. He also finds his situation clarified by this process of exploration and begins to see relationships between his various reactions.

In place of anxiety and worry and feelings of inadequacy, the client develops an acceptance of his strengths and weaknesses as being a realistic and comfortable point of departure for progress in maturity. Instead of striving desperately to be what he is not, the client finds that there are many advantages in being what he is and in developing the growth possibilities which are genuinely indigenous.

It is these values in *catharsis* which make it truly therapeutic in counseling. The counselor endeavors to create a releasing atmosphere in which the individual may express himself. The client finds that expression leads also to the releasing of new forces within himself, forces which heretofore had been utilized in maintaining defensive reactions.

Even if counseling goes no further than this phase of free expression, it is helpful and constructive. It is this fact which makes the type of counseling described here most satisfactory for short-contract counseling. The counselor is often faced with the situations in which he knows that he will be limited to but one interview, or in which he is sure that he cannot carry on any extended treatment. In such instances, the common practice is to be completely directive. Since time is short, the counselor quickly grasps the problem as he sees it, giving advice, persuading, directing.

The results of such directive approach are almost inevitably and thoroughly bad. If, however, the counselor makes use of this limited time to free the client to "talk out" his attitudes, positive results ensue. The client leaves without, to be sure, any artificial "solution" to his problem, but with his situation much more clearly defined in his own mind, with possible choices clarified, and with the comforting reassurance that someone has understood him and, in spite of his problems and attitudes, has been able to accept him.

A study made by E. H. Porter and recorded in Rodger's book reflects the characteristics of the Directive group, the Non-Directive group and techniques comon to both groups.

Counselor Techniques Characteristic of the Directive Group

- Counselor defines the interview situation in terms of diagnostic or remedial procedures.

Example. "I don't know what your trouble is, but we can get at it in part through the tests you take and in part through what we do here in the interview."

- Counselor indicates topic but leaves development to client.

Example. "Would you care to tell me a little more about that?"

- Counselor indicates topic and delimits development to confirmation, negation, or the supplying of specific items of information.

Example. "How long ago was it that you took it?" "Here or at home?" "What course was that in?"

● Counselor identifies a problem, source of difficulty, condition needing correction, etc., through test interpretations, evaluative remarks, etc.

Example. "One of your difficulties is that you haven't had a chance to compare yourself with others." Interprets test results, but not as indicating a problem, source of difficulty, etc.

Example. "This indicates that 32 percent of college freshmen read the test material more rapidly than you did."

● Expresses approval, disapproval, shock, or other personal reaction in regard to the client.

Example. "Good! Grand! That's a nice start."

● Counselor explains, discusses, or gives information related to the problem or treatment.

Example. "Well, I don't think that's the only reason. Some people who know a great deal about it get just as nervous as the ones who don't."

● Counselor proposes client activity, directly, or through questioning technique, or in response to question of what to do.

Example. "I think that you ought to quit that job and put as much time in on your schoolwork as possible."

● Counselor influences the making of a decision by marshaling and evaluating evidence, expressing personal opinion, persuading pro or con.

Example. "Well its up to you, but I'd at least give it a try."

● Counselor reassures the client.

Example. "Now you may run across a lot of difficulty, but don't let it discourage you. You'll come out all right."

Counselor Techniques Characteristic of the Non-Directive Group

● Defines the interview situation in terms of client responsibility for directing the interview, reaching decisions, etc.

Example. "And sometimes people find that by talking over their problems with someone else they get a much better picture."

● Counselor responds in such a way as to indicate recognition of expression of feeling or attitude in immediately preceding verbal response.

Example. "And that makes you feel pretty low."

● Counselor responds in such a way as to interpret or recognize feeling or attitude expressed in some way other than in the immediately preceding response.

Example. "Maybe you didn't want to come this morning."

Techniques Common to Both Groups

● Counselor uses lead which forces the choosing and developing of topic upon client.

Example. "What's on your mind this morning?"

- Counselor responds in such a way as to indicate recognition of subject content.

Example. "And that test comes up Tuesday." "Humph! So neither method worked."

- Counselor indicates decision is up to client.

Example. "That's up to you."

- Counselor indicates acceptance or approval of decision.

Example. "I think you're on the right track there."

The techniques most frequently employed, as compiled by Porter, follow in order of frequency.

Techniques Most Frequently Employed

Directive Counselor Group:

- Ask highly specific questions, delimiting answers to yes, no, or specific information.
- Explains, discusses, or gives information related to the problem or treatment.
- Indicates topic of conversation but leaves development to client.
- Proposes client activity.
- Recognizes the subject content of what the client has just said.
- Marshals the evidence and persuades the client to undertake the proposed action.
- Points out a problem or condition needing correction.

Non-directive Counselor Group:

- Recognizes in some way the feeling or attitude which the client has just expressed.
- Interprets or recognizes feelings or attitudes expressed by general demeanor, specific behavior, or earlier statements.
- Indicates topic of conversation but leaves development to client.
- Recognizes the subject content of what the client has just said.
- Asks highly specific questions, delimiting answer to yes, no, or specific information.
- Explains, discusses or uses information related to the problem.
- Defines the interview situations in terms of the client, responsibilities.

Psycho-Analysis:

Sigmund Freud, who worked and lived most of his life in Vienna, is known as the father of Psycho-Analysis. He spent nearly fifty years developing and modifying his theories.

Leslie Stevenson of the United Kingdom gets to the core of Freud's philosophies in the *Seven Theories of Human Nature,*[35] the essence of which is reported here.

Freud maintained that individual well-being or mental health depends on a harmonious relationship between the various parts of the mind, and between the person and the real world in which he has to live. The ego has to recognize id, super-ego, and external world, perceiving and choosing opportunities for satisfying the instinctual demands of the id without transgressing the standards required by the super-ego. If the world is unsuitable and does not give any such opportunities, then of course suffering will result, but even when the environment is reasonably favorable, there will be mental disturbance if there is inner conflict between the parts of the mind. So neurosis results from the frustration of basic instincts, either because of external obstacles or because of internal mental imbalance.

There is one particular mental misadaptation which is of crucial importance in the causation of neurotic illnesses, and this is what Freud called repression. In a situation of extreme mental conflict, where a person experiences an instinctual impulse which is sharply incompatible with the standards he feels he must adhere to, it is possible for him to put it out of consciousness, to flee from it, to pretend that it does not exist. So repression is one of the so-called 'defense mechanisms,' by which a person attempts to avoid inner conflicts. But it is essentially an escape, a pretense, a withdrawal from reality, and as such is doomed to failure. For what is repressed does not really disappear, but continues to exist in the unconscious portion of the mind. It retains all its instinctual energy, and exerts its influence by sending into consciousness a disguised substitute for itself—a neurotic symptom. Thus the person can find himself behaving in ways which he will admit are irrational, yet which he feels compelled to continue without knowing why. For by repressing something out of his consciousness he has given up effective control over it; he can neither get rid of the symptoms it is causing, nor voluntarily lift the repression and recall it to consciousness.

As we should expect from his developmental approach to the individual, Freud locates the decisive repressions in early childhood. And as we might expect from his emphasis on sexuality, he holds them to be basically sexual. It is essential for the future mental health of the adult, that the child successfully passes through the normal stages of development of sexuality. But this does not always proceed smoothly, and any hitch in it leaves a predisposition to future neurosis; the various forms of sexual perversion can be traced to such a cause. One typical kind of neurosis consists in what Freud called 'regression,' the return to one of the stages at which childish satisfaction was obtained.

---

[35]Reprinted with permission – Oxford University Press, Oxford, England.

There is much more detail in Freud's theories of the neuroses, into which we cannot enter here, but we have already noted that he can attribute part of the blame for them on the external world, and so we should look a bit more at this social aspect of his diagnosis. For the standards to which a person feels he must conform are one of the crucial factors in mental conflict, but these standards are (in Freud's view) a product of the person's social environment—primarily his parents, but including anyone who has exerted influence and authority on the growing child.

It is the instillation of such standards that constitutes the essence of education, and makes a child into a member of civilized society; for to be civilized requires a certain control of the instincts, a sacrifice of instinctual satisfaction in order to make cultural achievements possible. But the standards instilled are not automatically the 'best' or most rational conducive to individual happiness. Certainly, individual parents vary widely, and maladjusted parents will be likely to produce maladjusted children. But Freud was prepared to entertain the possibility that the whole relationship between society and the individual has gotten out of balance, that our whole civilized life might be neurotic. Even as early as 1909, he asserted that our civilized standards make life too difficult for most people and that we cannot deny a certain amount of satisfaction to our instinctual impulses. So there is a basic in the writings of Freud himself for those later Freudians who diagnose the main trouble as lying in society rather than in the individual.

Prescription

As usual, prescription follows from diagnosis. Freud's aim was to restore a harmonious balance between the parts of the mind, and between the individual and his world. The latter might well involve programs of social reform, but Freud never specified these in any detail; his everyday practice was the treatment of neurotic patients by psycho-analysis. The word 'psycho-analysis' refers at least as much to Freud's method of treatment as to the theories on which that treatment is based. It is this method which we must now examine.

The method developed gradually out of Breuer's initial discovery that one particular hysterical patient could be helped by being encouraged to talk about the fantasies which had been filling her mind, and could actually be cured if she could be induced to remember the 'traumatic' experiences that had apparently caused her illness in the first place. Freud started using this 'talking cure,' and assuming that the pathogenic memories were always somewhere in the person's mind even if not ordinarily available to consciousness, he asked his patients to talk freely and uninhibitedly, hoping that he could interpret the unconscious forces behind what they said.

He encouraged them to say whatever came into their mind, however absurd (the method of 'free association'). But he often found that the flow of associations would dry up, and the patient would claim to know nothing more, and might even object to further inquiry. When such 'resistance' happened, Freud took it as a sign that he was really getting near the correct interpretation of the repressed complex. He thought that the patient's unconscious mind would somehow realize this and try to prevent the painful truth being brought into consciousness. Yet only if the repressed material could be brought back into consciousness could the patient be cured, and his ego given back the power over the id which it had lost in the process or repression.

But to achieve this happy result could take a long process, involving perhaps weekly sessions over a period of years. The analyst must try to arrive at the correct interpretation of his patient's condition, and present them at such a time and in such a way that the patient can accept them. The patient's dreams will provide very fruitful material for interpretation, for according to Freud's theory the 'manifest' contest of a dream is always the disguised fulfillment of repressed wishes, which are its real or 'latent' content.

Faulty actions can also be interpreted to reveal their unconscious causation. As one would expect from the theory we have summarized, the interpretations will very often refer to a person's sexual life, his childhood experiences, his infantile sexuality, and his relationships to his parents. Clearly all this demands a relationship of peculiar confidence between patient and analyst, but Freud found that much more than this happened; in fact, his patients manifested a degree of emotion towards him that could almost be called falling in love. This phenomenon he labelled 'transference,' on the assumption that the emotion was somehow transferred to the analyst from the real-life situations in which it was once present, or from the unconscious fantasies of the patient. The handling of such transference is of crucial importance for the success of the analysis, for it itself can be analyzed and traced back to its sources in the patient's unconscious.

The goal of psycho-analytic treatment can be summarized as self-knowledge. What the cured neurotic does with his new self-understanding is up to him, and various outcomes are possible. He may replace the unhelathy repression of instincts by a rational, conscious, control of them (suppression rather than repression); or he may be able to divert them into acceptable channels (sublimation); or he may decide that they should be satisfied after all. But there is no possibility at all of a result that is sometimes feared by the layman—that primitive instincts when unleashed will take over completely—for their power is actually reduced by being brought into consciousness.

Freud spent his life treating individual neurotic patients. But he never thought that psycho-analytic treatment is the answer to every human problem. When grappling speculatively with the problems of civilization and society he was realistic enough to realize their extreme complexity and to abstain from offering any panacea. But he did hold that psycho-analysis had much wider applications than just the treatment of neurotics. He said 'our civilization imposes an almost intolerable pressure on us and it calls for a corrective,' and speculated that psycho-analysis might help to prepare such a corrective.

REFERENCES

American Dance Therapy Association. Explanatory Brochure.

Blatner, H. A. *Acting-In: Practical Applications of Psychodramatic Methods.* Springer Publishing Co., Inc., 1973.

Fleming, J. D. "How to Hire and Fire a Shrink." *Self Magazine,* Aug. 1979.

James, M. and D. Jongeward. *Born to Win.* Addison-Wesley Publishing Co., Inc., 1971.

Marcuse, F. L. *Hypnosis: Fact and Fiction.* Penguin Books Ltd. (England), 1959.

Morrison, J. H. and J. J. O'Hearne. *Practical Transactional Analysis in Management.* Addison-Wesley Publishing Co., Inc.

Rodgers, C. R. *Counselling and Psychotherapy.* Houghton Mifflin Co.

"The Nondirective Method as a Technique for Social Research."

Stevenson, L. *Seven Theories of Human Nature.* Oxford University Press, 1974.

Chapter 32

Resource Listings – Organizations and Materials

One of the greatest assets, available to any group worker, is a ready reference list of organizations to be contacted on an "as needed" basis for help and intervention in both crisis situations and normal day to day activity.

The author has compiled a listing of organizations and other material, beyond the references and additional readings, contained in the chapters. Obviously such a list could never be all-inclusive. However, there are comparable and counter-part organizations, similar to those listed, throughout the country. For instance, the New Jersey Department of Health has prepared a bibliography of health literature for community leaders (contained herein). A similar bibliography is available in many, if not most, other states.

Alcoholism Information

If help is needed with an alcohol problem, the group worker is advised to contact their state division of alcoholism or their state department of mental health. The following organizations may also be contacted for information and help:

- The National Council on Alcoholism (NCA)
  733 Third Ave
  New York, New York 10017
  (Consult telephone book for local chapter.)
- Alcoholics Anonymous (AA) World Services, Inc.
  Post Office Box 459
  Grand Central Station
  New York, New York 10017
  (Consult telephone book for local groups.)
- The National Clearinghouse for Alcohol Information (NCALI)
  Box 2345
  Rockville, Maryland 10852
- The National Congress of Parents and Teachers Alcohol Education Project
  700 North Rush Street
  Chicago, Illinois 60611

- Al-Anon Family Groups
  115 East 23rd Street
  New York, New York 10010
- Alcohol and Drug Problems Assocation of North America
  (formerly the North American Association of Alcoholism Programs)
  1101 Fifteenth Street, N.W.
  Washington, D.C. 20005
- Veterans Administration
  Alcohol and Drug Dependent Service
  810 Vermont Avenue, N.W.
  Washington, D.C. 20420
- The Salvation Army
  120 West 14th Street
  New York, New York 10011
- Rutgers
  The State University of New Jersey
  Rutgers Center of Alcohol Studies
  New Brunswick, New Jersey 08903

Sources of Sex Education

- American Assocation of Sex Educators and Counselors
  815 Fifteenth Street, N.W.
  Washington, D.C. 20005
- American Social Health Association
  1740 Broadway
  New York, New York 10019
- E. C. Brown Center for Family Studies
  1802 Moss Street
  Eugene, Oregon, 07403
- Educational Foundation for Human Sexuality
  Montclair State College
  Upper Montclair, New Jersey 07047
- Institute for Family Research and Education
  760 Ostrom Aveue
  Syracuse, New York 13210
- Institute for Sex Education
  18 South Michigan Avenue
  Chicago, Illinois 60603
- Planned Parenthood World Population
  810 Seventh Avenue
  New York, New York 10017

- National Council of Churches
  Commission on Marriage and the Family
  475 Riverside Drive
  New York, New York 10027
- Synagogue Council of America
  Committee on the Family
  235 Fifth Avenue
  New York, New York 10016
- Sex Information and Education Council of the U.S.
  84 Fifth Avenue
  New York, New York 10023
- United States Catholic Conferences
  Family Life Bureau
  1312 Massachusetts Avenue, N.W.
  Washington, D.C. 20003

Dance Therapy Materials

Dance therapy data can be obtained by writing or calling the American Dance Therapy Association, Suite 230, 2000 Century Plaza, Columbia, Maryland 21044.

Bibliography (1974)

Books, articles and films on dance therapy theory, practice and research, movement fundamentals, body image, non-verbal communication, other therapeutic approaches, child development, group work, creativity and art, psychology and psychiatry and literary and cultural dimensions. Compiled and edited by Joanna G. Harris and Judy Beers.

Newsletter

Six letters yearly. Contains communications from ADTA President and membership, regional news, film and book reviews, student section, theory and philosophy and listing of courses and workshops available. Edited by Floretter Orleans.

American Journal of Dance Therapy

This publication is the official journal of the American Dance Therapy Association. Dance therapy is defined as "the psychotherapeutic use of movement as a process which furthers the emotional and physical integration of the individual." The journal publishes original contributions related to the clinical use of dance therapy with a wide variety of populations, theoretical considerations which provide a framework for dance therapy intervention, and research in dance therapy.

Drug Abuse Prevention and Treatment Coordinators (State Level)

- Commissioner
  State Department of Mental Health

135 South Union Street
Montgomery, Alabama 36130
(205) 265-2301

- Commissioner
Department of Health & Social Services
Pouch H-05F
Juneau, Alaska 99811
(907) 586-3585
- Manager
Drug Abuse Section
Bureau of Community Services
2500 East Van Buren Street
Phoenix, Arizona 85008
(602) 255-1239
- Director
Arkansas Office of Alcohol & Drug Abuse Prevention
1515 West 7th Street
Little Rock, Arkansas 72202
(501) 371-2604
- Secretary
Health and Welfare Agency
915 Capitol Mall, Room 200
Sacramento, California 95814
- Executive Director
Department of Health
4210 East 11th Avenue
Denver, Colorado 80220
(303) 320-1167
- Executive Director
Connecticut Alcohol & Drug Abuse Council
90 Washington Street
Hartford, Connecticut 06115
(203) 566-4145
- Secretary
Department of Health & Social Services
1901 North du Pont Highway
New Castle, Delaware 19720
(302) 421-6101
- Director
Department of Human Resources
1329 E. Street, N.W.
Washington, D.C. 20004

- Secretary
  Department of Health and Rehabilitation Services
  1317 Winewood Boulevard
  Tallahassee, Florida 32301
  (904) 488-7721
- Commissioner
  Department of Human Resources
  47 Trinity Avenue
  Atlanta, Georgia 30334
  (404) 656-5680
- Director
  Department of Health
  1270 Queen Emma Street
  Honolulu, Hawaii 96813
  (808) 548-7655
- Director
  Department of Health & Welfare
  700 W. State Street
  Boise, Idaho 83720
  (208) 384-2336
- Executive Director
  Illinois Dangerous Drugs Commission
  300 North State Street
  Chicago, Illinois 60610
  (312) 822-9860
- Commissioner
  Department of Mental Health
  5 Indiana Square
  Indianapolis, Indiana 46204
  (317) 633-7570
- Director
  Iowa Department of Substance Abuse
  Liberty Building, Suite 230
  418 Sixth Avenue
  Des Moines, Iowa 50319
  (515) 281-3641
- Secretary
  Department of Social & Rehabilitative Services
  State Office Bldg., 6th Floor
  Topeka, Kansas 66612
  (913)296-3925

- Secretary
  Department for Human Resources
  275 East Main Street
  Frankfort, Kentucky 40601
  (502) 564-7130
- Assistant Secretary
  Division of Hospitals
  Weber Bldg., 7th Floor
  200 Lafayette Street
  Baton Rouge, Louisiana 70804
  (504) 342-2575
- Commissioner
  Department of Human Services
  Statehouse
  Augusta, Maine 04330
  (207) 289-3701
- Secretary, Department of Health & Mental Hygiene
  201 West Preston Street
  Baltimore, Maryland 21201
  (301) 383-3959
- Commissioner
  Commonwealth of Massachusetts
  Department of Mental Health
  160 N. Washington Street
  Boston, Massachusetts 02114
  (617) 727-5600
- Director
  Department of Public Health
  3500 North Logan Street
  Lansing, Michigan 48909
  (517) 373-8600
- Commissioner
  Department of Public Welfare
  658 Cedar, 4th Floor
  St. Paul, Minnesota 55155
  (612) 296-2701
- State Department of Mental Health
  619 Robert E. Lee Office Building
  Jackson, Mississippi 39201
  (601) 354-7031
- Acting Director
  Department of Mental Health

2002 Missouri Boulevard
Jefferson City, Missouri 65101
(314) 751-3070

- Director
  Department of Institutions
  1539 11th Avenue
  Helena, Montana 59602
  (449-3930
- Chairman
  Nebraska Commission on Drugs
  Post Office Box 94726
  Lincoln, Nebraska 68509
  (402) 471-2691
- Director
  Department of Human Resources
  Kinhead Building
  505 East King Street
  Carson City Nevada 89710
  (702) 885-4790
- Director
  Office of Substance Abuse
  3 Capitol Street, Room 405
  Concord, New Hampshire 03301
  (603) 271-2754
- Assistant Commissioner
  Alcohol, Narcotic & Drug Abuse
  Department of Health
  129 E. Hanover Street
  Trenton, New Jersey 08608
  (609) 292-5760
- Chief, Substance Abuse Bureau
  Behavioral Health Services
  Health & Environmental Department
  Post Office Box 968
  Santa Fe, New Mexico 87503
  (505) 827-5271
- Director
  New York State Division of Substance Abuse Services
  Executive Park South
  Albany, New York 12203
  (518) 457-2061

- Secretary
  Department of Human Resources
  325 North Salisburg Street
  Raleigh, North Carolina 27611
  (919) 733-4534
- State Health Officer
  N.D. State Department of Health
  Capitol Building
  Bismarck, North Dakota 58505
  (701) 224-2767
- State Methadone Authority
  Ohio Department of Mental Health & Mental Retardation
  65 South Front Street
  Columbus, Ohio 43215
- Commissioner
  Department of Mental Health
  Post Office Box 53277
  Oklahoma City, Oklahoma 73105
  (405) 521-2811
- Administrator
  Mental Health Division
  2575 Bittern Street, N.E.
  Salem, Oregon 97310
  (503) 378-2671
- Executive Director
  Governor's Council on Drug & Alcohol Abuse
  2101 North Front Street
  Harrisburg, Pennsylvania 17120
  (717) 787-9857
- Director, Department of Mental Health, Retardation, and Hospitals
  600 New London Avenue
  Cranston, Rhode Island 02920
  (401) 462-3201
- Director
  South Carolina Commission on Alcohol & Drug Abuse
  3700 Forest Drive
  Columbia, South Carolina 29204
  (803) 758-2521
- Secretary Department of Health
  Joe Foss Building
  Pierre, South Dakota 57501
  (605) 773-3361

- Commissioner
  Department of Mental Health
  501 Union Building
  Nashville, Tennessee 37219
  (615) 741-1921
- Executive Director
  Texas Department of Community Affairs
  210 Barton Springs Road
  Austin, Texas 78704
  (512) 475-2431
- Executive Director
  Department of Social Services
  150 West North Temple, Room 310
  Salt Lake City, Utah 84110
  (801) 533-5331
- Director
  Agency of Human Services
  State Office Building
  Montpelier, Vermont 05602
  (802) 241-2220
- Assistant Commissioner
  Virginia Department of Mental Health & Mental Retardation
  Post Office Box 1797
  Richmond, Virginia 23214
  (804) 786-5313
- Chief of Drug Section
  Department of Social & Health Services
  OB-43E
  Olympia, Washington 98504
  (206) 753-3073
- Director
  Department of Health
  State Capitol
  Charleston, West Virginia 25305
  (304) 348-3616
- Drug Abuse Program Policy Specialist
  1 West Wilson Street
  Madison, Wisconsin 53702
  (608) 266-2717
- Director
  Substance Abuse Program
  Hathaway Building, Room 457
  Cheyenne, Wyoming 82002
  (307) 777-7115

Drug Enforcement Administration (U.S. Dept. of Justice)
Regional Offices

North Eastern Regional Office
555 West 57th Street
New York, New York 10019
(212) 399-5151
- Canada
  - Montreal
  - Toronto
- Connecticut
- Delaware
- Maine
- Massachusetts
- New Hampshire
- New Jersey
- Pennsylvania
- Rhode Island
- Vermont

South Eastern Regional Office
8400 N.W. 53rd Street
Miami, Florida 33166
(305) 591-4870
- Alabama
- Arkansas
- Florida
- Georgia
- Kingston, Jamaica
- Louisiana
- Maryland
- Mississippi
- North Carolina
- Puerto Rico
- South Carolina
- Tennessee
- Virginia
- Washington, D.C.

North Central Regional Office
1800 Dirksen Federal Building
219 South Dearborn Street
Chicago, Illinois 60604
(312) 3353-7875

Indiana
Iowa
Kansas
Michigan
Minnesota
Missouri
Nebraska
North Dakota
Ohio
South Dakota
West Virginia
Wisconsin

South Central Regional Office
1880 Regal Row
Dallas, Texas 75235
(214) 767-7203

Arizona
Colorado
New Mexico
Oklahoma
Utah
Wyoming

Western Regional Office
Suite 800
350 South Figueroa Street
Los Angeles, California 90017
(213) 688-2650

Alaska
Canada
    Vancouver
Guam
Hawaii
Idaho
Montana
Nevada
Oregon
Washington

Films — Entertainment

Many youth groups are into 'film festivals' as a source of fund raising or just plain fun. There are many source companies that specialize in film rentals. Many public libraries have a film loan department and can be counted upon to provide hours of entertainment without charge.

On a national level there are a number of film rental companies that provide excellent mail order service. Twyman Films Inc. of 4700 Wadsworth Road, Box 605, Dayton, Ohio 45401, is one of such companies. Other Twyman Films addresses are:

Los Angeles
149 Detroit Street
Los Angeles, California 90036
(800) 543-9594

Dayton
4700 Wadsworth Road
Box 605
Dayton, Ohio 45401
(513) 276-5941
(800) 543-9594

New York
Room 803
45 West 45th Street
New York, New York 10036
(800) 543-9594

Graduate School Admission Tests

We have talked somewhat about college entrance practice tests earlier in this text. The author feels that there may also be some interest in the youth group environment in preparing for graduate school. Arco Publishing Company also provides help for this need to wit:

- Graduate Business Admission Test

Complete guide for passing and entering the professional school of your choice. Thousands of practice questions. Sample tests.

- Law School Admission Test

An essential review book for anyone taking the LSAT to gain law school admission. Every phase of the exam is covered in this book which contains over 3000 LSAT-type questions in law interpretation, nonverbal reasoning, graph, chart and table interpretation, reading comprehension, writing ability, cultural background. A highlight of the text is the inclusion of complete Trial Aptitude Tests which simulate closely the actual Law School Aptitude Test.

- How to Pass High on the Graduate Record Examination

This study guide was written for those who wish to succeed on the Graduate Record Examination. Included are questions which closely simulate the exam –

4000 GRE-type practice questions and answers. Trial tests are in biology, education, history, literature, and mathematics.

- Medical College Admission Test

Preparation for entire Medical College Entrance Exam. Over 3000 practice questions with answers are given. Study sections include Biology, Chemistry, Physics, Arithmetic, Algebra, Geometry, Social Studies, Literature, Art, Music, Psychology, Philosophy, etc. Actual Trial Tests are included, as well as tips on how to score high.

All books are available at your bookseller or directly from ARCO PUBLISHING COMPANY, INC., 219 Park Avenue South, New York, N.Y. 10003.

Health and Mental Health

Health Education Materials[36] and the organizations that offer them was prepared by the Health Insurance Institute. This booklet was based on a survey by the Health Insurance Institute which asked insurance companies, health organizations, medical associations, health-related businesses and many others to list their publications.

(Copies of this list can be acquired from the Health Insurance Institute, 1850 K Street, N.W., Washington, D.C. 20006.)

Accident Prevention:

- American Insurance Association
  Engineering and Safety Service
  85 John Street
  New York, New York 10038
  (Pamphlet, film list)
- American Red Cross
  Meyer Mathis, Director
  Office of Systems Analysis, Information & Statistics
  (Contact: Local Chapter)
  (Films, leaflets, pamphlets, textbooks)
- The Country Companies
  Jim Williams, Associate Director—PR
  P.O. Box 2020
  Bloomington, Illinois 61701
  (Booklets)
- Institute for Safer Living
  American Mutual Liability Insurance Company
  Wakefield, Massachusetts 01880
  (Pamphlet)

[36]Compiled from a brochure developed by the Health Insurance Institute, American Council of Life Insurance.

- Metropolitan Life Insurance Company
  Health and Safety Education Division
  One Madison Avenue
  New York, New York 10010
  (Pamphlet, film)
- National Easter Seal Society for Crippled Children and Adults
  2023 W. Ogden Avenue
  Chicago, Illinois 60612
  (Pamphlet)
- National Society to Prevent Blindness
  Cerisse M. Anderson, Associate Writer
  79 Madison Avenue
  New York, New York 10016
  (Pamphlet, film)
- Public Affairs Committee, Inc.
  381 Park Avenue South
  New York, New York 10016
  (Pamphlets)
- Aetna Life & Casualty
  Public Relations Department
  151 Farmington Avenue
  Hartford, Connecticut 06115
  (Pamphlets, film)
- Connecticut General Life Insurance Company
  Hartford, Connecticut 06152
  (Pamphlet)
- Johnson & Johnson
  501 George Street
  New Brunswick, New Jersey 08901
  (Pamphlet)
- Liberty Mutual Insurance Company
  Public Relations Department
  175 Berkeley Street
  Boston, Massachusetts 02117
  (Pamphlets)
- National Safety Council
  Director of Public Information
  425 N. Michigan Avenue
  Chicago, Illinois 60611
  (Films, pamphlets, posters)

- Prudential Insurance Company of America
  Public Relations Department
  Box 36
  Newark, New Jersey 07101
  (Pamphlets, film)

Allergies:

- American School Health Association
  Thomas D. Foster
  P.O. Box 708
  Kent, Ohio 44240
  (Reprint)
- Asthma & Allergy Foundation of America
  801 Second Avenue
  New York, New York 10017
  (Pamphlets, films)
- National Institute of Allergy and Infectious Diseases, NIH
  Information Office
  Room 7A-32-Bldg. 31
  Bethesda, Maryland 20014
  (Pamphlets)
- Public Affairs Committee, Inc.
  381 Park Avenue South
  New York, New York 10016
  (Pamphlets)
- Superintendent of Documents
  U.S. Government Printing Office
  Washington, D.C. 20402
  (Pamphlet)
- Superintendent of Documents
  U.S. Government Printing Office
  Washington, D.C. 20402
  (Pamphlet)

Birth Defects:

- The National Foundation—March of Dimes
  1275 Mamaroneck Avenue, or Box 2000
  White Plains, New York 10602
  (Pamphlets)
- National Society to Prevent Blindness
  70 Madison Avenue
  New York, New York 10016
  (Pamphlets)

- Public Affairs Committee
  381 Park Avenue South
  New York, New York 10016
  (Pamphlets)

Cancer:

- American Cancer Society
  Walter James, Vice President
  Public Education
  777 Third Avenue
  New York, New York 10017
  (Pamphlets, films, speakers)
- American Medical Association
  P.O. Box 821
  Monroe, Wisconsin 53566
- American School Health Association
  Thomas D. Foster
  P.O. Box 708
  Kent, Ohio 44240
  (Reprint of Journal of School Health special issue)
- Prudential Insurance Company of America
  Public Relations Department
  Box 36
  Newark, New Jersey 07101
  (Pamphlets)
- Public Affairs Committee
  381 Park Avenue South
  New York, New York 10016
  (Pamphlets)
- Superintendent of Documents
  U.S. Government Printing Office
  Washington, D.C. 20402
  (Pamphlet)

Cerebral Palsy:

- National Easter Seal Society for Crippled Children and Adults
  2023 W. Ogden Avenue
  Chicago, Illinois 60612
- Public Affairs Committee, Inc.
  381 Park Avenue South
  New York, New York 10016
  (Pamphlets)

- Superintendent of Documents
  U.S. Government Printing Office
  Washington, D.C. 20402
  (Pamphlets)
- United Cerebral Palsy Association
  66 East 34th Street
  New York, New York 10016

Child Care and Development:

- American Home Economics Association
  2010 Massachusetts Avenue, N.W.
  Washington, D.C. 20036
  (Pamphlets)
- American Hospital Association
  Department of Order Processing
  940 North Lake Shore Drive
  Chicago, Illinois 60611
  (Pamphlets, books, audiocassette, slides, films, poster, reprints.)
- Asthma and Allergy Foundation of America
  801 Second Avenue
  New York, New York 10017
  (Pamphlets)
- Cystic Fibrosis Foundation
  3379 Peachtree Road, N.E.
  Atlanta, Georgia 30326
  (Leaflets, film)
- Johnson & Johnson
  501 George Street
  New Brunswich, New Jersey 08901
  (Pamphlet, folder and chart)
- Mental Health Materials Center
  419 Park Avenue South
  New York, New York 10016
  (Pamphlets)
- Metropolitan Life Insurance Company
  Health and Safety Education Division
  One Madison Avenue
  New York, New York 10010
  (Pamphlets, film)
- National Congress of Parents & Teachers
  700 N. Rush Street
  Chicago, Illinois 60611
  (Pamphlets)

- National Easter Seal Society for Crippled Children and Adults
  2023 W. Ogden Avenue
  Chicago, Illinois 60612
  (Pamphlets)
- National Society to Prevent Blindness
  79 Madison Avenue
  New York, New York 10016
  (Pamphlets, film)
- Prudential Insurance Company of America
  Public Relations Department
  Box 36
  Newark, New Jersey 07101
  (Pamphlet)
- Public Affairs Committee
  381 Park Avenue South
  New York, New York 10016
  (Pamphlets)
- Superintendent of Documents
  U.S. Government Printing Office
  Washington, D.C. 20402
  (Pamphlets)
- Tampax, Incorporated
  Department HI
  P.O. Box 7001
  Lake Success, New York 11042
  (Pamphlets, teaching guide and reprints, anatomical charts)

Cystic Fibrosis:

- Cystic Fibrosis Foundation
  3379 Peachtree Road, N.E.
  Atlanta, Georgia 30326
  (Pamphlets, films)
- National Genetics Foundation, Inc.
  9 West 57th Street
  New York, New York 10019
  (Fact Sheet)
- Public Affairs Committee, Inc.
  381 Park Avenue South
  New York, New York 10016
  (Pamphlets)

Dental Health:

- American Dental Association
  Bureau of Health Education and Audiovisual Services

211 E. Chicago Avenue
Chicago, Illinois 60611
(Pamphlets)

- Association for the Advancement of Health Education
  Dr. William Kane, Executive Director
  1201 16th Street, N.W.
  Washington, D.C. 20036
  (Book)
- Johnson & Johnson
  501 George Street
  New Brunswick, New Jersey 08901
  (Pamphlet)
- Metropolitan Life Insurance Company
  Health and Safety Education Division
  One Madison Avenue
  New York, New York 10010
  (Pamphlet)
- National Dairy Council
  6300 N. River Road
  Rosemont, Illinois 60018
  (Pamphlet)
- National Easter Seal Society for Crippled Children and Adults
  2023 W. Ogden Avenue
  Chicago, Illinois 60612
  (Pamphlets)
- Public Affairs Committee, Inc.
  381 Park Avenue South
  New York, New York 10016
  (Pamphlet)
- Superintendent of Documents
  U.S. Government Printing Office
  Washington, D.C. 20402
  (Pamphlet)

Diabetes:

- American Diabetes Association
  1 West 48th Street
  New York, New York 10020
  (Pamphlets)
- American Foundation for the Blind
  Arthur Zigouras
  15 West 16th Street
  New York, New York 10011
  (Pamphlets)

- American Medical Association
  P.O. Box 821
  Monroe, Wisconsin 53566
  (Pamphlets)
- Juvenile Diabetes Foundation
  23 East 26th Street
  New York, New York 10010
  (Films, pamphlets)
- National Genetics Foundation
  9 West 57th Street
  New York, New York 10019
  (Fact sheet)
- National Society to Prevent Blindness
  79 Madison Avenue
  New York, New York 10016
  (Pamphlets)
- Prudential Insurance Company of America
  Public Relations Department
  Box 36
  Newark, New Jersey 07101
  (Pamphlets)
- Public Affairs Committee, Inc.
  381 Park Avenue South
  New York, New York 10016
  (Film)
- Superintendent of Documents
  U.S. Government Printing Office
  Washington, D.C. 20402
  (Pamphlet)

Drug Abuse:

- American School Health Association
  Thomas D. Foster
  P.O. Box 708
  Kent, Ohio 44240
  (Pamphlet)
- Association for the Advancement of Health Education
  Dr. William Kane, Executive Director
  1201 16th Street, N.W.
  Washington, D.C. 20036
  (Book, films)
- Connecticut General Life Insurance Company
  Hartford, Connecticut 06152
  (Pamphlets)

- Kemper Insurance Companies
  Communications and Public Affairs
  Long Grove, Illinois 60049
  (Pamphlets)
- National Clearing House for Drug Abuse Information
  Room 10A-56
  5600 Fishers Lane
  Rockville, Maryland 20857
  (Pamphlets, films)
- Pharmaceutical Manufacturers Association
  Consumer Services
  1155 15th Street, N.W.
  Washington, D.C. 20005
  (Booklet, flyer, curriculum guide, slides)
- Prudential Insurance Company of America
  Public Relations Department
  Box 36
  Newark, New Jersey 07101
  (Pamphlets)
- Public Affairs Committee, Inc.
  381 Park Avenue South
  New York, New York 10016
  (Pamphlets)

Environmental Pollution:

- Public Health Service
  Environmental Health Service
  U.S. Dept. of Health, Education & Welfare
  Rockville, Maryland 20857
  (Pamphlets, reprints)

Epilepsy:

- Epilepsy Foundation of America
  1828 L Street, N.W., Suite 406
  Washington, D.C. 20036
  (Pamphlets, reprints, paperback, cassettes and slides, films)
- National Genetics Foundation
  9 West 57th Street
  New York, New York 10019
  (Fact sheet)
- Public Affairs Committee, Inc.
  381 Park Avenue South
  New York, New York 10016
  (Pamphlets)

- Superintendent of Documents
  U.S. Government Printing Office
  Washington, D.C. 20402
  (Pamphlet)

Eyesight:

- American Foundation for the Blind
  Arthur Zigouras
  15 West 16th Street
  New York, New York 10011
  (Catalogues of films and publications)
- Better Vision Institute, Inc.
  230 Park Avenue
  New York, New York 10017
  (Pamphlets)
- National Society to Prevent Blindness
  79 Madison Avenue
  New York, New York 10016
  (Pamphlets, films)
- Public Affairs Committee, Inc.
  381 Park Avenue South
  New York, New York 10016
  (Pamphlets)
- Superintendent of Documents
  U.S. Government Printing Office
  Washington, D.C. 20402
  (Pamphlet)

Family Life Education:

- American Home Economics Association
  2010 Massachusetts Avenue, N.W.
  Washington, D.C. 20036
  (Pamphlets)
- American School Health Association
  Thomas D. Foster
  P.O. Box 708
  Kent, Ohio 44240
  (Book)
- Kimberly-Clarke
  Life Cycle Center
  Neenah, Wisconsin 54956
  (Pamphlets)
- Mental Health Materials Center
  419 Park Avenue South

New York, New York 10016
(Pamphlets)

- National PTA
  700 N. Rush Street
  Chicago, Illinois 60611
  (Pamphlets)
- Public Affairs Committee, Inc.
  381 Park Avenue South
  New York, New York 10016
  (Pamphlets)
- Tampax, Incorporated
  Department HI
  P.O. Box 7001
  Lake Success, New York 11042
  (Pamphlets)

First Aid:

- American Insurance Association
  Engineering and Safety Service
  85 John Street
  New York, New York 10038
  (Pamphlets, film list)
- American Red Cross
  (Contact local chapter)
  (Films, leaflets, pamphlets, textbooks)
- Metropolitan Life Insurance Company
  One Madison Avenue
  New York, New York 10010
  (Wall card)
- National Society to Prevent Blindness
  79 Madison Avenue
  New York, New York 10016
  (Pamphlet)
- Public Affairs Committee, Inc.
  381 Park Avenue South
  New York, New York 10016
  (Pamphlets)

Foot Health:

- American Podiatry Association
  Publications Section
  20 Chevy Chase Circle, N.W.
  Washington, D.C. 20015
  (Book)

- Public Affairs Committee, Inc.
  381 Park Avenue South
  New York, New York 10016
  (Pamphlets)

General Health:

- Aetna Life and Casualty
  Public Relations Department
  157 Farmington Avenue
  Hartford, Connecticut 06115
  (Pamphlets, films)
- American Medical Association
  P.O. Box 821
  Monroe, Wisconsin 53566
  (Pamphlets)
- American Physical Fitness Research Institute
  824 Moraga Drive
  Los Angeles, California 90049
  Attention: Grusha D. Paterson, M.A.
  (Posters, film, tapes, books, bulletin, pamphlets, reprints)
- American Red Cross
  (Contact local chapter)
  (Films, leaflets, pamphlets, textbooks)
- Kimberly-Clarke
  Life Cycle Center
  Neenah, Wisconsin 54956
  (Pamphlets)
- Liberty Mutual Insurance Company
  Public Relations Department
  175 Berkeley Street
  Boston, Massachusetts 02117
  (Pamphlets)
- Mental Health Materials Center
  419 Park Avenue South
  New York, New York 10016
  (Pamphlets)
- Metropolitan Life Insurance Company
  Health and Safety Education Division
  One Madison Avenue
  New York, New York 10010
  (Pamphlets, cards, posters)
- Pharmaceutical Manufacturers Association
  Consumer Services

1155 15th Street, N.W.
Washington, D.C. 20005
(Pamphlets)

- Provident Indemnity Life Insurance Company
  c/o George Bonsal
  2500 Dekalb Pike
  Norristown, Pennsylvania 19401
  (Pamphlet)
- Prudential Insurance Company of America
  Public Relations Department
  Box 36
  Newark, New Jersey 07101
  (Pamphlet)
- Public Affairs Committee, Inc.
  381 Park Avenue South
  New York, New York 10016
  (Pamphlet)

Genetic Disease:

- National Genetics Foundation
  9 West 57th Street
  New York, New York 10019
  (Brochures, pamphlets)
- National Tay-Sachs & Allied Diseases Assoc., Inc.
  122 East 42nd Street, Suite 3705
  New York, New York 10017
  (Books, pamphlets)
- The Paul Revere Life Insurance Company
  William G. Rickard, M.D.
  Vice President & Medical Director
  18 Chestnut Street
  Worcester, Massachusetts 01608
  (Pamphlet)
- Public Affairs Committee, Inc.
  381 Park Avenue South
  New York, New York 10016
  (Pamphlet)

Health Careers:

- American Hospital Association
  Department of Order Processing
  840 N. Lake Shore Drive
  Chicago, Illinois 60611
  (Pamphlets, posters)

- American Osteopathic Association
  Public Relations Department
  212 E. Ohio Street
  Chicago, Illinois 60611
  (Pamphlets)
- American Physical Therapy Association
  1156 15th Street, N.W.
  Washington, D.C. 20005
  (Pamphlets)
- American Podiatry Association
  Council on Education
  20 Chevy Chase Circle, N.W.
  Washington, D.C. 20015
  (Pamphlets)
- American School Health Association
  Thomas D. Foster
  P.O. Box 708
  Kent, Ohio 44240
  (Pamphlets)
- National Health Council
  1740 Broadway
  New York, New York 10019
  (Pamphlets)
- National Association for Retarded Citizens
  P.O. Box 6109
  2709 Avenue E. East
  Arlington, Texas 76011
  (Pamphlets)
- The Paul Revere Life Insurance Company
  William G. Rickard, M.D.
  Vice-President & Medical Director
  18 Chestnut Street
  Worcester, Massachusetts 01608
  (Pamphlets)
- Pharmaceutical Manufacturers Association
  Consumer Services
  1155 15th Street, N.W.
  Washington, D.C. 20005
  (Pamphlets)
- Public Affairs Committee, Inc.
  381 Park Avenue South
  New York, New York 10016
  (Pamphlets)

Hearing:

- American Speech & Hearing Association
  Career and Information Services Section
  10801 Rockville Pike
  Rockville, Maryland 20857
  (Pamphlet)
- National Easter Seal Society for Crippled Children and Adults
  2023 W. Ogden Avenue
  Chicago, Illinois 60612
  (Pamphlet)

Heart Disease:

- American Heart Association
  Inquiries Section
  7320 Greenville Avenue
  Dallas, Texas 75231
  (Pamphlets, brochure)
- Metropolitan Life Insurance Company
  Health and Safety Education Division
  One Madison Avenue
  New York, New York 10010
  (Card & Poster)
- National Dairy Council
  6300 N. River Road
  Rosemont, Illinois 60018
  (Pamphlets)
- National Easter Seal Society for Crippled Children and Adults
  2023 W. Ogden Avenue
  Chicago, Illinois 60612
  (Pamphlets)
- National Genetics Foundation
  9 West 57th Street
  New York, New York 10019
  (Fact sheet)
- Prudential Insurance Company of America
  Public Relations Department
  Box 36
  Newark, New Jersey 07101
  (Pamphlets)
- Public Affairs Committee, Inc.
  381 Park Avenue South
  New York, New York 10016
  (Pamphlets)

- Superintendent of Documents
  U.S. Government Printing Office
  Washington, D.C. 20402
  (Pamphlet)

Hodgkins Disease:

- Leukemia Society of America
  211 E. 43rd Street
  New York, New York 10017
  (Pamphlets, audiovisual material on a loan basis)

Hospital Services:

- American Hospital Association
  Department of Order Processing
  840 North Lake Shore Drive
  Chicago, Illinois 60611
  (Pamphlets, posters)
- American Osteopathic Association
  212 E. Ohio Street
  Chicago, Illinois 60611
  (Pamphlets)
- Public Affairs Committee, Inc.
  381 Park Avenue South
  New York, New York 10016
  (Pamphlets)
- Superintendent of Documents
  U.S. Government Printing Office
  Washington, D.C. 20402
  (Pamphlet)

Kidney Disease:

- American Medical Association
  P.O. Box 821
  Monroe, Wisconsin 53566
  (Pamphlets)
- National Kidney Foundation
  2 Park Avenue
  New York, New York 10016
  (Pamphlets)
- Public Affairs Committee, Inc.
  381 Park Avenue South
  New York, New York 10016
  (Pamphlets)

Leukemia:

- American Cancer Society
  Walter James/Public Relations
  777 Third Avenue
  New York, New York 10017
  (Pamphlets, films, speakers)
- Leukemia Society of America
  211 E. 43rd Street
  New York, New York 10017
  (Pamphlets, audiovisual materials on a loan basis)
- Public Affairs Committee, Inc.
  381 Park Avenue South
  New York, New York 10016
  (Pamphlet)
- Superintendent of Documents
  U.S. Government Printing Office
  Washington, D.C. 20402
  (Pamphlet)

Mental Health:

- American Hospital Association
  Department of Order Processing
  840 N. Lake Shore Drive
  Chicago, Illinois 60611
  (Pamphlets)
- American School Health Association
  Thomas D. Foster
  P.O. Box 708
  Kent, Ohio 44240
  (Book)
- Association for the Advancement of Health Education
  Dr. William Kane, Executive Director
  1201 16th Street, N.W.
  Washington, D.C. 20036
  (Book)
- Mental Health Association
  1800 N. Kent Street
  Arlington, Virginia 22209
  (Pamphlets, films)
- Metropolitan Life Insurance Company
  Health and Safety Education Division
  One Madison Avenue
  New York, New York 10010
  (Pamphlets, films)

- National Association for Retarded Citizens
  P.O. Box 6109
  2709 Avenue E. East
  Arlington, Texas 76011
  (Pamphlets)
- Public Affairs Committee, Inc.
  381 Park Avenue South
  New York, New York 10016
  (Pamphlet)

Multiple Sclerosis:

- National Multiple Sclerosis Society
  205 East 42nd Street
  New York, New York 10017
  (Pamphlets)
- Superintendent of Documents
  U.S. Government Printing Office
  Washington, D.C. 20402
  (Pamphlets)
- Wheat Flour Institute
  1776 F Street, N.W. #184
  Washington, D.C. 20006
  (Booklet)

Occupational Therapy:

- Public Affairs Committee, Inc.
  381 Park Avenue South
  New York, New York 10016
  (Pamphlets)

Parkinson's Disease:

- Public Affairs Committee, Inc.
  381 Park Avenue South
  New York, New York 10016
  (Pamphlets)
- Superintendent of Documents
  U.S. Government Printing Office
  Washington, D.C. 20402
  (Pamphlets)
- United Parkinson's Foundation
  220 S. State Street, Room 1710
  Chicago, Illinois 60604
  (Booklets, newsletters)

Rehabilitation:

- American Association for Rehabilitation Therapy, Inc.
  P.O. Box 93
  North Little Rock, Arkansas 72116
  (Pamphlets)
- American Cancer Society
  Walter James, Public Education
  777 Third Avenue
  New York, New York 10017
  (Pamphlets, speakers, film)
- American Foundation for the Blind
  Arthur Zigouras
  15 West 16th Street
  New York, New York 10011
  (Film)
- American Home Economics Association
  2010 Massachusetts Avenue, N.W.
  Washington, D.C. 20036
  (Pamphlets)
- American Physical Therapy Association
  1156 Fifteenth Street, N.W.
  Washington, D.C. 20005
  (Pamphlets)
- Public Affairs Committee, Inc.
  381 Park Avenue South
  New York, New York 10016
  (Pamphlets)

Respiratory Disease:

- American Lung Association
  1740 Broadway
  New York, New York 10019
  (Pamphlets)
- Public Affairs Committee, Inc.
  381 Park Avenue South
  New York, New York 10016
  (Pamphlets)

School Health:

- Allergy Foundation of America
  801 Second Avenue
  New York, New York 10017
  (Pamphlets)

- American School Health Association
  Thomas D. Foster
  Box 708
  Kent, Ohio 44240
  (Text, curriculum guides)
- Association for the Advancement of Health Education
  Dr. William Kane
  1201 16th Street, N.W.
  Washington, D.C. 20036
  (Mimeograph)
- National Society to Prevent Blindness
  79 Madison Avenue
  New York, New York 10016
  (Pamphlets, films)
- Prudential Insurance Company of America
  Public Relations Department
  Box 36
  Newark, New Jersey 07101
  (Pamphlet)
- Public Affairs Committee, Inc.
  381 Park Avenue South
  New York, New York 10016
  (Pamphlets)
- Tampax, Incorporated
  Department HI
  P.O. Box 7001
  Lake Success, New York 11042
  (Pamphlets)

Smoking:

- American Cancer Society
  Walter James, Public Education
  777 Third Avenue
  New York, New York 10017
  (Pamphlets, films, speakers)
- American Lung Association
  1740 Broadway
  New York, New York 10019
  (Pamphlets)
- American Medical Association
  P.O. Box 821
  Monroe, Wisconsin 53566
  (Pamphlets)

- National Clearing House for Smoking and Health
  U.S. Public Health Service
  5600 Fishers Lane
  Rockville, Maryland 20857
  (Pamphlets)
- National Dairy Council
  6300 N. River Road
  Rosemont, Illinois 60018
  (Pamphlets)
- Public Affairs Committee, Inc.
  381 Park Avenue South
  New York, New York 10016
  (Pamphlets)
- Superintendent of Documents
  U.S. Government Printing Office
  Washington, D.C. 20402
  (Pamphlets)

Tuberculosis:

- American Lung Association
  1740 Broadway
  New York, New York 10019
  (Pamphlets)
- National Institute of Allergy and Infectious Diseases
  Information Office
  Room 7A-32-Bldg. 31
  Bethesda, Maryland 20014
  (Fact sheet)
- Public Affairs Committee, Inc.
  381 Park Avenue South
  New York, New York 10016
  (Pamphlets)
- Superintendent of Documents
  U.S. Government Printing Office
  Washington, D.C. 20402
  (Pamphlets)

Venereal Disease:

- American Social Health Association
  260 Sheridan Avenue
  Palo Alto, California 94306
  (Pamphlets, films)
- Connecticut General Life Insurance Company
  Hartford, Connecticut 06152
  (Pamphlets)

- National Institute of Allergy and Infectious Disease
  National Institutes of Health
  Room 7A-32-Bldg. 31
  Bethesda, Maryland 20014
  (Pamphlet)
- The Paul Revere Life Insurance Company
  William G. Rickard, M.D.
  Vice President & Medical Director
  18 Chestnut Street
  Worcester, Massachusetts 01608
  (Pamphlet)
- Public Affairs Committee, Inc.
  381 Park Avenue South
  New York, New York 10016
  (Pamphlets)

Film Sources and Resources – Educational and Instructional

Write for free catalogs. Some of these films are free; some have modest rental fees. Many are intended primarily for sale but may be obtained for preview.

- Aevac, Inc. (filmstrips)
  1500 Park Avenue
  South Plainfield, New Jersey 07080
- Aims Instructional Media Services Incorporated
  626 Justin Avenue
  Glendale, California 91201
- Alfred Higgins Productions, Inc.
  9100 Sunset Boulevard
  Los Angeles, California 90069
- American Films, Inc.
  866 Third Avenue
  New York, New York 10022
- American Educational Films
  132 Lasky Drive
  Beverly Hills, California 90212
- American Journal of Nursing Co.
  Educational Services Division
  10 Columbus Circle
  New York, New York 10019
- Avis Films, Inc.
  904 E. Palm Avenue
  Burbank, California 91501

- Benchmark Films, Inc.
  145 Scarborough Road
  Briarcliff Manor, New York 10510
- Carousel Films, Inc.
  1501 Broadway
  New York, New York 10036
- Churchill Films
  662 North Robertson Boulevard
  Los Angeles, California 90069
- Classroom World Productions
  14 Glenwood Avenue
  P.O. Box 2090
  Raleigh, North Carolina 27602
- Colour Images Unlimited, Inc.
  4060 South Tamarac Drive
  Denver, Colorado 80237
- Concept Media
  1500 Adams Avenue
  Costa Mesa, California 92626
- CRM McGraw-Hill Films
  110 15th Street
  Del Mar, California 92014
- Educational Activities, Inc.
  Box 392
  Freeport, New York 11520
- Eye Gate House
  146-01 Archer Avenue
  Jamaica, New York 11435
- Films Incorporated
  Film and Tape Division
  733 Green Bay Road
  Wilmette, Illinois 60091
- Grove Press
  196 West Houston Street
  New York, New York 10014
- Guidance Associates
  757 Third Avenue
  New York, New York 10017
- Health and Welfare Materials Center
  801 2nd Avenue
  New York, New York 10017

- International Film Bureau
  332 South Michigan Avenue
  Chicago, Illinois 60604
- Learning Corporation of America
  1350 Avenue of the Americas
  New York, New York
- MacMillan Films, Inc.
  34 MacQuesten Parkway South
  Mount Vernon, New York 10550
- McGraw-Hill Films
  1221 Avenue of the Americas
  New York, New York 10020
- Mead Johnson Laboratories
  Meetings & Exhibits Dept.
  Evansville, Indiana 47721
- Medfact, Inc.
  1112 Andrew Avenue, N.E.
  Massilon, Ohio 44646
- Medi Cine' Sales Corp.
  2525 E. 28th Street
  Indianapolis, Indiana 46218
- Metropolitan Life Insurance Co.
  Health and Welfare Division
  One Madison Avenue
  New York, New York 10010
- J.B. Lippincott Company
  East Washington Square
  Philadelphia, Pennsylvania 19105
- National Audiovisual Center
  General Services Administration
  Washington, D.C. 20409
- National Film Board of Canada
  1251 Avenue of the Americas
  New York, New York 10020
- National Foundation March of Dimes
  1275 Mamaroneck Avenue
  White Plains, New York 10605
- National Multiple Sclerosis Society
  Upstate New York Chapter
  114 South Warren Street
  Syracuse, New York 13202

- National Safety Council
  425 North Michigan Avenue
  Chicago, Illinois 60093
- Paramount Communications
  5451 Marathon Street
  Hollywood, California 90038
- Perennial Education, Inc.
  1825 Willow Road
  P.O. Box 236
  Northfield, Illinois 60093
- Phoenix Films, Inc.
  470 Park Avenue South
  New York, New York 10016
- Pictura Films
  111 Eighth Avenue
  New York, New York 10011
- Psychological Cinema Register
  Special Services Bldg.
  Pennsylvania State University
  University Park, Pennsylvania 16802
- Public Relations Film Library
  General Motors Corp.
  1-101 General Motors Bldg.
  Detroit, Michigan 48202
- Pyramid Films
  Box 1048
  Santa Monica, California 90406
- ROCOM
  1 Sunset Avenue
  Montclair, New Jersey 07042
- Society for Visual Education, Inc.
  1345 Diversey Parkway
  Chicago, Illinois 60614
- Scott Graphics Incorporated and Educational Division
  104 Lower Westfield Road
  Holyoke, Massachusetts 01040
- Teach'em Inc.
  625 N. Michigan Avenue
  Chicago, Illinois 60611
- The Media Guild
  118 South Acacia
  Box 881
  Solana Beach, California 92075

- Trainex Corporation
  11016 Garden Grove Boulevard
  P.O. Box 116
  Garden Grove, California 92642
- Unicef
  331 East 38th Street
  New York, New York 10016
- Walt Disney Educational Media Co.
  500 S. Buena Vista Street
  Burbank, California 91521
- University of Iowa Audiovisual Center
  C215 East Hall
  Iowa City, Iowa 52240
- Wombat Productions
  Little Lake, Glendale Road
  P.O. Box 70
  Ossining, New York 10562
  (special order formats)
- Xerox Films, Inc.
  245 Long Hill Road
  Middletown, Connecticut 06457

Your state health department, universities, medical schools, drug houses, and national professional societies are additional resources.

There are also reference sources on the reference shelves of most libraries (e.g., Educators Guide to Free Films, Educators Progress Service, Randolph, Wisconsin).

Film Libraries and Media Centers

- ABC Media Concepts
  1330 Avenue of the Americas
  New York, New York 10019
- State Department of Education
  771 South Lawrence Street
  Montgomery, Alabama 36104
- Alaska State Department of Education
  Division of State Libraries & Museums
  Pouch G
  Juneau, Alaska 99801
- Arizona Department of Education
  1535 West Jefferson
  Phoenix, Arizona 85007

- Delaware Dept. of Public Instruction
  Instructional Services Branch
  The Townsend Building
  Dover, Delaware 19901
- District of Columbia Public Schools
  Presidential Building
  415 12th Street, N.W.
  Washington, D.C. 20004
- Kansas State Dept. of Education
  Kansas State Education Building
  120 East 10th Street
  Topeka, Kansas 66612
- Mass. Film & Media Service Corp.
  Fitchburg State College
  160 Pearl Street
  Fitchburg, Massachusetts 01420
- State Department of Education
  P.O. Box 480
  Jefferson City, Missouri 65101
- Nebraska Department of Education
  301 Centennial Mall South
  Box 94987
  Lincoln, Nebraska 68509
- New York State Education Dept.
  Bureau of Education Communications
  Albany, New York 12234
- Instructional Programming
  Florida State Dept. of Education
  Instructional Television & Radio
  Tallahasse, Florida 32304
- Idaho Department of Education
  Len B. Jordan Office Building
  Boise, Idaho 83720
- Division of Educational Media
  State of North Carolina
  Dept. of Public Instruction
  Raleigh, North Carolina 27602
- State of North Dakota
  Department of Public Instruction
  Bismarck, North Dakota 58505
- Oklahoma State Dept. of Education
  Oliver Hodge Education Building

2500 North Lincoln – Room 353
Oklahoma City, Oklahoma 73105

- Oregon State Department of Education
  942 Kabcaster Drive, N.E.
  Salem, Oregon 97310
- Film Center
  Rhode Island College
  Providence, Rhode Island 02908
- Audio Visual Library
  S.C. State Dept. of Education
  1513 Gervais Street
  Columbia, South Carolina 29201
- South Dakota Dept. of Public Safety
  Division of Highway Safety – Film Library
  118 West Capitol Avenue
  Pierre, South Dakota 57501
- Educational Media Center
  Tennessee Department of Education
  Building 308, 11th Avenue
  Smyrna, Tennessee 37167
- Curriculum Development Coordinator
  Utah State Board of Education
  250 East Fifth South Street
  Salt Lake City, Utah 84111
- State of Virginia
  Department of Education
  Bureau of Teaching Materials
  Richmond, Virginia 23216
- State of West Virginia
  Department of Education
  Charleston, West Virginia 25305
- Wyoming State Department of Education
  State Office Building West
  Cheyenne, Wyoming 82002

Cameras

- Eastman Kodak Company
  343 State Street
  Rochester, New York 14608
- Edixa Camera Corp.
  705 Bronx River Road
  Bronxville, New York 10708

Sources of Equipment

- American Photographics Instrument Company
  10 East Clarke Place
  Bronx, New York 10452
- Calcumet Scientific, Inc.
  1590 Touhy Avenue
  Elk Grove Village, Illinois 60007
- Demco Educational Corp.
  P.O. Box 7488
  Madison, Wisconsin 53570
- Denoyer-Geppert Company
  5235 Ravenswood Avenue
  Chicago, Illinois 60640
- Educational Supply and Specialty Company
  2823 E. Gage Avenue
  Huntington Park, California 90255
- General Electric Company
  Lamp Division
  Nela Park
  Cleveland, Ohio 44112
- M. Grumbacher, Inc.
  460 West 34th Street
  New York, New York 10001
- Mitten Designer Letters
  85 Fifth Street
  New York, New York 10003
- National Card, Mat and Board Co.
  P.O. Box 2306
  City of Industry, California 91746
- National Council of Teachers of Mathematics
  1906 Association Drive
  Reston, Virginia 22901
- Nystrom
  Division of Carnation
  3333 Elston Avenue
  Chicago, Illinois 60618
- Quik-Set, Inc.
  3650 Woodhead Drive
  Northbrook, Illinois 60062
- Redikut Letter Company
  12617 South Prairie Avenue
  Hawthorne, California 90250

- Smith-Victor Corp.
  Lake and Colfax Street
  Criffith, Indiana 46319
- Tablet and Ticket Company
  1021 West Adams Street
  Chicago, Illinois 60607
- MacMillan Science Company
  8200 South Hoyne Avenue
  Chicago, Illinois 60620
  Tuxtox/Cambasco
- Wrico
  The Wood Regan
  Nutley, New Jersey 07110

Health and Mental Health – Public Affairs Pamphlets

The Public Affairs Committee is a nonprofit educational organization founded in 1935 "to develop new techniques to educate the American public on vital economic and social problems and to issue concise and interesting pamphlets dealing with such problems."

The Public Affairs Committee[37] publishes many pamphlets of vital interest. The author has identified the following to be of special interest to workers and volunteers. Write to Public Affairs Committee, 381 Park Avenue South, New York, New York 10016.

No. 552 – Runaway Teenagers
No. 541 – Helping Children Face Crisis
No. 537 – Unmarried Teenagers and Their Children
No. 523 – Motivation and Your Child
No. 520 – Preparing Tomorrow's Parents
No. 515 – Drugs–Use, Misuse, Abuse
No. 512 – Talking It Over Before Marriage
No. 506 – You and Your Alcoholic Parent
No. 504 – Helping the Handicapped Teenager Mature
No. 499 – The New Alcoholics: Teenagers
No. 490 – Parents and Teenagers
No. 479 – Helping the Child Who Cannot Hear
No. 476 – Talking to Preteenagers About Sex
No. 464 – How to Cope With Crisis
No. 454 – Help for Your Troubled Child

---

[37]The Public Affairs Committee Inc., 381 Park Ave. South, New York, N.Y. 10016.

No. 445 – Helping Your Child Speak Correctly
No. 438 – Parent-Teenager Communication
No. 405 – Helping the Slow Learner
No. 369 – What Can You Do About Quarreling?
No. 305 – Tensions–And How to Master Them
No. 527 – Abortion: Public Issue, Private Decision
No. 509 – Woman's Changing Place: A Look at Sexism
No. 85 – The Races of Mankind
No. 540 – Behavior Modification
No. 539 – Marijuana: Current Perspectives
No. 538 – Understanding Stress
No. 517 – VD–Epidemic Among Teenagers
No. 498 – Health Foods: Facts and Fakes
No. 480 – Rights of Teenagers as Patients
No. 463 – Health Care of the Adolescent
No. 392A–The Rehabilitation Counselor
No. 364A–Overweight–A Problem for Millions
No. 352 – Serious Mental Illness in Children
No. 584 – Children and Drugs
No. 588 – To Combat and Prevent Child Abuse and Neglect
No. 573 – Smoking–A Habit That Should Be Broken
No. 579 – Assaults on Women: Rape and Wife Beating
No. 580 – Understanding and Dealing With Alcoholism
No. 581 – Schools and Parents–Partners in Sex Education
No. 586 – Violence in Our Schools
No. 589 – Pressures on Children

Internal Revenue Service – Tax Instruction Material Coordinators

Call your local I.R.S. office listed under U.S. Government in phone book. (Try contacting the district public affairs officer or chief, taxpayer service division.)

Jobs For The Hard to Employ

Write to Committee for Economic Development, 477 Madison Avenue, New York, New York 10022.

Jobs – Occupational Outlook Quarterly and Other Material

Looking Ahead to A Career, 1978-79 Edition . . . a 35mm color film strip and accompanying cassett tape narrative produced especially for young people. Cartoons, photographs, and charts are used to explain industrial and occupational trends, the occupational cluster system, sources of job openings, and the employment outlook for college graduates. Running time: 27 minutes. Cassette tape has both audible and inaudible film advance tone. Price: $12.50, complete. Sold only by BLS regional offices, listed below. Check or money order must be made payable to the Bureau of Labor Statistics.

Education and Job Leaflets:

A series of five leaflets that list jobs that require specified levels of education. Titles are jobs for which . . .

High School Education is Preferred, But Not Essential
High School Education is Generally Required
Apprenticeships Are Available
Junior College, Technical Institute, or Other Specialized Training is Usually Required
College Education is Usually Required

For each job listed, information is included about the qualifications and training needed and the employment outlook to 1985. Free from any regional office of BLS.

Motivational Leaflets:

A series of 11 leaflets on careers:
Clerical jobs
Ecology
English
Foreign languages
Health (without a college degree)
Liberal arts
Math
Mechanics
Outdoors
Science
Social science

Each discusses the types of jobs that may be available to persons with an interest or proficiency in a particular academic subject or field. Free from any regional office of BLS.

Display Posters:

Four color posters that encourage young people to plan careers. Free from any regional office of BLS.

All material except the Occupational Outlook Quarterly may be ordered from any regional office of the Bureau of Labor Statistics. Payment must accompany the order, with check or money order for publications made payable to the Superintendent of Documents. Checks for the film strip should be made payable to the Bureau of Labor Statistics. The Occupational Outlook Quarterly may only be ordered from the Superintendent of Documents.

Bureau of Labor Statistics Regional Offices

- 1603 Federal Office Building
  Boston, Massachusetts 02203
- 1515 Broadway
  New York, New York 10036
- P.O. Box 13309
  Philadelphia, Pennsylvania 19101
- 1371 Peachtree Street, NE
  Atlanta, Georgia 30309
- 230 South Dearborn Street
  Chicago, Illinois 60604
- 555 Griffin Sq. Building
  Dallas, Texas 75202
- 911 Walnut Street
  Kansas City, Missouri 64106
- 450 Golden Gate Avenue
  Box 36017
  San Francisco, California 94102

Jobs – Dictionary of Occupational Titles

Offices which can provide further information on the Dictionary of Occupational Titles:

Regional Offices:

Address inquiries to Regional Administrator, and Training Administration, U.S. Department of Labor.

- Room 1707
  J. F. Kennedy Building
  Boston, Massachusetts 02203
- Room 316
  555 Griffin Square Building
  Dallas, Texas 75202
- 6th Floor
  230 South Dearborn
  Chicago, Illinois 60604
- Room 405
  1371 Peachtree Street, NE
  Atlanta, Georgia 30309
- Room 3713
  1515 Broadway
  New York, New York 10036
- Federal Building, Room 1000
  911 Walnut Street
  Kansas City, Missouri 64106

- Box 36084
  San Francisco, California
  94102
- Room 1145 Federal Office
  Building
  909 First Avenue
  Seattle, Washington, 98174
- P.O. Box 8796
  Philadelphia, Pennsylvania
  19101
- 16122 Federal Office Building
  1961 Stout Street
  Denver, Colorado 80202

State Occupational Analysis Field Centers:

Address inquiries to: Supervisor, (State) Occupational Analysis Field Center. (For Arizona, address Manager, Employer Relations Section.)

- Arizona Dept. of Economic Security
  P.O. Box 6123
  Phoenix, Arizona 85005
- California Employment Development Dept.
  1525 South Broadway – Room 233
  Los Angeles, California 90015
- Florida Department of Commerce
  402 Reo Street – Suite 108
  Tampa, Florida 33609
- Michigan Employment Security Commission
  7310 Woodward Avenue
  Detroit, Michigan 48202
- Missouri Division of Employment Security
  505 Washington Avenue
  St. Louis, Missouri 63101
- New York Department of Labor
  Two World Trade Center – Room 7270
  New York, New York 10047
- North Carolina Employment Security Commission
  P.O. Box 27625
  Raleigh, North Carolina 27611
- Texas Employment Commission
  TEC Building
  Austin, Texas 78778
- Utah Department of Employment Security
  P.O. Box 11249
  Salt Lake City, Utah 84147
- Washington Employment Security Department
  300 West Harrison
  Seattle, Washington 98119

- Wisconsin Department of Industry
  Labor and Human Relations
  P.O. Box 2209
  Madison, Wisconsin 53702

Jobs – Helpful Sources for Career Information

Compiled by the New York Life Insurance Company, 51 Madison Avenue, New York, New York.[38]

Agriculture:

- American Society of Agricultural Engineers
  2950 Niles Road, St. Joseph, Michigan 49085
- American Society of Agronomy
  677 South Segoe Road, Madison, Wisconsin 53711
- American Society of Animal Science
  c/o David C. England, Department of Animal Science
  Oregon State University, Cornvallis, Oregon 97331
- American Society of Plant Physiologists
  9650 Rockville Pike, Bethesda, Maryland 20014
- National Association of Animal Breeders
  401 Bernadette Dr., P.O. Box 1033, Columbia, Missouri 65201
- National Association of County Agricultural Agents
  203 W. Nueva, Room 310, San Antonio, Texas 78207
- Society for Range Management
  2760 W. Fifth Avenue, Denver, Colorado 80204
- Soil Conservation Society of America
  7515 N.E. Ankeny Road, Ankeny, Iowa 50021
- Farm and Industrial Equipment Institute
  410 N. Michigan Avenue, Chicago, Illinois 60611
- National Farm and Power Equipment Dealers Association
  10877 Watson Road, St. Louis, Missouri 63127
- American Society of Farm Managers and Rural Appraisers
  210 Clayton Street, Denver, Colorado 80206
- Agribusiness Council
  20 East 46 Street, New York, New York 10017
- National 4-H Council
  150 North Wacker Drive, Chicago, Illinois 60606

---

[38]Careers in a Changing World – A series of booklets produced for the public by New York Life Insurance Co., New York City, to help young people choose productive and satisfying careers. This is part of New York Life's public service program.

- Future Farmers of America
  National FFA Center
  Box 15160, Alexandria, Virginia 22309
- Agriculture Council of America
  1625 I Street, N.W., Suite 708, Washington, D.C. 20006
- National Association of Supervisors of Agricultural Education
  Room 910, 65 South Front Street, Columbus, Ohio 43215
- National Vocational Agriculture Teachers Association
  Box 4498, Lincoln, Nebraska 68504
- National Association of Colleges and Teachers of Agriculture
  c/o Dr. J. C. Everly
  608 West Vermont, Urbana, Illinois 61801
- American Bankers Association
  1120 Connecticut Avenue, NW, Washington, D.C. 20036
- Sales and Marketing Executives International
  380 Lexington Avenue, New York, New York 10017
- National Association of State Universities and Land Grant Colleges
  One DuPont Circle, Suite 710, Washington, D.C. 20036
- Farm Credit Administration
  490 L'Enfant Plaza East, S.W., Washington, D.C. 20578
- Extension Service, U.S. Department of Agriculture
  14th and Independence Avenue, S.W., Washington, D.C. 20250
- Foreign Agricultural Service, U.S. Department of Agriculture
  14th and Independence Avenue, S.W., Room 4933
  Washington, D.C. 20250
- Personnel Division, U.S. Department of Agriculture
  14th and Independence Avenue, S.W., Washington, D.C. 20250
- American Institute of Certified Public Accountants
  1211 Avenue of Americas, New York, New York 10036

Finance, Advertising and Management:

- National Association of Accountants
  919 Third Avenue, New York, New York 10022
- American Advertising Federation
  Bureau of Research
  1225 Connecticut Avenue, N.W., Washington, D.C. 20036
- American Association of Advertising Agencies
  200 Park Avenue, New York, New York 10017
- American Bankers Association
  1120 Connecticut Avenue, N.W., Washington, D.C. 20036
- National Consumer Finance Association
  Education Services Division
  1000 16th Street, N.W., Washington, D.C. 20036

- American Federation of Information Processing Societies
  210 Summit Avenue, Montvale, New Jersey 07645
- Associations for Systems Management
  24587 Bagley Road, Cleveland, Ohio 44138
- Data Processing Management Association
  505 Busse Highway, Park Ridge, Illinois 60068
- American Society for Public Administration
  1225 Connecticut Avenue, N.W., Washington, D.C. 20036
- Institute of Life Insurance
  277 Park Avenue, New York, New York 10017
- Financial Executives Institute
  633 Third Avenue, New York, New York 10017
- Administrative Management Society, Publications Department
  World Headquarters, Willow Grove, Pennsylvania 19090
- American Society for Personnel Administration
  19 Church Street, Berea, Ohio 44017
- Public Relations Society of America
  845 Third Avenue, New York, New York 10022
- National Association of Purchasing Managements
  11 Park Place, New York, New York 10017
- National Secretaries Association
  2440 Pershing Road, Suite G-10, Kansas City, Missouri 64108
- American Institute of Architects
  1735 New York Avenue, N.W., Washington, D.C. 20006
- American Society for Testing and Materials
  1916 Race Street, Philadelphia, Pennsylvania 19103
- American Society of Civil Engineers
  345 East 47th Street, New York, New York 10017
- American Society of Mechanical Engineers
  345 East 47th Street, New York, New York 10017
- American Society of Heating, Refrigerating and
  Air-Conditioning Engineers
  345 East 47th Street, New York, New York 10017
- American Society of Sanitary Engineering
  960 Illuminating Building, Cleveland, Ohio 44113
- Associated General Contractors of America
  1957 E Street, N.W., Washington, D.C. 20006
- National Association of Home Builders of the U.S.
  15th & M Streets, N.W., Washington, D.C. 20005
- National Society of Professional Engineers
  2029 K Street, N.W., Washington, D.C. 20006

- Society of American Registered Architects
  Suite 1710, 180 North Michigan Avenue, Chicago, Illinois 60601
- Superintendent of Documents
  U.S. Government Printing Office, Washington, D.C. 20402
- U.S. Department of Labor
  3rd Street & Constitution Avenue, N.W.
  Washington, D.C. 20210
- AFL-CIO National Headquarters
  815 16th Street, N.W., Washington, D.C. 20006
- National Association of Women in Construction
  2800 West Lancaster Avenue, Fort Worth, Texas 76107

The groups that follow are only a few of the many sources of information about art careers. They may be a helpful starting point.

Arts and Related Activities:
- Actors' Equity Assocciation
  165 West 46th Street, New York, New York 10036
- American Association for Health, Physical Education, and
  Recreation Dance Division
  1201 Sixteenth Street, N.W., Washington, D.C. 20036
- American Council on Education for Journalism
  School of Journalism
  University of Missouri, Columbia, Missouri 65201
- American Crafts Council
  44 West 53rd Street, New York, New York 10019
- American Federation of Arts
  41 East 65th Street, New York, New York 10021
- American Federation of Television and Radio Artists
  1350 Avenue of the Americas, New York, New York 10019
- American Institute of Graphic Arts
  1059 Third Avenue, New York, New York 10021
- Associated Councils of the Arts
  1564 Broadway, New York, New York 10036
- Council of American Artists Societies
  112 East 19th Street, New York, New York 10003
- John F. Kennedy Center for the Performing Arts
  2700 F. Street, N.W., Washington, D.C. 20037
- Magazine Publishers Association
  575 Lexington Avenue, New York, New York 10022
- National Academy of Design
  1083 Fifth Avenue, New York, New York 10028

- National Art Education Association
  1916 Association Drive, Reston, Virginia 22091
- National Association of Broadcasters
  1771 N. Street, N.W., Washington, D.C. 20036
- The Newspaper Fund
  P.O. Box 300, Princeton, New Jersey 08540
- Public Relations Society of America
  845 Third Avenue, New York, New York 10022
- Screen Actors Guild
  7750 Sunset Boulevard, Hollywood, California 90046
- Television Information Office
  845 Fifth Avenue, New York, New York 10022
- Writers Guild of America
  1212 Avenue of the Americas, New York, New York 10036

Sources of Information About Careers in the Natural Resources:

- American Fisheries Society
  5410 Grosvenur Lane
  Bethesda, Maryland 20014
- American Forest Institute
  1619 Massachusetts Avenue, N.W.
  Washington, D.C. 20036
- American Geological Institute
  5205 Leesburg Pike
  Falls Church, Virginia 22041
- American Institute of Biological Sciences
  1410 Wilson Boulevard
  Arlington, Virginia 22209
- American Institute of Planners
  1776 Massachusetts Avenue, N.W.
  Washington, D.C. 20036
- American Meteorological Society
  45 Beacon Street
  Boston Massachusetts 02108
- American Ornithologists' Union
  National Museum of Natural History
  Smithsonian Institution
  Washington, D.C. 20560
- American Society of Agronomy
  677 South Segoe Road
  Madison, Wisconsin 53711
- American Society of Landscape Architects
  1750 Old Meadow Road
  McLean, Virginia 22101

- American Society of Range Management
  120 South Birch Street
  Denver, Colorado 80222
- Marine Technology Society
  730 M Street, N.W.
  Washington, D.C. 20036
- National Environmental Health Association
  1600 Pennsylvania
  Denver, Colorado 80203
- National Recreation and Park Association
  1601 N. Kent Street
  Arlington, Virginia 22209
- National Sanitation Foundation
  Attn: Educational Division
  NSF Building
  3475 Plymouth Road
  Ann Arbor, Michigan 48106
- National Wildlife Federation
  1412 16th Street, N.W.
  Washington, D.C. 20036
- The Nature Conservancy
  1800 North Kent Street
  Arlington, Virginia 22209
- Society of American Foresters
  5400 Grosvenur Lane
  Washington, D.C. 20014
- Soil Conservation Society of America
  7515 N.E. Ankeny Road
  Ankeny, Iowa 50021
- United States Environmental Protection Agency
  401 M Street, S.W.
  Washington, D.C. 20460
- Water Pollution Control Federation
  2626 Pennsylvania Avenue
  Washington, D.C. 20037

Sources of Career Information in Manufacturing:

- American Management Associations
  Career Information Services
  135 West 50th Street
  New York, New York 10020
- National Career Information Center
  American Personnel and Guidance Association

1607 New Hampshire Avenue, N.W.
Washington, D.C. 20007

- American Petroleum Institute
  2101 L. Street, N.W.
  Washington, D.C. 20037
- American Iron and Steel Institute
  1000 16th Street, N.W.
  Washington, D.C. 20036
- American Society of Mechanical Engineers
  345 East 47th Street
  New York, New York 10017
- American Society for Engineering Education
  Suite 400
  1 Dupont Circle
  Washington, D.C. 20036
- National Association of Wholesaler-Distributors
  1725 K Street, N.W.
  Washington, D.C. 20006
- American Institute of Baking
  400 East Ontario Street
  Chicago, Illinois 60611
- American Paper Institute
  260 Madison Avenue
  New York, New York 10016
- National Society of Professional Engineers
  2029 K Street, N.W.
  Washington, D.C. 20006
- Manufacturing Chemists Association
  1825 Connecticut Avenue, N.W.
  Washington, D.C. 20009
- American Chemical Society
  1155 16th Street, N.W.
  Washington, D.C. 20036
- American Society for Testing and Materials
  1916 Race Street
  Philadelphia, Pennsylvania 19103
- Society of Manufacturing Engineers
  20501 Ford Road
  Dearborn, Michigan 48128
- Aerospace Industries Association of America
  1725 De Sales Street, N.W.
  Washington, D.C. 20036

- National Aerospace Education Association
  Middle Tennessee State University, Box 59
  Murfreesboro, Tennessee 37132
- Foreign Industry Association
  1121 Illuminating Building
  Cleveland, Ohio 44113
- Graphic Arts Technical Foundation
  4615 Forbes Avenue
  Pittsburgh, Pennsylvania 15213
- Printing Industries of America
  1730 North Lynn Street
  Arlington, Virginia 22209
- Society of the Plastics Industry
  355 Lexington Avenue
  New York, New York 10017
- Manufacturers' Agents National Association
  Suite 509
  3130 Wilshire Boulevard
  Los Angeles, California 90010
- National Association of Manufacturers
  1776 Street, N.W.
  Washington, D.C. 20006
- Institute of Food Technologists
  221 North LaSalle Street
  Chicago, Illinois 60601
- American Society of Safety Engineers
  850 Busse Highway
  Park Ridge, Illinois 60068
- Sales and Marketing Executives
  International
  380 Lexington Avenue
  New York, New York 10017
- National Association of Purchasing Management
  11 Park Place
  New York, New York 10007
- Motor Vehicle Manufacturers Association of the U.S.
  320 New Center Building
  Detroit, Michigan 48202
- National Machine Tool Builders' Association
  7901 West Park Drive
  McLean, Virginia 22101

- Training Manager
  National Tool, Die and Precision Machining Association
  9300 Livingston Road
  Washington, D.C. 20022
- International Association of Mahinists and Aerospace Workers
  1300 Connecticut Avenue, N.W.
  Washington, D.C. 20036
- International Union, United Automobile, Aerospace and Agricultural Implement Workers of America
  8000 East Jefferson Avenue
  Detroit, Michigan 48214
- Society of Automotive Engineers
  400 Commonwealth Drive
  Warrendale, Pennsylvania 15096
- Computer and Business Equipment Manufacturers Association
  1828 L Street, N.W.
  Washington, D.C. 20036
- American Federation of Information Processing Societies
  210 Summit Avenue
  Montvale, New Jersey 07645
- American Textile Manufacturers Institute
  Suite 2124
  400 South Tryon Street
  Charlotte, North Carolina 28285
- American Apparel Manufacturers Association
  1611 North Kent Street
  Arlington, Virginia 22209
- Electronic Industries Association
  2001 I Street, N.W.
  Washington, D.C. 20006
- International Union of Electrical, Radio and Machine Workers
  1126 16th Street, N.W.
  Washington, D.C. 20036
- American Pharmaceutical Association
  2215 Constitution Avenue, N.W.
  Washington, D.C. 20005
- National Association of Trade and Technical Schools
  2021 L Street, N.W.
  Washington, D.C. 20036
- Printing Industries of America, Inc.
  1730 North Lynn Street
  Arlington, Virginia 22209

- National Association of Printers and Lithographers, Inc.
  570 Seventh Avenue
  New York, New York 10018
- American Newspapers Publishers Association
  1160 Sunrise Valley Drive
  Reston, Virginia 22091
- Education Council for the Graphic Arts Industry
  4615 Forbes Avenue
  Pittsburgh, Pennsylvania 15213
- National Art Education Association
  National Education Association
  1916 Association Drive
  Reston, Virginia 22091
- Photographic Art and Science Foundation
  111 Stratford
  Des Plaines, Illinois 60016
- National Association of Broadcasters
  1771 N Street, N.W.
  Washington, D.C. 20036
- Corporation for Public Broadcasting
  1111 16th Street, N.W.
  Washington, D.C. 20036
- Federal Communications Commission
  1919 M Street, N.W.
  Washington, D.C. 20554
- Also: Lovejoy's Career and Vocational School Guide

Sources of Information in Transportation:

- American Trucking Associations, Inc.
  1616 P Street, N.W., Washington, D.C. 20036
- Association of American Railroads
  1920 L Sreet, N.W., Washington, D.C. 20036
- National Maritime Union of America
  36 Seventh Avenue, New York, New York 10011
- International Organization of Masters, Mates and Pilots
  39 Broadway, New York, New York 10006
- Personnel Operations Division
  Federal Aviation Administration
  800 Independence Avenue, S.W., Washington, D.C. 20591

The American Trucking Associations, Inc., publishes a Directory of Transportation Education in U.S. Colleges and Universities which lists transportation programs ranging from a single course to entire departments at more than 600 colleges, universities and junior colleges. Available free from address above.

Also, automobile companies, airlines, railroads, bus companies, local transit companies publish career and educational material. Inquire at your local dealer or ticket office.

Sources of Information about Careers in Consumer Service and Homemaking:

- National Association of Plumbing-Heating-Cooling Contractors
  1016 20th Street, N.W., Washington, D.C. 20036
- Apprentice Program, U.S. Department of Labor
  200 Constitution Avenue, N.W., Washington, D.C. 20210
- American Society of Interior Designers
  730 Fifth Avenue, New York, New York 10019
- Society of American Florists and Ornamental Horticulturists
  901 N. Washington Street, Alexandria, Virginia 22314
- Culinary Institute of America
  Albany Post Road, Hyde Park, New York 12538
- American Veterinary Medical Association
  930 N. Meacham Road, Schaumburg, Illinois 60196
- Shoe Service Institute of America
  222 West Adams Street, Chicago, Illinois 60606
- American Home Economics Association
  2010 Massachusetts Avenue, N.W., Washington, D.C. 20036
- Extension Service, U.S. Department of Agriculture
  14th Street and Independence Avenue, S.W.
  Washington, D.C. 20250
- Day Care & Child Development Council of America
  1012 14th Street, N.W., Room 1105, Washington, D.C. 20005
- National Association for the Education of Young Children
  1834 Connecticut Avenue, N.W., Washington, D.C. 20009
- National Association of Social Workers
  1425 H Street, N.W., Suite 600, Washington, D.C. 20005
- American Dietetic Association
  430 N. Michigan Avenue, Chicago, Illinois 60611
- National Consumer Finance Association
  1000 16th Street, N.W., Washington, D.C. 20036

Sources of Information About Careers in Public Service:

- U.S. Customs Service
  1301 Constitution Avenue, N.W., Washington, D.C. 20229
- FBI
  9th Street & Pennsylvania Avenue, N.W., Washington, D.C. 20535
- International Association of Chiefs of Police
  11 Firstfield Road, Gaithersburg, Maryland 20760

- Agricultural Research Service
  U.S. Department of Agriculture
- Day Care & Child Development Council of America
  Room 1105, 1012 14th Street, N.W., Washington, D.C. 20005
- National Association for the Education of Young Children
  1834 Connecticut Avenue, N.W., Washington, D.C. 20009
- National Association of Social Workers
  Suite 600, 1425 H Street, N.W., Washington, D.C. 20005
- Food and Drug Administration
  5600 Fishers Lane, Rockville, Maryland 20852
- U.S. Civil Service Commission (Office of Personnel Management)
  1900 E Street, N.W., Washington, D.C. 20415

Sources of Information about Careers in Marketing and Distribution:

- American Marketing Association
  222 South Riverside Plaza
  Chicago, Illinois 60606
- American Advertising Federation
  1225 Connecticut Avenue, N.W.
  Washington, D.C. 20036
- American Association of Advertising Agencies
  200 Park Avenue
  New York, New York 10017
- Sales and Marketing Executives International
  Student Education Division
  380 Lexington Avenue
  New York, New York 10017
- National Retail Merchants Association
  100 West 31st Street
  New York, New York 10001
- National Association of Wholesale Distributors
  1725 K Street, N.W.
  Washington, D.C. 20006
- Direct Mail Marketing Association
  6 East 43 Street
  New York, New York 10017
- National Association of Realtors
  155 East Superior Street
  Chicago, Illinois 60611
- Council on Opportunities in Selling
  c/o Sales Management Magazine
  633 Third Avenue
  New York, New York 10017

- American Management Association
  135 West 50 Street
  New York, New York 10020
- American Collegiate Retailing Association
  College of Business
  Rochester Institute of Technology
  1 Lomb Memorial Drive
  Rochester, New York 14623
- Office of Information
  U.S. Department of Labor
  Washington, D.C. 20212
- Sales Promotion Executives Association
  2130 Delancey Street
  Philadelphia, Pennsylvania 19103
- Association of National Advertisers
  155 East 44 Street
  New York, New York 10017
- Business and Professional Women's Foundation
  2012 Massachusetts Avenue, N.W.
  Washington, D.C. 20003
- American Council of Life Insurance
  1730 Pennsylvania Avenue, N.W.
  Washington, D.C. 20006
- Market Research Association
  P.O. Box 145, Grand Central Station
  New York, New York 10017
- National Automobile Dealers Association
  2000 K Street, N.W.
  Washington, D.C. 20006
- National Food Brokers Association
  NFBA Building
  1916 M Street, N.W.
  Washington, D.C. 20036

Special Labor Force Reports

The Bureau of Labor Statistics conducts a continuing program of special studies designed to reveal selected characteristics of workers, such as work experience and educational attainment. These studies are published in a series of Special Labor Force Reports. Copies may be obtained, while the supply lasts, upon request to the Bureau of Labor Statistics, Inquiries and Correspondence, Room 1539, Washington, D.C. 20212. The following reports have been issued since August 1975:

Number

180 Students, Graduates, and Dropouts in the Market, October, 1974
181 Work Experience of the Population 1974
182 Multiple Jobholders in May 1975
183 Marital and Family Characteristics of the Labor Force, March 1975
184 Going Back to School at 35 and Over, October 1974

185 Employment and Unemployment During 1975
186 Educational Attainment of Workers, March 1975
187 Length of Working Life for Men and Women, 1970
188 Long Workweeks and Premium Pay, 1975
189 Families and the Rise of Working Wives – An Overview, 1950-75

190 Women Who Head Families: A Socioeconomic Analysis, March 1975
191 Students, Graduates, and Dropouts in the Labor Market, October 1975
192 Work Experience of the Population, 1975
193 Educational Attainment of Workers, March 1976
194 Multiple Jobholders, May 1976

195 Weekly and Hourly Earnings Data from the Current Population Survey, May 1967-May 1976
196 Long Hours and Premium Pay, May 1976
197 New Labor Force Projections to 1990
198 The Labor Force Patterns of Divorced and Separated Women, March 1975
199 Employment and Unemployment in 1976

200 Students, Graduates, and Dropouts in the Labor Market, October 1976
201 Work Experience of the Population, 1976
202 The Extent of Job Search by Employed Workers, May 1976
203 Year-Round Full-Time Earnings in 1975
204 Going Back to School at 35 and Over, October 1976

205 Children of Working Mothers, March 1976
206 Marital and Family Characteristics of the Labor Force in March 1976
207 Absence from Work – Measuring the Hours Lost, May 1973-76
208 Labor Force Trends: A Synthesis and Analysis and a Bibliography
209 Educational Attainment of Workers, March 1977

210 Job Search of the Unemployed, Mqy 1976
211 Multiple Jobholders in May 1977
212 Emploiyment and Unemployment Trends During 1977
213 Women Who Head Families: A Socioeconomic Analysis, March 1977
214 Long Hours and Premium Pay, May 1977

215 Students, Graduates, and Dropouts in the Labor Market, October 1977
216 Marital and Family Characteristics of Workers, March 1977
217 Children of Working MOthers, 1977
218 Employment and Unemployment During 1978: An Analysis
219 Marital and Family Characteristics of Workers, 1970-78

220 Divorced and Separated Women in the Labor Force – An Update
221 Multiple Jobholders in May 1978
222 Job Search of Recipients of Unemployment Insurance
223 Students, Graduates, and Dropouts in the Labor Market, October 1978
224 Work Experience of the Population in 1977

225 Educational Attainment of Workers – Some Trends From 1973 to 1978

To begin looking into job opportunities and study offerings in the fields of recreation, you can write to the following for brochures and booklets:

- National Recreation & Park Association
  1601 North Kent Street
  Arlington, Virginia 22209
- National Therapeutic Recreation Society
  1601 North Kent Street
  Arlington, Virginia 22209
- National Industrial Recreation Association
  20 North Wacker Drive
  Chicago, Illinois 60606

National Education Association Handbook

The NEA Handbook is published annually as a tool for leaders in the field of education. It is designed to help them build a more effective education profession through use of services and participation in programs of the National Education Association, its departments, and state and local affiliates. It is both a directory of names and addresses and a source of information concerning objectives, structure, and activities of the NEA and affiliated associations. One is urged to keep it handy for reference throughout the school year and to share it with colleages.

Write to:

- National Education Association of the United States
  1201 Sixteenth Street, N.W.
  Washington, D.C. 20036

Runaway Programs

The National Youth Work Alliance, 1346 Connecticut Avenue, N.W.,

Washington, D.C. 20036, publishes a most informative book titled—*National Directory of Runaway Programs.*

The National Youth Work Alliance (YWA) is a nonprofit membership organization representing more than 1,000 community based youth service agencies through affiliated state and local youth service coalitions across the country. These agencies range in size and sophistication from small, primarily volunteer-operated hotlines to large youth services agencies offering a variety of services. Each agency, however, shares the common philosophy of providing accessible, non-stigmatizing services and offering young people the opportunity to participate in the development, provision, and evaluation of these services. There are three categories of membership in NYWA: *Affiliated Members* are statewide and metropolitan coalitions of community based youth serving agencies; *Associate Members* are community based youth service agencies located in states or metropolitan area lacking a coalition affiliated with NYWA: *Supporting Members* are individuals or agencies, either public or private, who subscribe to NYWA's newsletter, *Youth Alternatives.*

Newsletter

Youth Alternatives, NYWA's acclaimed monthly newsletter, reports on issues and events in the nation's capital and across the country which affect youth and youth workers. In-depth coverage is provided on federal, state, and local activities under the Juvenile Justice and Delinquency Prevention Act, the Youth Employment Act, and the Runaway Youth Act; as well as in such areas as networking and coalition building, fundraising, alcohol and drug abuse, child abuse and neglect, foster care, juvenile law, research, and much more. In addition, each issue contains listings of new resources, job opportunities, and upcoming conferences and meetings. Write for a free sample issue.

Publications and Seminars

NYWA offers publications and intensive two-day seminars on a variety of topics of vital interest to youth workers. These include:

- Local and federal fundraising for community based youth services
- Juvenile justice
- Youth employment
- Youth services management and administration
- HEW youth services
- Participating in and influencing state and federal youth policies
- Alternative programs
- Youth services planning

National Youth Workers Conference

Each summer NYWA sponsors the National Youth Workers Conference, a three-day training conference for all those who work with youth. To minimize costs the conference is held on university campuses in alternating sections of the country. Previous conferences have had well over 1,200 participants and close to 100 workshops.

Other Resources Include:

Books

Single copies of the following may be received free of charge from the Youth Development Bureau, HEW, Room 3260, DHEW North Building, 330 Independence Avenue, S.W., Washington, D.C. 20201.

- *Runaway Youth – From What to Where – The Status of Runaway Children.* Completed in 1975, this report is a study of all states' statues, judicial decisions and attorney generals' opinions. Publication No. 26046.
- *National Statistical Survey on Runaway Youth.* This report consists of three parts: data on runaway incidence; descriptive analysis of runaways; and classification system. Publication No. 26048.
- *Catalog of Federal Youth Programs.* The catalog is a comprehensive directory of federal programs for direct and indirect services to youth. Publication no. 26051.
- *Doing It.* A collection of articles on issues, problems and viable solutions concerned with the provision of effective human services in programs servicing runaway youth. Publication No. 26053.
- *Runaway Youth – Annual Report on Activities Conducted to Implement the Runaway Youth Act.* This report comments on activities conducted by DHEW during FY 1977. The report is submitted annually to Congress. Publication No. 26054.

Single copies of the following OJJDP publication may be requested free of charge from Document Orders, National Criminal Justice Reference Service, P.O. Box 6000, Rockville, Maryland 20850.

- *Responses to Angry Youth.* An examination of the cost and service impacts of deinstitutionalization of status offenders states. Shelf No. 45306.

The following publications may be purchased from the National Youth Work Alliance, 1346 Connecticut Avenue, N.W., Washington, D.C. 20036.

- *Adolescent Life Stress as a Predictor of Alcohol Abuse and Runaway Behavior.* Prepared after a three-year national study this book presents significant implications for prevention and programming.
- *It's Me Again: An Aftercare Manual for Youth Workers.* This book contains detailed sections on needs assessment and plan long-term care, and generating resources.

Relevant Governmental Agencies

- Youth Development Bureau (YDB)
  Department of Health, Education, and Welfare
  330 Independence Avenue, S.W.
  Washington, D.C. 20201

Part of the Administration for Children, Youth and Families, Office of Human Development Services, administers a broad range of social and rehabilitation services and human development programs designed to deal with the problems of specific populations. Runaways are one of the major concerns.

- Office of Juvenile Justice and Delinquency Prevention
  (OJJDP) Law Enforcement Assistance Administration
  Department of Justice
  633 Indiana Avenue, N.W.
  Washington, D.C. 20531

Administers juvenile justice and delinquency prevention program in accordance with the Juvenile Justice Act of 1974. Includes the National Institute for Juvenile Justice and Delinquency Prevention, which performs research, serves as a clearinghouse, develops standards, and develops training.

General Information Sources

- Child Welfare Resource Information Exchange
  2011 I Street, N.W., Suite 501
  Washington, D.C. 20006 (202) 331-0028

Provides bibliographic searching on many topics including counselling, diversion, and teenage parents. Publishes a newsletter which outlines new publications and programs.

- National Clearinghouse for Alcohol Information
  P.O. Box 2345
  Rockville, Maryland 20852
  (301) 468-2600

Offers free pamphlets, bibliographies, and prevention posters on alcohol for the general public. Citation cards, and latest research findings available to professionals. (HEW operated)

- National Clearinghouse for Drug Abuse Information
  5600 Fishers Lane
  Rockville, Maryland 20857
  (301) 443-6500

Offers pamphlets and prevention posters to the general public. Many items available in Spanish. Extensive bibliographies provided to professionals. (HEW operated)

- National Criminal Justice Reference Services
  P.O. Box 6000
  Rockville, Maryland 20850
  (202) 862-2900

Provides bibliographic searching and single copies of LEAA publications to individuals, agencies and organizations involved in prevention and reduction of crime. Provides a Selective Notification of Information Service which presents books, documents and seminars (some are free). (LEAA sponsored)

- National Institute of Mental Health
  Public Inquiry Section
  5600 Fishers Lane
  Rockville, Maryland 20857
  (301) 443-4517

Provides mental health pamphlets, posters, and referral information for the general public. Literature searches available to professionals and graduate students. (HEW operated)

- The National Youth Alternatives Project, Inc.
  1341 Connecticut Avenue, N.W., Room 502
  Washington, D.C. 20009
  (202) 785-0764

Sports Equipment

There are a multitude of athletic equipment stores and manufacturers in all states and/or regions—many of which offer special discounts to youth groups. Here again, as in film rentals, there are a number of companies that look to a national mailorder market and provide interesting and colorful catalogs for the group workers' use. One of these companies is the J.F. Hammett Co., Physical Education Division, P.O. Box 545, Braintree, Massachusetts 02184. Hammett also provides workshops in Movement Education, Music and Rhythm and Gymnastics (write Hammett for particulars).

Other such companies are Wolverine Sports, P.O. Box 1941, 745 State Circle, Ann Arbor Michigan 48104 and SPORTIME, A division of Select Service and Supply Co. Inc. 2905 E. Amwiler Rd. Atlanta, GA 30360.

Student Aid

There are a variety of federally funded and supported programs to help those students who are in need of and qualify for student aid.

A prime source for information relating to such aid is the *Student Consumer's Guide: Six Federal Financial Aid Programs 1980-81*. This is a ready reference booklet explaining the loan, grant, and workstudy plans offered by the Bureau of Student Financial Aid, Box 84, Washington, D.C. 20044. However, recent alterations in the student aid programs and qualifications for such aid may well change the overall student aid availability. Group workers must acquaint selves re: such alterations.

Mental Health – Therapy Organizations and Source Information

Some of these organizations maintain local offices in large cities. Look for them in the white pages of your phone book. If they're not listed there, contact national headquarters or the medical school or psychology department at your local university.

- American Academy of Psychoanalysis
  40 Gramercy Park N.
  New York, New York 10010
  (212) 477-4250
- American Association for Marriage and Family Therapy
  924 W. Ninth Street
  Upland, California 91786
  (714) 981-0888
- American Association of Sex Educators, Counselors and Therapists
  Suite 304
  5010 Wisconsin Avenue, NW
  Washington, D.C. 20016
  (202) 686-2523
- American Psychiatric Association
  1700 18th Street, NW
  Washington, D.C. 20009
  (202) 797-4900
- American Psychological Association
  1200 17th Street, NW
  Washington, D.C. 20036
  (202) 833-7600
- Association for Advancement of Behavior Therapy
  420 Lexington Avenue
  New York, New York 10017
  (212) 682-0065
- Group for the Advancement of Psychiatry
  419 Park Avenue South
  New York, New York 10016
- Joint Information Service (of APA and NAMH)
  1700 18th Street, NW
  Washington, D.C. 20009
- Mental Health Materials Center
  419 Park Avenue South
  New York, New York 10016

- Mental Health Association
  1800 N. Kent Street
  Arlington, Virginia 22209
- National Association for Retarded Citizens
  P.O. Box 6109
  Arlington, Texas 76011
- Psychological Cinema Register
  Pennsylvania State University
  University Park, Pennsylvania 16802
- New York University Film Library
  26 Washington Pl. (Press Annex Building)
  New York, New York 10003
- Indiana University
  Audiovisual Center
  Bloomington, Indiana 47401
- Mental Health Materials Center
  419 Park Avenue South
  New York, New York 10016
- National Clearinghouse for Drug Abuse Information–NIDA
  1140 Rockville Pike
  Rockville, Maryland 20852
- National Clearinghouse for Mental Health Information–NIMH
  5600 Fishers Lane
  Rockville, Maryland 20857
- National Council on Alcoholism
  2 Park Avenue
  New York, New York 10016
- Office of Child Development
  Division of Public Education
  P.O. Box 1182
  Washington, D.C. 20013
- President's Committee on Employment of the Handicapped
  Washington, D.C. 20210 (all materials free)
- Public Affairs Committee, Inc.
  Publishers of Public Affairs Pamphlets
  381 Park Avenue South
  New York, New York 10016
- Perennial Education
  1825 Willow Road
  Northfield, Illinois 60093
- NAMH Film Service
  (National Association for Mental Health)

P.O. Box 7316
Alexandria, Virginia 22307

Professional Organizations

- American Rehabilitation Counseling Association
  1605 New Hampshire Avenue, NW
  Washington, D.C. 20005
- American Psychological Association
  Divisions 17 and 22
  1200 Seventeenth Street, NW
  Washington, D.C. 20036
- National Rehabilitation Counseling Association
  1522 K Street, NW
  Washington, D.C. 20005

Associations for Handicapped Persons

- Muscular Dystrophy Associations of America
  810 Seventh Avenue
  New York, New York 10019
- National Easter Seal Society for Crippled Children and Adults
  2023 West Ogden Avenue
  Chicago, Illinois 60612
- National Foundation for Birth Defects
  (formerly the March of Dimes)
  Box 2000
  White Plains, New York 10602
- National Multiple Sclerosis Society
  205 East 42nd Street
  New York, New York 10017
- National Rehabilitation Association
  1522 K Street
  Washington, D.C. 20005
- United Cerebral Palsy Associations, Inc.
  66 East 34th Street
  New York, New York 10016

Rehabilitation Agencies

- International Association of Rehabilitation Facilities
  5530 Wisconsin Avenue
  Washington, D.C. 20015

- International Society for the Rehabilitation of the Disabled
  219 East 44th Street
  New York, New York 10017

Vocational Rehabilitation

- American Occupational Therapy Association
  6000 Executive Boulevard
  Suite 200
  Rockville, Maryland 20852
- Department of Health, Education, and Welfare
  Rehabilitation Services Administration
  Washington, D.C. 20201
- Goodwill Industries of America
  9200 Wiscon Avenue
  Washington, D.C. 20014
- State Divisions of Vocational Rehabilitation

Education

- Association for Children with Learning Disabilities
  5225 Grace Street
  Pittsburgh, Pennsylvania 15236
- The Council for Exceptional Children
  1920 Association Drive
  Reston, Virginia 22091
- Department of Health, Education, and Welfare
  Office of Education
  Bureau of Education for the Handicapped
  Washington, D.C. 20202
  "Closer Look"
  Box 1492
  Washington, D.C. 20036
- National Rehabilitation Counseling Association
  1522 K Street, NW
  Washington, D.C. 20005
- State and Local Boards of Education

Recreation

- American Association for Health, Physical Education, and Recreation
  Unit on Programs for the Handicapped
  1201 16th Street, NW, Washington, D.C. 20036

- Camps: contact your state or local Society for Crippled Children and Adults (Easter Seal), Association for Retarded Citizens, or United Cerebral Palsy Association.
- Indoor Sports Club
  1145 Highland Street
  Napoleon, Ohio 43545

Venereal Disease Prevention Programs

Consultants:

Services provided by American Council for Healthful Living, 43 Main Street, Orange, New Jersey 07050 (formerly Venereal Disease Service Org.)

Educational Services

- Inservice Courses & Workshops–
  for teachers, nurses and health educators
- Symposia–
  for medical & paramedical practitioners
- Educational Sessions–
  for community and professional groups
- Rap Sessions and Skits–
  for youth groups
- Educational Materials–
  "Foundations for Decision Making", K-12 VD Teachers Guide
  "9 Common Sexually Transmitted Diseases" – Leaflet
  "Syphilis–the facts made simple"–slide presentation for elementary and secondary schools
  "VD Newsletter"–A bimonthly publication
  Films, slides, posters, assorted brochures and technical information
  VD Hotline
  (201) 674-7476
  9 to 5 Weekdays
  Information and referral service

Virtually every populated area in the nation has some free social hygiene clinics where all treatment and information is handled confidentially. An example of this type of service is that provided by the Health Services Administration of the Department of Health, New York City. Free clinics are available (which incidently do not require parental consent for examination and treatment of minors).

Other Reading Material

- An Educational Approach to Venereal Disease Control, by Florence Bennell. A teacher guide for grades 7 through 12. The National Press, Palo Alto, California.
- Plain Facts About VD, Western Electric, Sunnyvale, California 94086.
- Sex & Birth Control: A guide for the Young, by James E. Lieberman, M.D., and Ellen Peck. Includes comprehensive chapter on VD. Thomas Y. Crowell Co., New York, New York.
- Some Questions and Answers About VD; Today's VD Control Problem 1974; and VD Facts for Everybody, American Social Health Association, 1740 Broadway, New York, New York 10019.
- VD Facts for Teenagers, Operation Venus. Call "VD" Hot Line in your state.
- VD: Facts You Should Know, by Andre Bianzaco, MD. Self-instruction booklet for grades 7 through 12; teacher notes available. Scott, Foresman and Co., Glenview, Illinois.
- V.D.: It Could Happen to You. Booklet on prevention and treatment, written for young adults. New Readers Press, New York, New York.

For Medical Information

- The Practicing Physician Confronts VD, American Social Health Association or Pfizer, Inc., c/o Science and Medicine Publishing Co., Inc., 515 Madison Avenue, New York, New York 10022.

Every state publishes VD literature; group workers should contact their local or state health department.

Films About Venereal Disease

- A Half a Million Teenagers
  16 minutes, color. Explains how organisms of gonorrhea and syphilis enter and affect the body; the symptoms. Need for prompt treatment is stressed. Churchill Films, 662 N. Robertson Boulevard, Los Angeles, California 90069.
- Her Name Was Ellie, His Name Was Lyle
  30 minutes B/W. Directed at urban teenagers, film shows roles of private physician and health department in treatment and in tracking down sources of infection and contacts. Stresses infectious nature of VD and need for prompt treatment.
  Precision Films Laboratories, Inc., 21 West 46th Street, New York, New York 10036.
- How to Keep From Catching VD
  20 minutes, color. Explains symptoms of syphilis and gonorrhea, effects of

untreated VD, preventive measures that may reduce risk. Teacher guide available. Jarvis Couillard Associates, 142 Paseo De Gracia, Redondo Beach, California 90277.

Volunteer Services:

The following resource organizations are concerned with voluntary actions:

- Association for Administration of Volunteer Services
  P.O. Box 4584, Boulder, Colorado (303) 443-2100
- Association of Voluntary Action
  Scholars – S-211 Henderson Human Development Building
  Pennsylvania State University
  University Park, Pennsylvania 16802 (814) 865-1717
- Association of Volunteer Bureaus c/o
  United Way
  801 North Fairfax
  Alexandria, Virginia 22314
- National Center for Voluntary Action (NCVA)
  1214 16th Street, N.W.
  Washington, D.C. 20036 (202) 467-5560
- National Collaboration for Youth
  1666 Connecticut Avenue, N.W.
  Washington, D.C. 20009 (202) 659-0516
- National Commission on Resources for Youth, Inc.
  36 West 44th Street
  New York, New York 10036 (212) 840-2844

Miscellaneous Matter

The ARCO Publishing Company, Inc., 219 Park Avenue, South, New York City 10003, publishes other books in a general category that are designed to instruct and entertain and which the group worker might find adaptable for group use.

The Public Affairs Committee, Inc. 381 Park Ave. South, New York, N.Y. 10016, mentioned earlier in this book (along with recommended pamphlets and booklets) is a non-partisan, non-profit organization dedicated to the development of new techniques to educate the American public. They direct their efforts toward examining vital economic and social problems and issuing of concise and interesting pamphlets dealing with such problems.

Public Affairs pamphlets today deal with family relationships and child development, health and mental health and race relations, among many others. Group workers would do well by tapping this resource avenue. A catalog of full and updated material can be secured by writing to the Public Affairs Committee.

Chapter 33

Armed Forces Opportunities

The armed forces offer such a plethora of occupational fields, the author felt it best to set up a special chapter referring to such occupations. In addition, the group worker many times will be asked about educational opportunities both in the military and after military service. Such a group worker might well contact the local armed forces recruiting office for the purpose of assembling enlistment information as well as details about current educational opportunities.

For instance, in recent years, young men and women have been offered the opportunity to join the Army and take advantage of an unusual offer called the Veteran's Educational Assistance Program, VEAP for short. Quite simply VEAP is a savings plan for continuing education. A soldier who chose to participate in VEAP contributed up to $75.00 of each months pay. In return, the government matched each dollar two for one. The personal investment was limited to $2700.00. Combined with the government's matching funds, the basic VEAP amounted to as much as $8100.00. The army recently came out with an additional "education bonus" for certain qualified people for an enlistment of 2 years, 3 years or 4 years. For those that qualify, a $14,100 education fund (for a 4 year enlistment) can be accumulated. Comparable programs can be found in the other services. The Marine Corps has a Tuition Assistance Program (TAP) designed to give financial help to Marines who are willing to take college courses during off-duty time.

The Navy has a program titled "Navy Campus." The objective of this program is to enable Navy men and women to pursue their education, *at all levels,* wherever they may be stationed. This is a system for managing and coordinating all the Navy's off-duty and on-duty educational programs. This assures that naval personnel achieve fullest academic and career development—while in the service and later, if they choose, in civilian life.

It is important for the youth worker, if he is to be effective in this area, to place himself on the mailing list of an armed forces publication called "Profile." Profile (USPS 436-170) was published monthly October through December and February through April by the High School News Service, a Department of

Defense activity at Norfolk, Va. The purpose of this magazine was to inform young people and guidance personnel about benefits, opportunities, privileges and programs of military service. Distribution was free directly to Junior and Senior High Schools, colleges, libraries and career centers requesting the service.

Other material, such as "A Guide to Navy Educational Opportunities" and "Enlisted Education Programs of the Marine Corps" can be picked up at the local recruiting centers.

Enlistment Programs

Programs offered by the military services differ in length of enlistment and opportunites for selection of specific training and assignments. Each service has its own recruiters who determine eligibility of applicants.

Applicants born overseas of an American parent or parents are required to provide proof of citizenship. A birth certificate, Social Security card and high school diploma or GED equivalent are required for enlistment (women must have a high school diploma except for those applying to the Air Force). Aliens require proof of lawful entry for permanent residence. Parental or guardian consent is required for all applicants between 17 and 18 years old.

After preliminary processing, applicants are sent at government expense to an Armed Forces Examining and Entrance Station (AFEES) for a physical examination and the Armed Services Vocational Aptitude Battery (ASVAB). The ASVAB tests are not given to individuals who have previously been tested in high school or by a mobile AFEES team.

Army Enlistments

Army enlistments are from two to six years for applicants 17 (with high school diploma) to 34 years old. Applicants for specific options are given separate qualification tests. Qualified high school graduates may choose training for any of approximately 350 jobs, plus a unit or area of choice from world-wide assignments. At enlistment, they are given a written guarantee for training in their chosen jobs, provided requirements for course attendance are met and school quotas are available. They may also receive a monetary enlistment bonus for enlisting and completing training in some combat areas (infantry, armor and field artillery) or other designated skills.

Applicants who have a civilian skill which is needed by the Army may also receive entry at pay grade E-3. They are then eligible for further accelerated appointment to grade E-4 after satisfactory performance in an Army unit. Those who have completed high school training in skills needed by the Army may be enlisted in grades E-2 or E-3 and appointed to E-4 after eight weeks of satisfactory performance in a unit.

Army applicants may qualify to delay their actual entrance on active duty for up to 365 days to obtain training in a specific skill.

Navy Enlistments

Navy enlistments are for two, four, five or six years, depending on the program an individual is qualified to enter. Age requirements are 18 (with high school diploma or GED for women) to 30. Math and science backgrounds are particularly helpful for those who enter nuclear, advanced electronics or advanced technical programs. There are more than 60 skill areas available in the Navy.

Qualified persons may request a specialty field with a guarantee of service school training. Advanced pay grades (E-2 and E-3) are available to some vocational school graduates, applicants who have one or two years of college, enlistees in certain technical programs, ROTC personnel and those in the "Enlist a Buddy" program. Navy applicants may delay reporting for active duty for up to 365 days.

Air Force Enlistments

Air Force enlistments are for four or six years for applicants 17 to 27 years old (inclusive). The two basic enlistment options are the Guaranteed Training Enlistment Program (GTEP) and the Aptitude Area Enlistment Program.

In the GTEP, qualified applicants may select from more than 150 specialties and are guaranteed training and their first duty assignment in the GTEP skill.

Under the Aptitude Area Enlistment Program, applicants may select one of four career areas (mechanical, administrative, general or electronics) based on the results of the ASVAB tests. Job selection is done during basic military training, based on the needs of the Air Force, the individual's aptitude scores, civilian education and experience and personal desires.

More than 50 GTEP skills are available in the six-year enlistment option which guarantees accelerated promotion to pay grade E-3 after successful completion of the six-week basic military training course. Six-year enlistees in limited fields may also select a "3 x 3" option which guarantees retraining at the three year point into another field for which the enlistee is qualified and a vacancy exists.

Other enlistment options include guaranteed base of choice (in the U.S. and some foreign countries) in certain GTEP skills and the Buddy Flight option which guarantees basic military training together for applicants of the same sex who wish to enlist at the same time.

The Air Force Delayed Enlistment program allows applicants to become qualified in certain skills and delay their entry on active duty for up to 365 days, based on individual qualifications and projected vacancies in the service.

Marine Corps Enlistments

Marine Corps enlistments are for three, four or six years. Ground and aviation enlistment options and sub-programs which guarantee assignment to certain groups of occupations are available to qualified applicants. There are provisions in these programs for appointment to pay grade E-2 for applicants who have completed at least one semester of college with a minimum C+ average. An enlistment of six years guarantees a choice of certain occupational fields, areas of assignment and promotions.

Enlistees are tested to determine their aptitudes and interests. Specialized training is granted on the basis of these tests, according to Marine Corps needs. Age requirements for enlistment are from 17 to 28.

Coast Guard Enlistments

Coast Guard enlistments are for four years. Under the Guaranteed School Program, qualified applicants can be given a choice of a specific occupational training program in writing before they enlist (provided class openings are available). They may also delay entry on active duty for up to 12 months. Those with special training in a needed skill may enlist under an advanced promotion program in which they will be promoted to pay grade E-4 or E-5 immediately after recruit training. Enlistment age requirements are 17 through 25 for those with no prior military service.

Armed Forces Occupational Fields

Armed forces career or occupational fields can be defined as groups of related jobs in which enlisted personnel are trained and employed. A number of fields are similar among all services in training provided and skills and duties required. Career fields are listed in occupational handbooks which can be secured at any armed forces recruitment center; and in addition to job descriptions cite related civilian occupations.